Reality Bites BACK

the
Troubling
Truth
about Guilty
Pleasure
TV

Jennifer L. Pozner

SEAL PRESS

Praise for *Reality Bites Back*

"*Reality Bites Back* is a cogent, witty, exhaustively researched look at how your reality-TV sausage gets made. Since reality programming is likely to continue down its slippery slope, the book's forward-thinking call for more media literacy and less televised stereotyping couldn't come at a more crucial time. TV can still be a guilty pleasure, but that doesn't mean it can't also be an informed one."
—ANDI ZEISLER, Editorial Director, Bitch Media

"A landmark study of one of the most misunderstood, vitally important aspects of popular culture. Mixing superb extensive research with crystal clear writing (and a scathing wit), Jennifer Pozner demonstrates not only the entirely fabricated nature of so-called 'reality' television, but illustrates how its gender, racial, and class narratives are deeply reactionary. This book will disabuse any honest reader of the notion that reality TV is just escapist and innocent. An indispensable tool for teachers of media and popular culture. I will use it in my classes."
—SUT JHALLY, Professor of Communication, University of Massachusetts– Amherst; Executive Director, Media Education Foundation

"Pozner delivers the goods by comprehensively analyzing race, class, and gender in reality shows, offering viewers concrete steps to deconstruct racist messages and build their own healthier media alternatives. A must-read for all avid TV watchers, and those who love us."
—Rinku Sen, Publisher, *ColorLines* magazine; President and Executive Director, Applied Research Center

"Media is a form of sustenance for our society. Our television 'diet' consists of fables that leave women looking damaged and destructive. How do you change the game? First you understand it. Pozner's *Reality Bites Back* is a chance to understand why reality television is so dominant, and how that shapes our interactions with each other and the world."
—Farai Chideya, radio and television personality; author, *The Color of Our Future* and *Kiss the Sky*

"Jennifer L. Pozner provides a decoder ring for understanding how today's most popular TV shows manipulate what we think about ourselves and others. Revealing complicated issues of body image, sexuality, money, race, and gender, *Reality Bites Back* is a smart and witty lesson in media literacy. Readers who are new to the topic will come away with a clear understanding pop culture politics. Those more familiar with the subject will find updated examples and deep analysis. Pozner is a clever writer with a keen eye for the issues that matter. Expect to be both edified and entertained."

—SHIRA TARRANT, PhD, author, *Men and Feminism;* Associate Professor, Women's, Gender, and Sexuality Studies, California State University, Long Beach

"*Reality Bites Back* is a MUST READ for committed reality TV addicts and those frustrated by the onslaught of these shows. A comprehensive, well-researched, intelligent look at voyeur culture and what reality television tells us about our cultural understanding of race, class, gender, and status."

—SAMHITA MUKHOPADHYAY, Executive Editor, Feministing.com

"An incredible resource for media educators. From concrete examples of destructive messages in specific programs, to media literacy activity ideas, to a thorough resource guide, it offers an evidence-based analysis of reality TV without demonizing its audiences for watching. Pozner empowers viewers to confront sexist, racist programming in ways that are fun, meaningful, and doable for young people. I can't wait to share *Reality Bites Back* with teen filmmakers."

—MAILE MARTINEZ, Program Manager, Reel Grrls, Seattle

"Jennifer Pozner does a brilliant job exposing reality TV's troubling hyperconsumerist messages, and offers common sense ways to fight back. As a feminist, a mom, and an educator, it frightens me how easily we have allowed reality TV to define beauty, intelligence, and what we should own."

—VERONICA I. ARREOLA, VivalaFeminista.com

Reality Bites Back

The Troubling Truth about Guilty Pleasure TV

Some material in this book has been adapted from the previously published articles by the author:

"Evil Dead: Feminist bloggers bring the hammer down on *Top Model* necrophilia," *Bitch:* Feminist Response to *Pop Culture* magazine, Issue no. 36, Summer 2007.

"Triumph of the Shill, Part 1: Product Placement Runs Amok in Movies about Product Placement Run Amok," Issue 23, Winter 2004, and "Triumph of the Shill, Part 2: Reality TV Lets Marketers Write the Script," Issue 24, Spring 2004, both *Bitch* magazine.

"The Unreal World: Why women on 'reality TV' have to be hot, desperate and dumb," *Ms. Magazine,* Fall 2004.

Published by
Seal Press
A Member of the Perseus Books Group
1700 Fourth Street
Berkeley, California

Library of Congress Cataloging-in-Publication Data

Pozner, Jennifer L.
  Reality bites back : the troubling truth about guilty pleasure tv / by Jennifer L. Pozner.
    p. cm.
  ISBN 978-1-58005-265-8
  1. Reality television programs—Social aspects. 2. Reality television programs—Political aspects. 3. Women on television. 4. Sex role on television. 5. Minorities on television. I. Title.
  PN1992.8.R43P69 2010
  791.45'3—dc22
                                        2010010376

9 8 7 6 5 4

Cover and interior design by Domini Dragoone
Printed in the United States of America by Edwards Brothers
Distributed by Publishers Group West

For Mason Wicks-Lim (age five), who said, while watching

a Nickelodeon video, "Mom, can we turn this off?

I feel like they're trying to sell me something."

And for Elizabeth Martinez (age six), who observed the announcement

of the Emmy Awards nominees for writing and asked,

"So, is this the mens' writing awards?"

If we were all as engaged, aware, and critical media consumers

as these kids are, I wouldn't have had to write this book!

Contents

INTRODUCTION
Resisting Project Brainwash...8

CHAPTER ONE
Unraveling Reality TV's Twisted Fairytales..........33
Cinderellas and Cautionary Tales

CHAPTER TWO
Get Comfortable with My Flaw Finder.....................60
Women's Bodies as Women's Worth

CHAPTER THREE
Bitches and Morons and Skanks, Oh My!...................97
What Reality TV Teaches Us about Women

CHAPTER FOUR
This Is Not My Beautiful House!.................................133
Class Anxiety, Hyperconsumerism, and Mockery of the Poor

CHAPTER FIVE
Erasing Ethnicity, Encoding Bigotry.........................161
Race, Pre– and Post–*Flavor of Love*

CHAPTER SIX
Ghetto Bitches, China Dolls, and Cha Cha Divas......196
Race, Beauty, and the Tyranny of Tyra Banks

CHAPTER SEVEN
Beautiful Corpses, Abusive Princes 212
Violence against Women as Glamorous, Romantic Reality

CHAPTER EIGHT
"I Would Be a Servant to Him" 239
New Millennium, Same Old Backlash

CHAPTER NINE
The World According to CoverGirl 273
Advertiser Ideology Goes 3-D

CHAPTER TEN
Fun with Media Literacy! 300
Drinking Games, Deconstruction Guides, and Other Critical Thinking Tools

CHAPTER ELEVEN
What Are You Going to Do? 325
How *You* Can Transform the Media—Starting Today

RESOURCE GUIDE 347

NOTES 352

INDEX 371

Introduction

Resisting Project Brainwash

> The whole process of watching television [has] social significance. Television provides us with pictures of the world, of our world, and the knowledge that most of these pictures are fictional does not immunize us from believing in them. The beliefs we form become part of the context within which we understand who we are. To understand prime-time television, then, is to understand an important part of the way we view the world and ourselves.
>
> —SUT JHALLY AND JUSTIN M. LEWIS, *Enlightened Racism*[1]

Nearly every night on every major network, "unscripted" (but carefully crafted) dating, makeover, lifestyle, and competition shows glorify stereotypes that most people assume died forty years ago. Follow me into the rabbit hole of reality TV, and let's take a look at how television's Svengalis want us to see ourselves.*

On ABC's *The Bachelor* and NBC's *Who Wants to Marry My Dad?* fifteen to twenty-five interchangeable hotties compete for the chance to marry a hunky lunkhead they don't know from Adam. Weepy waifs line up to be objectified for a living (or simply for a moment) on the CW's *America's Next Top Model*. Branded "ugly ducklings," appearance-obsessed sad sacks risk their health to be surgically altered on Fox's *The Swan* and E!'s *Dr. 90210*. Starved women get naked for Oreos and men gloat about "dumb-ass girl alliances" on CBS's *Survivor*. Women of color are ostracized as deceitful divas on NBC's *The Apprentice*, lazy or "difficult" on ABC's *Wife Swap*, and "ghetto" train wrecks on VH1's *Flavor of Love*

---

* *Reality Bites Back* investigates reality TV series that aired from 2000 to 2010. For simplicity's sake I often use the present tense, even when referring to shows that aren't still on the air. For a listing of the debut year and original network for each series analyzed in this book, see RealityBitesBackBook.com.

and *I Love New York*. And through it all, slurs like "bitch," "beaver," and "whore" are tossed around as if they're any other nouns.

Who do we have to thank for this?

Meet Fox exec Mike Darnell, who *The Washington Post* suggests "may be the most influential man working in television."[2] The phrase "shit-eating grin" could have been coined for this once-disgraced, now-embraced king of bottom-feeder reality TV schlock. Back before we all succumbed to American idolatry, reality television wasn't a prime-time-dominating genre with its own Emmy category—it was simply one low-rated, unscripted MTV soap opera called *The Real World*. In just two hours on February 15, 2000, Darnell changed all that, with *Who Wants to Marry a Multi-Millionaire?* The special, which predated the game-changing *Survivor*, was a hybrid of Miss America and a mail-order bride parade. With executive producer Mike Fleiss of Next Entertainment, Darnell brought fifty brides-to-be to Las Vegas to be auctioned off to a complete stranger. They sashayed in swimsuits, tittered nervously, and answered pageant-style questions to assess their moral fortitude and sexual prowess in thirty seconds or less. Groom Rick Rockwell was hidden as he and the audience determined who deserved "the biggest prize of all . . . a brand-new multimillionaire husband." Nurse (and future *Playboy* centerfold) Darva Conger, Rockwell's eventual choice, got her first glimpse of her "fiancé" moments before they were legally wed on-air. Nearly 23 million viewers tuned in.

"Best show ever," Darnell gushed when it snagged a whopping 28 share rating.* They'd exceeded their own expectations, Fleiss raved:

> Mike and I . . . knew that the National Organization for Women would hate us. That this would be the most controversial show ever! We thought it was all good, but it got so hot, so crazy red-hot. They said it was the most talked-about show since Roots! It was the lead sketch on Saturday Night Live.[3]

---

* Nielsen ratings, which determine TV ad rates, analyze the habits of sample viewers. Nielsen defines a rating as "a percent of the total universe, either of total television households or total number or persons in a given demo," and a share as "the percent of households or persons using television at the time the program is airing." By "universe," they mean total number of households that own televisions.[4]

Alas, it was a short honeymoon—for the Rockwells, and for Fox.

Conger annulled their never-consummated nuptials after The Smoking Gun website reported that Rockwell* had a history of abusing women. A former girlfriend filed a restraining order against Fox's "Prince Charming" after he vandalized her car, broke into her home, and "threw me around and slapped me and hit me in the face . . . he said he would find me and kill me."[5]

At the time, Darnell was just Fox's "specials guy," responsible for such classy celluloid concoctions as *When Animals Attack!* and *World's Scariest Police Chases*. When Rockwell's sordid past came to light, Darnell was bashed as a chauvinistic, manipulative ratings-whore who betrothed an unsuspecting woman to a potential wife beater. When Rockwell's violent past was uncovered, Darnell was full of fake contrition, saying, "This is the worst day of my life."[6] The entertainment press called him the P. T. Barnum of television, and many speculated that he would—or, at least, should—lose his job over the sensationalistic spectacle. Fox was widely criticized by newspapers, magazines, broadcast, and online media as sinking to an abysmal new low. In the wake of the damaging PR hit, the network canceled a planned rebroadcast, declined to take *Multi-Millionaire* to series, and promised to back away from such exploitative fare in the future.[+]

Yet the damage had been done. UPN bid to make *Multi-Millionaire* into a series, but executive producer Fleiss turned them down. Instead, he took his and Darnell's desperate-to-be-housewives premise to ABC, masked its misogyny in the trappings of "fairytale romance," and launched the landscape-altering dating franchise *The Bachelor* in March 2002.[#] The entertainment press heralded the series as "a reality revolution, ushering a soap-opera concept into prime-time." It became ABC's highest-rated show among eighteen- to forty-nine-year-olds, every network's target demographic.[7] What was once considered inappropriate and

---

* Who wasn't a real estate investor, as Fox claimed, but a failed comic actor and B movie writer of *Attack of the Killer Tomatoes!*
+ Darnell's boss, the chairman of Fox Entertainment Television, swore, "I'd rather fail with quality than succeed with garbage." Then he approved the sleaze-fest *Temptation Island.*[8]
# ABC aired fourteen seasons of *The Bachelor* by 2010—each Prince Charming was white, as were the vast majority of women pursuing them.

culturally corruptive became a staple as every network scrambled to duplicate *The Bachelor*'s ratings success—with Fox taking the lead at lowering the bar.

By February 2003, Fox was devoting a whopping 41 percent and ABC 33 percent of their sweeps offerings to reality shows. These percentages increased over the years,* limiting the number of quality comedies and dramas available to viewers and reducing opportunities for union-represented actors, writers, and crew.[9] Instead of firing their previously shamed reality guru, Fox promoted Darnell to executive vice president of alternative programming,+ and he wasted no time generating such lurid gems as:

- *Temptation Island* (2001): Real-life couples were separated and set up with scores of scantily clad "tempters" hired to coax them into adulterous sex— with every soft-porn-for-prime-time caress captured for our prying eyes.

- *Joe Millionaire* (2003): Women are shallow, greedy gold diggers who deserve to be lied to, ridiculed, and humiliated for our collective amusement.

- *Married by America* (2003): Women got engaged to strangers by slipping their ring fingers through a matrimonial glory hole in a wall on a TV soundstage. Then: bedroom cams!

- *Bridezillas* (2003): "Out-of-control brides," Darnell promised, "become insane" on this Fox special. Segments were separated by such charming screen titles as "Life's a Bitch and Then You Marry One." Later became a WE series.

- *The Swan* (2004): makeover-cum-beauty pageant series gave plain-looking women with low self-esteem a battery of medically risky plastic surgery procedures, mocked their physical pain during recovery and emotional wounds during faux "therapy," and pitted them against one another in a beauty pageant.

With these—but especially with his original *Millionaire* stunt, which laid the groundwork for Fleiss's *The Bachelor*—Darnell established the standard for how a decade of reality programming would represent women and men and

---

* See Prime-Time Programming Lineup by Network, on page 282.
+ He eventually became president of alternative entertainment, reportedly "free to greenlight reality series pilots and specials," with "creative control" over Fox's lineup.[10]

marginalize people of color. While some of his shows flopped (for example, the Monica Lewinsky–hosted *Mr. Personality,* where a woman dated men in creepy masks), many have scored landscape-altering ratings and big bank from advertisers. With 40 million viewers, the finale of *Joe Millionaire* was the third-most-watched television episode of the entire decade.[11] Rival networks plumbed their inner frat boys to replicate his formulas.

The Real World's devolution clearly illustrates the spill-over effect on content across the TV dial. First broadcast in 1992, the show originally featured diverse casts and explored issues such as racism, homosexuality, HIV/AIDS, and abortion with something resembling care. Discussions addressing these identities and issues often illuminated rather than reinforced prejudice. During the 2000s, the series used sensationalized sexism, racial prejudice, homophobia, sloppy hookups, and drug and alcohol addiction as the main viewership draws. As cultural critic Latoya Peterson writes, "Growth. Development. An actual exchange of ideas" used to be major components of *The Real World,* which now seems to "specifically cast for racists, assholes, and agitators . . . it's like a formula. Every season has some huge racial altercation. Every season has some kind of woman trying to sleep her way into self-esteem. Every season has a guy coping with a breakup angrily."[12]

Why the shift? For one thing, TV execs believe that the more they bait advocacy groups like NOW, the NAACP, and GLAAD, the more controversy a show will generate. Offensiveness = hype = increased eyeballs for advertisers and cash for networks, making outrageous bigotry less a by-product of reality TV than its blueprint. Let Fleiss explain: The first thing he and Darnell thought when they heard about Rockwell's violent past was, "Great! More publicity! Mike said, 'We gotta get out in front of this!' I'm like, 'Absolutely! Fuck! It's a restraining order! Let's get an interview with the girl! We'll put it on as part of the special!' We had a whole plan, because that's the way we like it!" Hindsight makes most people wiser. Fleiss . . . not so much. Three years after the fact, he told a reporter that "In retrospect, I don't feel like we did anything wrong on that *Multi-Millionaire* show, when you see that, hey, on *Married by America* they had somebody who was already married . . . we were just there first." The next time you see *The Bachelor* passing out the long-stems, consider that the producer of reality TV's longest-running "fairytale romance" franchise sees no difference between wedding a woman to a violent stranger and the fact that "one of the final girls had like done fetish films" [sic] on *Joe Millionaire.*[13]

What do Darnell's Hollywood peers think of his corrosive influence on the television landscape? As early as 2000, *The New York Times* predicted that "he would be avidly sought out if Fox ever let him go," especially "where his touch with male viewers would be appreciated." After *Joe Millionaire* and *American Idol,* competitors overlooked his gutter-grazing rep and declared their admiration. "He's a genius," WB Chairman and CEO Jamie Kellner pronounced. UPN tried to steal Darnell away from Fox, offering to appoint him as their head of programming. CBS President and CEO Les Moonves stated, "Any network would like to have Mike Darnell on their team."[14]

Why? Because nothing—not creative quality, not social impact, and certainly not accountability to the public—matters to corporate media companies other than the financial bottom line.

Therein lies the secret to Darnell's perpetual shit-eating smirk. No matter how crass or asinine his concepts, no matter what twisted new fantasies he dreams up in pursuit of a 40 percent ratings share, he'll have free rein as long as he remains a cash cow for Fox, which has explicitly encouraged him to "push the limits with impunity."[15] Meanwhile, the rest of the networks continue to race to meet him in the gutter.

When Hollywood "pushes the limits," it's usually bad news for women. That has been increasingly true with reality TV, our most vivid example of a pop cultural backlash against women's rights and social progress. If at first this sounds extreme, that is precisely because "A backlash against women's rights succeeds to the degree that it appears *not* to be political, that it appears not to be a struggle at all," as Susan Faludi explained in *Backlash: The Undeclared War Against American Women.*[16]

The Myth of
"Giving People What They Want"

Even as I write this, I can hear predictable responses: It's the public's fault! I've heard that song before. Whenever they're criticized for airing emotionally exploitative or politically incendiary reality shows, networks parrot Mike Darnell's claim that "We're giving people what they want, pushing the envelope to match tastes."

Michael Hirschorn, the brain trust behind VH1's *Charm School* and *A Shot at Love with Tila Tequila,* blames female consumers. "If women didn't want these shows, they wouldn't get made," he told Jezebel.com.[17]

I call bullshit.

One of the entertainment industry's biggest myths is that media companies bombard us with ad-rich, quality-poor unscripted programming simply because we demand it. Not so. These shows exist for only one reason: They're dirt cheap. It can cost an average of 50 to 75 percent less to make a reality TV show than a scripted program. Sometimes even less: In 2001, NBC paid $9 million per hour for *The West Wing,* while *The Weakest Link* clocked in at $500K per episode. This is why witty, inventive shows beloved by loyal audiences in the modest/low millions get yanked off the air lickety-split before they get to develop and retain a major following (for example, Fox's quirky space Western *Firefly,* or ABC's *Commander in Chief,* about the first woman president), while low-rated unscripted series often get to languish on the dial.*

For example, *The Pickup Artist* (which taught awkward guys how to erode women's self-esteem to manipulate them into sex) premiered to a measly 673,000 viewers and never reached higher than a 1.3 rating among eighteen- to forty-nine-

---

* *Commander in Chief* averaged 16.5 million viewers and was the number one show on Tuesdays in 2005, until it went up against *American Idol.* ABC shelved it for months. In a new time slot it drew between 6.5 and 8.2 million viewers—not stellar, but not abysmal. Verdict? Canceled. In 2002, Fox chose the Friday night ratings graveyard for *Firefly,* an intricately written show from Joss Whedon, creator of cult hit *Buffy the Vampire Slayer.* They aired episodes out of order, making the premise and characters hard to follow. Yet an average of 4.7 million viewers still managed to find it every week; more would have if the network hadn't undermined it. Verdict? Fox canned it after eleven episodes, never airing the final three. Outraged fans sent DVD sales soaring, and a feature film, *Serenity,* followed. It remains a much-missed favorite, featured on numerous "Best of the Decade" lists.[18]

year-olds. Those are sad numbers even for cable—yet it still got picked up for a second season. TV by the Numbers, a website that analyzes Nielsen data relative to program renewals and cancelations, concluded that some unscripted shows survive "with very low numbers" because they're "so cheap that they are expected to do little more than fill air time and produce little in the way of viewership."[19]

Add an immense funding stream from embedded advertising, and it's party time. Unscripted programs aren't just cheap to *make:* They can be major moneymakers before they ever appear on-screen. "The economics of it are incredible—it can sustain a lower rating," crowed NBC's programming exec (and later chairman) Jeff Gaspin in 2001. It was a prescient explanation of NBC's decisions regarding *The Apprentice,* every episode of which is built around brands such as Burger King, Dove, Sony, Verizon, and Visa. Season 1 of *The Apprentice* was a hit in 2004 with 20.7 million viewers, but plummeted as people lost interest each year. Half its audience vanished by season 4, but since sponsors were paying "upwards of $2 million *per episode* to have their products incorporated into plot lines," NBC kept it in their lineup for two more seasons. When it dropped to 7.1 million viewers (great for a cable outlet like VH1, dismal for a former network smash hit), the peacock network finally dropped the show from the fall 2007 lineup. That didn't sit well with Ben Silverman, the new co-chairman of NBC's entertainment division.* A former reality producer and product placement emissary, he sprinkled D-list fairy dust on the poorly performing shill-fest and revived it as *The Celebrity Apprentice* in 2008. Season 9 aired in 2010.[20]

"Steeped in Some Social Belief"

Enamored of reality TV's high ratings, low production costs, and product placement revenue, media owners and producers typically reject the notion that there's any social relevance to these shows. Darnell is adamant about this. "I get asked, 'What do you think the social responsibility of your shows is?'" but "The truth is,

---

* Silverman was one of the masterminds behind *The Restaurant,* which was produced and funded entirely by advertisers, who offered the program for free to NBC.

I'm in entertainment, not in news. I don't know what the social responsibility of *Seinfeld* is." As long as "the buzz gets going" and it's "big TV," he says, "I will do almost anything for a good number."[21]

Occasionally, though, reality producers reveal a truth they'd prefer to hide. Noting that *Temptation Island* and *Joe Millionaire* were Fox's highest-rated programs in 2001 and 2003, *Entertainment Weekly* asked him the secret to his success: "The reality business is a delicate science," he insists, "you need a premise that's easy to understand, *that's steeped in some social belief,*" and that earns the reaction of, to quote Darnell: "'Oh, my god!' or 'What's wrong with you?'" (emphasis mine). He reiterated this to *Variety:* "The biggest reality shows we've done, other than 'Idol,' have been social ideas."[22]

This is key. It's true that millions of people have become reality TV junkies, initially drawn in by a sort of cinematic schadenfreude.* That "What's wrong with you?" reaction is the viewer's equivalent of rubbernecking at an accident. Sometimes it makes us laugh, sometimes it shocks us, but we're unable to turn away from the cathartic display of other people's humiliation. Often it makes us feel superior: No matter how bad our problems may be, at least *we* aren't as fill-in-the-blank (pathetic, desperate, ugly, stupid) as those misguided enough to sign up for such indignities on national TV. It's easy to feel like we haven't hit bottom compared to the dregs of humanity on *Rock of Love Bus.* We revel in the bizarre antics, pitiful tears, wild hookups, and self-loathing insecurities. We vicariously savor all the delicious melodrama of high school cliques and office gossip, with none of the guilt. These are normal, human emotions, masterfully manipulated by folks like Darnell, Fleiss, and Hirschorn.

After a long, stressful day, it can be comforting to zone out with mindless entertainment . . . even the kind produced by Mindless Entertainment, makers of *The Surreal Life.* Some reality shows can even be edifying, offering insights into diverse communities and customs through travel and cultural exchange *(The Amazing Race, Meet the Natives: USA),* or focusing on talent and ingenuity

---

* *Schadenfreude* is a German word that means "taking pleasure in the misfortune of others."

(*Project Runway, Top Chef*). But even the most salacious reality shows can be compelling. With their larger-than-life premises, they provide the same platform for fantasy and escapism as romance novels and comic books. If we're unlucky in love, we can pretend we're the dating show princess being whisked away to happily ever after, or the one lucky dude in a hot tub with twenty horny chicks. If we have body image issues, we can imagine ourselves as a glamorous *Top Model*. If we're broke, how appealing to dream of winning a million-dollar record deal on *American Idol* or dropping insane amounts of cash on clothes, cars, or mansions on *What Not to Wear, The Real Housewives,* or *Million Dollar Listing.*

But while the schadenfreude and escapism factors may get us to tune in, that's not what *hooks* us. On a more subconscious level, we continue to watch because these shows frame their narratives in ways that both play to and reinforce deeply ingrained societal biases about women and men, love and beauty, race and class, consumption and happiness in America. Which raises the question: *What are these "social beliefs" that Mike Darnell and his counterparts are exploiting for the profit of networks, product placers, and media owners?* What are the implications of a nation of viewers gulping down the influential genre's gendered myths as readily as we do the Cokes hawked on every episode of *American Idol*—and what can we do about it?

This book is my answer to those questions.

People love to ask why we watch these shows by the millions, and why thousands audition to participate—areas ripe for sociological study. But as a journalist and media critic, what I find most relevant is what we've learned from a decade of unscripted programming. Too often what passes for discussion about reality TV is limited to "Wow, that bitch was crazy!" or "Should this dater/singer/ model be eliminated?" We need a deeper debate in this country about the meaning and implications of reality TV's backlash against women's rights and social progress. *Reality Bites Back* aims a critical, analytical lens at how women are portrayed throughout a form of entertainment often dismissed as harmless fluff. I demonstrate how these "guilty pleasures" foment gender-war ideology, with deep significance for the intellectual and political development of a generation of viewers. Additionally, I examine the ways race, class, and commercialism intersect and complicate depictions of women throughout the genre.

In January 2007, *CBS Evening News* reported that more people watched *American Idol* on Fox than saw President Bush's State of the Union speech on ABC, NBC, and CBS combined. They critiqued how "train wreck TV" relies on humiliation, using VH1's *I Love New York* as a prime example. In response, Michael Hirschorn, formerly VH1's executive VP of original programming, argued that "resistance to reality TV ultimately comes down to snobbery." The man who brought the minstrel show back to prime time with *Flavor of Love* claimed the genre serves a higher purpose. Reality TV "has engaged in hot-button cultural issues—class, sex, race—that respectable television, including the august CBS Evening News, rarely touches," he wrote in *The Atlantic Monthly.* As such, it "presents some of the most vital political debate in America, particularly about class and race."[23]

It's a convenient rationalization from a man who went on to form his own production company, Ish Entertainment. (*Ish* is a popular slang term for *shit.* He couldn't have chosen a better name.) Hirschorn's claim that this low-brow form serves a high-brow function is just the sort of bait-and-switch I hope to help you unpack.

It's true that corporate news outlets have become more likely to report on Paris Hilton's breakups than racial disparities in healthcare, the pay gap for women, or how poverty compounds women's inability to leave violent relationships. But rather than adding depth, reality TV exacerbates media's superficiality. As you'll see, Hirschorn's argument falls apart when we look at how hot-button issues are presented in unscripted programming. Like nearly all reality producers and network execs, this ish-pusher fails to acknowledge that these shows are very intentionally cast, edited, and framed to amplify regressive values around gender, race, and class, underscore advertisers' desire to get us to *think less* and *buy more,* and create a version of "reality" that erases any trace of the advances made during the women's rights, civil rights, and gay rights movements.

As I illustrate in chapter 4, reality TV skews America's economic realities beyond recognition. Unsurprisingly for a genre that allows advertisers to work with producers to create and craft content, product-placement string-pullers aim to convince us that expensive frivolities such as couture gowns, cuisine, and design are "not luxuries," but lifesavers. This message runs through lifestyle series (*The Real Housewives* franchise), makeover shows (*Extreme Makeover: Home Edition*), and competitions (*The Apprentice, Project Runway*). Right when millions of Americans were losing their homes, jobs, and health insurance, cable networks asked us to root for real estate agents and speculators (*Flip That House, Million Dollar Listing*). In this context, low-income women's struggles to feed, clothe, shelter, and educate themselves and their kids become fodder for mockery on *American Idol* and *America's Next Top Model*—when they're not erased entirely.

Gender and class biases are inextricably linked with racial bigotry in this realm, as discussed in chapter 5. Women of color are quickly dismissed tokens on network dating shows like *The Bachelor*, while makeover shows like *The Swan* "fix" ethnic features and *American Idol* makes African American and Latina girls straighten their kinky hair. With the arrival of *Flavor of Love* in 2006, producers began using racism as a bedrock for unscripted programs. Since then, blaxploitation shows from the *Flavor* franchise to criminals-make-good series like *From G's to Gents* revived minstrel-era archetypes of mammies, jezebels, and shucking-and-jiving clowns. And then there's *America's Next Top Model*, whose problematic race and gender imagery merits extended analysis in its own chapter, 6.

Race and class biases have been acute in some series and minimal in others. Yet this new television genre was built on a foundation of garden-variety misogyny. Crude and regressive ideas about women were present in *Multi-Millionaire* in early 2000 and persisted through MTV using a clip of a woman getting punched in the face to promote the debut of *Jersey Shore* in late 2009. This is due not only to the visions of folks like Darnell and Fleiss but also to the story-driving influence of embedded advertisers, whose business model has always relied on representing women as objectified and subservient.

Because sexism is so thoroughly infused in the DNA of reality TV, *Reality Bites Back* analyzes how this form of entertainment defines "Women," and how it constructs gender roles within various contexts, including body, romance, marriage, home, and work. And because "Woman" is not a monolithic group, we cannot understand reality TV's antifeminism without also looking at the genre's treatment of race and class.

Still, there are limitations to this analysis. I've monitored more than one thousand hours of unscripted programming over ten years* and supplemented that primary source material with extensive journalistic research. Yet, with an ever-growing number of series on the dial, it would be impossible to watch every reality show or comprehensively cover every bias that merits attention. Despite a handful of emerging academic anthologies and papers,[24] there has not yet been a mainstream, single-author media criticism book about the significance of reality TV for women. *Reality Bites Back* intends to connect thematic dots between reality TV attacks on women's social, sexual, and political power and the treatment of women in news media and politics. I am laying this groundwork not as the final word, but as the beginning of a larger conversation.

I hope to offer you a new way to look at reality programming regardless of your entry point to this discussion. Are you a TV fan, not a media geek or political activist? *I do not judge you for enjoying reality TV.* My critique is aimed at the powerful entities that choose to define reality in ways that suit their interests, regardless of what is healthy or dangerous for our culture. I hope this nuanced introduction to feminist media analysis prompts you to ask questions and bring a more active eye to what you watch. *Reality Bites Back* also aims to stimulate deeper debate among academics, social justice activists, media makers, and journalists about the nature and meaning of the most talked-about form of entertainment

---

* Deciding which shows to monitor versus omit was a difficult process. In the end, I chose to focus on series potentially available to the widest audiences: shows airing between 2000 and early 2010 on the free broadcast networks (ABC, NBC, CBS, Fox, CW, and the now-defunct UPN and WB), several cable networks available to most media markets (VH1, MTV, Bravo, TLC, Style), and a few entries on three "women's programming" networks (Lifetime, Oxygen, and WE). Additionally, I have not monitored the parenting, youth, mental health, addiction, crime and law enforcement, cooking, travel, and celebutaunt reality subgenres.

at the turn of the century. If you don't see your favorite guilty (or not so guilty) pleasure within these pages, I hope you'll use this book as a starting point rather than an end in itself. Use the tips in chapters 10 and 11 to encourage debate in your own blogs, zines, local TV reporting, microradio broadcasts, and other independent media.

Framing Reality . . .

Media both shape and reflect cultural perceptions of who we are, what we're valued for, what we want, what we need, what we believe about ourselves and others—and what we should consider "our place" in society.

According to audience reception research[25] by communication scholars Sut Jhally and Justin Lewis, "Television affects how viewers make sense of the world. It is not usually one episode or one series that influences the way we think; it is the aggregate of messages that enter our minds. These messages are part of our environment and . . . ubiquitous, are consumed as automatically and unconsciously as the air we breathe."[26]

This does not mean we're all affected the same way by any particular message in, say, any single episode of *America's Next Top Model*. We each bring our intellects, identities, and experiences to everything we watch, which affects the way we enjoy, interpret, or internalize media messages. Though we're unique individuals who react differently to specific TV shows, our ideas are inescapably shaped by our participation in collective culture and society. We live in a commercially controlled, media-saturated era, one in which a small handful of owners have consolidated power over the means of production and distribution of not just entertainment television but also broadcast and print journalism, film, music, video games, and communication technologies.* The influence of all this media is systemic and affects how we think and feel in ways we don't always recognize, even—sometimes especially—when we consider ourselves immune.

---

* Who sits at the top of this mega-merged heap? Find out with *Columbia Journalism Review's* interactive "Who Owns What" guide at CJR.org and the media ownership charts at FreePress.net.

In 1992, University of Massachusetts–Amherst researchers conducted a "major qualitative audience study" to evaluate how *The Cosby Show* affected social and political attitudes of fifty-two focus groups (twenty-three Black, twenty-six white, three Hispanic). Their findings remain highly relevant today. In-depth interviews revealed that "many viewers were so engaged with the situations and the characters on television that they naturally read beyond the scene or the program they were discussing and speculated about them as real events and characters. . . . The implications of this are profound. We can no longer assume that the content of TV fiction does not matter simply because TV viewers understand that it is fiction."[27] Viewers' identification with characters and situations in the sitcom seemed to directly impact their opinions about people of color, and about public policies impacting race and class status in America. As a result:

> Many of us know that most television is fiction, yet we see television as a key source of information about the world we live in. It is simultaneously real and unreal. We may know, for example, that television exaggerates the scale of violent crime for dramatic purposes; nevertheless, studies show that the more television we watch, the more violent we assume the world to be. Our awareness of exaggeration, in other words, is only momentary.
>
> This grants TV producers and program makers the enormous luxury of power without responsibility. They have the means to influence our view of the world without ever claiming to do so. Most television, goes the gigantic disclaimer, is (after all) nothing more than "entertainment." This grants an insidious form of poetic license, apparently innocent because it is achieved with our complicity . . . an unwitting form of manipulation that occurs because we, as TV viewers, suspend our disbelief so automatically that we forget that we are in a state of suspension.[28]

Remember, the authors were describing a sitcom viewers knew was fictional, written by screenwriters and performed by actors. Now consider the potential impact of contemporary unscripted programming. Many of us are aware that reality shows play fast and loose with context and editing. We know they're at least somewhat "fake."* That knowledge doesn't stop us from passing judgment about the behavior and personalities of people who appear on reality TV. Just like 1980s audiences related to fictional shows as "real events and characters," today we talk, blog, write, and read about reality TV participants as if we *know* them. Google through fan sites and you'll find thousands of comments debating whether "this bitch" or "that whore" should be eliminated from dating shows, or rooting for a "smart guy" or "sweet girl" to win competitions. Tabloid media play along, despite knowing that some cast members are actors and all are edited beyond real-life recognition. From *USA Today* to *Access Hollywood*, rejected *Bachelors, Bridezillas,* and *Apprentices* are treated as if they actually are the two-dimensional caricatures they appeared to be on their shows.

News media further this mass delusion. "Reality shows are, at their cores, social experiments," *Newsweek*'s Joshua Alston wrote, and "are largely agenda-free: there's no writer pulling the strings (for the most part). There are real people reacting in real and unexpected ways. Sometimes those reactions will be ugly."

This is patently untrue. Unscripted programming isn't "social experimentation"—it's just an easier, quicker, cheaper way to fill airtime with content created by nonunion labor. A major misconception during the 2007 Hollywood writers' strike[29] was that we'd see more reality television because networks needed material produced without writers. But *all reality shows employ writers*— just underpaid, nonunion ones. As for string-pullers, advertisers regularly instruct writers to script dialogue about their products.[30] We also can't overlook the ideological agendas of executive producers like Fleiss, who base shows on the desire to make women extremely unhappy: "It's a lot of fun to watch girls crying," Fleiss has said. "Never underestimate the value of that."

---

* The distinctions between what is "real" and what is not, between creative story and commercial pitch, are especially blurry for children, who are less likely to be aware of production tricks, selective casting, and editorial deception in reality TV—or manipulative practices in advertising and other forms of media. This is why media literacy education, discussed in chapters 10 and 11, is crucial.

When reporters pretend these shows are *social* rather than *commercial* experiments, the public can't be blamed for underestimating the depth of deception involved. The central conceit—that participants are "real people" experiencing "real emotions"—is used to hide the storytelling work of casting directors, writers, editors, videographers, and production teams, as well as advertisers who contribute to visuals, dialogue, and plot development. Behind-the-scenes maneuverings are hidden off-camera, and the remaining veneer of authenticity allows networks to package this programming almost as psuedo-documentaries.

As a result, reality TV pretends to tell us, not only what our lives are like as turn-of-the-century Americans, but who we supposedly *are,* writ large.

... Framing Gender

So, what do reality TV producers want us to believe about ourselves, and about "our place" in society? Each chapter explores a distinct "social belief" Darnell, Fleiss, Hirschorn, and their cohorts exploit to convince us that women and people of color "are" certain things. For example, that no matter how old women are, they're "hot girls," not self-aware adults with intellectual, social, or sexual agency.

What other ideas are sold alongside the name-brand colas, cars, and cosmetics shilled within show content? There's a series to reinforce every conceivable gender stereotype.

"The claws come out" in chapter 3, wherein we learn that "women are conniving, deceitful, and vicious," that men should beware "money-grubbing gold diggers," and that sisterhood is not powerful, it's spiteful. Here and in chapter 8, we see how a performative version of heterosexual women's sexuality is used as a bargaining chip, reviving double standards about "good girls" and "sluts." Of course, they're only "good girls" if they're straight. The marginalization and pornification of lesbians and bisexuals comes up in chapter 1, which explores the trappings of reality romances. Dating shows infantilize adult women with childlike princess imagery and insist the only criteria men need to qualify as Mr.

Right are firm asses and even firmer financial portfolios. This chapter takes on the crippling notion that men are unworthy of love if they are not rich.

Chapter 2 details how picture-perfect reality TV women are picked apart for every real or imagined physical imperfection, especially related to weight, ethnicity, and nonconformity. Far from objecting to their objectification, reality TV women are portrayed as wanting nothing more than to achieve advertisers' impossible ideal of beauty. Producers erase any signs of women's individuality momentarily, via *Top Model*'s airbrushes, and permanently, via *Extreme Makeover*'s scalpels . . . all in the name of "liberation."

Yet as I argue in chapter 3, reality TV producers are diametrically opposed to women's liberation, portraying the female population as ditzy and inept workers, wives, and mothers. It's a hop, skip, and a jump to the notion of single women as pathetic losers who can never be happy or flourish financially without husbands (even abusive ones). Chapter 8 delves into the deeper political implications of reality TV's backlash ideology, showing how compulsory domesticity and female subservience are core values in the reality universe, as is a limited interpretation of masculinity.

Reality TV isn't simply *reflecting* anachronistic social biases, it's resurrecting them. This genre has done what the most ardent fundamentalists have never been able to achieve: They've created a universe in which women not only *have* no real choices, they don't even *want* any.

A NOTE ON "WOMEN," GENDER IDENTITY, AND SEXUAL ORIENTATION

Imagine a reality TV show in which the pronouns used to describe people were based on each participant's self-identified gender, rather than on visual judgments. For that matter, imagine if transgender people were simply *present* in reality television—without their gender identity being treated as confusing or laughable.

Now, consider how different the reality TV landscape might be if its producers and writers did not define "Woman" as almost uniformly heterosexual, desperate, and domestically inclined. If straight, lesbian, and bisexual women were shown dating whomever they desired—and falling in love, breaking up, having sex, or abstaining—on their own terms and without judgment. Or if our favorite shows followed ethnically diverse women of different ages with a wide range of social values, body types, styles, and ambitions.

That's what the boob tube could look like if reality TV featured a cross-section of *real* American women. Instead, this highly manipulative form of entertainment is created to showcase embedded sponsors' products, and the "social ideas" used to advertise those products. To service those goals, producers exclude or punish those who flout conventional ideas about "proper" gender identity, presentation, or behavior. This is why, unless otherwise noted, whenever I describe or quote women on reality shows, or discuss the genre's depictions of "women" in general, it's safe to assume I'm referring to straight women who were born female—because this is how the genre defines "Woman."

Lies, Damn Lies, and Editing

Before Mike Fleiss was a reality TV kingpin, he was a frustrated sports reporter. Journalism didn't agree with him, though: "I was being restricted by the facts all the time! I felt like I couldn't really do anything creative."[31] Nowadays, Fleiss doesn't let pesky "facts" get in the way on *The Bachelor* and *The Bachelorette*. If the truth isn't working, he and his staff just get . . . "creative."

"We shoot 100% of the time and air 1% of what we shot," then edit "the really good stuff" to suit their purposes, an anonymous *Bachelor* producer told NPR. "We have even gone so far as to 'frankenbite,' where you take somebody saying, 'of course I'd like to say that I love him' and cutting the bite together to say 'of course I love him.' . . . [It's] misleading to the viewer and unfair to the cast member, but they sign up for this."[32]

Though this technique is commonplace, most reality show runners want us to believe that, as *Laguna Beach* executive producer Tony DiSanto claims, "we never make up something that hasn't happened." Actually, they

do. On *The Dating Experiment,* when a woman didn't like a guy the producers chose for her, they asked her to name her favorite celebrity. "She replied
that she really loved Adam Sandler. Later . . . they spliced out Sandler's name
and dropped in audio of her saying the male contestant's name," according to *Time* magazine media critic James Poniewozik. Voiceovers are also
potentially sketchy. "If [there's] a shot of a girl walking into the kitchen for
no reason while her bite plays in VO, you might want to ask questions," an
America's Next Top Model producer told *Television Without Pity.*[33]

What reality fan doesn't assume that the *Hills* girls and the *Real Housewives* show up where and when producers instruct? When eight women in
bikinis in an Australian hot spring simultaneously shave their legs with Skin-
timate Gel on *Outback Jack,* we realize that's staged. Yet most of us remain
unaware of practices like Frankenbiting. Even fewer understand that *pretty
much every part of a reality show* is manipulated to support producers' chosen
narrative. As *Time* tells it, "Quotes are manufactured, crushes and feuds constructed out of whole cloth, episodes planned in multiact 'storyboards' before
taping, scenes stitched together out of footage shot days apart."[34]

It starts with the gatekeepers. "Casting is the single most important ingre-
dient in the success of any reality show," explains Adam Shapiro, *Big Brother*'s
executive producer. Hirschorn wants us to believe this assembly process is
benign. He claims that although there's "probably a little bit of truth to" the
"conventional wisdom . . . that there's the evil reality TV producers who are
manipulating everything," mostly casts just . . . *happen:* "We just have our nets
out and we're catching a lot of dolphins."[35]

How naive does he think we are? Within the industry, it's understood
that producers seek out people they believe will behave in hypersensitive,
bizarre, or stereotypical ways. Critical thinkers aren't desirable; those prone
to verbal outbursts, physical aggression, or addiction are. The more overly
emotional or mentally unstable a cast member, the higher the potential for
buzz-generating conflict, so casting directors keep key clichés in mind.

Contestants are molded into predetermined stock characters, such as "The Weeper," "The Bitch," and "The Angry Black Woman." They behave as they do not just because strong, independent, and (god-forbid, feminist) women are typically excluded, but as a result of structural techniques designed to break down their defenses. Contestants are usually not allowed to see friends or family, read the news, surf the Internet, watch TV, listen to their own music, have private phone conversations, or go for walks, dates, or job interviews without camera crews. "It's like a women's penitentiary," one *Top Model* contestant said. They're kept sleep-deprived and underfed, plied with alcohol, then prodded to spew petty grievances in on-camera "confessionals." Voila: catfights, tears, crazy antics. Other times, staff psychologists "are more apt to spark fights than to prevent them." *American Idol* contestants confide their fears and jealousies to Fox-provided counselors, who then feed this information to producers. "It is pretty satisfying to watch the kids go to crazy town," a *Bachelor* producer says.

Oh, and those writers I mentioned earlier? While they don't create traditional scripts for characters to memorize,* they craft dialogue that can be fed to participants in a pinch (like Paris Hilton's schtick on *The Simple Life*), or popped into scenes after a series has stopped filming (as on *The Restaurant*). They coach contestants to deliver monologues on specific topics: A staffer instructed *Paradise Hotel* participants to "tell me you're sexy and you'll do anything to prove it," turning them intro improv actors. Emily Sinclair, a story editor for *Survivor, Extreme Makeover: Home Edition, Paradise Hotel,* and *Are You Hot?* sums up her role this way: "It's us being the puppeteers."[36]

And if there still aren't enough sparks? Editors just "take something black and make it white," as reality editor Jeff Bartsch told *Time.* Bait-and-switch is par for the course. "Footage has to be manipulated cleverly and often, so it's really in my job description to know where all the bodies are buried," a *Top Model* producer says. "If the show is done well, you wouldn't even know my job exists, because it would just feel like watching people do stuff."[37]

---

* Participants are made to read line-for-line ad copy, though.

Between all their Frankenbiting, editing, and product shilling, no wonder reality freelancers (including video editors, writers, and others) have been organizing for representation in the Writers Guild of America. In 2005, the WGA filed two class action lawsuits against producers and networks alleging wage violations and "sweatshop conditions" on eleven shows, including *The Bachelor, The Bachelorette, Joe Millionaire,* and *Trading Spouses.* By 2008, reality writers filed more than twenty labor complaints with the state of California against various reality producers, also with the help of the WGA.*

The bulk of *Reality Bites Back* breaks down the gender, race, and class stereotypes sold to us by reality TV's "puppeteers" and shows how regressive "social ideas" function together as backlash against women. But chapter 9 moves from reality TV content to media economics: You'll learn who is creating this contemporary cultural attack, who benefits from it, and why.

What impact might this deceptively produced alternate "reality" have on viewers' intellectual and critical instincts, over time? Until significant communications research is conducted, we can't be certain. But my experiences doing media literacy education raise concerns.

Where Have Our Critical Filters Gone?

As part of my work as executive director of Women In Media & News, I began discussing sexism in reality TV with high school and college students in 2003, just after *The Bachelor* started cheerfully asking, "Who will get sent home brokenhearted?" and skinny-minnies started stripping down on *Top Model.* Since then, I've spoken with thousands of students at more than eighty schools in more than half the states in America. I've seen a change in both the substance and the tone of responses to this form of television—and to its gendered ideology. Although anecdotal, these interactions may be telling.

In the early '00s, young people had exceptionally critical responses to my reality TV clip reel. They found show premises to be "ludicrous," "vile," and

---

* Named defendants in these lawsuits included Fox, ABC, CBS, WB, TBS, and five production companies, including Darnell's longtime collaborators Rocket Science Laboratories and Fleiss's Next Entertainment.[38]

"completely unrealistic." They'd gasp, groan, or grumble to one another when cameras intrusively zoomed in on rejected bachelorettes' tear-stained faces, or on plastic surgeons' scalpels cutting into insecure mothers' bodies. They'd laugh when announcers described manipulative scenarios as "every girl's dream!" They were funny, wisecracking about the overuse of seemingly scripted phrases like "emotional connection" and "I'm not here to make friends!" in show after show. They were angry, asking "Where do they get off treating women like that?" Most important, they saw right through the networks' fairytale facades. "It's like they want us to think feminism never happened," a Fordham student told me. "Do they think we're stupid enough to believe this shit is real?"

Eight years later, I find stark differences in young people's responses to similar TV clips. Today's teens and young adults grew up watching reality shows as uncritically as their parents watched *The Cosby Show* in the '80s and *Happy Days* in the '70s. At least among those who've spoken with me, their ability to discern production tricks—and their critical responses to gendered, raced messages within media "texts"—seems to have suffered as a result. Women's and ethnic studies majors sometimes express offense at some of the content, but many other young women and men tell me that shows like *The Bachelor* and *Flavor of Love* are "hilarious," "just TV, so no big deal," or more disturbingly, "realistic." I'm dismayed at how often I hear people mouthing the justifications media executives use to deflect accountability for biased content. They say that producers "are just showing us the way dumb-asses act," and since they "can't put words in people's mouths" (a false assumption, as Frankenbites attest), any problematic representations are the fault of participants, not the responsibility of the networks that air these shows. "If these skanks want to act like they have no self-respect, that's not the show's fault," an MIT student insisted. Students of color who expect and demand ethical practices from government and business have nevertheless said it's "important" to "support" shows like *Flavor of Love* or *The Real Housewives of Atlanta,* because their primarily African American casts bring visibility to our mostly white TV landscape. When I ask about the bigoted representations of Black, Latino, and Asian people on minority-led reality shows, students too often say that people of color "should learn how to behave," and if "they act the fool," then "of course the cameras will keep rolling." What media companies should do seems less of a consideration.

Now when I screen clips, instead of snickering at cheesy narrators or blatant product placements that disrupt the flow of a show, students giggle when women sob after being dumped, when beautiful girls are badgered about their bodies, and when women of color go off on violent tirades. Girls used to ask me about the social and economic forces that might compel a woman to volunteer to have her appearance, personality, or romantic prospects savaged on TV. Now, girls regularly tell me they're dieting to audition for *Top Model.* Reality shows are appointment TV on many campuses I've visited. This pastime sometimes affects academic priorities and impacts the way educators work: A college in Boston rescheduled my visit because they'd inadvertently planned the lecture on an *American Idol* night, and no one shows up for events when *Idol*'s on. The Millennial Generation seems to be getting more cynical ("Of course it's all bullshit, but it's funny. *Whatever.*") but less skeptical. That kind of mind-set makes advertisers salivate.

Viewers have many reasons for enjoying all forms of media, and unlike reality producers, I do not think stupidity is one of them. Young adults are not sheep soaking up media messages in unison. Young feminist and social justice activists are a testament to that, often producing their own documentaries and political remix videos and using social media and technology to draw attention to human rights issues, improve their local communities, and advocate for public policies they believe to be important.

Yet intelligence and savvy do not immunize Millennials—or their parents or grandparents—from being ideologically and commercially influenced by media messages. I am concerned at the increasingly uncritical ways I've seen students react to media over the last decade. I'd like to see serious scholarly investigation into what impact reality television's portrayals of gender, race, class, sexuality, and consumerism may have on the expectations and worldview of viewers who've come of age with these shows.

In 2007, the Pew Research Center reported that 81 percent of eighteen- to twenty-five-year-olds stated that being rich is the first or second most important goal in life for their generation, and 51 percent chose fame. Only 30 percent identified helping people in need as their peers' top priorities; and just 22 percent said community leadership.[39] My guess is that the wealth and semicelebrity status lavished on reality TV participants over the course of a decade has played a role in Millennials' goals.

Viewers of all ages do ourselves a disservice by watching reality TV with our intellects on pause. We can enjoy the catharsis and fantasy these shows offer, but unless we keep our critical filters on high, we leave ourselves open to serious manipulation.

Don't Get Depressed, Get Active

Beyond recognizing that very little is "real" in reality TV, my goal is to arm you with the knowledge you need to understand and challenge the bigoted "social ideas" pushed by pop culture. So in chapter 10, you'll find tools you can use to empower your friends, family, and community to become more conscious media consumers. From reality TV drinking games to tips on how to write a protest letter to guidelines for deconstructing media content, you'll learn how fun fighting propaganda can be.

Ultimately, I want to encourage you to seek accountability from media companies that promised us "reality," and instead delivered a contemporary cultural attack on four decades of social progress. That's why I've turned over the conclusion to leading media justice activists, independent media producers, and educators. Each of these inspiring women and men offers you a unique way to effect positive change. In the end, I hope you will be amused, outraged, engaged, and ready to take action.

As for me, I invite you to check out RealityBitesBackBook.com, where you can debate the reality TV you love, hate . . . or love to hate. Maybe together, we'll make a viral video series about TV fans protesting integrated advertisers, or chaining themselves to Mike Darnell's, Mike Fleiss's, or Michael Hirschorn's desks to demand better programming. In honor of those "evil geniuses," we can call it *When Reality TV Viewers Attack!*

Chapter One

Unraveling Reality TV's Twisted Fairytales

Cinderellas and Cautionary Tales

Careful the wish you make. . . . Careful the path they take—wishes
come true, not free. Careful the spell you cast. . . . Sometimes the
spell may last beyond what you can see and turn against you.

—INTO THE WOODS

I can't believe I'm saying this, but I do believe in fairytales.

—ZORA, the "winner" on *Joe Millionaire*

The palace ballroom was massive, and they had it all to themselves. Lush royal green curtains fell over towering windows. Candles flickered on the mantel. Hundreds of golden lights glittered from a lavish chandelier spanning nearly the entire ceiling.

They seemed like the perfect couple. Like all good princes, Evan was tall, dark, and handsome. And, like every true princess, Zora had lustrous hair and a pure heart. As he took her in his arms and began a slow waltz, she gazed up at him as if he were the answer to all her dearest dreams.

Music swelled as they kissed. If you listened very carefully, you'd swear you could hear bluebirds chirping in the background, as if Cinderella's animated helpers themselves might be the ones to roll out the words *The End* in calligraphy on the screen above the pair as the camera panned out and the credits rolled.

And then they never saw each other again.

See, it's like this: No one ever skips off together into the sunset on reality TV, and Evan Marriott was not exactly a prince among men. In reality, he was just some schmo with a thin bank account and a full head of hair, hired by Fox to play the part of a single, moneyed stud looking for love on the "gold diggers get theirs" dating show, *Joe Millionaire*.

And what about Zora Andrich, the sweet-natured "good girl" who "won" the privilege of being selected by a guy who had done nothing but lie to her from the moment she met him? Turns out Evan was never the least bit interested in her, heartstrings-tugging finale notwithstanding. On the postshow interview circuit, he let it slip that he chose her only because "I had to pick one of the girls," and the producers wanted Zora, a schoolteacher who did charity work, in order to stage a convincing fairytale ending. During an appearance on *Live with Regis and Kelly,* Zora confirmed that their "relationship ended as soon as the set lights went out."[1] That was 2003. Seven years later, we're still inundated with reality TV shows pitching us fairytales, and we're still eating it up to the tune of millions of viewers per night.

As practiced storytellers, reality TV producers like Mike Darnell and Mike Fleiss (who we met in the introduction) understand that old cliché about being able to catch more flies with honey than vinegar. They know they can lure more viewers with the promise of possibility—romantic, economic, or otherwise—than with overt misogyny. That's why they package their parade of sexist stereotypes as the embodiment of the "perfect fairytale."

"This show really is kind of a reality version of Cinderella," Ken Mok, executive producer of *America's Next Top Model,* told E!'s *True Hollywood Story,*[2] describing a UPN-turned-CW series that regularly tells gorgeous, insecure young women that they're too fat, too flawed, and, in the case of girls of color, too "ghetto" to make it as an advertiser's muse.

This formula pops up wherever women are pivotal to a series: The central conceit of Fox's *The Swan,* for example, was that "ugly ducklings" would be sliced and diced into "beautiful swans," as if pitting emotionally unstable plastic surgery patients against one another in a bizarro–world beauty pageant were a modern Hans Christian Andersen fable rather than prime-time exploitation of body dysmorphia.

Nevertheless, "I felt like a princess!" has been a constant refrain from female reality stars, starting with the first winner of *America's Next Top Model,* Adrianne Curry,[3] and echoed by competitors every season thereafter. It doesn't take much to prompt this exact proclamation—and not just from would-be models. Sometimes we hear it from bona fide stars, as when actress Debra Messing giddily described feeling "like a princess" on the red carpet after being frocked for an awards show by fashion stylist Rachel Zoe, on Bravo's eponymous *The Rachel Zoe Project.* Other times, it's a favorite phrase of star fuckers. For one of the fame-seekers on *Paris Hilton's My New BFF* (MTV, natch), getting her hair cut according to the heiress's specifications made her "feel like a princess."*

Really? Being bossed around by Paris Hilton is Cinderella treatment?

Well, yes, in the unreal world of "reality television," where virtually *anything that happens to any woman—no matter how crass, vindictive, or fleeting*—can be presented as an idealized fairytale, so long as it is done *to* a woman rather than achieved *by* one.

On dating shows like ABC's *The Bachelor,* prospective princesses sit on their aimless, tiny behinds, fend off fellow ladies in waiting, and hope to be whisked away by a network-approved knight in shining Armani. Stay-at-home moms, waitresses, and crime scene investigators depressed about their appearances are physically transformed by scalpels and silicone on programs like ABC's *Extreme Makeover* and Fox's *The Swan.* But the much-vaunted "journeys of self-discovery" these women undergo rarely involve much activity on their part. On *Extreme Makeover,* self-esteem is induced by surgeons, hairstylists, and makeup artists rather than the psychological heavy lifting of therapy. On *The Swan,* weight loss is the result of liposuction and tummy tucks rather than lifestyle-changing diet

---

* It wouldn't be fair to call just any reality show participants "star fuckers." But on any given episode of *Paris Hilton's My New BFF,* young women and men willingly jump through humiliating hoops just for the "prize" of being momentary "best friends" with the paparazzi's muse.

and exercise. Fashionistas on less physically intrusive makeover series such as TLC's *What Not to Wear* and Bravo's *Tim Gunn's Guide to Style* instruct mom-jeans wearers that beauty comes from product-placement cosmetics and clothing, not from within—which is why participants' overhauled "personal style" ends up reflecting producers' and advertisers' choices instead of their own tastes.

In real life, situations in which women have such little agency would be seen as pitiable, not enviable—yet in reality TV we're prompted to believe that this is the stuff dreams are made of. This is never in as stark relief as when series center on (the flimsiest approximations of) love.

Princes for Hire, Princesses for Sale: Constructing the Fairytale

Just as in those classic stories from Disney to the Brothers Grimm, romance and finance are inextricably linked in dating, mating, and marriage shows, in which a bevy of doormat-y "gorgeous girls" is invariably paired with one supposedly "rich, successful" single man, as in this typical, scene-setting montage from season 2 of ABC's *The Bachelor:*

> *"Aaron, a successful twenty-eight-year-old bank vice president, was intro-duced to twenty-five beautiful bachelorettes in hopes that one of them would become his wife."*

> *Voiceover clip from Aaron: "I just had twenty-five supermodels walk by me. What do you say? They're all beautiful; they all have so much going for them. I can't find a flaw in any of them. They're all into me, which is wonderful. I never thought I would be so lucky."*

Yep, they're all supermodels, and they're all "into him," whomever "him" happens to be. That, of course, is what princesses are expected to be: available, pretty, eager . . . and easily impressed.

"I understand each one of you is in love with him," *Bachelor* host Chris Harrison says in mock-somber tone to a room of angsty bachelorettes on the show's fourth installment. True to Grimms' form, we're never really shown *why* these irrationally attached lasses have gone all googly-eyed over relative strangers. The guys, after all, rarely expend any real effort to win their hearts. (Not that they need to: These men are almost afterthoughts, there to fulfill the role of symbolic Everyman without whom Everywoman's life is supposedly incomplete.) And mirroring the minimal information traditional fairytales impart about the dashing prince, reality programs rarely reveal much about their harem masters' hopes and dreams beyond their desire to feel up as many princesses as possible in hot tubs, limos, and "fantasy suites."

There's a reason the male heroes of these shows don't usually get all that emotionally invested: They're not meant to. For the most part, a desire to fall in love and settle down isn't among the criteria producers look for when casting Prince Charming. Evan Marriott got the *Joe Millionaire* gig, he explained to *Entertainment Weekly,* because "They needed a guy that was in construction but didn't have kids, hadn't been in jail, wasn't on drugs. And basically I fit the bill. They said they would pay me $50,000, and I said, 'Where do I sign?' I wasn't looking for the love of my life."[4] That, then, was *Joe*'s biggest lie of all. Viewers were told from the outset that Evan would be duping twenty women about his income bracket to determine whether they were "in it for true love" or just "greedy gold diggers." Yet the show's deeper deception was that Evan ever had any intention of finding a wife, or a girlfriend—or even anything more than a paycheck—from the program. And he was hardly alone in his disinterest in commitment. Dating show dudes tend to ooze insincerity while spouting platitudes about finding "the right girl for me," like every Abercrombie-looking, line-throwing player at every bar on any given night.*

---

* Every once in a while a show doesn't even bother to hide it. For example, challenges on VH1's *The Pickup Artist* involve teaching socially awkward and unattractive guys how to "run game" on— translation: lie to—women to get as many numbers from or make out with as many babes as possible within a designated time period.

Deviations from this script are rare. It wasn't until season 13(!) in 2009 that *The Bachelor* chose a star who honestly seemed to want to find a wife.* In contrast, dating shows emphasize women's matrimonial motivations with a nearly endless stream of marriage-minded femmes professing some variation of the belief that being the last girl standing at a network altar—even though they'd be standing there with a virtual stranger—will make all their dreams come true.

While they don't genuinely offer their hearts, reality TV men *do* play the proud provider. It hardly matters that what they provide is not theirs to give; they are simply handsome shills (for products as well as ideas), offering well-orchestrated infomercials disguised as courtship rituals. "This Tacori diamond ring symbolizes forever for me. I just hope that she will accept it," snowboarder Jesse Csincsak said on the finale of *The Bachelorette*'s fourth season. He chose the 2.3-carat platinum and diamond engagement band for his potential paramour, DeAnna Pappas, with the help of a spokesperson for Tacori, which has provided jewelry for the *Bachelor* franchise for years.[+] During their "romantic journeys," these bachelors hand over many a prettily wrapped box containing various items advertisers have paid—or provided free in exchange for publicity—to position as fairytale linchpins. Starry-eyed future brides are dolled up in Badgley Mischka and Nicole Miller gowns; festooned with millions of dollars worth of Tacori, Harry Winston, and Chopard diamonds; chauffeured in $100,000 Maseratis; and swept off to book-your-spa-stay-now resorts by beaus who use Marqui Jet cards.

---

* Even then, the "fairytale" was beyond twisted. After ABC spent months hyping *Bachelorette* castoff and single dad Jason Mesnick as a family-minded wife seeker who "found the love of his life," viewers did see this *Bachelor* propose to Melissa Rycroft, who agreed to become insta-stepmom to his four-year-old son—only to watch him dump her and get back together with previous dumpee Molly Melaney on the live reunion show that aired literally one hour after the finale. ABC televised *Jason & Molly's Wedding* in 2010, like they did with *Bachelorette* Trista Rehn and Ryan Sutter's nuptials in 2003, as "proof" that their nineteen-season franchise "works."

[+] Incidentally, if Tacori wants to "symbolize forever" in the minds of the potential ring-buying public, the company might want to reconsider branding itself as the bling of choice for a franchise that's one-in-thirteen (*The Bachelor*) and one-in-five (*The Bachelorette*) where weddings are concerned. DeAnna did accept the costly rock, oh yes, but "forever" translated to roughly four months: They split shortly after their "we've set a date!" announcement on ABC's reunion episode—and far before most couples would have finished paying off the ring. That's still about three months longer than the lifespan of the engagement of *Bachelor* number 12, Matt Grant, to aspiring actress Shayne Lamas. But while *The Bachelor, Joe Millionaire*, and their ilk don't tend to reward participants with true "happily ever after" endings, these shows definitely deliver fairytale-esque windfalls for advertisers who ♡ free PR for their products and services.

They're not kidding about booking your spa stay now, by the way. Viewers who want to travel in these misguided daters' luxurious footsteps—and are willing to blow $5,580 and up for five days, not including airfare—can plan "a posh, all-inclusive Bachelor Getaway package" at Kamalame Cay island, by clicking the "As Seen on *The Bachelor"* link at Bahamas.com.[5] And for those of us who don't have the cash for a luxe getaway, we can buy a pair of "Frankie & Johnny Fairytale Wedding" pajamas for $79 from various websites using that ubiquitous "As Seen on *The Bachelor"* tag. The sizing is for adults, even though the pink cotton PJs are decorated with childlike illustrations of diamond rings, pumpkin carriages, castles, hearts, and flowers, and of course, princesses kissing frogs.

Dating shows aren't the only subgenre where commerce is the key to the fairytale. Sometimes the promise of a lucrative job prompts such illusions *(America's Next Top Model, American Idol, The Apprentice);* other times a lower-rent version of happily ever after is offered via a new wardrobe that fits better than what a working mom can afford on a thrift store budget *(What Not to Wear).* And sometimes what contestants consider a "fairytale" can be downright heartbreaking, as when a plastic surgery show provided a root canal to a poor woman whose teeth were rotting after a decade without health insurance—but only if she agreed to undergo around a dozen unnecessary cosmetic procedures.

Mistaking the Trappings for Love

When they're not marketing brand-specific jewelry, clothing, vacations, or dental veneers, reality TV shows advertise the same ideology about gender roles found in traditional fairytales. Both visual and verbal indicators are used to underscore the notion that women are poor damsels who can't take care of themselves, while men are all-powerful studs ever ready to rescue them.

There's something truly ridiculous about watching grown women masquerading as would-be princesses, abdicating all choices to a guy they hardly know and hoping their passivity will help them snag some suburban Prince Charming. This infantilization is especially ludicrous when the "girls" languishing in husband-hunting harems are mothers in their forties with mortgages, careers, and kids in college, as they've been on *Who Wants to Marry My Dad?* and *Age of Love.*

These messages aren't exactly subtle. *Joe Millionaire* is first introduced as he gallops toward his admiring throng on a stallion, looking like Gaston, the muscle-bound, animated hunk from Disney's *Beauty and the Beast.* As for *Joe's* lovely suitors, we first encounter them squealing "Ohmigawd! It's a *castle!*" as they arrive at the mansion.

Preferring not to leave viewers' interpretation of this theme to chance, Fox assembled a montage to frame their *Joe Millionaire* reunion special. It began with the caption "The Fairy Tale" floating across the screen in wedding-invitation-style calligraphy, followed by seventeen out-of-context clips from "gold diggers" dishing about their Cinderella fantasies:

"We were put in a situation to see if we could find romance in a fairytale."

"We're gonna be in a fairytale."

"In my fairytale, when you know, you know."

"I expect the fairytale."

"There's this guy who resembles a fairytale prince riding up on a horse."

"I can appreciate the fairytale idea now."

"And it's happening—it's so real!"

"As far as the fairytale part of it?"

"It's going to be a fairytale."

"I'm a big fan of romance and fairytales."

"It's a fairytale come true."

"Fairytale."

"Fairytale."

"Fairytale."

"Fairytale."

"Fairytale."

"Fairytale."

As if this montage didn't sufficiently deflate these adults, it ended with one final cast member musing in full-on baby talk, "It's a *jour*-ney. It's a *fai*-rytale." (Viewers subjected to this barrage might be forgiven for feeling less like they were being sold a fairytale and more like they were being trained at a school for unusually dense puppies.)

Where Fox partially passed this off as tongue in cheek, ABC's packaging of *The Bachelor* has always been disingenuously earnest. As the *Los Angeles Times* noted, despite failing to actually produce long-term pairings, the show pretends to be "absolutely irony-free."[6] In one "where are they now?" clip, host Chris Harrison reminded the audience that sweet-natured bridal castoff Gwen had "watched her journey on season 2 of *The Bachelor* unfold like a fairytale, complete with horse-drawn carriage." No shit—they actually roll tape of this babe riding off in a buggy decorated with Christmas lights to resemble the fairy-godmother-procured pumpkin carriage of cartoon fame. "I do feel like Cinderella," Gwen says in her poufy princess ball gown.

After a while, the narrator's breathless promises that every upcoming episode will contain "the most romantic rose ceremony *ever!*" ring hollow. It's a letdown to fans—the viewership equivalent of a restaurant promising culinary delicacies and delivering greasy takeout. Talk about a recipe for heartburn.

The faux sincerity embedded in the structure of reality TV's flagship dating show is insulting to its audience, who are lied to as boldly as are its contestants. During season 11, for example, producers knew full well the twist hidden from viewers until the finale: For the first time in series history, bachelor Brad Womack *rejected each and every bachelorette,* preferring to walk away single. Yet, despite his full house of broken hearts, the first episode opened with the narrator proclaiming that "in the end, only one woman *will become* Mrs. Brad Womack," followed by edited audio snippets of the show's star pledging, "I'm here to find true love. *I will* find my wife."

All these pricey props and "princess for a day" primpings work manipulative magic on contestants. Sequestered from the outside world during weeks and sometimes months of filming, they respond predictably. When Billie Jeanne Houle, a sexually exuberant, free-spirited bartender, was seduced on *Married by America,* she thought it was her TV-arranged fiancé who was winning her heart. In reality, producers simply seized on her eagerness to fall in love to cajole her into believing she was living a real-life fairytale.

Here's the formula: First, take a naive beauty who longs to get married and offer her a gorgeous guy who says he shares that wish. Next, send her to a series of bridal gown fittings, let her select a wedding ring, and eventually have her write vows with the other half of this arranged marriage equation. Throw in a healthy heaping of liquor-lubricated sex scenes and, voilà, "love"—reality TV style. "When we got to the show it just happened to be that we clicked. You got gourmet chefs, you got Jacuzzis, you got all the alcohol you could want. *I really fell for the whole experience,"* Houle told *Entertainment Weekly* (emphasis mine).[7] Time and time again, this is how it's done.

In a limo on the way to a date on a luxury yacht, a bubbly brunet gushed, "I have the dress, I have $1 million worth of jewelry on me, I have the prince, and I am feeling like Cinderella at the ball." How could she *not* feel fireworks when fourth-season *Bachelor* Bob Guiney kissed her, considering how producers *literally shot fireworks* over their heads as the couple gazed at a starry horizon?

Such seeming attempts at posthypnotic suggestion appear to provoke Pavlovian responses in the women of reality TV (drape with diamonds, sprinkle fireworks, commence swooning), essentially telling female viewers that the measure of a man's love can only be found in the gift receipts in his wallet. Not only shouldn't we *expect* mental, emotional, or political rapport with our boyfriends, we're told, we shouldn't even *want* such a connection. Just as troubling, reality television teaches boys and men that without an array of posh and cheesily metaphoric props, most bachelors have nothing genuine to offer women.

Which brings us to the tenth season of *The Bachelor,* when an ingenue named Tessa Horst expressed doubts about remaining on the show. She liked Naval Lieutenant Andy Baldwin just fine when they were alone, but she vented, "When I'm back home and wondering about group dates that I'm not on, I get fed up with it." Andy was increasingly aware that Tessa was getting ready to opt out of CrazyTown if she didn't feel "a real connection" with him soon. Since this potential cardinal sin of female agency diverges from the usual script (princesses aren't supposed to rescue themselves, after all), Prince Andy was tasked with luring the errant cutie safely back into his court. "[Tessa] doesn't want to go the distance unless she knows that I truly am interested in her," he told the cameras. "Tonight I need to convince her that I'm a man that she wants. I'm nervous, but I gotta go out there and give my all."

So, how would our *Bachelor* boy get the job done? Was he funny enough to seduce her with that evergreen aphrodisiac, laughter? Would he attempt to bond over mutual shared interests, politics, or family stories? Perhaps he'd offer her new insights into his dreams, his worldview, his character?

Er . . . no.

Remember, a man's character is considered irrelevant in the Bachelorverse (as are humor, intelligence, and fidelity). So when Andy needed to "give his all," he resorted to the only tools producers put at his disposal: "the fairytale date." (Or, as obsequious host Chris Harrison promised, "One pretty woman . . . gets the *most romantic date, ever!*")

First, Andy summoned Tessa to their first solo outing with a note instructing her to "Come as you are. I'll take care of the rest." Next, amid the jealous glares of all her evil stepsister competitors, he presented her with a $2 million Chopard diamond necklace, earrings, and bracelet set to wear for the night.* From there, the pair sped off in a $600,000 Saleen S7 Twin Turbo to a Nicole Miller boutique, where cameras lingered on the storefront's marquee and fashionable mannequins. "I thought along with your diamonds you could use a very elegant dress," Andy said, as if he had anything to do with it. But, par for the television course, such

---

* But not to keep. The luxury jeweler's product placement deal with ABC involves bachelorettes only donning such baubles on screen as free promotion for the brand. I've never been able to figure out why, season after season, the women swoon over these limited-time offers. Okay, quick question to my male readers: If you surprised your girlfriend or your wife with a gorgeous necklace as a gift but then said, "It'll look beautiful on you when we go out to dinner, but you're going to have to return it to the store before we go home," level with me—aren't the chances good you'd be sleeping on the couch?

distinctions didn't seem to bother the formerly dubious Tessa, now giddy at the chance to model a series of designer cocktail gowns, while the *Bachelor* showered her with compliments. "This whole date I've wanted someone to pinch me. I think it's every girl's dream to, like, be brought over diamonds, and brought to a dress store, and pick out anything you want. I'm just excited!" she gushed.*

So, let's recap: To keep Tessa from walking off the show, a worried Andy has to "pull out all the stops" to show her "that she's truly special to me." Instead of sharing more of his authentic self with her, he simply offers a parade of product placement goods and activities as a proxy for actual feelings. Nevertheless, this stream of artifice does the trick. "It's been an amazing, amazing, amazing date, and while I still have some reservations and doubts, he's really putting himself out there, and I think it's pushing me to do the same thing," the formerly frustrated beauty tells the cameras. By the end of the night she's fully convinced and lets him know she wants to bring him home to meet her parents.

Apparently "putting yourself out there" is defined in the Bachelorverse as "maxing out your spending limit."

Hear that, guys? If you want a woman to fall in love with you, don't worry about baring your soul or risking your heart. Just get out your credit card and prepare to score, because the girl of your dreams doesn't care about who you really are. Not that it matters, since you don't really care about her, either, so long as she looks hot in a halter top.

Pushing Culturally Ingrained Buttons

If reality dating shows portray women (and men) so shabbily, why do so many of us continue to watch them?

---

* The resemblance to the shopping scene in the classic "hooker with a heart of gold" flick, *Pretty Woman*, was uncanny—and not just because host Chris Harrison called Tessa a "pretty woman." There was Andy doing his best impression of Richard Gere's rich john buying fashions for—and affection from—Julia Roberts's prostitute, Vivian, updated by Tessa twirling for her bachelor's approval. Viewers are supposed to come away with warm fuzzies about how "lucky" Tessa was to be cast as a "real-life" *Pretty Woman*. We're just supposed to forget that Vivian was a call girl, and that it's not exactly the epitome of romance when a wealthy egotist trades cash for a hooker's body and eventually her heart. At least Richard Gere knew to limit expectations when he gave Julia Roberts a $250,000 choker to wear for just one evening: "I don't want you to get too excited. It's only a loan," he said.

DISNEY FROM
CRADLE TO GRAVE

It's fitting that *The Bachelor,* which revived the princess fantasy for prime time, airs on Disney-owned ABC. In the 1970s, feminists began rethinking fairytales, creating new children's stories with heroines like Atalanta, who explores the world before getting married. They hoped to pique kids' imaginations and teach them that strength, adventure, and love are available to boys and girls alike.

Atalanta doesn't live here anymore. Today, Disney wants women from cradle to grave, and they're using their media properties to keep us in their thrall. They get us from preconsciousness: Before we're old enough to speak in complete sentences, our parents read us Disney's instructive morality plays about what it means to be "good little princesses" and "strong, daring boys." They intrigue us as preadolescents with Cinderella and Snow White costumes at Halloween and Disney on Ice: Princess Classics shows at the local skating rink. As teens, *Hannah Montana* on the Disney channel teaches us that girl power = merchandizing.

Infantilizing us is so profitable that *The Bachelor* has attempted to provoke psychological regression in adults for fourteen seasons and counting. As the show's popularity has grown, Disney's commercial fairytale imagery has woven its way from network TV to cable. Brides on WETV's *My Fair Wedding with David Tutera* twirl with glee in "Kirstie Kelly for Disney Fairy Tale Weddings" dresses. (Want to walk down the aisle in a ball gown named after Princesses

Ariel, Belle, or Jasmine? You can—for a few thou.) Tutera even hosted a WE TV special called *Disney Dream Weddings* and spent a full hour hawking Disney's "destination wedding" packages, including his own high-end "Couture Collection." He and other Disney spokespeople effused about all the "magic" you can buy if you have Your Special Day at Disney World. This and other WE series such as *Platinum Weddings* want you to know that you, too, can ride up to your ceremony in a theme-park pumpkin carriage, say your vows in Cinderella's Castle, and dance alongside a dozen waltzing Princes Charming and Snow Whites in full Disney regalia. All it costs is a hundred grand.*

Disney has mastered media synergy to implant and co-opt our fantasies from pre-K to our wedding day. I wonder if they're planning to stop there. Sleeping Beauty dozed for a hundred years in a glass coffin . . . can a Disney-branded line of caskets be far behind? Perhaps when reality TV shows have been on the air long enough for women to start dying from complications from their *Extreme Makeovers,* they'll be buried in Disney couture coffins. And then we'll all watch the funeral procession on ABC, during sweeps.

---

* Viewers responded just as Disney hoped they would. "I just watched an incredible television special on the Disney Dream Wedding and I just have to share the great information in this with you!" a rapt viewer blogged. "I honestly cannot think of a better way to spend your living fairytale than in the one place where fairytales and dreams come true every day!"[8]

I'm asked this question constantly, by everyone from seasoned entertainment journalists to tenured professors of psychology to students who attend my media literacy workshops. Everyone seems to want one simple, clean answer. I can't offer that. We tune in for numerous reasons, some conscious (mockery of reality series' typecast characters is an amusing sport for many viewers) and some subconscious (from fantasy escapism to the superiority we feel when watching human train wrecks display their shortcomings under a national spotlight).

That said, I begin this book by discussing reality TV's overreliance on fairytale narratives because this is the saccharine coating that masks the genre's chauvinistic and anachronistic ideas about women and men, about love and sex, about marriage and money. As we saw earlier, Fox was panned as reaching a new low when they aired *Who Wants to Marry a Multi-Millionaire?* but by repackaging the very same concepts under a fairytale gloss, ABC struck programmatic gold with *The Bachelor*.

Why? Because this genre that calls itself "unscripted" is carefully crafted to push all our culturally ingrained buttons. In the case of dating shows, it's precisely all the pretty-pretty-princess twaddle that allows us to accept these regressive notions as palatable, even ideal. Dating back to our earliest childhood instructions on gender, the call to these contrivances is powerful. The psychological underpinnings of fairytale imagery provoke a strong emotional response, and thus compel us to keep watching.

But at what cost?

For men, as Andy and Tessa's experience illustrates, reality TV's warped fairytales reinforce a limiting vision of masculinity in which they must be stoic providers of both pleasure and financial comfort, responsible for not only their own happiness and success but also that of their female companions. Male viewers learn relatively quickly that they should not expect (or desire) women as partners in love and in life, only as beautiful, compliant subjects in need of social, sexual, and interpersonal direction.

For women, these representations conjure our earliest memories—of the stories our parents read to us before bed, of the cartoons that danced in our imaginations, telling us what we could (and should) look forward to when we grew up. No matter how independent we might be as adults, how cynical we consider ourselves, or how hard we've worked to silence external cultural conditioning, decades of sheer repetition make it extremely difficult to fully purge societal standards from our psyches. Simply put, it's damn near impossible to live completely outside the culture, no matter how well we try to shield ourselves from its impact. Buried deep inside many adult, single, heterosexual women's minds is that internalized, conformist voice humming, "Someday my prince will come."* It's an external tune borne of cultural conditioning, one that we may reject or work to silence. Even if some of us are soothed by its melody ("chick flick," anyone?), most of us don't live our lives in deference to it. Yet as many relationship counselors can attest, countless romantically dissatisfied women beg therapists to help them figure out why they haven't found their Prince Charming yet.

Regardless of where we fall on this continuum—from conscious refusal to let childish notions inform our love lives to enthusiastic embrace of fantasies we've nursed since we were little girls—producers play on these deep-seated ideas about gender, love, and romance for ratings. This, in part, is what Mike Darnell was talking about when he told *Entertainment Weekly* that the secret to airing a successful reality TV show is to create a premise that is "steeped in some social belief."⁹ And, as we'll soon see, similar stereotypes about race, class, beauty, and sexual orientation are endemic, even necessary, to reality TV—in all its forms.

Exclusivity, Conformity, or Banishment

While reality TV picks at emotional wounds about the loneliness, poverty, and desperation that Grimms and Disney have told us await strong-willed women, the genre also reinforces the punitive proscriptions for their "bad" girls in these classic stories. With few exceptions (Disney's *Mulan* and Tiana of *The*

---

* Of course, the costar of many lesbian and bisexual women's "one great love" fantasies is another princess. But just like Disney, reality TV producers—with only a couple of cable exceptions—prevent lesbians and gays from participating in the classic romantic fairytale. We'll get to that in a moment.

Princess and the Frog are two; the ogre Fiona from DreamWorks' *Shrek* is another), fairytale females who stand up for themselves, or who are confident, active, or powerful, are typically depicted as bitchy, catty, cruel, and unworthy—and they are almost always punished for their sins. Only the prettiest, most passive girls, without agency or voice, without ambition or individuality, are rewarded with love, financial success, and the ultimate prize: being picked by the prince.*

And so it goes in reality TV, where women are portrayed as virtually interchangeable in body type and personality alike. Those who deviate from the norm in appearance or behavior are immediately banished. These prefab fairytales are exclusive to a fault, and anyone who hopes to qualify must subscribe to a litany of regressive social mores. Producers act as gatekeepers, allowing inside only those participants who conform to the strict gender, ethnic, and sexual codes that this genre is attempting to recodify as American "reality."

Do you transgress these codes by daring to have a healthy relationship with food? Are you simply larger than a size 6? Well, ladies, you're not allowed to visualize yourself as a princess—or even a member of her court. Only thin, often surgically enhanced women have been cast on network dating shows, which we'll discuss in more detail in the following chapter. The only exception came in the summer of 2009, when average-size and heavier women were cast to compete for the heart of a three-hundred-pound real estate dude on *More to Love,* a "plus-size" dating show from the minds that brought us *The Bachelor* and *Joe Millionaire.* Though they promoted the show as a *Bachelor*-style fairytale with a bit of extra padding, producers framed the women as self-loathing losers who could do little more than sob about hating their bodies, stuff their faces with meat on a stick, and declare that their weight prevented them from ever having a happy relationship.

The princess crown is also off-limits to women of color, who are underrepresented and typically eliminated after just a couple of episodes on network

---

* Grimms-turned-Disney classic *Sleeping Beauty* wins the love of her prince—and gets jogged out of a curse-induced coma—simply by resting prettily in her glass coffin. At least her slumber was the result of a spell, not something she chose for herself. In Disney's "modern" fairytale *The Little Mermaid,* heroine Ariel willingly—literally—gives up her voice to mutely woo her beloved with her "feminine wiles."

reality casts. Women of color are, however, very present in cable dating shows—where the fairytale packaging is missing. There's zero earnestness in the framing of programs like VH1's *Flavor of Love, I Love New York, Real Chance of Love,* or MTV's *For the Love of Ray J,* for example, which celebrate the exploitation of both women and men of color, each in different ways (as we'll see in chapter 5). Likewise, there has never been a Black, Asian, Latino, Native American, or Middle Eastern *Bachelor,* nor have men of color headlined any dating shows on network television, where such programs are sold as offering a chance at finding "true love." When men of color are the stars of their own dating shows, it's only on cable nets, where salacious hookups and racist throwbacks to Stepin Fetchit are much more the focus than classic notions of romance.

Are you lesbian, gay, or bisexual? In the world of reality TV, Americans can see people like you decorating homes *(Top Design),* designing clothing *(Project Runway),* cutting hair *(Shear Genius),* whipping people into shape *(Work Out),* telling sloppy straight men how to dress *(Queer Eye for the Straight Guy),* being campy divas *(RuPaul's Drag Race* on Logo*),* navigating the globe *(The Amazing Race),* and eating bugs *(Survivor),* but you can never seek "fairytale love." Oh, you can get laid, as on VH1's STD-chasing *A Shot at Love with Tila Tequila* and *A Double Shot at Love,* where dating challenges involved bikini foam parties and licking hot fudge off mannequins, but *love?* That's out of the question.

Among broadcast and widely viewed cable networks, only four high-profile queer-themed reality TV dating shows have aired in the genre's first full decade, two starring gay men and two starring bisexual women. Series starring bisexual women choosing between lesbians and straight men have played to straight male fantasies. Both incarnations of MTV's *A Shot at Love* with drunken calendar girls have featured busty, bi babes with long fingernails and a penchant for feeling each other up in full view of panting, horny dudes. While those hormonal performances may help destigmatize hookups between mostly-straight sorority girls who enjoy teasing their boyfriends with a little "hot girl-on-girl action," they hardly validate authentic lesbian and bisexual desire. MTV's storytelling leaves little room for genuine yearning for romantic love between women, much less "happily ever after." The debut episode of *A Shot at Love with Tila Tequila* was framed as the pinup girl's quest to figure out whether she wanted to be "with a man or a woman." But bisexuals are not confused about which gender they want to be with; they are sexually and romantically attracted to both women and men.* By portraying Tila as trying to "choose" whether to be a lesbian or to have a heterosexual relationship, MTV rendered bisexuality into the exact misconception bisexuals have long fought: the notion that they can or should "pick a side" or "get off the fence."

Still, *A Shot at Love* was the only mainstream-accessible dating show to even hint that not all women are interested in men. By early 2010, no major network had aired a single lesbian or a transgender dating series. Viewers can find such programming options only on Logo, a network launched by Viacom in 2006 to target the LGBT audience. Logo's dating shows *Curl Girls, Gimme Sugar,* and *Gimme Sugar: Miami* have diverged from reality TV's cult of compulsory heterosexuality and have featured more ethnically diverse casts than most network romances. Still, these shows placed more emphasis on the fun and drama of dating than the pursuit of genuine love and partnership. More groundbreaking was Logo's *Transamerican Love Story,* starring transgender actress and writer Calpernia Addams, who sought love among a pool of straight, gay, bisexual, and transgender men with the help of her best friend, trans activist Andrea James. Unfortunately, institutional biases and media economics combine to keep millions of television viewers from being able to watch Logo programming. For example, Comcast has blocked Logo from its channel lineup in conservative-leaning media markets such as Jackson, Mississippi, and Monroe, Louisiana, and DISH customers didn't have access to Logo until 2009—well after *Curl Girls, Gimme Sugar,* and *Transamerican Love Story* had aired.

---

* Of course, even the categories of "woman" and "man" themselves are limited. As discussed in chapter 8, reality TV hews extremely closely to the "gender binary," which does not encompass the many variations in gender presentation and gender identity present in the human experience. For tips on how to combat media bias against transgender people, see Julia Serano's suggestions in chapter 11.

Gay male dating shows have been light on happily ever after and heavy on cultural fears and stereotypes. On Bravo's cruel *Boy Meets Boy,* a bachelor thought he was going to have a chance to find same-sex bliss among a group of men he believed were all gay. The catch? Half were secretly straight actors setting him up to be rejected. Then came Fox's *Playing It Straight,* where a straight woman had to guess the sexual orientations of her male suitors based on whether they "acted gay" or seemed to behave like "normal" (i.e., "red-blooded heterosexual American") guys. If a gay man fooled her, he'd win a million bucks and she'd go home empty-handed; if she chose a straight man at the end, they'd split the money between them. The pretense of romance fell away as the bachelorette was "expected to be more of a detective than a fair maiden," trying to use her "gaydar" to decipher whether a man might be a big old homo because he owned a hair drier or danced well.[10] Gay men embraced the closet, modeling presumptions of straight, macho masculinity and renouncing their true sexuality, while heterosexual men attempted to turn themselves into the clichéd limp-wristed queen from popular film and sitcoms.* *Playing It Straight* was such a ratings flop that Fox yanked it after only three episodes, offering the series online years later on a pay-per-download basis. That was still more airtime than was received by the ill-fated gaysploitation special *Seriously, Dude, I'm Gay,* which Fox touted as "a heterosexual male's worst nightmare: turning gay overnight." The show was to follow the foibles of straight men moving into gay men's apartments to "immerse themselves in 'the gay lifestyle'"—defined by the network as bunking in West Hollywood lofts, dancing at gay clubs, and going on a "romantic blind date with another man." If after all this they successfully conned "a jury of their queers" (as well as their friends and families) into believing that they were out and proud homosexuals, they'd win a chunk of cash. Fox's press release called it

---

* Though *Playing It Straight* reveled in homophobic stereotypes about gay men, it also unintentionally crystallized how cultural expectations of masculinity—both gay and straight—are all performative rather than innate. Unfortunately, producers squandered the opportunity to explore culturally constructed gender presentation, instead creating a narrative that "ultimately served the interests of the heterosexual" status quo by reinforcing stereotypes, othering gay participants, and "maintaining heterosexuality's dominant status."[11] (RuPaul's *Drag Race* offers a much more compelling look at gender performance.)

"outrageously satirical," "hilarious," and "socially provocative." But they didn't count on the well-organized outrage of GLAAD, the Gay & Lesbian Alliance Against Defamation, which blasted the "backward" premise as raising red flags. The show was canceled before it went to air.[12]

Clearly, the level of ethnic, sexual, and behavioral uniformity required of potential castmates excludes a huge portion of the American public from the "reality" landscape, and "others" anyone who diverges from TV's cult of white, middle class heteronormativity. Just another way in which these shows are inauthentic in their depictions of modern life.

Humiliation:
The Flip Side of the Fairytale

Unfortunately for those who *are* allowed into this genre's surreal world, the fairytale is conditional. Reality TV exacts a steep price in exchange for the fantasy of happily ever after for *one* woman (however short-lived). That price is humiliation of *all* women.

Now, it's undeniable that reality TV producers love nothing more than to make fools of their cast members. Any five minutes from NBC's *Fear Factor*—which has made male and female contestants alike guzzle liquefied rats from a blender, gobble live cockroach and maggot sushi, and stick their heads into gallons of raw sewage—is proof enough that humiliation is aimed willy-nilly at any contestant who dares to appear on these sorts of game shows. But the goal of competition-based series like these is to shock or gross out viewers, not to sway them ideologically. For that sort of cerebral impact we need to turn to mating and makeover shows, where blatant degradation of women *as women* is persistent and inescapable.

The practice of humiliation functions structurally throughout gender-based series. It works both implicitly through show premises (for example, that scores of women are desperate enough to fight and weep over strangers just to avoid the shame of being single and female) and explicitly through manipulative editing, lying to contestants, and production tricks employed to portray women as stupid, pathetic losers. In fact, reality TV's humiliation of women is so systematic that it's almost mathematical. The formula is right out of those "if/then" logic proofs from high school math class:

IF A = *advertising is at the root of the proliferation of these programs,*

AND B = *one of the ultimate ideological goals of reality TV is to bring back outdated biases about women's rightful place in society,*

THEN C = *humiliation is both the preferred strategy of programmers (the means by which those goals are achieved) and the outcome (the emotional impact on show participants, and the implicit warning to female viewers).*

Humiliation is the tactic by which reality TV spreads antifeminist backlash ideology. As a structural device, it is used to offer women an ugly, unstated, and all-too-clear message: "This is where independence leads, ladies—to failure and misery."

This cautionary tale is present at every stage. It starts with the season opener of series such as *The Bachelor*, when one single dude is told how handsome and manly and *perfect* he is by twenty-five overdressed, overeager chicks who emerge from a couple of limousines as if from glammed-up clown cars. Our first introductions to these women assure us that they have no sense of self beyond a willingness to please some guy—*any* guy.

From there, we watch women sink to sickening depths as they perform one mortifying stunt after another in pursuit of male validation. City girls stick their hands up cows' asses to prove their romantic fitness for a cute country bumpkin on Fox's *Farmer Wants a Wife*. On VH1's *Real Chance of Love*, they're ordered to muck out a barn filled with horse, sheep, pig, and goose manure, while the cocky brothers they're vying to date mock them from a distance.* Though most reality

---

* This was a scene recycled from a *Joe Millionaire* episode filmed at a horse stable five years earlier, proving that in the reality TV universe, the image of women knee-deep in shit never goes out of style.

show stunts aren't so stinky, "group dates" are a staple. Like a flashback to some horrid high school popularity contest, women are made to jockey for "one-on-one time" to sell themselves as the prettiest, most easygoing, and most lovable of the bunch in five minutes or less, before one of their competitors can interrupt with a stream of insults.

For every shiny, happy moment where a wide-eyed waif gets to play-act as Cinderella at the ball, we get a litany of bitter, nasty scenes where dozens of female castmates are tormented as mercilessly as Cinderella was before she met her fairy godmother. Reality TV women are debased in any number of ways. They cry in limos after being kicked to the curb. They hyperventilate when the guy they've known for, oh, three hours says he doesn't see forever in their future. They abandon their belief systems to suit their men: For example, a vegetarian described eating meat for the first time in twelve years just because Andrew Firestone (star of *The Bachelor*'s third season) fed it to her. "My stomach will probably never be the same, but at least I touched his hand," she said, grateful for crumbs. After she got the heave-ho, she batted her big, brown eyes at the camera and moaned: "You wanna see a girl that's crushed, you got her."

The cautionary tale of female humiliation is embedded in the DNA of reality television. Whole series are dedicated to it. Take Fox's *Married by America,* where gorgeous would-be bride Billie Jeanne Houle (discussed earlier) was jilted at the altar of an elaborate sham of a "wedding" with all the fairytale trimmings. We watched her excited pursuit of the "perfect" bridal gown, the "perfect" ring, and the "perfect fairytale love." The catch? The groom clearly never cared about her or intended to marry her—and viewers knew this from the start. "Silly bimbo!" we were primed to laugh (and cringe) as we watched the naive sexpot fall for, fawn over, and fuck her distant but randy "fiancé."

After weeks of buildup, the inevitable happened: She said "I do" in earnest vows in front of her family, friends, and millions of viewers—and he replied, in effect, "Um... no thanks." Cameras pursued her as she fled the scene, a sobbing blur of satin, tulle, and smeared mascara. "When I woke up this morning I felt like all my dreams were gonna come true. I felt so alive and so happy," Billie Jeanne cried, choking out her words before collapsing in a heap. Viewers were treated to approximately ten full minutes of bawling—that's major prime-time real estate devoted to our voyeuristic peek into the misery of a woman *set up to feel this very way.*

Eventually, the moment producers had been waiting for all season finally arrived. Granted no privacy or ability to seek solace from her friends, the hysterical bride hid in a closet in an attempt to elude the show's intrusive glare. No luck. Fox's unblinking celluloid eye found her cowering there, still in her gown and veil. As her crying and shaking finally subsided, she stared off into space, glass-eyed and emotionally broken. "I'm a joke," she whispered. Not wanting that little gem to go by unnoticed, producers slapped Billie Jeanne's self-flagellating comment into a caption under her despairing face.

And there you go. The money shot in porn flicks usually involves male ejaculation. In reality TV dating shows, it comes when cameras zoom in on the tear-soaked face of some woman shattered by romantic rejection.* Producers bank on such scenes to reinforce the notion that single women are simpering spinsters who can never possibly be fulfilled without husbands. From casting to editing to reunion shows, everything builds to that moment when some sad sack sobs miserably from embarrassment and self-doubt, bemoaning her broken heart. Glowing about the star of their fourth season, *Bachelor* producer Mike Fleiss told *Entertainment Weekly* that he was thrilled with the opening episode because "Normally, there's nothing more challenging than getting girls to cry when they've only known the guy for three hours. Not this time."

---

* Humiliation is also among the top payoffs on shows like *America's Next Top Model* (when formerly confident women finally break down in a mass of self-doubt after repeated denials of their beauty) and in talent competitions like *American Idol* (where low-income young women—single moms who work at places like Wal-Mart are series staples—are mocked for dreaming that music might help them escape a dismal economic future).

Showcasing these moments is exactly what's behind the "Women Tell All" reunion specials ABC airs before every *Bachelor* finale. It's a simple premise: Producers bring back all the rejectees and force them to sit with strained smiles as montages of their most pitiful moments play for a live studio audience. Handy-dandy split screens offer close-ups of their disgraced faces as they watch clips of themselves making out with, professing undying love for, and then being unceremoniously dumped by that season's star. The goal is to make TV's sexiest sacrificial lambs squirm uncomfortably, accept their place as the butts of our collective jokes, and possibly start to cry all over again. All the while, the host says in mock concern, "Wow, that must be uncomfortable for you to watch." Cue applause from the live studio audience.

This suffering is part of what viewers tune in to see, learning from promo ads that this or that particular season will feature "more crying girls than *ever!*" And the narrators deliver, framing most dating series' premieres and finales with promises that "hearts were broken along the way," over clips of women whimpering, "What have I done wrong? What did I do to deserve this?" and the ever-popular cautionary tale, "I'm not going to be okay!"

Because humiliation is their money shot, when producers find a woman like Heather, a thirty-one-year-old flight attendant petrified of ending up like one of "those horror stories, forty and single!" they milk her for all she's worth. "I think tomorrow I'll be okay, but tonight it's like, 'God, I'm a loser.' That's what you feel like. I wonder, what is so wrong with me that someone cannot love me for who I am?" she blubbered tearfully to the ubiquitous confessional cam after being eliminated by *The Bachelor*. ABC reran that clip numerous times, just like Fox made the most of Billie Jean's left-at-the-altar aftermath.

That's just the kind of anxiety reality TV hopes to inspire in female viewers. After all, as advertisers have long understood, it's far easier to shill cosmetics and clothing—not to mention Match.com and Bally Fitness memberships—to insecure women scared of being alone than it is to self-confident people who believe they're beautiful, lovable, and capable of being happy just as they are.

So Much for Happily Ever After

Part of the danger of the "hey, look over here!" misdirection of beautiful princesses and brave princes is that it dissuades us from thinking critically about the dangerous messages these shows are sending.

Structurally, reality television's sweet fairytale imagery coupled with its dark, degrading underpinnings work to convince the audience that the women we see on these shows have no self-respect. And because a central premise is that contestants are "real people" behaving as they normally would in "real life," the none-too-subtle implication is that women *in general* may not deserve any more respect than is shown to the ones on the TV.

Worse yet, the cumulative effect of this one-part-honey, ten-parts-vinegar formula is that it leaves female viewers with the impression that exploitation, contempt, and emotional abuse are just par for the course of women's romantic experience. "You have to kiss a lot of frogs before you find your prince," the old saying goes; in reality TV's updated version, happily ever after only occurs when men have all the power and women do all the groveling.

Perhaps saddest of all, "true love"—that ultimate payoff promised by classic fairytales—is wholly absent from these crass, commodified mating dances. In the classic fables, once the heroine was whisked away by the prince, she was assured a life of happiness, adoration, and wealth, so long as she abandoned anything resembling ambition, independence, or individuality. This uneven exchange doesn't serve women (or men) well, for reasons too numerous to elaborate here.* But at least Disney's princesses ended up with "true love" that was sure to last "forever more." In contrast, these revisionist fairytales from the likes of Mike Darnell and Mike Fleiss demand all the same self-sacrifice from their female protagonists—but they deny them actual love.

Virtually all of us, women and men, young and old, straight, gay, or bi, feel

---

* For more discussion of gender roles in fairytales—and more egalitarian models—see *Don't Bet on the Prince: Contemporary Feminist Fairy Tales in North America and England* and the 1970s-era *Free to Be . . . You and Me* recordings and books.

a very human yearning for affection and intimacy. There's nothing wrong with that, and everything wrong with the way reality TV producers manipulate these needs. To understand how deeply this genre bastardizes our earliest depictions of desire, think back for a moment to a time when you were an innocent child having *Cinderella* read to you at bedtime, or when Disney's *Snow White* magically danced on the big screen. Try to remember how you felt as you imagined your perfect fairytale romance, that magical moment when your true love would ride up and whisk you away to happily ever after (or, if you were a little boy, when you imagined doing the whisking).

Now, as you recall those childhood daydreams, tell me: Was the Prince Charming of your fantasies some shallow, egotistical, lying dimwit who stuck his tongue down twenty-five other women's throats until he reluctantly settled for you? And if you hoped to grow up to be the prince, did you yearn to leave a trail of broken hearts behind you as you screwed your way through a throng of insincere hotties?

That's the thing about fairytales . . . they're not real. Of the dozens of reality couples who've pledged to "make each other happy for the rest of our lives" on ABC, NBC, Fox, VH1, and MTV, only three—the first *Bachelorette,* the thirteenth *Bachelor,* and the pair from *Outback Jack*—ended up married. After all the happily-ever-after buildup, after all the pathetic pandering to be picked, nearly every dating show hero has dumped his chosen "princess," even those from shows with proposals at the end. (No one married anyone's dad, either.) It shouldn't come as a shock that tennis champ and *Age of Love* star Mark Philippoussis ended up with luv, not love, from the NBC series or that Evan "$50,000? Where do I sign?" Marriott admitted that aside from one uncomfortable reunion segment, he has "never seen the girl" he chose even once since *Joe Millionaire* wrapped production.[13] Aside from these three outliers, the pattern is always the same: Every feted TV couple announce their breakup just as soon as they are no longer contractually obligated to canoodle on the couch in postshow interviews on *Access Hollywood* and *The View*. Even the yentas who used to sit on the stoop of my Brooklyn apartment building wanting to fix up every pretty girl they met with their bucktoothed nephews and balding accountant sons would have been more trustworthy matchmakers.

There's a silver lining here, though, if you look hard enough for it. The one positive thing I can say about reality TV's dating shows is that, read a certain way, they can be seen as a strong argument for legalizing gay marriage. Stay with me . . . opponents of gay marriage claim that granting equal legal rights to gay couples would degrade the sanctity of a sacred familial institution. What they don't seem to notice is that *Who Wants to Marry a Multi-Millionaire? Married by America,* and *The Bachelor* have been degrading the notion of marriage on prime time for an entire decade . . . especially during sweeps. If desperate, lonely women can get engaged—and sometimes even legally wed—to complete strangers who pluck them from harems on national TV for the profit of advertisers and corporate media, then perhaps we should consider allowing committed gay couples who actually love one another, own homes together, and raise families together to marry their life partners. Just a thought.[14]

In the end, reality TV's twisted fairytales are terribly unromantic at their core. They've popularized a trivial and depressing depiction of the concept of love itself. Real love involves a foundation of respect, honesty, and trust, concepts wholly missing from the pale imitations hawked to us by the folks who script "unscripted" entertainment. The equation Fat Wallet + Skinny Chick = Love robs us all of our humanity and erases the possibility of true emotional connection.

But who needs true emotional connection when you can have—or be—a "perfect 10"?

Chapter Two

Get Comfortable with My Flaw Finder

Women's Bodies as Women's Worth

People that say, you know, "beauty's from within"—they're liars.
They're usually ugly people that say that.

—Former NBA player John Salley, judge on

ABC's *All American Girl,* explaining why hotness is crucial

for contestants hoping to be voted viewers' "dream girl."

Miss America died, and no one seemed to care.

After half a century as the shimmering symbol of American womanhood (and a lightning rod for feminists opposing women's "seen but not heard" objectification), she finally succumbed to the fate that awaits all faded icons: irrelevance. The contest had been aired annually on network TV since 1954,* and a record high of 85 million viewers watched the Cinderella-themed *Miss America Pageant* on CBS in 1960. That mammoth audience had shrunk by 65 percent by 1979. With ongoing protests from women's rights groups and as women entered the worlds of business and politics in increasing numbers, interest in the beauty contest waned. Seventeen million people saw Vanessa Williams become the first African American woman to take the crown in 1983. Viewership continued to plummet, with newspapers in the mid-'80s reporting that "the grande dame of pageants," now "often called frivolous and dated," seemed less and less alluring to advertis-

---

* The *Miss America Pageant* began in 1921. It aired on ABC from 1954 to 1956, CBS from 1957 to 1965, NBC from 1966 to 1996, and ABC from 1997 until its final network broadcast in 2005. As this book goes to press, ABC is in talks to potentially broadcast the pageant in 2012.

ers.[1] Fifty years after its broadcast debut, the pageant was widely seen as a relic of a more archaic time. By 2004, only a paltry 7.1 million people bothered to tune in when it aired on ABC. With ratings so anemic, ABC dropped the pageant in 2005; NBC, CBS, Fox, UPN, and the WB also passed. Once the epitome of femininity to whom all girls should aspire, Miss America was DOA on network TV.

It could have ended there. After decades of feminist progress and anti-pageant organizing (and cable channels fragmenting network audiences), who would have noticed its absence? But feminist progress is anathema to reality TV, which prefers to stifle, ignore, and ultimately erase women's hard-won gains. So cable network TLC resurrected the "grande dame of pageants"—as a reality series called *Miss America: Reality Check* in 2008 and *Miss America: Countdown to the Crown* in 2009.* We used to see these beauty queens graded on their bikinied bods, toothpaste smiles, and platitudes about Loving World Peace during just one night of network TV per year. But thanks to TLC, we got to watch all fifty state winners—many of whom only participate in the pageant system to get money for college—live together for a month, while they were "groomed" in fashion, makeup, and hairstyling by "experts" from *Us Weekly* and *What Not to Wear*.+ They navigated a gauntlet of challenges designed to teach them "how to represent themselves as role models in today's modern world" and determine if they had "what it takes to be Miss America, a relatable and individual it girl who can connect with today's modern woman."[2]

How do reality TV producers find "role models" for "today's modern woman"? Why, by making contestants compete in shopping tasks and "a swimsuit trivia contest in which participants who get a question wrong jump into the pool."[3]

It's only fitting that reality TV would bring Miss America back from the dead. A decade of unscripted programming has taught us that life is a beauty

---

* TLC aired *Miss America* again in 2010, without a reality series attached, and with Rush Limbaugh as a judge.
+ My snark is aimed at the message the televised pageant has sent about beauty and about what it means to be a woman—not at its participants, who often compete because it's their only route to a higher education. The Miss America Organization is the world's largest provider of scholarship assistance for young women. In 2009 alone, they made $45 million in cash and scholarships available to more than twelve thousand young women—but only those considered attractive enough to compete in beauty contests.

contest for every woman. Viewers learn that girls and women who win this genetic lottery (and those buoyed by scalpels and silicone) will be lusted after by lovers regardless of personality and sought after by employers regardless of professional skills.

In this Darwin-esque survival of the prettiest, we learn to pity the poor girl who isn't "hot"—for she's destined to be unloved, unsuccessful, and unhappy.

And what does it take to be considered "hot" in the world of reality TV? What kind of beauty is valued, validated—or simply visible at all—in "unscripted" programming? The requirements resemble those advanced in an average issue of *Vogue:*

- YOUNG: Twenty-four-year-olds are berated as "dried-up" on *America's Next Top Model;* a forty-year-old single mom is considered laughable as *The Cougar* while the forty-eight-year-old star of *Who Wants to Marry My Dad?* is called a catch.

- WHITE, WESTERN: Women of color are invisible on most network reality shows, minus quickly eliminated tokens. Cable series with more diverse casts invoke race-based beauty hierarchies, portraying African American, Latina, and biracial women with lighter skin tones and straightened hair as more desirable than those with darker skin and kinky locks.

- SKINNY, OFTEN UNHEALTHILY SO: Trim, conventionally pretty women and girls are berated as fat (therefore "ugly") on dating shows. Bodies that appear anorexic are praised on modeling competitions, even as judges carefully mouth empty warnings—aimed more at network lawyers than viewers—that eating disorders are *bad.* Not even four-year-olds are exempt: A judge on a baby beauty pageant series explained that although kiddie bikinis are A-OK for swimwear contests, they draw the line at thongs because "It's just really hard to pull off . . . a perfect body in a thong."

- SURGICALLY ALTERED: So many fake breasts grace dating show hot tubs that the shows might as well be subtitled *Implants on Parade.* (These are de rigueur on series such as *Extreme Makeover* and *Dr. 90210,* which rarely mention the health risks of boob jobs or other dicey elective procedures.)[4]

- HYPERSEXUALIZED: Hugh Hefner's rotating girlfriends are barely dressed on *The Girls Next Door,* unsurprising on a series-long product placement for

Playboy. Worse, to vie for a job on *The Apprentice,* businesswomen must look like pinups. If that's off-putting, it's downright disturbing when first-graders in midriff-baring costumes mimic hip-pumping, chest-shimmying Dallas Cowboy Cheerleader–style dance routines on *Toddlers & Tiaras.*

There are exceptions, of course: *She's Got the Look,* a modeling competition for the thirty-five-and-over set, showed viewers that "gorgeous" doesn't have an expiration date. And, in one of the only truly progressive developments in reality television, pre- and postoperative male-to-female transgender cast members redefined and expanded perceptions of beauty by their very presence on MTV's *The Real World: Brooklyn* and season 11 of *America's Next Top Model.*

Such positive glimmers are rare. Most of the time, reality television none-too-subtly instructs viewers that a limited, advertiser-approved "ideal" of beauty is the primary—possibly the sole—measure of women's worth.

Beauty in Commercial Media

Of course, reality TV isn't the first advertiser-driven form of U.S. media to impose these restrictive standards. But to understand just how ugly the role of beauty has become in reality television, let's look at how youth, thinness, and whiteness are privileged in nearly every form of commercial media.

An enduring Hollywood double standard allows extremely young, extremely thin women to play lead roles opposite wizened senior citizens like Jack Nicholson and Clint Eastwood as virile box office leads, while relegating actresses their own age to sexless spinsters and nosy grandmas. Anne Bancroft was only six years older than Dustin Hoffman when she played Mrs. Robinson, the predatory proto-"cougar" of the 1967 film *The Graduate.* More than forty years later, even A-listers can't escape this cinematic insult: Angelina Jolie was just one year older than Colin Farrell when she played his hot mama in *Alexander,* while Rachel Griffiths was five years *younger* than on-screen son Johnny Depp in *Blow.* This bias fueled an oft-quoted joke from 1996 chick flick *The First Wives Club:* When asked why she didn't play parts her own age, Goldie Hawn's character yells, "My own age?! You don't understand. There are only three ages for women in Hollywood: babe, district attorney, and *Driving Miss Daisy*."[5] (My addendum: There are only five female characters of color in Hollywood: hooker, crime victim, maid, "sassy" sidekick, and Tyler Perry in drag.)

It's not just film. In TV news, pouty lips, tight bods, and shampoo-commercial hair now seem like resume requirements for many female news anchors, who might as well be renamed The Bodacious Babes of Broadcast. In contrast, paunchy, balding, aging male newscasters, analysts, pundits, and talk show hosts are on-air staples. In sports reporting, female athletes are not only underrepresented but nearly always sexualized, garnering coverage based more on their looks than their abilities. Traditionally "hot" competitors (like blond bombshell Anna Kournikova, who has never won a singles tennis tournament) become media and advertising darlings, while African American world tennis champs Venus and Serena Williams, who don't conform to the white = cute beauty "ideal," receive far less coverage.*

Dangerously underweight women have dominated entertainment TV ever since small-screen starlets such as Calista Flockhart, Courteney Cox, and Lara Flynn Boyle started wasting away on late-1990s sitcoms and dramas such as *Ally McBeal, Friends,* and *Law & Order.* The phenomenon has become so noticeable that actresses whose lovely round heads perch atop sticklike bodies are now called symbols of "lollipop syndrome."

This unfortunately termed trend coincided with—and likely arose in part due to—an ever-growing obsession with female celebrities' weights by tabloid magazines such as *Us Weekly* and *People* and infotainment shows like *Access Hollywood* and *Entertainment Tonight.* Gossip rags and tabloid TV have pumped up sales and ratings by scrawling *FAT!!!* over the figures of even such generally slim and (traditionally) gorgeous models, singers, and actresses as Tyra Banks, Jessica Simpson, Renee Zellweger, and Kate Winslet. When media brand stars with

---

* A search of broadcast transcripts in the Nexis.com news database conducted in September 2009 showed 993 and 985 stories referencing Serena and Venus Williams, respectively, compared with 1,643 stories mentioning Anna Kournikova.

this new Scarlet F, they intend it as the worst sort of pejorative, a statement that wearing a dress size above 0 is now a crime. Falling short of one brand of physical perfection is treated as a moral failing for which girls and women (celebrities and average citizens alike) should be publicly, repeatedly flogged. In this vicious media culture, paparazzi stalkers armed with unflattering camera angles are just meting out deserved punishment.

One red carpet moment from the 2009 Emmys offers an objective measure of how much the goalposts have shifted in the last decade: "Congratulations on being a size 0," *American Idol* host (and *E! News* schmoozer) Ryan Seacrest praised *The Office* star Jenna Fischer. In the '80s, mass media trained women to think they were undesirable if they weren't "a perfect size 8." Today, reality TV, like tabloid mags and entertainment "news," harasses women who can't squeeze into size 2s. The specter of the tiny "double zero" (a less-than-nothing size that wasn't even sold until the mid-2000s) now looms large as aspirational.

It wasn't always this way. As recently as the 1970s through the early '90s, pretty but not necessarily skinny, age-appropriate actresses were very much at home on the small screen. Erin Moran, Tempestt Bledsoe, Shannen Doherty, and Tatyana Ali played cute but healthy teenagers with actual flesh on their bones on *Happy Days, The Cosby Show, Beverly Hills: 90210,* and *The Fresh Prince of Bel-Air.* In the late '80s, Black women of a variety of ages, shapes, and sizes, from thin to athletic to full-figured, were all considered vibrant and sexy on *A Different World.* 1988 saw *Roseanne* deflating the conventional wisdom that American audiences wouldn't embrace a sitcom headlined by a fat actress and forty-two-year-old Candice Bergen premiering as the tough-as-nails *Murphy Brown,* whose age was positioned as a prize of experience. And who couldn't appreciate the feisty exploits of those sexy seniors on *The Golden Girls?* By the early '90s, *Living Single* stars Queen Latifah and Kim Coles played attractive, self-confident women whose plus-size figures were seen as fabulous, not as a hindrance to their self-esteem, careers, or love lives. Even Jennifer Aniston and Courteney Cox were significantly curvier when *Friends* premiered in 1994.

Unfortunately for them, President Bill Clinton signed the Telecommunications Act of 1996, heralding a severe wave of media consolidation and leading a deregulated industry to prioritize profit above every other factor in media production. The impact on content was immediate, as were the unintended consequences industry deregulation held for women's bodies. Low-cost (and lower-quality) infotainment shows such as *Access Hollywood* and *E! News*—among the media's most ardent fat-shaming bottom feeders—both debuted later that same year. Mass media culture, already a purveyor of unrealistic beauty ideals, became a compulsive enforcer of ever-more-unhealthy images. And so we watched our *Friends* shed dress sizes week by week, shrinking to stunningly coiffed ghosts of their former selves, while networks green-lit new series built around already emaciated female leads (*Ally McBeal* being the most famous example). Bye-bye, voluptuous ladies of *Living Single*, hello petite *Girlfriends*. And in a form of neighborhood beautification we could all do without, the CW evicted those healthy '90s *Beverly Hills* teens and made scarily skinny Lolitas the new tenants of *90210*.

How are women perceived and depicted by the sponsors of all these media products? As with the programming itself, expectations for the form and function of women's bodies are becoming increasingly extreme. Decades ago, fast food chains featured appealing women in suggestive poses. Now, hedonistic blonds hump hamburgers (or prepare to "blow" them) in Carl's Jr. and Burger King TV commercials. And I'm hardly the first to note that nearly every ad (and probably half the editorial copy) in most glossy women's mags props up women's insecurities about the deep, unsightly flaws supposedly present in parts of our bodies we'd never have thought to be concerned about—"cankles," anyone?—in the hope that we'll try to "fix" ourselves with their sponsors' products. Perhaps worst of all, fashion advertisers continue photographing skinny, wide-eyed ingenues as if they'd been beaten, bound, gagged, raped, and even murdered, believing this equation of violence with beauty sells clothes and shoes.[6]

Media scholars such as pioneering advertising critic Jean Kilbourne have long studied how deeply these sorts of media images affect girls' and women's self-esteem. In 2007, the American Psychological Association's Task Force on the Sexualization of Girls found "associations between exposure to narrow representations of female beauty (e.g., the 'thin ideal') and disordered eating attitudes and symptoms. Research also links exposure to sexualized female ideals with lower self-esteem, negative mood, and depressive symptoms among adolescent girls and women." Frequent exposure to physically unrealistic and hypersexualized media imagery, the APA determined, can carry negative cognitive and emotional consequences for girls and have serious impacts on girls' mental and physical health, their sexuality, and their attitudes and beliefs.[7] In *Can't Buy My Love: How Advertising Changes the Way We Think and Feel,* Kilbourne makes clear that while advertising doesn't cause mental illnesses such as anorexia or bulimia any more than it causes alcoholism, its "images certainly contribute to the body-hatred so many young women feel and to some of the resulting eating problems" they experience. By "promot[ing] abusive and abnormal attitudes about eating, drinking, and thinness," advertising "provides fertile soil . . . in which these diseases flourish."[8]

Advertising's self-interested conflation of women's beauty with women's worth existed well before the dawn of television. In the 1920s and 1930s, in periodicals such as *Ladies' Home Journal,* Camay Soap ran a didactic ad campaign titled, "The Beauty Contest of Life." Ominous headlines blared, "The Eyes of Men . . . The Eyes of Women Judge your Loveliness every day." There was no escape, Camay warned. Another ad pitted "You against the Rest of Womankind . . . in keen rivalry with other women, it's the girl with the flawless skin who wins." In a typical illustration, a happy, wholesome girl is drawn in cheery colors surrounded by a sea of male suitors, while a spinster sits shunned on the side of the page, shrouded in gray, punished for choosing the wrong soap.

Women of color face added bigotry in beauty ads. From the early twentieth century on, white-owned beauty companies advertised hair relaxers and skin-lightening products as ways Black women could correct their looks to resemble white standards. Black-owned companies marketed some of the same products "as a modern, healthy, progressive way for black women to care for their hair," stressing not only glamour and sex appeal but also "promot[ing] personal grooming, including hair straightening, as a route to racial uplift—as a way for African American women to use their appearance to help raise the collective and individual fortunes of black people." Similarly, Asian women today are targeted by the plastic surgery industry for "corrective" "Asian eyelid surgery," and by advertisers pushing skin lighteners as keys to both beauty and success.*[9]

Advertisers' core messages about women's beauty, and about our place in the world, have not changed significantly since Camay's insulting early-twentieth-century campaign. They simply use more sophisticated linguistic and visual codes to achieve the same psychological results, poisoning our cultural psyche.

Reality television, therefore, is just the newest format for the dissemination of traditional advertiser values. But if such images and ideas have been and continue to be present in movies, on the boob tube, in journalism, and in nearly every form of corporate media, why should we care *specifically* about unhealthy beauty standards embedded in the DNA of reality TV? And why should we pay particular attention to the body image issues that these shows promise to provoke in viewers?

Because reality TV carries these beauty myths further, and may be even more damaging, than traditional forms of media. As culturally corrosive as these images have been in previous forms of media, they become exponentially more dangerous when offered as "reality." Most viewers understand to varying degrees that reality television is an edited form of entertainment. Yet we also largely accept the genre's insistence that its cast members are "real people" who "actually believe" the cherry-picked, contextless comments we hear them make—and who "really behave" as they appear to—on these shows. (If you've ever thought, "Where do they *find* these people!?" or "What a freak/

---

* An ad for Imadeen skin-lightening pills pictures a lovely Asian model sprawled in bed, saying, "My secret to beautiful skin? I swallow."

loser/bitch!" when watching clips of shows like *Flavor of Love, The Bachelor,* or *America's Next Top Model,* you already know what I'm talking about.) This highly manipulated form of unscripted programming presents deeply problematic stereotypes as being *just the way it is* in the "real world."

That insidious veneer of authenticity allows reality TV's sponsors to ply their persuasive magic while our shields are down. Oh, we notice particularly clumsy product placement close-ups on name-brand cars and cell phones. But reality fans less readily recognize ideological indoctrination. Over the past decade, integrated marketers have worked hand in hand with entertainment producers and broadcast and cable networks to craft a generation's worth of programming around much the same fundamental dogma about gender, race, class, and sexuality that has permeated ads for eighty years.

Is it any surprise, then, that reality TV not only shills sponsors' products but also presents self-esteem-crushing beauty myths as a crucial part of "every girl's fairytale?"

Pretty Princesses, Conditional Love

With that unpleasant history behind us, it's time to focus on women's bodies in reality TV. Let's start where the genre did: with "love," or its calculated approximation. Our first introduction to "reality" romance was the Fox shocker *Who Wants to Marry a Multi-Millionaire?* which aired in February 2000. Coexecutive producer Mike Fleiss and Fox exec Mike Darnell added an arranged-marriage twist to a classic beauty pageant formula, topping it off with an any-woman-can-be-bought gloss. Each perky participant strutted her stuff like Miss America, hoping to snare some random rich dude. The groom's looks were insignificant, of course, but the way potential brides filled out their bikinis was of critical importance in determining who'd be good wife material and who was out of the romantic running.

Multi-Millionaire and its progeny, *The Bachelor,* set the racial template for a decade of network reality romance programming: white groom chooses from majority-white sorority; token African American, Latina, and Asian women are quickly eliminated; viewers learn that desirability is the domain of white women. This mold has been broken only on cable, beginning with the relatively late arrival of VH1's blaxploitation series *Flavor of Love* in 2006. Women of color, primarily African American and Latina, then became a staple among cable dating show casts (Asian and Native American women, however, are still severely underrepresented). With Black men anointed as their bachelors, cable shows began portraying curvy figures and ample asses as enviable for women and lust-worthy for men.* Previously nearly invisible, women from a wider range of ethnicities, shapes, and sizes were suddenly snogging in VH1 and MTV hot tubs just like white women had done for years on ABC and Fox. Even among cable casts with more racial and size diversity, Eurocentric beauty standards still reign: The lighter a woman's skin color, the straighter her hair, the thinner her nose and lips, the sexier and "more classy" she is considered. (Biracial women with classically Western features and so-called "good hair" rank just under white women in reality TV's race-based beauty hierarchy.)

Ever since *Millionaire,* nearly every reality TV dating show has reinforced the idea that women are unworthy of love and happiness if they are not stereo-typically beautiful. *Married by America* confirmed this when cameras followed a made-by-TV couple into their new bedroom. Begging her withholding "fiancé" for sexual validation, a curvy woman whispered insecurities amplified by captions: "Do you just not have the desire to kiss me?" Originally sexually aggressive, Denise crumbled: "I don't understand. I'm successful. I have a good personality. Or, do you want me to wear sexier clothes and lose thirty pounds, too?"+ Denise gave Fox exactly what they wanted: a tear-stained clip they could run during

---

* Here, the pendulum swings to the objectifying extreme, portraying Black and Latina women's asses as the most significant thing about them. Whole segments of *Flavor of Love 2* were devoted to winner London "Deelishis" Charles's booty, complete with slo-mo video and cheesy Barry White–sounding narration as she walked. After appearing on the show, she released a line of jeans for curvy women, recorded a music video for a song called "Rumpshaker," and charges $19.95 per month for online access to photo galleries of her nude, oiled-up ass.

+ Denise's body wasn't as much an issue for the couple as Fox intended it to appear. In fact, it was her faux-fiancé's penchant for female passivity that caused the friction. Stephen told producers that he'd be attracted to her if she just let him Be A Man and make all the moves. But editors emphasized Denise's body image insecurities to fit into reality TV's "average-size women are pathetic" narrative, blaming her appearance—rather than Stephen's subscription to 1950s notions of "appropriate" sexuality—for their lack of chemistry.

numerous episodes to remind viewers that the rounder a woman's hips, the more alone she's destined to be.

Lest viewers miss the message that physical appearance is the only thing that qualifies women for love, producers state it flat-out. During an on-air introduction, *The Bachelor*'s executive producer, Mike Fleiss, spelled out the most crucial characteristic women must possess to win a slot in his harem: "When we're looking for the bachelorettes, we take all kinds of things into consideration. There are psychological tests, there are blood tests, *but most important—they have to look good in the hot tub*."

Cameras immediately cut away from the smirking show runner to a lengthy T&A montage of bikini-clad babes emerging in slo-mo from a pool, droplets of water glistening off their cleavage. A cheesy soft-porn soundtrack played while lenses zoomed onto thong-covered butts and jiggleless boobs.

Ironically, Fleiss's brazen declaration came during an episode introducing the fourth season of the franchise, when *The Bachelor* was a funny but overweight guy who (as host Chris Harrison reminded us) was nicknamed "Fat Bob" during his stint as suitor to Trista Rehn on *The Bachelorette*. Given his own bevy of bony babes, Bob said, "When I was on *The Bachelorette* I was at the heaviest point I've ever been in my entire life . . . but I was very proud of the fact that I was chosen to be on that show—I knew it was because of my personality. I knew it was because of my character."

Sad, isn't it? Even for a guy the show demeaningly dubbed "Fat Bob,"* producers selected thin, silicone-enhanced lookalikes, with few distinguishable differences in personality. Why? Because, as Fleiss said, character can't help a chick "look good in the hot tub."

Conventionally beautiful women are not interchangeable in the real world, as they are on these shows. Exceptionally attractive women can be brilliant, funny, and capable of all the successes and failures of the rest of humanity. But women with

---

* Let me be clear: It is not okay to hurl insulting epithets at male reality stars, either. Juvenile bullying is offensive regardless of the target's gender. On the majority of dating shows, however, male stars have been spared the harsh, appearance-based judgments leveled against their female counterparts, aside from a few notable exceptions (i.e., *Average Joe*, *The Millionaire Matchmaker*, *Beauty and the Geek*).

self-esteem grounded in their intellect, humor, and individuality are generally considered liabilities to reality casting directors, regardless of their looks. Much more attractive to bookers and producers are stunners whose self-esteem is so rooted in their appearance that their physical insecurities can be easily triggered, then edited into stock reality TV characters: The Weeper, whose self-doubt is played for laughs. The Antagonizer, whose confidence is framed as arrogance. The Slut, whose strategic use of sex appeal we're meant to condemn. Through their beauty-based bravado and anxiety, participants become vessels on whose bodies and from whose lips these shows can reinforce antifeminist backlash values. However their self-doubts play out on-screen, women are often cast because they buy into cultural beauty myths that devalue their worth as individuals, as partners, as lovers.

Once already-insecure dating show contestants are selected, they're never allowed to forget that their looks are all that matter. And neither are viewers, who listen in as even movie-star-looking blonds epitomizing the young, Eurocentric "ideal" worry that they aren't perfect enough to be desired, appreciated, and— most important on these shows—*chosen.* "After meeting the girls, I'm just floored. They're beautiful, gorgeous, and *skinny!* Everything you would never want to go up against," an anxious Marilyn Monroe double fretted on *The Bachelor.* "That's intimidating to me, thinking, 'Am I going to measure up to these girls?'"

Some love-themed series are built entirely around this "am I going to measure up?" anxiety. NBC's *Age of Love* pitted twentysomething "kittens" against fortysomething "cougars" for the attention of a thirty-year-old tennis champ with poor conversational skills and a penchant for jailbait. Tessa, a bouncy twenty-three-year-old with a pet dog that could fit in her purse but a chest that couldn't be contained by a mere shirt, offered this toast to her elders: "Cheers to the extra bitches and their crows' feet and their saggy boobs. Did I say stretch marks? Did I mention stretch marks? Loose skin? Did I say tummy tucks?" That episode's final shot featured "decrepit" Angela sobbing upon elimination: "I'm forty years old . . . at my age the time period's getting a little bit shorter. I don't want to miss out on everything. I just want to find that one."

Even when women have married "that one," reality TV tells us that they should never get too comfortable. On an episode of *Wife Swap,* a mother who works as a doctor and does roller derby for fun trades places with a beauty-salon-aholic mom who enters her thirteen-month-old baby in pageants and cleans her house in stilettos. The doc asks her "new husband," Tim, whether he'd love his wife less "if she became allergic to peroxide and she wasn't so blond" or was no longer a size 3. "Fat girls need lovin', but just not by Tim," he snapped. She pressed on, wondering if Tim would at least encourage his wife to stop exposing herself to "increased rates of cancer" from regular visits to "genuinely unhealthy" tanning beds.[10] "I love that dark skin tone," he replied. "My wife sold me that package of who she was, and she needs to maintain that package. I love the blond look, and that's the way it needs to stay."

Just More of the Same

In 2009, Fox promised viewers an empowered, compassionate alternative: *More to Love,* a plus-size dating show produced by Fleiss with help from his old *Multi-Millionaire* partner, Mike Darnell. The series opened with faux populism. "The AVERAGE woman on a dating show: size 2," an announcer read as those words were captioned above a *Bachelor*-style bikini montage. Cut to footage of voluptuous women and the caption, "The AVERAGE American woman: size 14. All that is about to CHANGE."

It was a lovely premise . . . but a suspicious promise from producers with two of the most misogynistic track records in Hollywood. In promo interviews, Fleiss described the series (nicknamed "The Fatchelor") as "the dating show for the rest of us. . . . We want to send the message that you can be the size you are and still be lovable." Added Darnell, "Why don't the real women—the women who watch these shows, for the most part—have a chance to get on these shows and find love, too?"[11]

Why? Really? To paraphrase that classic '80s antidrug PSA, "From you! We learned it from watching you!" Fleiss and Darnell are the industry leaders in keeping all but skinny, white women off network dating shows. No wonder *More to Love* reinforced the very stereotypes they pretended they were trying to challenge. After co-opting the language of liberation and fat acceptance, they stocked the cast with self-loathing ladies who sobbed about never having a boyfriend and hating their bodies, and hyperventilated when forced to wear swimsuits. Plus-size women who embrace their curves, have happy dating histories, and enjoy exercise, vegetables, and sex exist in the real world—but not on this show. Instead, viewers were treated to near-constant shots of zaftig women chowing down on pizza or meat-on-a-stick and crying about how they'd be doomed to a spinster's life if the three-hundred-pound male star didn't pick them.

That's because statements like "You don't have to be thin to be loved" were just talking points to Fleiss, who never believed that average and larger-than-average women could be sexy. In prepress interviews, he kept slipping up: These women have "experienced dating a different way than the beautiful—than the stick-thin girls have." Translation: Fat women aren't beautiful; stick-thin girls are. When he told reporters that *More to Love* was "an inspirational show," that was his code for "We think it'd be a freaking miracle if you Fatty McFatterson viewers out there ever got a date, so we're giving you a fantasy show in which some dude actually wants to make out with chicks who look like you. Eww. And, you're welcome."[12]

All these self-loathing fat women, inevitably rejected "cougars," and insecurity-ridden "beautiful people" are framed as cautionary tales to female viewers. You can never be content without a man, and even if you find one there's always someone younger, hotter, and thinner waiting to steal him (and your happiness) away. So remember, gals, if you want love, don't waste your time studying for a degree, pursuing a financially and personally satisfying career, or developing your talents—you'd do better to eat rarely, exercise often, and for the love of God, remove those fine lines by any means necessary!

Modeling Beauty:
Cutting Women Down to Size

Just in case female reality viewers are self-assured enough to reject the notion that they must conform to some socially sanctioned ideal or be in perpetual competition with other women, a variety of modeling, makeover, and beauty pageant shows exists to disabuse them of their confidence.

Even those at the top of society's beauty hierarchy don't emerge unscathed. "Get comfortable with my flaw finder!" a smarmy judge sniped on ABC's short-lived *Are You Hot? The Search for America's Sexiest People*. What's a "flaw finder?" Oh, that's the laser pointer judges aimed at "problem areas" on the bodies of bombshells in bras and panties to determine who was a smokin' 9.9 and who a lowly 5.6 in the categories of "face," "body," and "sex appeal." This parade was coed, but the "flaw finder" was used most often (and most viciously) on women. Entirely new categories of "ugly" were invented to knock gorgeous gals down a few pegs. "I don't see any part of your leg touching between the hip and the knee," one confused contestant was told. "This is a point-scoring system!" Meanwhile, "I've got a burrito cooking down south and it's almost ready" passed as praise from judge and D-list soap star Lorenzo Lamas.

At least Lamas was aiming his erection jokes at adults.

On shows like WeTV's *Little Miss Perfect* and TLC's *Toddlers & Tiaras*, hypersexualized children win crowns for "Prettiest Eyes" and "Most Beautiful." *T&T*'s opening title screen uses a quick-flip chart to swap different kids' lips, eyes, noses, foreheads, chins, and hair to make one "perfect" little girl. Pageant moms say they want their five- and ten-year-olds to be "natural," while adorning them with hundreds of dollars' worth of makeup, spray tans,* hair extensions, false eyelashes, press-on nails, fake teeth (called "flippers"), and more makeup than an entire sorority would use in a month. A *Toddlers &*

---

* "I just want her to be as natural as possible in the glitz pageant," the mother of a seven-year-old Black girl says, as her daughter's teeth are chattering and bikinied body is shivering in a spray tanning booth. While this would be questionable in general, why a Black girl would "need" a tan is particularly perplexing.

Tiaras expert explains that if a girl wants to prove her beauty to the judges, she should be "Full of smiles. Never stop smiling. Just [be] kind of bubbly and giggly." Many women never outgrow these prescriptions for cosmetic and behavioral inauthenticity.

Adults on *What Not to Wear* are reprimanded for not learning those early lessons. Makeover subjects discover "people are always judging you," and the proper response is to never reject these external pressures. The stylists use words like "hootchie," "hooker," and "butch" to keep in line those who deviate from an "appropriate" feminine appearance, especially in episodes featuring women of color, straight women with short hair, and athletes.

But for the primary petri dish of toxic reality TV images of women and girls, we have to turn to *America's Next Top Model*. For fourteen seasons and counting, a generation of young women has tuned in to learn which bodies have value in our culture and which do not, who can claim beauty and who cannot. It provides a telling case study.

If women worry about metaphorically "measuring up" against their rivals on dating programs, those fears are literal on *ANTM*. Appearance-obsessed girls are weighed on scales like cattle at a 4-H fair, their measurements and weight plastered on the screen for the world to see. (Such weigh-ins are standard practice on imitators such as *Make Me a Supermodel* and *The Janice Dickinson Modeling Agency*, and opposite-land series such as *The Biggest Loser*, *Dance Your Ass Off*, and *Celebrity Fit Club*.) Frighteningly underweight girls are praised for their gangly physiques. A 5'10" waif is "Terrific!" at "114!"; an emaciated contestant clocks in at 105 pounds with a thirty-inch chest, twenty-five-inch waist, and jutting bones, garnering jealous gazes from fellow competitors. Predictably, these skeletal girls are upheld as paragons of not only beauty but also "health." At the same time, pretty model hopefuls far slimmer than most average women are derided as "plus-size" "big girls" at 5'8" and 130 pounds.

Of course, this is only "plus size" in some bizarre world where anorexia is the norm. It's also wildly inaccurate. Conflating appearance with wellness is a poor way to assess physical fitness. It is impossible to tell the condition of a person's heart, blood pressure, liver, or lungs just by looking at them, or even measuring them. What you'd never know from *ANTM* is that a physically active 158-pound, 5'10" woman can be in better medical shape than her 124-pound peer, according to the Centers for Disease Control.*

Though some statistical outliers can healthily fall below a body mass index of 18, for the majority of women the extremely low weight ranges praised on *ANTM* would pose serious risks—especially if they became underweight through anorexia or bulimia. Victims of such eating disorders (EDs) are at risk for anemia, reduced blood flow and slowed heart rate, loss of menstruation and fertility complications, muscle loss, bone problems such as osteoporosis, tooth decay, peptic ulcers, gastric or esophageal rupture, and kidney and heart failure.[13]

Yet *ANTM* and other modeling and weight loss reality shows give the false impression that *thin* is synonymous with *healthy*, and *fat* with *unhealthy*. This obscures the reality that extreme thinness can carry serious consequences, even death. Playing bait-and-switch with definitions of *health* and *fat* on modeling shows (and weight loss series, which we'll discuss later) can confuse viewers as to what healthy women's bodies actually look like. It can also contribute to body dysmorphic syndrome among girls and women who see their bodies as bigger than they really are (and therefore, they've been acculturated to believe, hid-

---

* Morbid obesity can carry negative medical consequences, but reality television often slaps the label of "obese" onto people who are only mildly overweight, further confusing the public as to what a dangerous weight is and isn't. The body mass index is used by the Centers for Disease Control to determine general "underweight," "normal," "overweight," and "obese" ranges. As Kate Harding points out at Shapely Prose, it calculates only height and weight without regard for other health factors such as diet, exercise, addiction, or illness. Though imperfect, the BMI is the most common tool health professionals use to initially assess what is and isn't considered a "healthy weight." According to the CDC, a 5'10", 158-pound woman has a BMI of 22.1, within the "normal" or healthy weight range for her height. At 124 pounds, a woman of the same height has a BMI of 17.8, which is considered unhealthily underweight. A BMI of less than 17.5 is used as an informal indicator to diagnose anorexia. *ANTM* contestant Elyse, the 114-pound model called "terrific" on the scale, had a BMI of 16.4; the CDC considers a BMI of 16 to be a potential indicator of starvation. It's possible that Elyse was naturally that thin with no ill health effect. Most women would not be.

eous). This mindset serves the diet and beauty industries well.* Eighty percent of American women are dissatisfied with their appearance, translating to Americans spending more than $40 billion on dieting and diet-related products each year, according to the National Eating Disorders Association.[14]

Exacerbating this distorted definition of "normality," *ANTM*'s lone "plus-size" slot tends to be filled by girls who aren't all that "plus-size" in the first place—even by already-strict modeling industry standards. Often sizes 8 and 10, these slightly more-bootylicious competitors have usually been smaller than the successful size 12 and 14+ women who model for plus-size divisions of leading agencies such as Ford 12+ and Wilhelmina Ten-20. Not to mention that in contrast with the industry's warped looking glass, the average American woman is 5'3", weighs 162.9 pounds, and wears a size 14.[15]

Three of *ANTM*'s first thirteen seasons didn't feature any full-figured contestants at all. As if to indicate that the series has room for only one kind of stunt-casting tokenism at a time, no "big girls" were included during the cycle featuring transgender model Isis, or the all-shorties cycle, when everyone was 5'7" or under. Viewers had to wait until the tenth season for a plus-size contestant to finally win. Tyra Banks boasted about how much good it would do young girls to see blond, curvy Whitney Thompson, "the first girl with some booty," take the crown. Yet her bluster couldn't erase the fact that for nearly a decade, her show has reinforced the same "narrow perceptions of beauty" she claims it is her "mission to expand," regarding both size and race.[16]

"Tyra and I understand the influence 'Top Model' has on a generation of young people, and we want to make sure we get the right message to our audience," Coexecutive Producer Ken Mok has said. Too bad *ANTM*'s content

* The Biggest Loser rakes in $100 million annually from merchandising. Ten million viewers per week watch people shed hundreds of pounds on the program, which claims to be about helping obese men and women get "healthy." Yet its extreme regimen—severe restriction of calories coupled with workouts that can last six hours per day—has led contestants to collapse, suffer dehydration or heat stroke, urinate blood, and be hospitalized. Unaffiliated physicians call the show exploitative and unsafe, and no wonder: Participants have to sign contracts stipulating that TBL does not guarantee "the qualifications or credentials of the medical professionals who examine me or perform any procedures on me . . . or their ability to diagnose medical conditions that may affect my fitness."[17]

runs counter to Banks's and Mok's lofty aspirations. Banks is extremely harsh in her treatment of models of color, as discussed in chapter 6. She cast only short women on season 13 though there are no jobs for them in the industry— yet, to date she's never done an all-plus-size season, despite the fact that the plus-size sector of the modeling industry is growing. By including nonwhite, nonemaciated, and transgender women as *Top Model* competitors, Banks presents the possibility that they, too, can be symbols of beauty—yet by focusing unrelentingly on their difference, she "others" them as abnormal, not truly beautiful after all. As this book goes to press, two of *ANTM*'s skinny-only seasons aired after Whitney won. The producers might as well have said, "Hey, we gave you your plus-size winner . . . now we never have to subject you to the sight of a grotesque size 10 in a swimsuit again!"[18]

Toccara's Story: When Weight and Ethnicity Meet on *Top Model*

Fan-favorite Toccara Jones literally ran into her cycle 3 audition bursting with humor, energy, and pride. "I'm Toccara, and I'm big, Black, beautiful, and loving it!" she told the judges with a snap. On her home video, she said she wanted "to encourage full-figured women to appreciate their bodies and know that they're beautiful." With evocative eyes, bold curves, and personality to match, Toccara was a rare exception: a *Top Model* contestant who actually fit her "plus-size" label, complete with a natural 38DDD bust that actually respected the laws of gravity. In a bathing suit at a pool party for semifinalists, the 5'9" pinup-in-the-making announced that if the show was looking for "something juicy, then here I am. I'm 180 pounds, and I'm carrying it *well*, and I'm loving it," she laughed. "They shouldn't be scared. Don't be scared, America!"

The audience wasn't scared at all—they were enthralled. Viewers voted her "CoverGirl of the Week" four times in a row (including the episode in which she was eliminated). It's likely that fans appreciated Toccara not only for her great looks and vivacious attitude, but for her uncompromising faith in herself. In a sea of frail waifs obsessing over nonexistent "flab" on their washboard stomachs, here, finally, was a woman who felt at home in her own skin. "I love myself. I love my shape. I love my curves," she declared. "Some people think that America's not 'ready' for a plus-size model. I'm here to break that norm. I'm gonna be the first Black plus-size model to be on the cover of twenty magazines!" She believed in her beauty, and it was hard to watch her and not share in that belief. Even her rail-thin competitors were envious. "I wish I was more like Toccara. She's fabulous. She has a confidence in herself," mused skinny, nineteen-year-old Norelle.

No plus-size model on *ANTM* has had a fraction of Toccara's sexy swagger or posing talent (not even winner Whitney Thompson, whose performance was sometimes lackluster, but whose blond hair and white skin made her a "safe" choice to grace the cover of show sponsor *Seventeen*). Judge Nolé Marin glowed about her progress: "She photographs absolutely amazing week after week." Studying the proofs of her topless pose for Lee One True Fit jeans, photo shoot director Jay Manuel (Mr. J) raved, "Toccara looks so perfect!" A wardrobe assistant agreed: "Not even one bad picture." She performed consistently well even when she was set up to fail. Producers often didn't provide clothing in her size. There were no bras to fit her and only a medium-size robe when the girls had to become living lingerie mannequins in a La Perla store window. When her competitors wore gorgeous designer gowns and fantasy getups such as "glamazon" or "seventeenth-century courtesan" for a Ford photo shoot, Toccara was thrown into the frumpy button-down shirt and slacks of a parking garage attendant. She knew the deal, and she wasn't having it. "I wanna know why all the girls were so nice looking and here I am looking like I work at Home Depot?" she asked the wardrobe director. As if a size 14 dress is as elusive as a unicorn, the snotty stylist barked back, "Do you think I'm going to be able get a rack . . . loaded with clothes in *your* size?" Toccara refused to take the blame for the stylist's lazy approach to her job. "You can't find something in my size, so I'm supposed to feel bad?"

Yes, unfortunately. On *ANTM* and similar series, plus-size models are set up for psychological manipulation. Off the bat, Tyra makes sure to say during each audition episode that she's casting the plus-size girl for "her personality" and "her strength" (i.e., not for her looks), and that she'll have to be "better than" the "normal" girls. The few Rubenesque hopefuls who make the cut handle the first rounds of fire with confidence and aplomb, eventually falling apart after being systematically ripped to shreds by judges, photographers, designers, and marketing execs. This deliberation about Toccara is typical:

> JUDGE JANICE DICKINSON: The car looks better than she does. If the body could just slim down 150 pounds, that would be good.
> TYRA BANKS: Then she'd be 30 pounds.
> DICKINSON: That would be better.
> DESIGNER AND GUEST JUDGE MARC BOUWER: She's not America's Next Top Model. It's ludicrous to think that she would be.
> JANICE: It will *never* be top model.

Eventually, this separate-and-unequal treatment finally began to crack her armor. "I'm just trying to stay positive, but it's hard . . . it hurts," Toccara cried on a friend's shoulder after the Ford shoot. This was the first moment of weakness she showed in seven weeks (unlike most tearful *ANTM* contestants). She admitted that they "made me feel so bad and ashamed." That week, she landed in the bottom two for the first time. She took it in stride. "I never let it break my spirit," she said the following week. And that's precisely why they sent her home at the end of the episode (she certainly hadn't "lost her drive" or "checked out," as Tyra claimed).

Toccara's self-confident truth ran counter to *Top Model*'s script for plus-size participants, who are set up to be broken down. Once they become sufficiently self-loathing, they are eliminated—supposedly for "losing their fire" or not believing in themselves enough. Underneath these bogus clichés, the judges mean, "We worked as hard as we could to erode your self-esteem, and now that you've finally internalized our nagging voices: sayonara, sister!"

This didn't work on Toccara. But producers held true to their alternative reality and, through Selective Editing Theater, led viewers to believe she was ousted because she had "become a ghost of her original self."

Try as they might, *Top Model* didn't break Toccara. Instead, she has been one of the series' most successful alums. Between 2005 and 2009 she signed with the prestigious Wilhelmina agency, graced the covers of numerous women's and men's magazines, and has appeared in *Vogue Italia, Ebony, Essence, Vibe,* and *Smooth.* She walked runways for BET, Hot 97, Alice & Olivia, and others. High-profile companies such as Target, Avon, Torrid, and Rocawear have hired her; Hennessy made her one of six celebrity "brand ambassadors." She shares a manager with hip-hop stars Missy Elliott and 50 Cent, and has been a correspondent and cohost on three BET shows and had cameos on the UPN sitcoms *Girlfriends* and *All of Us.*

To the rest of the mainstream media, Toccara is recognized as one of the most successful African American plus-size models working today. To reality TV producers, she's just a fat Black girl who needs to lose weight. In 2005 and 2008, VH1 paid her to join the casts of VH1's *Celebrity Fit Club* and *Celebrity Fit Club: Boot Camp.* (Modeling jobs are fewer and further between for women of color— and for plus-size models of any ethnicity—than for white women size 2 and under, which may explain why she accepted.) She worked hard and lost thirty-two pounds, but the cover girl was badgered by made-for-prime-time "therapists" and doctors who refused to believe she felt beautiful, framing her self-acceptance as "dysfunctional" "denial."

During one of my favorite moments from a decade's worth of reality programming, Toccara finally lost her cool and told off *Celebrity Fit Club*'s bullying panel. "All of y'all can kiss my ass if y'all don't like the fact that I like who the fuck I am," she screamed. "You're making people in real life think that I'm dysfunctional. *This,*" she said, gesturing at her hourglass figure, "is not dysfunctional. I look good!" When her cast members tried to calm her down, she yelled, "I bust my butt every week, but they don't see that. All they see is the fact that I say I love myself. That's an issue? *That's* an issue?" The show portrayed her outburst as a rant from an out-of-control diva who needed to "have some class." In reality, it was righteous rage at the idea that anyone overweight should hate themselves—and at the stacked deck orchestrated to enforce that principle.

"Pro-ana" Goes Prime Time

Luisel Ramos lived exclusively on lettuce and Diet Coke for three months before modeling at Uruguay's Fashion Week in August 2006. Just minutes after she stepped off the runway, the twenty-two-year-old model suffered a heart attack and died.

Ramos had been told by a modeling agency that she could make it big, but only if she lost weight. At the time of her death, she weighed 97 pounds and had a BMI of 14.5. The next month, Madrid Fashion Week organizers responded to Ramos's death by preventing models with BMIs under 18 (meaning, anyone with diagnostic signs of anorexia) from working Spain's catwalks. Soon after, Italian fashion designers banned size 0 models from runway shows. The stated intent was to stimulate an industry-wide shift away from promoting eating disorders and toward protecting the models' health, as well as that of the girls and women surrounded by their images. The ban came too late to save Ana Carolina Reston, a Brazilian model who subsisted only on apples and tomatoes and died of kidney failure in November 2006 after shooting an Armani catalog. She weighed 88 pounds.

Despite controversy and debate in the press, the American, British, and French fashion industries rejected Spain and Italy's call for minimum health requirements for models. However, a "Health Initiative" statement in 2007 from the Council of Fashion Designers of America offered recommendations including making healthy snacks available, creating workshops to help industry insiders recognize early warning signs of EDs, encouraging models with EDs to seek professional help, and not hiring kids fifteen and under for runway shows.

Four-term *ANTM* judge Janice Dickinson told the *New York Post* that these rather tepid recommendations were "bull." "I'm dying to find kids who are too thin. I've got 42 models in my agency and I'm trying to get them to lose weight. In fact, I wish they'd come down with some anorexia," the *Janice Dickinson Modeling Agency* star said. "I'm not kidding. I'm running into a bunch of fat-assed, lazy little bitches who don't know how to do the stairs or get their butts into the gym. . . . Models are supposed to be thin. They're not supposed to eat."[19]

This is the same attitude embraced by the "pro-ana" (and the lesser-known "pro-mia") community that promotes anorexia nervosa and bulimia nervosa as "lifestyle choices" rather than illnesses. On thousands of pro-ana websites, blogs, and social media networks, girls and women suffering from ED offer tips for ways to starve or purge without being caught, join in collective fasts, and post "thinspiration" photos and video of emaciated women like Luisel Ramos and Ana Carolina Reston . . . and Jaslene Gonzalez, the 110-pound, 5'8" winner of the eighth season of *America's Next Top Model*.* *ANTM* is a cherished source of "thinspiration" to "pro-ana" girls, who post contestants' pictures alongside crash diet tips on sites with names like "The Fasting Girl's Blog."[20]

When confronted with the dismal reality of ED, *ANTM* turns out story arcs heavy on drama and light on support. During cycle 3, a tall, slender teenager named Cassie Grisham admitted that she practiced self-induced vomiting after eating because she believed it was the only way she could have her dream career. "If I didn't want to be a model, I would eat whatever I wanted to and not worry about it," she said, but "I have this will to be skinny. And if people have a problem with it that's their problem, not mine." Cassie denied that she was bulimic, rejecting the word—but not the behavior. "An obsession with my weight" propels her to throw up "sometimes," she acknowledged, noting that she worries about food "24-7." "If it makes me happy to do this, then they shouldn't have a problem," she told the cameras, defiant. "I've grown up dreaming of being a model. . . . And great, there's plus-sized models; that's not for me."

After several episodes worth of hand-wringing about how the lovely young woman should take care of herself, did Tyra Banks make a palpable effort to get

---

* Jaslene has strongly denied that she has an ED.

her help? After playing Cassie's bulimia for melodrama, did *Top Model* take the opportunity to deglamorize the notion that EDs can transform a girl's appearance from average to extraordinary?

Nope. Not unless "help" is defined as a brief guest appearance by plus-size model Kate Dillon, who lectured the group that if they need to starve themselves, "This might not be the right career for any of you," and a brief visit from a nutritionist. Banks could have insisted that Cassie seek treatment as a condition of participating in the show, a move that might have set the nineteen-year-old on a path to breaking her "obsession" with weight and food. Could've, should've . . . didn't. Instead, *ANTM* sent her on go-sees with fashion industry insiders, cherry-picked their most cutting criticisms, and reran those clips for maximum humiliation. As she walked for Nanette Lepore, producers let us listen in on the designer's snide critiques, plastering, "She's not exactly a size 2" on-screen in captions to shame Cassie and viewers who identified with her. Worse still, designer Marc Bouwer scoffed that her hips were too big and her thighs too unsightly to wear his clothes, then whipped a measuring tape around her ass and pronounced her unacceptable, while she stood mortified before him. She said she felt "singled out," an experience that almost definitely reinforced her eating disorder.

Hoping for a redemptive climax to this tale? Sorry, we didn't get one. After the endless browbeating the (underweight) teen endured, it would have been cathartic to see Tyra unleash some whup-ass on Bouwer for demeaning her. And, sure, it would have been immensely powerful for millions of girls to hear the former Victoria's Secret supermodel encourage the teen to love and accept her own body as beautiful the way it is, without starvation and without shame. But instead of giving us one of those Very Special Moments, the show simply showed Cassie the door. Because, Tyra decreed, she didn't "want it" enough.

She didn't want it enough? This is a young woman who said she was "happy" to stick her finger down her throat if that's what it took. By banishing a bulimic for a lack of desire (especially after the show called negative attention to her hips, thighs, and butt), *ANTM* tacitly sent the message that Cassie *hadn't thrown up enough* to get the job done. Rather than using her struggle as an opportunity to educate, producers used every trick in their toolbox—measuring tapes, title screens, verbal put-downs, selective editing—to reinforce the internal dialogue of those who suffer from ED. Cassie wasted no time regurgitating Bouwer's appraisal: "I have very wide hips," the dejected girl said later that episode. "Marc Bouwer told me I was too big."

Cassie's experience on the show was unique only in that the weight-baiting began after she copped to bulimic behavior. A long line of drop-dead-gorgeous girls have been attacked on *Top Model* for "eating too much," being "chunky," or "letting themselves go."

Nineteen-year-old Keenyah Hill's legs went on for miles, her eyes seemed to pierce right through the photographer's lens, and her striking pictures drew praise for resembling groundbreaking African American supermodel Iman. Unfortunately for her, *ANTM* hadn't included any plus-size competitors that season, but they were still jonesing for someone to scorn as too fat for fashion. So when the lithe, 5'11" teen's stomach became slightly less concave over the course of thirteen stressful episodes, *Top Model* turned her into an unflattering caricature. Logic dictates that every participant would have eaten several meals each day, yet Keenyah was often the only person shown consuming more than a bite or two of food, giving a misleading impression that she was an out-of-control binger. Judges ridiculed her appetite and ordered her to diet. She became the object of intense *Top Model* mockery. In one photo shoot, she was made to pose as Gluttony incarnate, lying in a coffin full of bacon and doughnuts, covered in grease and sprinkles. In a later shoot for Lubriderm Ultra Moisturizing Lotion, she had to personify an elephant, while her competitors were costumed as graceful creatures (white models became long, lean giraffes and cute springbok deer, while a biracial model was a cheetah ready to pounce). Mr. J made sure they knew this was no accident. "I've picked an animal that I think represents each and every one of you," he announced. "Everybody else has these sexy little animals. I get to be the big, fat elephant! Ugh! . . . What is going on?" Keenyah asked, exasperated. This was hilarious to the gangly girl next to her, wearing a "Please Do Not Feed the Models" T-shirt.*

When formerly anorexic and bulimic Lauren "London" Levi put on some weight during cycle 12, Mr. J scolded the eighteen-year-old for this "really shocking" development. "It's just clear that you're not taking care of your body," he said. "As a model you're expected to treat your body like a temple." Then, the (still-svelte!) eighteen-year-old was eliminated.

In a postshow interview, London told *E! News Online* that she had suffered from eating disorders from the time she was in junior high, and it got "super severe" in her "senior year in high school, which was actually . . . right before I went on to the show." Her EDs would have been common knowledge prior to casting due to intake interviews. Additionally, London says she told her castmates about her recovery in conversations that never made it to air.[21] As sinister as it sounds, *Top Model's* editors, judges, and producers knew about her eating disorder—yet they ignored the implications for London's (and their audience's) health, preferring to run footage of a judge telling her she was "unprofessional" for failing to control her body and clips of London calling herself a "fat freak."

As London struggled to break the cycle of starving and purging and finally began to eat normally, her body reacted as it was meant to; flesh began to pad bone. The minute she started looking less gaunt, she was yelled at for "not taking care" of herself. Coming into *ANTM,* London's "self-confidence was already kind of shaky because of my experience with my [ED] beforehand," she told *E!*[22] After the life-lessons she learned on *Top Model,* it will likely be harder for her to respect her body's nutritional needs while maintaining a healthy self-image.

And what of the self-images of the millions of girls for whom becoming *America's Next Top Model* seems a more compelling dream than passing the bar, curing cancer, or writing the Great American Novel? More than one-half of

---

* Where were Keenyah and co. when *ANTM* transformed them into "sexy little animals"? That would be Cape Town, South Africa. We'll discuss the racial implications of this in chapter 6.

teenage girls skip meals, fast, smoke cigarettes, vomit, and/or take laxatives in an effort to lose weight; 46 percent of nine- to eleven-year-olds are "sometimes" or "very often" on diets, and 81 percent of ten-year-olds are afraid of being fat, according to the National Eating Disorders Association.[23] By leveling such criticisms against even those few statuesque, fresh-faced teens who embody the conventional "ideal" of beauty, reality TV modeling shows send female viewers an insidious message: If *they* fall short, the rest of you must be *grotesque.* How much more difficult must it be for *ANTM*'s viewers to be comfortable with their own bodies?

To be sure, a large and loyal audience is paying close attention. *America's Next Top Model* "is a young-female magnet," a programmer from the former UPN network said in 2005, when the show's fifth cycle was drawing nearly 5 million eighteen- to thirty-four-year-old female viewers and some of UPN's highest ratings ever. By 2009, *ANTM*'s thirteenth cycle premiere made CW the number one network on Wednesday night among women eighteen to thirty-four in fourteen major media markets from liberal New York to conservative Houston; the show also scored first among all adults eighteen to thirty-four in six major markets.[24]

With so many girls and young adults watching every week, it's no wonder that every time I've conducted a workshop on media images for high school or college students, young women have expressed strong feelings about the role *ANTM* has played in shaping their vision of beauty and whether or not they like the way they look.* From pro-ana sites to ED recovery groups, a wealth of anecdotal evidence points to the deep impact reality TV modeling shows can have on young women. As just one example, take this comment left by a fourteen-year-old girl on a mental health support website where bulimics share their stories:

---

* In my capacity as executive director of Women In Media & News, I've worked with hundreds of young women in media literacy workshops, and thousands of students have seen my multimedia presentations on images of women in reality television. I can't remember conducting even one lecture or workshop in which at least one girl has not admitted that *America's Next Top Model* has had some impact on her, either on her body image, on her perception of others, or on her perception that the way she looks will determine her chances for success romantically or professionally.

I was bulimic for a year which seems to pale in comparison to the 5-10 year bulimics who have shared their stories. I have always been interested in modeling. My mom is a photographer and has taken pictures of me since I was around 10. I have always been a normal weight (as in I have never been able to get rid of that "pudge") and slightly athletic. I'm not sure why I first became bulimic, All I knew was staying fit wasn't as easy as it was when I was more little. I am now almost 15. I love the show "america's next top model" . . . they are all so skinny. And even one of the girls got called out for her weight and I am bigger-ish than her. I am short, 5'1 and I weigh around 110. I can't bear to see my weight anymore. I want to weigh 98.[25]

Just like "aspirational," airbrushed advertising in women's magazines, reality TV beauty programming invites female viewers to envy models' unrealistic figures and, by proxy, their clothes, cosmetics, shoes, and lifestyle products. Every episode of *ANTM* is crafted around a marketing challenge: a photo shoot for Steve Madden shoes, a fashion spread for *Seventeen,* a TV commercial for CoverGirl cosmetics filmed inside a Wal-Mart, with each girl mouthing the same ad copy about the transformational properties of mascara or lipstick on repetitive loop for an hour.

Though impacts vary, decades of research have documented that women's self-esteem often drops with exposure to advertising and ad-driven media. As Kilbourne notes, numerous studies document the negative effect women's magazines, driven by fashion and beauty ads (the same advertisers who are *ANTM*'s main sponsors), have on girls and young women. Brigham and Women's Hospital "found that the more frequently girls read magazines, the more likely they were to diet and feel that the magazines influence their ideal body shape," while Stanford University and the University of Massachusetts "found that about 70 percent of college women say they feel worse about their own looks after reading women's magazines."[26] Another study focusing on TV found that for young women, "actual body size is in conflict with a mediated ideal body image and an unstable self-perceived body image" such that "watching even 30 minutes worth of television programming and advertising can alter a women's perception of the shape of her body."[27]

Is it any wonder that advertisers who have always employed female insecurity and racial stereotypes in attempts to ply their wares are now promoting misogynistic and racist ideas about beauty in the name of "reality"? Considering the results of studies tracking the effects of other forms of advertising on women's self-esteem, it stands to reason that reality TV programming built with and for fashion and beauty marketers would, over time, make girls and women feel less attractive and more dissatisfied with their bodies.

Beauty Qualifies Me

Once, while Ryan Seacrest wore a T-shirt with the slogan "Beauty Qualifies Me" on *American Idol,* it struck me that it would be fitting for producer Simon Fuller to give the same shirt to every female competitor. After all, the shapes and sizes of female vocalists' bodies are critiqued as thoroughly as their voices. For nine seasons, *Idol*'s most influential judge, Simon Cowell, made "lose weight!" a virtual mantra when addressing attractive young women who dream of being pop starlets.*

This has been especially true in his treatment of girls of color. Like season 2 hopeful Kimberley Locke, Black and Latina female *Idols* get sent through what I like to call "The Homogenator." They emerge from the style machine with their natural hair straightened, Western-looking hair extensions added, wearing fashion and makeup chosen to provide a less ethnic "image." Cowell's many swipes at 2003 finalist Jennifer Hudson's looks didn't stop her from rebounding with an Oscar-winning performance in *Dreamgirls,* a Grammy for her self-titled album, and a coveted spot on the cover of *Vogue.* At least Kimberley and Jennifer got to compete. Lisa Leuschner, a pretty redhead with an exceptional voice and a slightly rounded derriere, was not allowed to progress

---

* Cowell's comments often wander into overt bigotry as well. On one audition show, "after failing to understand that an Asian woman's name was 'Fong,' he called her 'ping-pong, or whatever your name is.'" a *San Francisco Chronicle* blogger notes.[28]

to the semifinals. The dictate came from Cowell: Her "voice is sensational. Really, really good," he said, but "you need to lose weight . . . I'm only saying to you what I would be saying to an artist if they were signed to my record label. You know, I say it to guys on my label. When they get overweight, I say, lose weight! Because this is an image business." Fellow judge Paula Abdul said Lisa was beautiful and that she didn't need to change, and she angrily asked Cowell, "Why do you keep perpetuating eating disorders?" This was his dismissive reply: "It's got nothing to do with an eating disorder. Absolutely nothing to do with that. . . . This is simply to do with what a record company would say to an artist, and I think you've got a very good voice. I do."

And then they sent her home. Especially galling? Cowell was lying about this double standard. During season 2, Cowell consistently urged viewers to vote for a morbidly obese guy, Ruben Studdard, telling him, "I think you should win this competition." Guest judges like Gladys Knight also gushed about his performances, calling him "The world's velvet teddy bear." And, lest anyone unfairly dock the talented tunester points based on his weight, Cowell offered this prime directive: "Sensational! I mean, the most important thing about you is, apart from being [a] great guy, you have a fantastic recording voice, and lest we forget, *this competition is about finding a recording artist*. Amazing!" Paula Abdul added, "And personality!" Simon's near-unfailing flattery of Ruben helped him take home the crown. It's great that he appreciated Ruben's voice—that's as it should be on a show that promotes itself as identifying "the best singers in the country." The problem is that *Idol* seems to be a singing contest when the competitors are male and a beauty pageant when they're female.

Also problematic was Simon's implication that his critique of Lisa wasn't *about* an eating disorder—it's just that she'd never succeed if she didn't develop one. Cowell is painted in the entertainment press as mean but honest, doling out harsh truths to clueless contestants. *American Idol* tells millions of young women who watch the show religiously, dreaming of being the next Kelly Clarkson, Carrie Underwood, or Fantasia Barrino, that no matter how talented they are, music is less about the sound of their voices than the size of their asses. Girls learn *Idol*'s version of "the truth": They'll never accomplish their goals if they don't look like (pre-shaved-headed) Britney or ultraglam Beyoncé. *Idol*'s fans disagree: They voted biracial seventeen-year-old Jordin Sparks, who had previously done plus-size modeling for Torrid, the sixth winner. The healthy, perky teen went on to release several award-winning records, yet was decried as an "obese" symbol of "diabetes [and] heart disease" on Fox News's *Your World with Neil Cavuto.*[29]

"The Beauty Is Worth the Pain"

Since "only liars and ugly people believe" that "beauty comes from within," (as *All American Girl* judge John Salley proclaimed), reality TV tells women that no measure is too painful or too dangerous to take in pursuit of ever-elusive, billboard-ad beauty. As Kim Zolciak said on *The Real Housewives of Atlanta,* "I get Botox since I was twenty-four. . . . The beauty is worth the pain."

Before they realized they could rake in more product placement cash by redecorating rundown houses on a *Home Edition* of *Extreme Makeover,* the original series rebuilt the faces and bodies of self-hating women (and the occasional man). The formula was crass and predictable. They'd begin with insulting sob stories about what "ugly duckling" "losers" each average-looking woman was. A panel of doctors would tell her she "needed" an absurd amount of plastic surgery procedures in a few short weeks, from tummy tucks to brow lifts, breast implants to liposuction, glossing over or ignoring medical risks. They'd mark her near-naked form like beef ready for slaughter, followed by explicit footage of the patient getting sliced, diced, and vacuum-sucked. As she lay vulnerable and drugged on the operating table, smug surgeons would chuckle, "I can do more in here in a few hours than she could do in a gym in three years." (Three years of healthy physical activity would be a horrible thing to encourage, wouldn't it?) Once well enough for a grand "reveal," she'd be rewarded with a party where her loved ones would finally applaud her artificial "after" appearance.

The same themes were present in Fox's depressing knockoff makeover and beauty pageant series *The Swan,* but leave it to Mike Darnell to make a degrading concept even more damaging. Each episode featured two "ugly ducklings" going under the knife then squaring off against one another in weekly beauty contests to determine which of the "losers" had been remade thoroughly enough—and who was still too plain—to compete in the final *Swan* pageant. Along the way, the show institutionalized eating disorders by forcing women who were barely overweight to go on twelve-hundred-calorie-a-day diets and work out for several hours per day. When one contestant protested the radical weight-loss regimen because "I think I look really damn good," her "coach" (*Swan* creator and executive producer Nely Galán, who was by no means qualified to provide emotional guidance) angrily attacked her self-acceptance as laziness.

The most sadistic reality series of the decade, *The Swan* sank to new lows by not only surgically hacking up domestic violence victims and poverty-stricken single mothers but also promising to "transform [them] from the inside out" via filmed "therapy" sessions. Who needs doctor-patient confidentiality, anyway? Privacy concerns were the least of the ethical breaches surrounding the show's sham psychology. Turns out the shrink, Dr. Lynn Ianni, was a poseur whose PhD came from a correspondence school described "as an unaccredited 'diploma mill' by congressional investigators."[30] With a ratings-hungry Fox executive producer and an "I'm not a doctor but I play one on TV" quack dishing out mental health tips, is it any wonder that the "counseling" *Swan* participants received was actually harassment ("Stick to the program!" "Stop complaining!")? Or that this "therapist" suggested that a boob job, liposuction, and other elective cosmetic procedures would help a former battered woman "break the cycle of violence," "build self-esteem," and "leave her past behind"?

Preying on the emotionally at-risk, plastic surgery shows nevertheless market themselves as liberating for women. On a self-congratulatory episode of *Extreme Makeover,* the host asked a panel of cosmetic surgeons on ABC's payroll, "There's a wave of plastic surgery around the country right now. Every magazine you see, every TV show, talks about plastic surgery. Do you think *Extreme Makeover* created this wave, or did the wave create *Extreme Makeover?*" One doc's reply spoke directly to *EM's* calculating frame. "This show has done a wonderful thing for plastic surgery and patients, because it brought it out of the closet. It's made it okay to have plastic surgery without hiding it, and that's an incredibly liberating thing for a lot of people in whom it makes a huge difference in their lives."*

Indeed, reality shows like *Extreme Makeover, The Swan, Dr. 90210, I Want a Famous Face,* and *Addicted to Beauty* have "done a wonderful thing" for this growing, multibillion-dollar industry: Americans spent just under $12 billion on cosmetic procedures in 2008 alone. According to the American Society for Aesthetic Plastic Surgery, women had 91 percent of cosmetic procedures in 2008—accounting for 10.6 million surgical and nonsurgical procedures. Teens eighteen and younger had 4 million breast augmentations in 2007, compared with one million in 1997. Cosmetic surgeries are becoming more common, in part because media have increasingly presented plastic surgery as a quick-and-easy pick-me-up, glossing over the pain and length of recovery processes and obscuring its inherent dangers. Cosmetic surgeries and nonsurgical elective aesthetic procedures can carry risks ranging from minor (such as temporary numbness or loss of sensation) to major, including ongoing pain, necrosis (tissue death), excessive bleeding and hematoma, deep vein thrombosis, infection, and even coma or death, as when a former Miss Argentina died after undergoing an attempted butt implant. And 4.6 percent of patients die after having bariatric surgeries just within the first year, according to the *Journal of the American Medical Association.*[31]

Yet this misleading and opportunistic programming has made "liberation" its consistent theme. Most episodes of *Extreme Makeover* and *The Swan* ended with a closing shot of a woman postsurgery saying that now that the fat's been sucked out of her thighs and pumped into her lips; now that she's had her breasts enlarged; her tummy tucked; her eyes, nose, chin, and cheeks altered, "I have the

---

* Ah, liberation. Isn't it nice that after four decades of feminist and gay rights activism, ABC is finally letting plastic surgery "come out of the closet" on national TV?

ability to pursue whatever it is I want to pursue. I can pretty much, you know, conquer whatever I want to," as one made-over mom marveled—as if being pretty is a vocation, rather than an attribute. Let's think about that: Improving one's appearance can certainly raise a person's self-esteem, but it doesn't confer new tangible skills. These women emerged from their makeovers no more or less able to accomplish anything they hadn't done before surgery.

So, here's where we return to those "deep social beliefs" Mike Darnell says successful reality shows are steeped in. The assertion that cosmetic surgery and other makeover shows provide a benevolent service only makes sense if you accept the premise that unattractive women can't do great things, while only pretty women can conquer the world. These shows package themselves as "liberating" for women because they want us to believe that beauty is the main thing, possibly the *only* thing, the female half of the world has to offer.

Which may be why reality TV has fallen increasingly in love with pageant series. From the kiddie spectacles of *Toddlers & Tiaras* and *Little Miss Perfect* to infamous antifeminist Rush Limbaugh as judge on TLC's 2010 *Miss America* pageant, these shows teach us that no matter what age, women will always be reduced to the sum of their prettiest parts.

But, ever so rarely, someone comes along and subverts reality TV's dominant beauty ideals. In 2008, VH1 aired *The Cho Show,* a sitcom-style unscripted vehicle for feminist comedian Margaret Cho.* In "Dr. 9021-Cho," she feigned an interest in plastic surgery, but chose to age gracefully instead, with body art and lots of sex with young hotties. In another episode, titled, "Cho Universe Pageant," she tells a story about a radio interviewer who once asked her, "What if you woke up tomorrow, and you were blond, and you had blue eyes, and you were 5'11", and you weighed one hundred pounds, and you were beautiful?" But since she and her friends find "beauty contest beauty" to be "so weird and foreign," they decide to stage their own version of a mother-daughter pageant, complete with celebrity judges. Contestants were drag queens and rockers with

---

* In 1994, Margaret starred in the sitcom *All-American Girl,* for which ABC demanded she lose weight to play a character based on herself.

pink Mohawks, and diverse in ethnicity, age, and body type. There was no swimsuit portion because, as Margaret explained, "Fuck that fucking bullshit!" In the end, there were tiaras for every contestant, because, "In the Cho Universe, we are all fucking beauty queens!"

It's not the format of reality TV shows that's the problem—it's what producers, advertisers, and network owners choose to do with the format that we must be wary of. *The Cho Show* proved that it's possible for reality TV to be funny, creative, and engaging, all without preying on participants' weaknesses or stoking gender, race, or class biases for cheap laughs. Unfortunately, unlike VH1's numerous seasons of the constantly rerun *Flavor of Love* franchise and spinoffs, *The Cho Show* aired only seven half-hour episodes.

As Margaret might say, fuck that fucking bullshit.

Chapter Three

Bitches and Morons and Skanks, Oh My!

What Reality TV Teaches Us about Women

Women are bitches.

Women are stupid.

Women are incompetent at work and failures at home.

Women are gold diggers.

How do we know? Because reality TV tells us so.

Academics often talk about "hegemony," the concept that describes how cultural stereotypes become unquestioned truth. In today's society, mass media is our prime purveyor of that cultural hegemony—by which I mean that media is largely responsible for *how* we know *what* we know. In other words, media shape what we think of as "the truth" about "the way things are."

In that context, reality television is as much a dissemination mechanism for ideological persuasion as it is a means of entertainment. I'm not talking about viewers believing that any one particular segment of "unscripted" (or traditionally scripted) entertainment is unvarnished reality; no solitary media moment has the power to totally transform our consciousness. It's more macro than that. Media is our most common agent of socialization, shaping and informing our collective ideas about people, politics, and public policy. Pop culture images help us determine what to wear, whom to date, how to vote, how we feel about our bodies, how we see ourselves, and how we relate to racial, sexual, socioeconomic, and religious "others."

Using the rubric of "reality" and authenticity, representations of groups of people on shows such as *The Real Housewives of Atlanta*, *The Bachelor*, and *Amer-*

ica's Next Top Model have amplified the power to define perceptions of identity. Though no single episode of those or their copycats can do widespread damage, the potential effects of this type of media are disturbing when taken as a whole. From multiple channels, with varied commercially constructed products pumping similar messages through sheer repetition for years, this form of media has the power to influence our notions of normalcy versus difference, convince us that certain behaviors are "innate" for different groups of people, and present culturally constructed norms of gender, race, class, and sexuality as "natural," rather than performances we've learned to adopt through societal education and expectation.

To illustrate the way media shapes what we think of as "the truth," imagine that you've never in your life met an American woman or girl. How would you perceive American women as a group, if your impression was formed solely through reality television?

There are certain things the genre tells us women are supposed to *just be*. Reality writers, editors, and producers utilize a number of tropes to define a set of characteristics they want us to believe are *innately female*. What does contemporary television say it means to be "real" women? What do women think, how do they behave, who *are* they, at their core?

"I Know Better Than to Trust Women"

Trope 1: Women are catty, bitchy, manipulative, and not to be trusted— especially by other women.

Once reality TV lays the groundwork of jealousy and insecurity by telling women that they can never physically measure up to an endless parade of younger, skinnier, sexier feminine rivals, producers are better able to convince women and girls that every other female is their natural adversary.

From "frenemies" on lifestyle series such as MTV's *The Hills* and Bravo's

The Real Housewives of Orange County (and *New York, Atlanta,* and *New Jersey*) to flat-out enemies on dating and modeling shows, reality television presents women as being in constant competition for romantic love, professional success, and personal fulfillment. Like the crabby villains in those old Scooby-Doo cartoons, everything a woman is supposed to want could be available to her . . . if not foiled by some meddling bitch.

"We're all enemies, vying for the same prize," one *For Love or Money* dater says of her sexed-up competitors. As proof, we're treated to endless scenes of love-starved ladies badmouthing one another to the lone Y chromosome in their midst. Contestants attempt to convince their would-be prince that one gal is too immature and unrefined for him, another too old and boring, while a third hottie is too wild and slutty—leaving only the gossiper herself as a "classy" enough bridal candidate. Talk about your twisted take on Goldilocks.

"Women tend to be jealous and catty and bitchy," one of *Joe Millionaire*'s so-called "gold diggers" insists. Another sneers, "I have never seen grown, independent, self-sufficient women act like such brats." Angry at such smack talk, a *Bachelor* babe explains that "girls can be conniving, deceiving, and just vicious!" The men they fight over hardly hold their harems in higher esteem: "All they wanna do right now is fight. But you know what? There's nothing like a good catfight," Flavor Flav smirked during *Flavor of Love*'s third season. Second-season *Bachelor* Aaron grumbled, "The vindictive nature of all the women is starting to show."

That's right—*all* the women. That's what reality TV does best: gender essentialism.* The concept of women's inherent cattiness is coded into commercials: "The backstabbing begins!" a dating show narrator promises, as the phrase

---

* Gender essentialism is a philosophical belief—often confused with biological "fact"—that "all women are" this way or that, and "all men" are bound to behave one way or the other. Essentialism privileges nature above nurture, genetics above culture, as the primary determiners of identity and behavior. Gender roles are assumed absolute and immutable, and deviation from "feminine" characteristics for females and "masculine" traits for males is considered "unnatural." Gender essentialist thinking has often been the basis of conservative, antifeminist attacks on women's advancement in education, sports, business, and politics—the argument being that women's essential natures are not predisposed toward successful participation in those arenas. At times, this form of thought in science and media has even posited that sexual assault is a "natural" act born of men's evolutionary development.[1]

"BACK STABBING!" screams from the screen in big, bold letters. "The claws were *bound* to come out when one man is involved with more than one woman," Chris Harrison, host of *The Bachelor*, announced in a montage.

Lest this prove too subtle, *Joe Millionaire* and other series have played sounds of hissing cats to underscore their gleeful promise that "the claws will come out!" When NY Giants quarterback Jesse Palmer was cast to make all the romantic passes, "coming soon" ads for *The Bachelor* featured glammed-up women in cocktail gowns on a ball field, dive-tackling a football made entirely of roses, again with the clamor of cats scratching in the background.* By season 7, ABC plastered the words "SIX CATTY WOMEN!" over half a dozen bachelorettes' headshots, described D-list actor/*Bachelor* Charlie O'Connell as "ONE SCARED PUPPY," and commanded, "LET THE CATFIGHTS BEGIN." A narrator announced this in circus-master tones as Charlie smirked, "This could get ugly," and "What's New Pussycat?" played in the background.

Feline madness was also promised on *Age of Love,* which pitted "kittens" in their twenties against "cougars" in their forties so that "each week, you'll see young versus old in a battle for love." NBC primed us to believe the "decrepit" older women were destined to fail this epic battle of the wildcats: In the premiere, the "kittens" hang out in their apartment hula hooping in bikinis, while the "cougars" sew needlepoint, read, and do the laundry (because that's what worn-out old crones do, yes?).

Trapped in a house in which they have no agency, no independent choice, and no contact with the outside world, harem girls on dating programs have literally nothing to do but get drunk and fantasize about snagging a diamond from their show's Harlequin-esque hunk. Rather than question his intentions (or, heaven forbid, the contrived scenario's unfairness), women, prodded by producers, redirect the shows' intrinsic frustrations inward, against themselves and one another. Take it from a former *Bachelor* producer, who described herself to NPR

---

* A rose equals a promise of potential love from the series' stud; don't get one, and your chance for happiness shrivels like a dead bouquet.

as having been "involved in every aspect of the production; I was heavily involved with casting, interviewing the cast, and following/driving story." On the condition of anonymity, she revealed to her friend Carrie Brownstein, riot grrrl icon and NPR contributor, how they get people to go "from seemingly normal to totally coo coo pants":

> In the private one on one interviews with a producer (like me) it is the producer's job to get the sh*t talking started, like "tell me honestly what you think of Sally"—if the interviewee does not want to respond in a catty way then the producer will usually go to the next level, like "well I personally think she is a self absorbed, attention starved skank," and then see if the person will take the bait . . . it is easy to start seeding conversations and gossip. Also, if the conversations linger too long on favorite movies and stuff the producers will step in and say, "ok we all know we signed up for a TV show—so if you don't start talking about something more topical then you can't have the sushi you requested tonight." The smarter cast members start to realize that everything can be bartered. Like, "I will give you a good one-on-one interview about Sally, IF you let me listen to my iPod for the rest of the day."[2]

And so they turn on each other, often based on off-camera misinformation, manipulation, and a false economy where trash talk is a participant's only currency. Gesturing a mock punch in the direction of a woman edited as that *Bachelor* season's resident villain, one hostile combatant says, "I want to kick her ass. I want to wring her neck. I want to so bad!" During a hunting lesson on Fox's *Farmer Wants a Wife*, a lily-white city girl aims her rifle at some tin cans and talks of preemptive war: "I fight for men the way they do in the Middle East. Before somebody blows me up, I blow them up."

Women's antagonism toward one another is portrayed as innate even when a man isn't in the mix—and, we learn, it starts early. A *Toddlers & Tiaras* promo announces, "If competition had a face, it would be hers," over B-roll of a tot made up like a Gabor sister. Children are selectively edited to appear bratty with their parents and catty with their competitors. Bossy li'l beauty queen Madison ("stage name": Tootie) competes in the ten-to-twelve category. She speaks about her split personalities in third person, treats her mom like a "slave," and says she enjoys pageants because she loves to beat other girls. After she is framed as the villain of the episode, fans dutifully attack her in web recaps with titles such as, "Your Kid Is a Brat and That's a Fact of Life!"*

We're told to watch out for claws on *America's Next Top Model*, on *Queen Bees* (where participants are meant to "learn inner beauty"), and on every season of Bravo's *Real Housewives* franchise. "Any time you put a bunch of ladies together who are not necessarily friends, there is going to be some drama," Tamra Barney, self-declared "hottest housewife in Orange County," wrote on a Bravo .com *Real Housewives* blog. "Catfights" are among the main viewership draws— and the primary promotional tactic—of *Housewives*. Editing plays up regional and ethnic stereotypes. Stuck-up snobbery and betrayal among wealthy white women is a major theme of *Orange County*. In contrast, we get "low-class" tantrums on *The Real Housewives of New Jersey*, in which Italian American women accuse each other of prostitution, kidnapping, and drug dealing while flipping over banquet tables. In *Atlanta,* African American *Housewives* get into verbal brawls with Black male employees and threaten and even hit one another. (One of the most talked-about scenes of season 2 was when divorcée Sheree Whitfield physically intimidates the only white cast member, Kim Zolciak, then tries

---

* A close, critical reading of *Toddlers & Tiaras* (like WE TV's *Little Miss Perfect*) could reveal the disturbing psychological effects of pageant participation on youth over time. It's almost as if the multiple children on each episode are not distinct individuals but representative of a universal Pageant Girl at different stages of her young life. Like a kiddie-horror version of *A Christmas Carol*, we see a time-lapse projection of their potential mental and emotional development. Viewers watch three- and four-year-olds, all smiles and sweet as can be, trying desperately to look pretty enough to please mommy, juxtaposed with the "bitchy" antics of older kids like Tootie, framed as demanding and spoiled. Interviews with judgmental parents convince us that for the foreseeable future, these girls will be valued primarily for how convincingly they wear fake eyelashes, fake tans, fake hair, fake teeth, and other artificial beauty "enhancers." They'll spend their childhoods commanded to "shake your booty" and "win for mommy." We're left to assume that these gentle, earnest kindergartners will inevitably become narcissistic, entitled ten-year-olds jaded before they reach third grade—just like Tootie. These shows would almost be cautionary tales . . . if the producers and networks didn't take such glee in demonizing not only the parents but also the children themselves.

to pull off Kim's wig. During another wildly popular incident, Kim called the police to allege that NeNe Leakes grabbed her neck and choked her. The fight, which occurred off-camera, was widely reported in the entertainment press and online.) Tellingly, the one castmate who wouldn't perform "diva antics" on cue was canned. DeShawn Snow, head of a girls' self-esteem foundation, was the only original cast member not asked to return to *Atlanta*'s second season—because Bravo considered her too dignified. A producer "said that I was 'too human for a circus show' and that because the show did so well, they are about to pump up the drama and they didn't think that I would fit in."* DeShawn was replaced by Kandi Burruss, a successful hip-hop songwriter who was repeatedly called "ghetto" throughout the second season.[3]

Producers ensure that women dutifully perform their bitch-tastic roles by egging them on with techniques that would make psyops intelligence officers proud. Based on interviews with two dozen reality TV stars, *The New York Times* reported that reality television has become "Hollywood's sweatshop," functioning behind the scenes like a "psychological experiment that keeps contestants off-balance and vulnerable . . . programs routinely use isolation, sleeplessness and alcohol to encourage wild behavior."+[4] And so, they snipe away. On dating and competition series, they attack each other in antagonistic confrontations ("You are all a bunch of catty-ass bitches!"—*Flavor of Love*). They conspire against each other like high school Mean Girls ("[She's] a ho and she's got to go. She's a total bitch!"—*Joe Millionaire*). They mouth off in hateful, bleep-filled "confessionals" ("You f–cking worthless c–nt. You are so . . . wasteful, bitchy, stupid . . . you're worthless. Your parents must be ashamed of you!"—*America's Next Top Model*). Whether they're sloshed and overtired or sober and alert, such angry outbursts are stoked and edited to "prove" that no matter how sophisticated or sweet her facade, nearly every woman is a selfish schemer deep down.

---

* In chapter 5, we'll hear about the "Angry Black Woman," another virulent facet of reality TV's "catty bitches" trope.

+ The same tactics used to produce the genre's oh-so-important "drama"—sleep deprivation, restriction of food, controlled environments that disallow communication with the outside world, and abuse of alcohol—are often used as elements of torture.

Lifestyle series manipulate us in the opposite direction. Women who truly dislike one another are portrayed as "real life" friends. Thrown together as cameras trail their semiscripted—yet supposedly authentic—lives, they are rude and unkind. They betray their so-called friends' trust, as when *The Hills* stars have semistaged arguments over men and jobs. The *Housewives* make fun of one another *(Atlanta)*, flirt with each other's men *(Orange County)*, and reveal embarrassing, scandalous secrets about members of their social circle *(New Jersey)*. "How can they treat each other that way?" we wonder, amused and disgusted, not realizing that the answer's simple: "None of us are friends," NeNe Leakes of *The Real Housewives of Atlanta* told *Jet*. "Friends don't do what we have done to each other on the show. You have not seen one of us get the other one's back. If you did see somebody get somebody's back, the next week they were talking about them. . . . We are all clearly associates."[5]

In contrast, competition show castoffs often speak fondly and at length in postelimination interviews about the bonds they developed with their fellow bachelorettes and *Top Models*. "I made some great friends on the show," Kortnie Coles of *ANTM* has said. "We still keep in touch and hang out and all that good stuff."[6] You'd never guess that from watching what seems like "all catty, all the time" behavior. That's intentional. Series producers who traffic in "drama" rarely allow viewers to see signs of real fondness and camaraderie between female castmates, whose mutual support is usually left on the cutting room floor. Instead, belying claims of "unscripted" storytelling, the phrase "I'm not here to make friends! I'm here to win!" echoes from the lips of numerous women through every season of nearly every "reality" series . . . ever since May 2003, when *America's Next Top Model* titled their second ever episode, "The Girl Who Is Here to Win, Not Make Friends."[7]

The moral of these sorry stories? If you don't want to get stabbed in the back, heed this canny *Bachelor* babe's advice: "I know better than to trust women."

Who benefits when women are conditioned not to trust one another? Reality TV depictions of women as inherently at war over female beauty and male booty mirror a broader media attack against women's solidarity. These shows put an entertaining spin on decades of corporate news coverage that pits women against one another socially and economically, diverting attention from true problems we could be allying to solve.

Before we ever witnessed a *Real Housewives* catfight, news media spent many years trying to convince Americans that women are each other's worst enemies. From an NBC morning news segment devoted to an author's quest to "blow the lid off sisterhood," we've learned that female rivalry is inescapable: "No matter what your life is like there's always some kind of competition between you and your friends or female coworkers. Even mother."*

Before *Age of Love*'s "kittens" and "cougars" came years of news stories egging on a generational divide among women. *Time, Newsweek, The New York Times Magazine,* and hundreds of other outlers have claimed that feminism is "dead" and a "failure." As this preferred media narrative goes, older women are disgusted by their daughters' supposed rejection of feminism, while Gen X and Gen Y women consider their foremothers irrelevant relics. These stories consistently ignore young, progressive women's activism alongside older feminist mentors in social justice movements for the rights of women, people of color, youth, workers, the LGBT community, immigrants, and the environment.[8]

Throw motherhood into the mix, and watch out. Print and broadcast media have spent the past twenty years pumping out nearly two thousand stories pitting "Mommy vs. Mommy" and decrying the "Scary Rise of the 'Sanctimommy.'"+ "The Mommy War" seems to have made its journalistic debut in July 1989, when the *Texas Monthly* declared that "Working moms view stay-at-home moms as idle and silly, traitors in the battle to encourage men to assume more responsibility at

---

* With dire headlines such as "MY BOSSES FROM HELL—AND THEY WERE ALL WOMEN," newspapers warn us that "The deviousness of a woman's mind hell-bent on destroying an employee is something to behold" because "Bitch Bosses . . . undermine other women, at every opportunity." Even women's magazines such as *Marie Claire* instruct readers that if they find themselves in a position to choose between a male or female employer, "your answer should most definitely be a man."[9]

+ A Nexis news database search shows 1,930 stories using the term "mommy wars" between June 27, 1989, and November 11, 2009.

home. Stay-at-home moms view working moms as selfish and greedy, cheating their own children out of a strong maternal bond." Ever since, headlines such as *The New York Times'* 2001 "LOVE & MONEY; Is My Mom Better Than Yours?" and 2003 "The Opt-Out Revolution" (which claimed that educated women were fleeing the workforce to stay home with their babies) have abounded.[10] These antagonistic trend stories persist despite being widely and repeatedly debunked. The actual evidence paints a very different picture. "The ballyhooed Mommy Wars exist mainly in the minds—and the marketing machines—of the media and publishing industry," according to E. J. Graff of the Schuster Institute for Investigative Journalism. The Bureau of Labor Statistics shows that "working mothers with infants ha[ve] held steady at 53.5 percent" since 2000, Graff wrote in *The Washington Post,* "and most of their stay-at-home peers don't hold it against them":

> Most women today have to work: it's the only way their families are going to be fed, housed and educated. A new college-educated generation takes it for granted that women will both work and care for their families—and that men must be an integral part of their children's lives . . . stay-at-home moms and working mothers aren't firmly opposing philosophical stances but the same women in different life phases, moving in and out of the part-time and full-time workforce for the few years while their children are young.[11]

It may not be accurate, and it may not be good for women's mental health, but ginning up a media-manufactured feud between women "is good for the news business. The Mommy Wars sell newspapers, magazines, TV shows and radio broadcasts," Graff continues. "An especially inflammatory article or episode can increase Web site hits, achieve 'most e-mailed' status, drag more outraged viewers or listeners to the phone lines and burn a media brand more deeply into consumers' minds."

That anxiety-breeds-ratings formula also sells reality shows—but we'll get to ABC's *Wife Swap* in a bit.

What is *The Bachelor* and its legion of copycat dating series, if not a manifestation of all those articles in women's mags like *Cosmo* and *Allure* warning older women to always be on guard lest some younger, sluttier floozy steal their men?* It's no coincidence that the same antiwrinkle creams and "age-defying" cosmetics that advertise in *Glamour* often run commercials during dating series.

In reality television as in corporate journalism, such representations divide and conquer. This isn't just about depriving women of female friendships to foster desperation for male affection. All social, academic, professional, and political gains women have made in this country—suffrage, legality and availability of contraceptives, gender equity in education and sports, criminalization of sexual harassment and acquaintance rape, protections against gender and race-based employment discrimination, among others—have been won through hard-fought collective struggle with other women. If women are conditioned to consider other women lying backstabbers, we are less likely to organize together for better working conditions or pay equity.+

Girls taught not to rely on each other will be less likely to want to play team sports together, or defend their rights to do so.# Similarly, we'd be loath to reveal to one another the kinds of painful or embarrassing experiences of workplace

---

* And oh, how the tabloids love to slap those fears onto the perfectly chiseled features of Evil Seductress Angelina Jolie, whose mere existence is used as evidence that even women as gorgeous and successful as Jennifer Aniston can have their lives destroyed when their husbands are powerless to resist the advances of conniving bitches.

+ For example, without talking to one another about their wages and working conditions, blue collar working women would not have been able to ban together in 2004 to file Dukes v. Wal-Mart Stores, Inc., then the largest-ever class action civil rights lawsuit. Representing more than 1.5 million women, the suit charged systemic discrimination against women in hiring, pay, and promotions.[12]

Women and girls have benefited greatly from the fierce legislative struggle that resulted in passage of Title IX of the Education Amendments of 1972, which required equal opportunities for girls and women in sports and education. As noted in *A Place on the Team: The Triumph and Tragedy of Title IX*, "At American colleges, more than two hundred thousand women are on varsity sports teams, up from a handful in 1971," and compose approximately 40 percent of high school and college athletes. And according to NOW, women earned just 7 percent of all law degrees, 9 percent of all medical degrees, and 13.3 percent of doctoral degrees before Title IX, but the law's legacy led to 47 percent of law degrees, 43 percent of medical degrees, and nearly half of all doctoral degrees being awarded to women. Despite its proven success, Title IX has been repeatedly attacked by conservatives hoping to roll back or eliminate this public policy and media outlets reporting that Title IX has waged a "War on Boys."[13] If women grow to believe reality TV's hype, they won't be as prepared to work together to prevent opponents from rolling back their educational and athletic equity.

assault that can lead to class action prosecution when we realize that we're not the only ones who have been mistreated. And, as every counselor who works with battered women knows, one of the primary ways an abuser gains control over his girlfriend or wife is by isolating her from her friends and family. If the notion that women are not to be trusted permeates our culture, will domestic violence victims feel they can turn to female allies for aid to escape abusive relationships—and will men and women be more or less likely to believe them when they describe their situations?

The consequences of this "women as bitches" trope are not just political. If we start to believe the common reality TV premise that it's better to hang out with men because "girls are jealous" and don't want other women to be happy, as *Charm School* and *Tough Love* castmates insist, we will miss out on the laughter and love that so often accompany deep female friendships. Female friends prop up our self-esteem in times of frivolity (bikini season, first-date jitters) and provide emotional support to help us survive life's inevitable crises (divorce, unemployment, death). Deep bonds between women can be crucial to our happiness and longevity: A 2006 study of nearly three thousand nurses with breast cancer found that "women without close friends were four times as likely to die from the disease as women with 10 or more friends."[14]

If millions of TV viewers believe that sisterhood is not powerful but spiteful, it becomes all that much harder for women to achieve any further social progress in America.

No One Wants to See a Brainiac in a Bikini: Women as Stupid

Trope 2: Women are stupid.

Women's intellectual inferiority is among reality TV's basest notions. Time and time again, we learn that the female half of the population is cringe-inducingly stupid. In embarrassing scenes across unscripted subgenres, women are portrayed as "the dumber sex." For women, we learn from one *Bridezilla*, "Thinking is a waste of time. Thinking is for people who have no brains."

Before we learn a thing about their personalities, we're predisposed to deem them inane, idiotic, or at best, naive for signing up for reality TV humiliation in the first place. Producers build on our derision by carefully casting women who are, let's just say, in no danger of being recruited to join Mensa. Once selected, editors play up their every ditzy interaction, leaving any expressions of intellect or clarity to the annals of unaired tape.

When the genre's gender templates were first being created, reality TV taught us that "dumb blonds" exist for our comedic pleasure. In 2002, E! encouraged us to snicker at addle-brained former *Playboy* Playmate (and former trophy wife of an eighty-nine-year-old oil billionaire) Anna Nicole Smith. The original reality TV train wreck, *The Anna Nicole Show* mocked the steady mental and physical decline of the buxom and seemingly stoned Smith, whose slurred speech and erratic behavior fueled the show's tagline, "It's not supposed to be funny. It just is." The cover of the first-season DVD described Anna Nicole—whose eventual drug overdose and death could have been forecast by this opportunistic spectacle—as "America's Guiltiest Pleasure."*

One year later, MTV introduced another reality option for those who wanted to laugh at "a clueless, rich blond bimbo" with none of *The Anna Nicole Show*'s tragedy-waiting-to-happen aftertaste. Welcome *Newlyweds*' star Jessica Simpson, who boggled our minds with how little seemed to be in hers. She told the secretary of the interior, "You've done a nice job decorating the White House." She believed Buffalo wings were made from Buffalo meat, not chicken—but her logic

---

* Broadcast and cable news were just as exploitative of Smith's death as E! was of her life. On the day Anna Nicole's lifeless body was found, nearly every major TV outlet devoted itself to what author Bob Harris called "wall-to-wall, 24 hour, dead stoner Playmate watch." In contrast, Harris noted the glaring absence of "some other things that happened on or around February 8, 2007, generally not covered by CNN, CBS, ABC, MSNBC, and Fox," including North Korea agreeing to shut down its nuclear plants, a tentative peace deal between warring Palestinian factions in the Middle East, and Iran test-firing its first ballistic missile capable of striking at U.S. ships in the Persian Gulf. "So you can see why Anna Nicole's death is getting all the coverage. Slow news day," Harris wrote.[15]

was always getting fouled up by fowl. In the series' debut, the pop star picked at a meal made from a can of Chicken of the Sea and asked her hubby, Nick Lachey, "Is this chicken, what I have, or is this fish? I know it's tuna, but it—it says Chicken by the Sea." From that infamous moment on, her every confused quote became proof that, as *Dateline* put it, "Saying something really dumb was now 'pulling a Jessica.'" Her presence on television was heralded as proof that the stereotype of the "'dumb blond' won't go away" because "maybe it's true." Her father went so far as to suggest that his daughter's queries were typical of silly broads everywhere. "Jessica represents all the questions that women across America want to ask their husbands but are afraid to," he told the *Arizona Daily Star*.[16]

At the same time, Fox was unveiling their Paris Hilton and Nicole Richie vehicle *The Simple Life*, which, for five seasons, reveled in the "rich bitch" heiresses' simpleminded ignorance (contrasted with their haughty elitism). Both Hilton and Simpson have said that they were just "playing characters" on *The Simple Life* and *The Newlyweds*. That's likely true. These media-savvy young women have intentionally played up their airhead images to heighten their fame and their already-overflowing bank accounts. It's a time-tested bait-and-switch: smart, professionally independent women become more successful by playing the part of the silly, dependent dimwit in the media. The phenomenally accomplished *I Love Lucy* star Lucille Ball, the first woman to head a Hollywood production company, is probably the most famous TV example.*

Reality producers may have cut their teeth on "dumb blonds," but they want viewers to believe female stupidity knows no racial limits. Five years after Joe Simpson told the press that his *Newlywed* daughter represented all American women, *The Real Housewives of Atlanta*—which features a predominately African American cast—revived the theme of husbands imparting knowledge to imbecilic wives. In one of the most talked-about scenes of the first season, NeNe

---

* By playing dumb as a strategic career move, Hilton and Simpson are the pop cultural counterparts to conservative antifeminist women who build lucrative professional journalism and political careers by telling average women that their place is in the home, such as Caitlin Flanagan (*To Hell with All That: Loving and Loathing Our Inner Housewife*) and Danielle Crittenden (*What Our Mothers Didn't Tell Us: Why Happiness Eludes the Modern Woman* author and former staffer of the right-wing Independent Women's Forum).

Leakes futilely attempted to help her nine-year-old son with his math homework. Since she was cowed by basic fractions, her husband, Gregg, had to step in to tutor his spouse right alongside their son. Alas, not even his helpfully drawn pie graphs and patient tone could bring her comprehension up to sixth-grade level:

GREGG: Three thirds make a whole. This is the pizza. Three thirds. If John ate one, Cole ate one, do you have half of it left?

NENE: Yeah. He said yeah!

GREGG: No, you have a third of it left.

NENE: No you don't!

GREGG [gently reads a line from the math textbook to underscore his point]: Sure you do, honey.

NENE: [confused] Okay . . .

GREGG: Would you rather have one third of something, or one half of something?

NENE: It just depends on what that something is. Still, I'm just, Gregg, I'm just—can we get a tutor?

While NeNe couldn't pass grade-school algebra, we were to understand that Kim Zolciak, the sole white woman on the show, couldn't pass elementary English. When she was asked, "How do you spell *cat?*" Kim's matter-of-fact reply was, "K-A-T." Producers pounce on such moments to portray the *Real Housewives of Atlanta* as fundamentally ignorant. Yet during *RHOA*'s entire first season, viewers never learned about original cast member DeShawn Snow's postgraduate divinity studies. Why? Because filming a competent, intelligent African American woman pursuing a master's degree would have broken producers' preferred narrative: that Black women (and their wealthy white lady friends) are gossipy idiots.

Regional accents and cultural slang are often used to brand women of color as unintelligent. On *America's Next Top Model*, Tyra Banks has told numerous Black girls that their speech patterns make them sound "ghetto," or inferior to

other (implied "normal-sounding") girls with standard anchorwoman-style dia-
lects. Danielle Evans, an African American teen from Arkansas, was browbeaten
for her Southern drawl. Dani had poise, charm, and a vocabulary to put her competitors to shame (they said they were "bitches" when they got mad; she described
herself as "cantankerous"). Yet Tyra harped on the eventual *ANTM* champ's
speech throughout the sixth season, referring to her as "the girl that takes beautiful pictures but the judges don't trust when she opens her mouth." Dani was a
liability to advertisers, Tyra said: "That voice cannot necessarily sell makeup."*

Despite show runners' best attempts to portray women—especially women
of color—as ignorant, every once in a while a moment of rebellious clarity slips
through the editorial cracks to disprove that depiction. Saaphyri, a low-income
Black woman whose story we'll hear more of in chapter 4, was portrayed as violent and crazy on *Flavor of Love 2*. Producers tried to stick with this script when
they brought her back for *Flavor of Love Girls: Charm School*, employing editing
and production devices to make her (and her fellow "classmates") seem unintelligent. But Saaphyri defied her "hood" packaging and became the queen of the
one-liners, displaying quick wit and regular rebellion against judges' class-based
insults. And during a business challenge, she was the "student" who figured out
how to solve a key problem, much to the surprise of the rest of the cast. She
quickly corrected their assumptions: "I feel that people take me as being stupid,
because they figure 'she's not a college graduate, her speech isn't perfect.' All that
together should equal dumb, but that's not the case."

Still, ever since Anna Nicole and Paris and Nicole, reality casting directors
have sought out female participants likely to "pull a Jessica." Producers pair them
with male counterparts who expect to exploit their assumed stupidity to get off,

---

* In "Is Tyra Banks Racist? The peculiar politics of *America's Next Top Model*," J. E. Dahl described an
episode in which Banks "singled Danielle out, imitating her delivery and demonstrating the difference
between an acceptable black Southern accent, and an unacceptable one. . . . Perhaps Tyra was simply
trying to toughen Danielle up: The fashion industry is run by white people, many of whom may think
'black' or 'country' accents are uncouth, a mark of poor upbringing. But shouldn't Tyra be using her clout
to challenge this stereotype?" Dahl asked. Yes. She should. Unfortunately, her actions rarely match her
rhetoric. We'll hear more about Banks's internalized racism, sexism, and other fashion industry legacies
in chapter 6.[17]

or to get over. Sometimes this plays out through sexual conquest: for example, tag-team daters Kamal and Ahmad Givens on VH1's *Real Chance of Love* act as if the less intelligent a woman is, the more likely they will be to bed her. Other times, financial gain is the goal, as when *Survivor: Samoa* castaway Russell Hantz bragged about "my dumb-ass girl alliance."

In 2009, TLC's *King of the Crown* brought us their version of a "dumb-ass girl alliance" between former Miss South Carolina Teen USA and her pageant coach, Cy Frakes. Before she became the marketing hook for this men-behind-the-pageant series, Caitlin Upton garnered major media ridicule and more than 40 million YouTube views for spouting gibberish about geography ("education, like, such as in South Africa and, uh, the Iraq, everywhere, like, such as") during the Miss Teen USA 2007 pageant. The premise of *King of the Crown* is that the beauty queen's internationally recognized incoherence damaged Frakes's "Complete Pageant Preparation" business, so he and his employees must now redeem themselves by guiding Upton (and their other clients) to victory once again. Frakes's sequined shirts and Southern aphorisms are only so compelling, so TLC promised more moronic mumblings from Upton as ratings bait. In a preview video, Frakes tells us his job is "to make sure the next time she opens her mouth, a brick doesn't fall out of it." Cameras immediately cut to Upton in "interview boot camp." What does she think of the swine flu epidemic? "All these people who don't take their antibiotics when they had the flu or the cold, it creates new, new cat-a-strophes." The series premiere implies that she really is as mindless as she seems. Her speech coach asks her opinion about the 2008 auto bailout (a major news story when the episode was filmed). Upton stares blankly, over har-dee-har-har music piped in by producers. He clarifies: "I mean, do you think the government should be bailing out automakers?" With a pained expression, Miss Teen South Carolina exhales deeply, then asks, "Auto [*blink*] makers?" "Yeah, like GM, Ford, Chrysler," her coach offers, voice tinged with pity and exasperation. This time Upton accompanies her blank stare with a long, low "Hmmmmnnn . . . mmmmmm" that sounds like the moan of a wounded animal.

In describing *King of the Crown,* my intent is not to trash the beauty queen's . . . seeming limitations . . . entertaining as they may be. Instead, the lesson we should take from this is that reality television makes stars out of certain kinds of young women (for example, those who don't even know what automakers *are,* much less understand the complicated economic issues involved with a recession-era governmental bailout), while leaving female scholars, business leaders, community advocates, and other high achievers off the dial.

While we don't get to see shows highlighting American women's brilliance, sometimes their inherent idiocy is the concept around which an entire series is built. On Ashton Kutcher's *Beauty and the Geek,* dim-witted hotties are paired with brainy but socially awkward boys, who are instructed to "teach" each other "valuable" life skills their partners "need." The men instruct the women in math, science, grammar, geography, technology, and how to not be stuck-up bitches. The women teach the men how to find the right pair of good-ass jeans, construct the perfect pickup line, and dazzle at cocktail parties with breaking news about which celebutant is diddling whose ex-boyfriend. The point of this "social experiment"? One gender's knowledge is vital to the workings of the world, while the other gender has a lock on all things superficial. Simply by benefit of being male, the "geeks" are supposed to know how to do things like pitch camping tents and fix cars (really? nerd boys are auto repair jocks?), while the "beauties" (code on the show for "bimbos") are presumed to have zero expertise beyond cute outfits and pop culture trivia. At the series' conclusion, the triumphant geeks emerge as newly well-rounded individuals with oh-so-much-better haircuts, fashion sense, and interpersonal confidence. The extent of the jiggly, giggly girls' "transformation" is summed up in end-of-episode gushing about how they've looked *deep inside* and learned that *even geeks* can be good people. Wait, let me get that Harvard application.

Dating shows, too, bend over backward to convince us that women are as dumb as a pile of rocks. On NBC's early reality series *Meet My Folks,* nubile young things attempted to win a European vacation fling with "the folks'" son.

Old-time game show host Wink Martindale was on hand to conduct a patronizing "smarts test," because "the parents would like to find out just how intelligent you ladies are." The girl with the highest number of correct answers, Martindale condescended in baby talk, "gets a *private wittle date* with Dan!" Martindale's tone wasn't the only thing juvenile about the scenario. "How many states are there in the United States?" he asked, tacking on "I know this one. I know this one!" before their replies. When a dippy pigtailed girl correctly answered, "When was the war of 1812?" he cooed, *"Veeery goood!"* in the same voice one usually uses to praise a potty-training toddler. But, like every good patriarch, Martindale was ready to scold. "That's embarrassing! I feel like I'm losing control here," he told one babe who didn't know which countries are separated by the Rio Grande. When another thought a year has 346 days, he snapped, "Are you blushing because you're embarrassed? Because if you're not, you should be!"

In a horrible catch-22, when reality TV women aren't embarrassingly stupid, they're condemned for *that,* too. Medical student Elyse was favored to be the first *Top Model* winner because her bony, underweight body was the preferred form of high-fashion designers. The comely future doc made it to the final episode, despite expressing frustration at "the most vapid conversations you've ever experienced going on around me all the time." But in the season finale, this is what Tyra Banks told the frontrunner just before eliminating her:

> *Elyse, your look is really strong for the fashion world—for the die-hard, hardcore fashion world. . . . Elyse, I admire your intelligence. I think you are so smart. But one thing with that intelligence is that it can intimidate people, and there's a way to use that intelligence in a way that doesn't feel like you're maybe putting down other people or sounding derogatory.*

After a long, silent pause for dramatic effect, Tyra sent Elyse packing. Her tiny couture bod made the grade, but her big, fat brain cost her the title, and the $100,000 that comes with it. Get that, girls? Your mind is a terrible thing to use.

Apparently, no one wants to see a brainiac in a bikini. One wonders how a med student slipped through the casting process in the first place. Not to worry; future seasons have mostly avoided participants prone to such pesky habits as critical thinking. A rare exception was third-season runner-up (and later *Ugly Betty* supporting actress) Yaya DaCosta, an academically accomplished African American graduate of Brown University. For the sins of expressing pride in her ethnic heritage, her intelligence, and her degrees in International Relations and African Studies, Yaya was framed as "arrogant" and "snotty." She represented a double whammy: not only intellectually driven, but Black; that's a losing combination in the reality TV universe, which prefers its women of color loud, ignorant, and, as they're too often described, "ghetto." (We'll learn more about Yaya in chapter 6.)

Mental acuity isn't considered cute on dating shows, either. Usually this message is sent through omission, when dozens of desperate women usually express little to no professional or intellectual ambition beyond lounging around McMansions, peacocking for male attention. Thinking for a living is seen as a romantic handicap. "I'm a rocket scientist," twenty-five-year-old Natasha said by way of introduction to bachelor Luke on the opener of plus-size dating series *More to Love*. "My goodness. That's a little bit intimidating," came Luke's quick response. "Oh! Sorry!" she giggled self-consciously. He sent her home at the end of the first episode.

As if there was ever any doubt.

The reign of the Ditz Queen in reality TV is an attempt to reinforce a deeply held social belief (here's looking at you, Mike Darnell!) that women have struggled for centuries to overcome. After all, less than one hundred years ago, American women were still denied the ability to vote, partly justified by the allegation that they were less intelligent than men.[18] Today, class action lawsuits are still being levied against Fortune 500 corporations that refuse to promote women out of secretarial and retail positions based on institutional biases that consider women not as mentally prepared as men for achievement and leadership. And as recently as 2005, Lawrence Summers, then the president of Harvard University, publicly declared that women's innate intellectual deficiencies are responsible for their disproportionate underrepresentation in the highest ranks of science, not the glass ceiling or other forms of systemic discrimination. Men, Summers said, are simply smarter. Summers left Harvard in part due to fallout from his blatant expression of bigotry against half his student population. Yet President Barack Obama awarded him his next gig, as director of the White House's National Economic Council.*

When pop culture underscores Summers's notion of women's mental inferiority to millions of Americans every week, continued efforts toward gender equity take a hit . . . as do young women growing up in a culture that would prefer they shut up and look pretty.

Weak Workers, Wicked Wives, Mediocre Moms: Women as Incompetent

Trope 3: Women are incompetent at work and at home.

The logical extension of women's stupidity is women's incompetence. From these shows, we learn that women are too intellectually, professionally, and socially unequipped to function effectively in the "real" world (not to mention *The Real World*).

Reality TV has very clear, archaic notions about what a "woman's place" is, and what it isn't: The personal sphere is singularly female, the public sphere predominantly male. Or, as one *Wife Swap* husband put it, fathers shouldn't do housework or cook for their children because "cavemen, the dad would go out there, work, and mom would stay home, cook, clean, and take care of the kids."

---

* Veronica Arreola, director of the Women in Science and Engineering (WISE) program at the University of Illinois at Chicago, put into context Summers's new role in the Obama administration. "Could the man who sold America on change seriously be considering appointing a man who suggested that Malia, Sasha and all of our daughters have a genetic disposition for not being able to [do] math? Sadly yes," she wrote.[19]

Women, the genre suggests ad nauseam, should be confined to their rightful realms of hearth and home (and, of course, hot tubs and strip clubs). But a funny thing happened on the way to prime time: Even when we've shed any last indicators of pesky ambition for the confinement of reality TV approved domesticity, we still can't perform our "natural" roles with any efficacy.

We're losers while we're single, imply *The Bachelor, More to Love,* and *Flavor of Love.* Of course, we're all the more pathetic if unmarried after thirty-five, as per cautionary tales such as *Age of Love, Who Wants to Marry My Dad?* and *The Cougar.*

We're terrors before we wed: "There's three kinds of Bridezillas stalking the streets of America: the Princess Bride, the Neurotic Bride, and the Obsessive Bride," a narrator warned in horror movie tones on the premiere episode of *Bridezillas.*

If we work outside the home (whether for fulfillment or from economic necessity), we're slovenly housekeepers and bossy tyrants to wimpy husbands. At least, that's what we learn about nearly every nonhomemaker among the two women traded like chattel on most episodes of *Wife Swap,* a televised version of those trumped-up "Mommy Wars."

We're piss-poor parents to our out-of-control children on shows like *Supernanny* and *Nanny 9-11,* where "experts" from central casting whip our rug rats into shape with well-chosen parenting book platitudes. Mothers are so witless, these shows posit, that strangers can accomplish more with our kids in just a few days than we could in all the years since we birthed them.

And as the *Real Housewives* are meant to illustrate, women with money are horrid human beings who care more about our implants, mansions, galas, and feuds than our kids, husbands, families, and communities. (Only a handful of women—including those with careers they downplay in order to call themselves "housewives"—participate in the filming of *The Real Housewives of Orange County,* yet producers clearly want us to believe the behavior of these few is representative of a great many. Why else would they include a random title screen reading, "7 million families live in gated communities" before a mansion's gate opens during the show's intro credits?)

As a whole, the reality TV landscape paints us as failures in the domestic domain that we're supposed to believe is our sole responsibility.

If this television genre wants us to believe that women can't even function in the classically female terrain of homemaker, wife, and mother—often described on *Wife Swap* as our "God-given roles"—just imagine how much worse its messages are about female performance in professional and public life.

In business competitions, producers carefully construct narratives in which women's good looks are their primary—sometimes their only—asset. Boob-power, not brainpower, is the key to women's success on *The Apprentice*, where ambitious (and always gorgeous) female executives are often shown relying on their physical appearances and, in some cases, their overt sexuality to compete against men's supposedly inherent problem-solving abilities. They flirt with clients to raise donations for charity. They flash their belly buttons to sell lemonade. They even drop their skirts to sell M&Ms . . . because they can't think of a better way to get men to give them money. By the same token, they're often portrayed as inept when unable to coast on the feminine wiles that, we are meant to understand, were partially responsible for their being cast in the first place.* If host and executive producer Donald Trump behaved toward female staffers of the Trump Organization the way he does on his show, promoting women for sexy stunts and ignoring or rewarding the sort of treatment women have received from male *Apprentice* candidates over the years, he'd be setting himself up for sexual harassment lawsuits.

With its emphasis on mock-professional marketing challenges for high-end corporate advertisers such as Marquis Jets, Lamborghini cars, and natch, the

---

* *Apprentice* fans with good memories may recall that Donald Trump fired Ivana, the second-season "job applicant" who showed male passersby her undies so they'd buy her candy bars, because he said she was no better than "a stripper." Yet in that same episode, Trump had no problem with Ivana's teammates Jennifer and Sandy dressing in tight little matching tops and heels to get men to "buy some candy from the eye candy." This, and a great many instances like it over the course of eight seasons of *The Apprentice*, was considered good business strategy . . . since women, we're meant to understand, need such schemes to compensate for the sort of inferiority Larry Summers says is our natural impediment.

Trump Organization, NBC's mainstay business competition has the undeserved reputation of being more sophisticated fare than cable reality sleaze-fests. Yet the same notions about women and work hawked on *The Apprentice* can be found at the low-rent end of the TV dial. Take *Flavor of Love Girls: Charm School,* which split contestants into teams for a "business lesson" in how to create and sell perfume. Inevitably for a franchise that revels in debasing women (especially women of color), the episode read more like a tutorial in workplace discrimination. A "CEO" chose a "skanky" woman to "work" for her team "because you are sexy and I think you will use your assets to your advantage." And so she did: Her team let random men sniff their cleavage as incentive to buy the scent and eventually stripped nearly naked on the sidewalk to market their perfume. "They did what they do—selling tits and ass. They just added perfume to the ho-selling business!" a competing *Flavor of Love Girl* groused. Never fear: *Charm School* "dean" Mikki Taylor, also *Essence* magazine's beauty director and cover editor, was on hand to reassure the audience that "us[ing] their sexuality to sell the perfume" was a perfectly acceptable sales strategy because "It was tasteful and not slutacious." Um, okay.

What did promise to be "slutacious"? The premise for the Fox "comedy/reality hybrid" show *Anchorwoman,* which simultaneously pinched two of my biggest pet peeves as a journalist and media critic: reality TV misogyny, coupled with the marginalization of qualified women in the news biz. It started with Fox giving busty blond bikini model and former WWE wrestler Lauren Jones a job as a local news anchor for KYTX, a flailing CBS news affiliate in Tyler, Texas. Until that point, Jones's most notable experience outside the wrestling ring was as one of "Barker's Beauties" on the game show *The Price Is Right,* and as "Hobo Bikini Model" on *Wonder Showzen.* Promotional materials called her an "über-vixen" and included pictures of the model perched seductively on a news desk wearing a low-cut, leopard-print halter top and red micromini. Pretty girl = ratings gold, CBS believed, so they let Fox convince them to give Jones a news gig . . . not *despite* her lack of journalistic expertise but specifically *because* of those nonexistent credentials, to serve as conflict-generating fodder for *Anchorwoman*. Here's how Fox's promotional material described the series:

> *Can this bombshell make it as a serious reporter? Will she save KYTX, or make it the laughingstock of the Lone Star State? Lauren wants to show everyone she's no airhead, and this is her big chance to prove she's more than just a pretty face. The entire newsroom thinks the boss has made a giant mistake. Reigning anchor Annalisa Petraglia is not about to lose her Queen Bee status to some L.A. hottie. News Director Dan Delgado is fit to be tied as his beloved journalistic standards go out the window. . . . How will it all turn out? Only the ratings will tell, so stay tuned. . . .*

How fun! A bikini model will try to read news copy from cue cards! Let's place bets on how badly she'll mangle the news! And, oooh, get ready for catfights from coworkers jealous that she's hotter than they are!

This may have been seen as "comedy/reality" by Fox, but it's anything but funny that for an entire month, residents of Tyler, Texas, had their local news delivered by someone with zero journalistic merit. It's bad enough that so many news stations hire "über-vixens" as "weathergirls"—now, thanks to reality TV producers, opportunistic station managers are casting them as pseudojournalists (if only for the amount of time it takes to film a reality series about the news). I wish this were the stuff of satire, as when *The Daily Show*'s Samantha Bee spoofed the sexualization of women in journalism as "N.I.L.F.: News I'd Like to F@#k." Even as scripted entertainment, Jones's appointment would be far-fetched, but as "real-life" practice, hiring a news anchor based solely on her looks and setting her up to fail, while placing women on her team into a hostile workplace environment, smacks of employment discrimination. At best this would be improper, at worst illegal. But the impact on the news—or on citizens who rely on it to make sound decisions about elections, legislation, health, and public life—hardly matters to Fox or CBS. Degrading pretty bimbettes in business settings is usually a reliable ratings draw to networks that have long since abandoned anything resembling "beloved journalistic standards."*

Anchorwoman managed the trifecta: all three tropes—women as catty, ditzy, *and* incompetent—squeezed into one show. Luckily, reality viewers never did learn whether this insult to women journalists everywhere had any impact on the news in Tyler, Texas—*Anchorwoman*'s ratings were so abysmal that Fox canceled it after just one episode.

Credibly delivering the news is just one of many things reality TV tells women we just can't do. We can't wait tables, clean hotel rooms, milk cows, catch crayfish, unload a casket from a hearse, or manage not to desecrate cremated ashes *(The Simple Life)*. We can't remove rat carcasses, inseminate pigs, sling fast food burgers, or avoid getting drunk as a nudist colony staffer *(New York Goes to Work)*. We can't engage in shrewd sales negotiations. ("Apparently stripper clothes are worth more than I thought, unless she gave him a blow job. Damn crack whore!" one *Flavor of Love Girl* says of the large dollar figure her competitor scored for her fashions from a male thrift store manager.) We can't serve and protect ("Female officers put people's lives at risk," a husband tells his "new wife," a cop, on *Wife Swap*). We can't work construction, or even assemble an out-of-the-box children's playground safely *(Charm School)*. We can't cook as delectably as men (there has been only one female *Top Chef* among the winners of the culinary show's first five seasons). We can't prepare healthy meals *(The Biggest Loser, Dance Your Ass Off* . . . then again, neither can male contestants on weight loss shows). We can't tell jokes without a handicap *(Last Comic Standing)*. We can't write or sing hip-hop *(Real Chance of Love, Ego Trip's The White Rapper Show)*. We can't even dress ourselves appropriately for work, play, or the simple task of not embarrassing our loved ones *(What Not to Wear)*.

---

* This stunt casting by CBS says as much about sexism in the media industry as it does about the cross-promotional degeneration of broadcast journalism and hypercommercial entertainment programming. As KYTX president and general manager Phil Hurley said of the controversy surrounding the show, "I'm still surprised at all the attention around the country on the journalism/entertainment issue. I've been around a long time and it's always been that way. It's entertainment, and we just weren't cutting any new ground here."[20]

THIS IS SHIRLEY CHISOLM'S LEGACY?

Correspondence between myself and Brian Gadinsky, executive producer of Fox's *Anchorwoman* and an executive producer on several seasons of *American Idol*, is telling. After reading a critique I wrote about *Anchorwoman*'s prospects for both sexism and unethical journalism, Gadinsky sent me this email, hoping to convince me that his show wasn't antifeminist. All spelling and punctuation [sic]:

wanted to tell you an interesting tidbit!

my mother, who passed away in 2000, was one floridas pioneer feminists and she served in the fla legislature for 22 years as a champion for abused women, women who wanted choice over their own bodies, women who were underpaid in the workplace, woman who wanted the ERA in the constitution, etc etc etc. . . . she was the first inductee into the florida womens hall of fame!!!

and so i was raised by her! i will never forget campaiging in 1972 for shirley chisholm for president!!

so for my creation to be slammed by a feminist organization certainly got my attention!

i asked my brother and sister awhile back if mom would be turning in her grave or laughing hystercally and we were unanimous it would be the latter. people need to lighten up! the irony is, as you will see on the show, you're all wrong.

just like my mom, lauren jones, being a woman, is completely marginalized and underestimated. in my show, like my mom did . . . she shows 'em . . . and shows

'em good . . . that she is a bright college grad and with her perseverance and hard work she will triumph and leave everyone dumbfounded. . . .

. . . keep writing about my show!!!! it premieres august 21!!!

my best wishes
 brian gadinsky

Hmm . . . I wonder what Gadinsky's mom and her fellow Florida Women's Hall of Famers would have said if they saw Fox's promo materials portraying Lauren Jones as an unintelligent hottie who doesn't deserve her job. But, maybe I *should* "lighten up." I mean, I'm sure this unqualified model-posing-as-journalist is just as ready to "show 'em good" as a groundbreaking feminist ERA-campaigning, Chisholm-voting, battered-women-protecting, pay-equity-advocating, abortion-supporting politician.

Or . . . not. Neither Gadinsky's late mother's political persuasions nor his excessive use of exclamation points negate the fact that he built and marketed a show based on the premise that hot women are brainless and unprofessional, while smart women are catty and jealous of pretty young things. The original blog post Gadinsky responded to appeared at WIMN's Voices. "Calling Texas TV viewers—WIMN needs your help! (Asinine 'Anchorwoman' sneek peek tonight makes mocking women journalists a primetime sport)," June 11, 2007.

With our limited initiative, intelligence, and ingenuity, reality TV tells us women are followers, not leaders. In ABC's post-9/11 reality docu-series *Profiles from the Front Line,* Jerry Bruckheimer's cameras followed members of the U.S. military in Afghanistan. The male heroes they chose to bring into our living rooms were brave soldiers, surgeons, and weapons inspectors. In contrast, the women they profiled were a blonde, ponytailed medic who bragged that military work keeps women thin, some grieving white war wives, widows, and moms who kept the home fires burning, and Sergeant First Class Danette Jones, an African American cook whose "job is to supervise the kitchen, ensure everything is getting done properly, and that the soldiers are happy and fed." Segment title captioned on the screen? "Mission: Breakfast."* Powerful men fight the wars, find the weapons, and heal the soldiers, while nurturing women deliver their medicine, keep their bellies full, and pray for their safe return. Check.

Bruckheimer wasn't the only big-name movie producer to bring Hollywood's double standards to the small screen. When women are, rarely, allowed to show true talent or skill, they're often portrayed as exceptions to the incompetent rule. This was the case with *On the Lot*, a highly hyped, low-rated quest for the next great American filmmaker, brought to us by Steven Spielberg and *Survivor* and *Apprentice* producer Mark Burnett. Throughout the series, judge Garry Marshall (director of *Pretty Woman, Runaway Bride,* and *Exit to Eden*) consistently gave male directors specific feedback about the quality or inadequacy of their short films, while offering mostly contentless comments to female directors. Marshall described those gals whose movies he fancied as credits to their gender; those whose work he found subpar were told they reflect poorly on "women filmmakers." Because, as we all know, female filmmakers were responsible for notorious box-office bombs such as *Howard the Duck, Showgirls, Glitter,* and *Gigli.* Oh, wait . . . +

---

* We'll hear more about this Bagram Air Base kitchen supervisor in chapter 5.

+ Executive Producer George Lucas was so embarrassed by his involvement with the widely panned *Howard the Duck,* directed by Willard Huyck in 1986, that he disowned the film. The 1995 cinematic failure *Showgirls,* directed by Paul Verhoeven, has become a camp classic, so bad that people looking to make fun of it while sloppy drunk can buy a DVD version packaged with shot glasses and drinking game instructions. *Glitter* and *Gigli,* built around Mariah Carey and Jennifer Lopez, respectively, were directed by Vondie Curtis-Hall in 2001 and Martin Brest in 2003—not even Mariah's voice or J-Lo's curves could save these eminently mockable flicks from being counted among the worst films of their decade.

Damning portrayals of women's incompetence at home and at work can send messages that are truly toxic to women's rights. If women are generally flakier, less talented, and less capable than men, why hire them, support their artwork, elect them as politicians, pay attention to their concerns as citizens, or respect them as equal life partners?*

On the domestic front, we're led to believe that if women would just quit their jobs and devote all their time to straightening out their bratty kids, they wouldn't need a *Supernanny* to swoop in and save the day. Yet there's rarely much indication that fathers should be considered equally responsible for the mental and emotional care of their children. On shows such as *Wife Swap,* financial provision is usually considered dads' primary purpose within the family, as well as the occasional meting out of discipline. Stay-at-home dads and home-schooling fathers are often called "wimps" and attacked as emasculated.

Casting directors shine an intentional spotlight on wives who say they are happy being "obedient" to controlling, sometimes verbally abusive husbands. (In reality, female servitude and male domination are often the first indicators of a pattern of escalating abuse in domestic violence relationships; in reality television, domineering men and subservient women are contentedly upholding "family values.")

When it comes to the public sphere, the messages become even more repressive to social progress. Why should we support antiharassment laws, viewers may wonder, if real women engage in, invite, and even rely on sexual behavior in the workplace? Through their ample product placements, Fortune 500 corporations such as Microsoft, Sony, Wal-Mart, and Home Depot tacitly approve the sexual-harassment-encouraging working conditions condoned on NBC's *The*

---

* The stereotypes reality TV does its best to revive are based on longstanding social biases. For example, the gender essentialist questions reality shows raise about women and work were at play in early 2010, when the New York State Bar Association announced that their annual meeting would feature a "distinguished panel of gentlemen from the legal field [who] will discuss the strengths and weaknesses of women in . . . their legal work." Originally titled, "Their Point of View: Tips from the Other Side," the planned all-male panel was revised to include female speakers. However, that didn't change its core idea that (unlike men) women are a monolithic group within the legal arena, and any obstacles they face are attributable not to systemic factors but to individual women who need "tips" to overcome their "weaknesses."[21]

Apprentice. Young women preparing to enter the workforce are groomed by such shows to expect that their looks will be as important as their resumes, and that they may have to put up with come-ons from male colleagues and bosses if they hope to keep their jobs. Meanwhile, male reality fans who aspire to The Donald's wealth are taught to regard their female colleagues as mentally deficient playthings. It's the same office ethos that rules the fictional advertising agency of AMC's 1960s period piece *Mad Men*—minus the feminist subtext included as a running critical commentary about the gender and racial injustices of that show's era. But unlike the writers and producers of *Mad Men,* the (nonunion) writers and producers of unscripted programming are intentionally replicating those mid-twentieth-century values in the name of "reality" and insisting that this is just the way the modern world works.*

In the reality TV universe, human beings are not a product of their environments and of cultural conditioning—they are simply acting out the roles preset for them by their DNA or their deity. "With millions of people watching shows like *What Not to Wear, Wife Swap* [and others]" author Shira Tarrant writes, "these become powerful vehicles for transmitting hegemonic ideals."[22] Over time, viewers may come to believe that women shoulder the bulk of the burden of housework and childcare because they're naturally predisposed to do so, and that men are biologically destined for the worlds of commerce, politics, and the military. At the same time, these shows underscore the myth that women's professional inferiority is responsible for their underrepresentation in corporate America's executive suites and boardrooms, rather than still-prevalent systemic discrimination in hiring, promotion, and pay.[23]

Reality shows exploring the personal and public spheres too often promote the idea that the institutional problems facing contemporary women are simply the result of each individual woman's poor choices at home and inability to perform up to par at work.

---

* The *Apprentice* shares another element with *Mad Men:* Both series include entire storylines devoted to selling the merits of specific name-brand airplanes, food, clothing, and other sponsors' products.[24]

But just like poverty (a socioeconomic condition resulting from institutional imbalances, reinforced by structural policies benefiting wealthy corporate and governmental interests), gender-based inequity is caused by societal circumstances and requires intentional public solutions, not just individual change.

I Ain't Sayin' She's a Gold Digger . . .

Trope 4: Women are gold diggers.

OK, so, reality TV has taught us that women are stupid, bitchy, incompetent idiots. What else is there? Oh, that's right—they're also "money grubbing, gold-digging whores."

At least, that's how Trish Schneider, the "most hated bachelorette in history," was described on season 5 of *The Bachelor.* Who's Trish, you ask? She's the babe who sinned against reality TV's version of womankind by mentioning she didn't want kids and wearing a retro-look T-shirt that said, "Gold digger: Like a hooker . . . just smarter."*

That slogan was the entire basis of Fox's *Joe Millionaire,* which didn't hide its contempt for female cast members. The show's conceit started with deceit: Producers tricked a couple dozen women into agreeing to participate by telling them they were going to star in a reality-based version of *Sex and the City* in France. Participants were misled by an ironically feminist pitch, finalist Sarah Kozer said on a Bravo exposé: "I wasn't aware that there was going to be a man there who was choosing amongst us. They had this female producer come to me and say 'We're so sick of the way women are being portrayed on reality TV. We want really confident, together, classy, sophisticated'" women.

What they really wanted were guinea pigs that could be sacrificed to the ratings gods. Contestants who thought they'd be trading spit with a spate of

---

* So memorable was this "gold digger" that Trish landed at number five on *TV Guide's* "Top 10 Reality TV Villains" list in June 2008.[25]

European Casanovas and girl talk with fellow castmates learned—too late—that they were there to compete for one man's affections. Once the cameras were rolling and they couldn't back out, they were told that the bloke had "inherited $50 million" and was "looking for love" with "someone he could trust," who didn't "want him only for his money." Of course, the conspiratorial inside joke between Fox and viewers was that Evan Marriott was a workaday construction jock with an annual salary of just $19,000—and contrary to his talk of trust, he'd be deceiving them for the duration of the show. From the get-go, producers played these women as laughingstocks, a series-long adventure in Schadenfreude. From the outset, our complicity made the joke complete.

A buzz-generating campaign to demonize these dames for our viewing pleasure started well before the series premiered. Fox's marketing strategy involved pretending to take their own "gold diggers v. true love" setup seriously one day and claiming to be a tongue-in-cheek send-up of reality TV clichés the next. Yet many corporate media outlets discussed the show's premise without irony. Headlines like "Gold Diggers Get Comeuppance on FOX Reality Show" were typical. Newspapers, magazines, and blogs ran stories implying that while *Joe* was a faker, the show realistically exposed the supposedly mercenary nature of single American woman. *USA Today* even used the show as a springboard for an online article headlined, "How to marry your own millionaire." Here's how the story opened: "What if Joe Millionaire really was filthy rich? Yes, we're waiting for [the finalists] to get their comeuppance when they learn he's just a poor construction worker. But wouldn't it be more fun if they really were going to land Mr. Moneybags?" The series garnered its share of criticism, but the entertainment press too often used *Joe Millionaire* as "proof" that, when it comes down to it, many—if not most—real women are merely greedy sluts who can't be trusted to do anything other than feign affection to use men for money.[26]

Producers were hardly subtle about it, marshaling female contestants' comments to underscore the message that "They're all gold diggers, I don't care what you say." Another competitor went further: "It was pretty cool to hear that he inherited $50 million," she said. "That's obviously appealing to women. Come on! I mean, *we're women!"* Contestants didn't do all the thematic dirty work—the first episode's narration set the tone. "Once this Average Joe has made his choice, he will have to confess the truth. Will love or money prevail?"

NBC framed crass copycat *For Love or Money* in an equally disparaging way. "Fifteen women are on a quest for *true love* that begins and ends in this palatial estate. But, there's a twist. What he can never know is that the girl he chooses will win *One. Million. Dollars!"* we learned from a Mr. Moviefone sound-alike in the show's opening montage. "Will these women lie, backstab, and break hearts for cold, hard cash?" Contestants were edited to suit producers' purposes. Pragmatic participants announced that "Smart girls finish rich," and "It's only about the money!" Mr. Moviefone returned with the final whammy: "The man *or* the money—they can't have both. See how far these women will go—for love, or money." At that, we spied a wide-eyed beauty batting her eyes and trying to convince prince-poseur Rob Campos to choose her, promising, "You will get the farthest with me."*

Marketing mean-spirited misogyny as mischievous fun paid off for Fox, as *Joe Millionaire* became a gargantuan hit. With 40 million viewers, the finale was not only Fox's most-watched show of 2003, it was the third-most-watched television episode of *the entire decade.* As Reuters reflected, why should networks tell women the truth "when fooling them is so much more fun?"[27] *For Love or Money* dominated its time slot with 12.9 million viewers, making its July 2003 finale that summer's number one reality series and the highest-rated entertainment program NBC had aired since 1999. Even though both networks failed to achieve strong numbers with their second seasons, the "gold digger" concept has influenced dating shows ever since, especially on later cable series such as VH1's *Flavor of Love, Real Chance of Love,* and *Rock of Love* franchises, and MTV's *For the Love of Ray J,* where the concept has been translated into Black and Latina women as "hos." Or,

---

* Oddly, the real twist of the show was that they *did* tell the guy about the money, giving him just as much motivation to choose among the women based on finances rather than feelings—yet his motivations were always assumed pure, while theirs were always presumed selfish.

as Tiffany "New York" Pollard described a competitor on *Flavor of Love:* "she's a gold digger, she's a slut, she's a whore . . . she's totally fake."

But why did Fox and NBC initially believe this premise had legs? Because they constructed *Joe Millionaire* and *For Love or Money* to play on virulent cultural hostility toward women—in particular, the notions that men should distrust female partners, women should be jealous of romantic rivals, and every woman has a price.

Packaged as fluffy fun, the premises of such programming fall apart without deep, irrational, and abiding prejudice. To get into such shows, viewers must assume that not only are women inherently stupid and heartless, but that they can *and should* "fall in love" under constant surveillance while being disparaged by the guy they're pursuing. After weeks of this sort of treatment, if the "lucky lady" chosen at the end doesn't profess pure, endless emotion for an offensive jerk, she's considered an evil "gold digger." Producers allow no room for the normal emotional response of anyone who, in reality, learned they'd been deceived and mocked by someone pretending to care about them. Any signs of anger, disillusionment, or disgust at their betrayal are either left on the cutting room floor or edited to make the aggrieved dater appear disappointed that she wasn't in for a financial windfall. Yet what person in her right mind could ever truly "fall in love" in a couple of camera-laden weeks with a himbo who was snogging fifteen of her friends and lying to her from the moment they met?

These shows posit women as inherently calculating and unfeeling about sex in ways they imply men are not. This is particularly manipulative when we consider that their male stars admit publicly, as Evan Marriott did, that they do shows like *Joe Millionaire* for paychecks, not life partners. The idea that women are mercenary when it comes to love is a convenient way to deflect uncomfortable, unacknowledged economic realities that complicate gender relations in and outside of the romantic sphere. Beyond the confines of the reality TV universe, it is by and large men who utilize the services of (female, male, and transgendered) prostitutes, and mostly men who stuff their hard-earned bills down exotic dancers' G-strings. Further, American men fuel an illegal, abusive, billion-dollar sex trade, in which women and children are sexually enslaved domestically and internationally for the equivalent of the cost of a couple of triple tall Starbucks lattes.[28] Women's bodies are still used by advertisers to sell everything from soap to SUVs. And as we'll see in chapter 4, women still make only 77 cents for every dollar men earn, an inequity that becomes even more steep for women of color. Women are more likely to be poor, less likely to own their own homes, and still face financial and institutional disparities in employment and healthcare, all widely documented aspects of the feminization of poverty. Such economic indicators are major draws for (straight, lesbian, and bisexual) women and girls who work in the sex industry, often from necessity, sometimes by choice, and sometimes under force or coercion.[29] At the same time, more and more blue- and white-collar working women are striving to be financially self-sufficient than ever before, as the age of first marriage continues to rise.[30] Reality TV producers want nothing to do with these economic realities, when it's so much easier and more lucrative to direct men's distrust and women's scorn onto so-called "gold diggers" and "hos."

The Bottom Line about Reality TV's "Bitches," "Morons," and "Incompetent Skanks"

Author Shira Tarrant argues that shows such as *Wife Swap* are "modern fables" that "are filled with repressive prescriptions about who we are." Because this genre "lacks any critical reflection on social injustice," Tarrant describes reality TV as "a component of what bell hooks calls the politics of domination."[31]

Media images have impact on adults as well as on youth, as any advertising executive can attest. Long-term exposure to tropes about women as stupid, incompetent, gold-digging bitches may begin to affect the way adults see themselves, their relationships to friends, loved ones, and coworkers, and their own place in public and private life.

According to Nielsen research,[32] U.S. television viewership hit record highs in 2008 and continues to rise. By 2009, the average American watched more than thirty-one hours of TV per week. Now, consider that reality shows are especially popular among young viewers. Typical U.S. teenagers watch three hours and twenty minutes of TV per day, "more than ever before," with reality shows being among their favorites.* If reality TV's tropes about women are troubling for adults, they're even more disturbing when we consider viewers who have grown up with these shows shaping their worldview. Young women and men who reached voting age in 2008 would have been just ten years old when reality shows such as *Who Wants to Marry a Multi-Millionaire?* and *Survivor* debuted. If they've had TVs in their homes (or on their computers), those young people have potentially consumed a steady diet of thousands of hours of programming in which female solidarity doesn't exist, women's problems are not structural but the result of individual weakness, and gender equality is a fiction. The likely psychological and political impact of this televised "reality," where the pursuit of women's rights is inherently futile, should be as obvious as it is damaging.

---

* Reality programming (or "participation/variety," as Nielsen calls the genre) is among the most popular entertainment options for teens, with *American Idol* being their top program in 2008—"as it was for everyone else," Nielsen notes.

Chapter Four

This Is Not My Beautiful House!

Class Anxiety, Hyperconsumerism,
and Mockery of the Poor

And you may find yourself behind the wheel of a large automobile

And you may find yourself in a beautiful house, with a beautiful wife

And you may ask yourself, "Well . . . how did I get here?"

—TALKING HEADS, "Once in a Lifetime"

Don Mueller, the forty-eight-year-old father at the center of NBC's *Who Wants to Marry My Dad?* seemed like a great catch. After all, he had good looks, three telegenic kids, and a sprawling Southern California mansion with a pool, a hot tub, and a six-car garage (the better to fit his red Ferrari convertible).

Welcoming a dozen potential stepmoms to the impressive estate they'd be sharing with his family for several weeks, twenty-two-year-old son Chris said, proudly, "This is our house."

Except . . . it wasn't.

Despite the entry sign that read THE MUELLERS and the family photos on the walls, the Muellers actually call Glendale, Cincinnati, home. Don does well for himself, running a map-printing business with more than one hundred employees, but while the dapper dad's real house is very nice, it's hardly palatial. There's no pool, no six-car garage, and no $165,000 sports car.

Don does own a hot tub, though.[1] That puts him way ahead of most of the contestants of the show's predecessor, *Meet My Folks,* where parents creepily selected their sons' or daughters' future sex partners from among a brood of opportunists who slept in their lavish homes, languished by their pools, and made out in their hot tubs. The catch? The ostentatious McMansions where the shows were filmed never belonged to "the folks." The precious keepsakes and trophies on the mantels? The high-end sofas on which they sat in judgment of the young daters hoping to win a free vacation fling with their kids? The Jacuzzis that sparked inevitable scandals? All staged, Executive Producer Scott Satin explained to *TelevisionWeek*.

Each episode of *Meet My Folks* featured a different cast of characters and a new sign above the front door bearing their name (for example, THE BLANKENSHIPS, who starred in the series opener).[2] Both shows shared a similar blink-and-you'd-miss-it disclaimer whizzing by during the closing credits:

PARTICIPANT FAMILY DOES NOT RESIDE AT FILMING LOCATION.

Satin told the press that fake homes were used on *Meet My Folks* because "When a girl brings home a boy to meet her parents, it's a lot more intimidating if you are in their own home." On the other hand, he chalked up Dad's extravagant new digs to logistics: the house needed to be big enough to accommodate the contestants and crew.[3]

That's his story, but I don't buy it. More likely, "the folks" on Satin's shows, and on so many others, are relocated from their own modest homes (or—*horrors!*—apartments) to erase anything so banal as an average, middle-class existence.

For immediate branding purposes, integrated marketers prefer upscale homes as the "sets" where their products will be showcased. Like the opulent, fifty-two-room Manhattan penthouse Donald Trump gloated about to the "job applicants" on *The Apprentice:* "If you are really successful . . . you'll all live just like this."* And taking a longer view, reality TV producers would rather we lust after the exorbitant lifestyles of pampered trophy wives and mistresses on Bravo's *The Real Housewives of Orange County* (and *New York, Atlanta,* and *New Jersey*), wealthy bachelors on *The Millionaire Matchmaker,* and a certain bad-toupee-wearing real estate mogul. The

---

* *The Apprentice* portrays extreme wealth as the key to professional, personal, and spiritual fulfillment. Trump is cast as the ultimate role model, with no acknowledgment that he has driven multiple companies and casinos into bankruptcy and has been sued for fraud.

"rich bitch" duo of ditzy trust fund brats on *The Simple Life* weren't presented to us simply as subjects for the kind of "dumb blond" mockery discussed in chapter 3; they were meant to be unconscious object lessons.* Paris Hilton and Nicole Richie's self-indulgent lives of frivolity and excess stoke our fantasies of wealth, power, and privilege—the very outlook advertisers always attempt to foster. Watching the bad behavior of heiresses, *Housewives,* and captains of industry on such shows plays on Americans' twin desires to hate the rich for having what most of us don't—and, ultimately, to *be* them.[4]

Unfortunately, that American dream of prosperity and plenty is getting farther out of reach for the vast majority of us. By the end of 2009, unemployment rates had risen to a staggering 10 percent, with 15.3 million people jobless. And even before the banking and housing collapses of 2008 and 2009, the gap between the wealthiest and poorest individuals had grown greater than our country has seen since the Great Depression: The top 1 percent of the population control 42.7 percent of the nation's wealth (and the bottom 80 percent of Americans control only 7 percent). That inequity is compounded by race and gender: People of color have 15 cents for every dollar of white wealth, according to United for a Fair Economy.[5] And as Meizhu Lui, director of the Closing the Racial Wealth Gap Initiative, writes, "Single women of working age between 18 and 64 have only 36 cents of wealth to the single man's dollar" and by "2004, single white women had around $24,000 in wealth, while African-American women at the median had only $2000 dollars to fall back on. And for Latinas? Nada." Women of color are also less likely than white women and men to have health insurance.[6]

In the face of these stark realities, the magnification and misrepresentation of affluence in reality television plays a dangerous game with our expectations, our desires, our spending patterns—and our country's economic stability.

---

* Fox debuted *The Simple Life* in 2003, early in the life of reality television. Paris and Nicole were dispatched to cities across America without benefit of their no-credit-limit platinum cards, where they had to interact with "real Americans" in trailers, small homes, farms, and factories—sort of like *The Beverly Hillbillies* in reverse. Producers used the spoiled heiresses' exaggerated disrespect for the middle- and low-income people they met as a twofer: Producers positioned the "dumb blonds" as ignorant, privileged brats, while viewers were encouraged to laugh at the blue-collar "yokels" framed as the "opposite" of Hilton and Richie.

Mocking the Poor

We've seen the crucial role finance plays in reality romance, but it's not only dating and lifestyle shows that are steeped in economic undercurrents. In reality TV, class issues run deeper than the transaction between commodified female body and privileged male provider, as seen on *The Bachelor* and *The Millionaire Matchmaker*. As middle-income mortgages are whitewashed away with mansions designed to make cast members appear admirably rich, producers play on the pathos of poverty for dramatic impact or, worse, for cheap laughs.

Such class anxiety is acute in competition shows, where financially strapped women are taunted with the dream of a better life. Broke but busty babes beg for a photo shoot payday on *America's Next Top Model,* proclaiming that posing nearly (or, sometimes, completely) nude for Tyra Banks's parade of integrated marketers is their only shot at economic security. Year after year, *American Idol* has gone even further, overtly making fun of low-income women's desperation to get out of dead-end jobs at McDonald's or Wal-Mart with paychecks that don't allow them to properly feed, clothe, and house their kids. From the hundreds of hours of filmed tryouts in numerous cities season after season, producers cherry-pick for scenes of young, poor single moms, often African American and Latina, who—just before painfully off-key performances—say they *just know* that *Idol* will be their stepping-stone to a better life. Then, after their inevitable ear-splitting auditions and cutting commentary from the judges, cameras follow the pitch-poor rejectees out of the *Idol* studios and down the block as they head home, cursing and crying about their dashed dreams, dragging sad toddlers behind them. All the while, *Idol* host Ryan Seacrest takes snarky swipes at their pathetic pipes. Thought you could escape poverty through song? Hilarious!*

If you're like most reality watchers, you've probably asked yourself why

---

* To be sure, men are subjected to humiliating commentary on *American Idol* as well, with judges poking fun at male singers' voices, personalities, clothes, and haircuts. In many ways, *Idol* is an equal opportunity exploiter. But there is something uniquely harsh and very gendered about the show's harping on single mothers' financial duress, especially when their children are also filmed—a tactic from which *Idol* has usually spared low-income fathers.

anyone would willingly volunteer to be humiliated on national television. Though some are actors (and others hope to be), for many participants fame is less of a motivator than the chimera of a more comfortable life without daily struggle to meet the most basic of human needs for themselves and their children. This is especially true of women of color, who, though marginalized in the reality TV population in general, seem to compose a major percentage of poor cast members. Nearly every season, both *Idol* and *Top Model* broadcast a familiar refrain from young women: "This is my only chance to . . . " fill-in-the-blank: get out of the "inner city"; leave my Nowheresville, U.S.A., hometown behind; provide a better life for my child; or, for some contestants, all of the above.

When ethnicity is factored in, reality TV's mockery of the poor becomes particularly ugly. VH1's unholy trinity of race-, class-, and gender-biased programming—*Flavor of Love, I Love New York,* and *Flavor of Love Girls: Charm School*—epitomizes this theme. The first season of *Charm School* claimed to offer training in "manners," "poise," and "grace under pressure" for "nasty, vicious, and rough-around-the-edges" (mostly) Black women.[7] Instead, it provides a telling case study in broadcast bigotry.

Through comments from comedian and host Mo'Nique, video montages, and promo ads, viewers were explicitly encouraged to believe that women of color are "low-class" both figuratively and literally. In the opening episode, a barrage of clips aims to reintroduce the *Flavor of Love* competitors as violent, ignorant whores. Mo'Nique explains that her job is to help "unruly" girls who "looked like hookers" become "refined women" by serving as "a mentor to guide them on a path toward self-respect." The first step on this lofty path? Dress adults in their late twenties and early thirties in naughty Catholic schoolgirl uniforms straight out of a fetish costume catalog.

The "students" are then informed that the last woman standing—supposedly the one who "grows" the most, though in actuality the one who creates the most drama for VH1—will win $50,000. Saaphyri, an unemployed black woman from "the hood," reacts with wonder and guarded hope. "To me, $50,000 is a home." That money, she muses, "would change my life tremendously. I'd be able to pay my rent, first of all, because right now my landlord is really waiting for that." When the judges ask her, "What do you really hope to take away from this experience, really?" she offers a heartfelt reply: "Something more than what I have right now. Last year I was on 54th and Briarhurst. And we didn't have floors because the pipes had broke. We couldn't cook. I didn't have anywhere to go. I was so depressed. I was like, 'This is horrible.'"

It was a rare moment for reality television, which generally leaves this level of insight about poverty on the cutting room floor. But since these shows are not set up to react in a human way to such revelations, *Charm School*'s smug, white, wealthy "dean," Keith Lewis (director of the Miss California Teen USA pageant) offered only condescension. "To have $50,000," he lectured, "is *nothing* compared to what you could get out of everything else."*

When Saaphyri expresses her anger at Lewis's remark, saying he "doesn't know what the hell he's talking about" because "$50,000 to me is like saying $5 million right now," producers freeze-frame the scene with the sound of a scratched-record, a TV-land indicator that something crazy has just occurred. This bit of audiovisual mockery was chosen to discount and even ridicule her honest expression of deep financial distress. For daring to admit that the prize money would offer her a far better chance at self-improvement than VH1's insincere "schooling," this formerly homeless woman was edited to appear money-hungry, crass, and "ghetto."

Exploitation in the name of etiquette has become a thematic staple on the numerous pseudo-self-help imitators *Flavor of Love Girls: Charm School* has spawned, from *Rock of Love: Charm School* to *The Girls of Hedsor Hall* to versions for men, such as *Tool Academy* and *From G's to Gents*.

---

* "Self-improvement" wasn't what VH1 was aiming for when they advertised *Charm School* this way: "Hair may be pulled. Spit may fly. Fists may land. But one thing is for sure, when these ladies stab each other in the back—it will be with the proper utensil."[8]

The Ideology of Conspicuous Consumption

When reality producers aren't painting low-income women of color as "ghetto hos," a popular label on VH1's *of Love* franchise* and a host of other shows, they're dangling symbols of wealth just out of contestants' (and the audience's) reach. As viewers, we're meant to grasp at the lifestyles held up before us like diamond-encrusted carrots dangling from platinum-plated sticks.

In the talent competition, fashion, and lifestyle subgenres, hypercommercialism isn't subtext, it *is* the text. Interior designers compete to create upscale rooms for eight grand a pop and furnish lofts for $187,000 on Bravo's *Top Design.* Fashion designers whip up red-carpet-caliber dresses on Bravo's *Project Runway,* where "it looked expensive!" is the judges' highest mark of praise.+ Style luminaries Oscar de la Renta and Diane von Furstenberg themselves show up on Bravo's *The Rachel Zoe Project* to plug their exclusive lines, from which any one item can cost more than most people spend on their entire wardrobes. On *Tim Gunn's Guide to Style* (again, Bravo), luxe clothing and accessory brands like Gucci and Prada (as well as midrange department stores such as Macy's) appear as catalysts for women to "achieve" major "life transformations"—synonymous for "getting new looks"—which are only complete once subjects are given an haute couture gown from a different designer's showroom each episode. Bravo's first major reality show, *Queer Eye for the Straight Guy,* did the same thing to men in 2003, hawking a ludicrously long line of fashion, personal grooming, and home furnishing products to a previously untapped demographic. On each episode, after having gotten the once-over from the *Queer Eye's* Fab 5, a formerly slovenly dude had the epiphany that all he needs to do to lure in the ladies is plunk down excessive amounts of cash for tubes of ritzy hair gel, bottles of lavender-scented misting spray for high-thread-count linens, and an apartment full of new furniture.

---

* *Flavor of Love,* debuting in 2006, became the bedrock of VH1's "celebreality" programming focus, along with its numerous dating show spinoffs and "rehabilitation" knockoffs, including: *I Love New York, Charm School, Real Chance of Love, New York Goes to Work, New York Goes to Hollywood,* and *Rock of Love.*

+ *Project Runway* debuted on Bravo in 2004 and over five seasons became a flagship series for the network, a turning point for Bravo branding itself as *the* destination for affluent viewers. *Top Chef, Top Design, Shear Genius,* and the *Real Housewives* franchise all arose after, and can be attributed to, *Project Runway's* success. After a protracted legal battle, *Project Runway* moved to the Lifetime network in the fall of 2009.

As culture scholar Shira Tarrant writes, "Change has a price tag" on make-over shows. "Because transformation is something you *buy*, not something you *are*," wealth is the distinguishing factor between those who "can pay to discover our True Self," and "the poor [who] can never *become*."[9]

Bravo may have branded itself as the go-to network for shop-o-rama reality shows, but it has hardly cornered the market: TLC's *What Not to Wear (WNTW)* was redoing women's wardrobes inside Bloomingdale's, Searle, and H&M stores for almost five years before the debut of Tim Gunn's better-mannered, higher-end copycat. Nearly three years before Bravo's *Top Chef* hopefuls competed to prepare the most impressive lobster, Kobe beef, and truffle delicacies, actors paid by NBC to pose as real-life customers, supped on the equivalent of a couple of months' rent over dinner and drinks for two at *The Restaurant* (this isn't "food," this is "cuisine," darling!). And *Extreme Makeover: Home Edition (EM: HE)* has been giving "deserving families" pricey appliances and decor from Sears since 2003, when the department store paid ABC more than $1 million for narrative integration into the series.[10] Through it all, participants are shown using the goods and services of integrated marketers; for example, Glad, GE, Butterball, and Diet Dr. Pepper are served up on *Top Chef*, while L'Oréal, TRESemmé, Bluefly.com, and Saturn are integral to *Project Runway*. But while the brands may shift from show to show, one thing is consistent: Contestants are constantly ordered to "make it" (the furniture, frocks, or food) "seem expensive" or "luxurious."

When compared with the heavy-handed chauvinism of *Joe Millionaire*, the vicious cruelty of *The Swan*, or the blatant racism of *Flavor of Love*, watching programs like *Project Runway* and *Top Design* can be a pleasure. In contrast to the typical format of preying on participants' shaky mental health or liquoring them up to stoke petty dramas, Bravo's competition shows prioritize something else: talent. We're blown away when *Project Runway*'s gifted cast produces stunning garments armed only with vegetables, flowers, duct tape, and their own imaginations. We're inspired to modify *Top Design* contestants' inventive ideas to beautify our own homes. We make New Year's resolutions to cook at home more often with recipes we saw on *Top Chef* (that is, when we're not encouraged to drop a few hundred per plate at five-star restaurants where meals are garnished with avocado foam and truffles).

By now it's no secret that I'm not a big fan of reality television. I've watched more than a thousand hours of "unscripted" programming since 2000 in my research for this book,* and I've found most of it painful *(Dr. 90210)*, aggravating *(The Bachelor)*, or mind-numbingly boring *(The Hills)*. But I would watch a show like *Project Runway* even if I didn't have to. Differences among participants' identities, whether in sexual orientation, ethnicity, or gender, are not only "tolerated," they're actually respected and appreciated. Challenges celebrate contestants' artistry rather than reveling in their weakness. Competitors create something fabulous under tight deadlines, using weird materials. It's like MacGyver meets Milan (*You've got ten hours to make a runway-ready outfit out of coffee filters from Gristedes, silver foil wrappers from Hershey's, and as many Saturn seatbelts as you want. Make it work!)*.+ Sure, small dramas are stirred up to fill time, but *Project Runway* is innovative, engaging, and accessible. To a lesser degree, the same can be said for Bravo's other lifestyle competition shows, where creativity is key even as infighting is encouraged. *Top Chef* may leave some viewers more hungry than entertained, but foodies really enjoy it. The editors at ApartmentTherapy.com, a popular interior design blog, regularly go gaga for *Top Design*.

By showcasing skill instead of shame, could it be that Bravo's kinder, gentler competition and lifestyle series have no negative social consequences? Is there finally a segment of the reality TV landscape that isn't bad for us?

I really wish the answer were yes. Unfortunately, though they may be less offensive and more enjoyable than so many of their "unscripted" peers, fashion and lifestyle series are crafted around the most fundamental tenets of

---

* *I know!* Fill in your own punch line here. The brain cells that would have been responsible for offering my own joke rotted away somewhere between seeing live cockroaches ingested on *Fear Factor* and watching them used as runway accessories on *America's Next Top Model*.

+ Each of these items has been used as raw material in *Project Runway* challenges sponsored by these grocery, candy, and car companies.

advertising—the premise that conspicuous consumption is the ultimate key to contentment and success. The higher creative quality of *Project Runway* and similar fare doesn't erase this underlying ideology; it just serves to make such messages more insidious.

This little corner of the reality TV universe is designed to maximize our desire for . . . *stuff.* Stuff of all kinds, the more expensive the better. These shows encourage us to lust after things we might have never thought we wanted or needed, even things we might have previously considered wasteful or distasteful. When *EM: HE* gave a six-bedroom, seven-bath, seven-television house to a family of four, ABC's lead designer, Ty Pennington, acted as if it's normal for folks of modest means to live in a home with three more TVs and bathrooms than people to use them.[11] During a Very Special Episode of *WNTW,* stylists Stacy London and Clinton Kelly surprised a record industry exec named Lisa with a "fashion intervention of a lifetime," giving her fifty grand to spend on a "dream wardrobe" in Paris. As it turns out, $50,000 doesn't go very far at Armani, Gucci, and Christian Lacroix: She returned home with only fifteen outfits, a few pairs of shoes, and a couple of handbags. "This is how the rich shop," Clinton told her.

Who needs a house so large it dwarfs its residents? Or, for that matter, why would any middle-class working woman blow the equivalent of several years of college tuition or rent or mortgage payments on just two small suitcases worth of designer labels? Even if she was only allowed to spend that massive sum on clothing, wouldn't she be better served with a whole closet full of stylish and well-made winter, spring, summer, and fall attire, from business to casual, formal gowns to nightgowns, shoes to accessories, all of which she could have easily bought for a tiny fraction of that amount?

Ah, but "need" really isn't the issue. Improving people's lives can be a happy side effect on some shows, as when *EM: HE* rebuilt flood-damaged homes of Hurricane Katrina survivors in New Orleans and Mobile, Alabama. The devastation that disaster caused to low-income people, especially residents of color, was so deep that this televised Band-Aid of corporate largesse was a blessing for a handful of flood victims. But make no mistake: Social compassion and material support are the feel-good *by-product* of this show, *not its primary objective*. When reality TV series present families or individuals with larger-than-life homes, lavish furnishings, and extravagant wardrobes, it's not ultimately about helping the people on the receiving end of these gifts. It's about showcasing the products themselves and cultivating the idea that such luxuries are the secret to happiness.

This normalization of the grandiose, this glorification of spending for spending's sake, contributes to a dangerously shortsighted and superficial mind-set that does not serve Americans well as individuals or as a nation. The more we internalize the idea that we *need* bigger homes, more-expensive clothes, indulgent cars, shoes, purses, couches, and more (always more) of everything, the less money we're saving and the more unstable our futures are becoming.

Recession? What Recession?

Reality TV is certainly not the first form of media to encourage overconsumption—that's what advertising has always done—but there's something particularly invasive and perverse about doing so in the name of "realism."

Today, some networks have made the stimulation of a socially irresponsible, spend-now-regret-later attitude in viewers their primary programming strategy. Bravo, with its stable of high-end lifestyle series, basically admitted as much in a 2007 ad campaign touting "The Bravo Affluencer Effect." The spots depicted Bravo viewers as plasticized Barbie- and Ken-style dolls with multiple credit cards peeking from their pockets, along with gadgets and clothing they bought after watching reality TV. In an attempt to sell itself as the network of choice for marketers looking to influence viewers' shopping habits via product placement, Bravo bragged that it had "TV's Most Affluent + Most Influential + Most Engaged Viewers," whom they depicted as shopaholic drones with "Intent to Purchase," "High Recall" of integrated sponsors' brands, and a willingness to spread "Word of Mouth" about these products to their peers. Each "Affluencer" doll was annotated with notes such as "Linen Blazer: Learned to 'make it work' by watching PROJECT RUNWAY" or, while standing in line at a store, "Remember? We saw it on Bravo." Best of all, the ads gloated, those who watch Bravo come "with 85% extra disposable income!" making them "A Media Buyer's Dream."[12]

To be clear, if you are a fan of *Top Chef* or *The Real Housewives, you* are the product being sold to advertisers; this is how Bravo sees *you.*

An unthinking cadre of consumers lined up to take their purchasing orders from reality television? That may indeed be an advertiser's dream, but the overconsumption it helps to motivate is proving to be a nightmare for our ability to thrive individually or nationally. In the mid-1980s, Americans saved more than 10 percent of their paychecks. Twenty years later not only were we not saving enough—we weren't saving *at all.* "Americans' personal savings rate dipped into negative territory in 2005, something that hasn't happened since the Great Depression. Consumers depleted their savings to finance the purchases of cars and other big-ticket items," the Associated Press found. "In other words, the typical American spent $100.60 for every $100 of take home pay," CNN Money reported. We would have been wise to heed the warning in this 2006 headline: "Americans spend every cent—and more; Critics say America's negative savings rate can't be sustained and see a recession coming. Are they right?"[13]

Indeed, they were right. Just weeks before Barack Obama's inauguration, *New York Times* op-ed columnist Paul Krugman, winner of the 2008 Nobel Prize for economics, couldn't have been more blunt about the state of our economy: "Let's not mince words: This looks an awful lot like the beginning of a second Great Depression."[14] Whatever we call the financial mess we were in at the end of the first decade of the twenty-first century—"Depression II" or something else—one thing's certain: The news was depressing. The United States was racing toward a deeper and more threatening recession than economists had seen since the 1930s, but you'd never know it from "reality" television, which persisted in overemphasizing the short-term pleasures of "having nice things" and hiding the long-term economic consequences of our nation's overconsumption. By late

2008, Rachel Zoe was still looking earnestly into the cameras of her eponymous Bravo series and telling viewers, "I don't understand saving for the rainy day. It's like, live now! Live like it's your last day, every day!"

While shows like *The Rachel Zoe Project* and *WNTW* have been instructing us to model ourselves after "how the rich shop," Americans are drowning in credit card debt.* As the crippling cost of healthcare is forcing hundreds of thousands of Americans into bankruptcy every year because they can't afford to pay their medical bills, *Dr. 90210* (E!) follows "the pampered world of Beverly Hills' most beautiful," for whom no number of elective plastic surgeries is too expensive or extreme in their quest to stay that way. We're working way into our twilight years because we're too poor to retire, yet on series from the *Real Housewives* franchise to MTV's *Paris Hilton's My New BFF*, "real life" is all about leisure. And when thousands of news outlets were using the word "staycation" to put a positive-sounding gloss over the fact that more and more of us can't afford to go on actual vacations, Bravo's *First Class All the Way* took "viewers inside the world of high-end luxury travel" where "no mission [is] too great, no corner of the world too remote, and no experience too immense."[15]

By the end of 2009 the economic crisis hadn't let up—nor had reality producers' diamond-tinted blinders. Just as 34 million Americans were receiving food stamps, Bravo rolled out the *Gossip Girl*–esque *NYC Prep*, about rich kids in "the top 1 percent" of the "elite." More such series are in the works. "Do you live in an amazing home with maids, a chef, a personal assistant or a driver? Is your job an intense social calendar and your hobby shopping at Gucci?" asked a 2009 casting call for *The Good Life*,+ described as a major network show with a potential gold-digger twist. "If you're getting pampered on someone else's dime," Allison Grodner Productions announced, "you could just be the girl we're looking for." Searching for the rich—that's what reality lifestyle producers do best.[16]

---

* On July 20, 2008, as part of "The Debt Trap," a "series about the surge in consumer debt and the lenders who made it possible," *The New York Times* reported, "Today, Americans carry $2.56 trillion in consumer debt, up 22 percent since 2000 alone, according to the Federal Reserve Board. The average household's credit card debt is $8,565, up almost 15 percent from 2000."[17]
+ Headline: "Now Casting Women Living Extravagant Lifestyles!"

In the "greed is good" 1980s,* *Lifestyles of the Rich and Famous* allowed us to peek into the opulent lives of ultrarich actors, athletes, and moguls, always ending with host Robin Leach famously wishing his audience "champagne wishes and caviar dreams." But the show's production values, format, and even its host were tongue-in-cheek about these flashy, wasteful *Lifestyles*. It was intended as a lark, an escapist fantasy; Leach never insinuated that this was "normal."

Today, dozens of reality shows aim to convince us that such lifestyles are not only desirable but reasonable—or worse, realistic. In direct contrast to our vanishing middle class, increasing poverty rates, and crumbling economy, such shows extol "a world where champagne wishes and caviar dreams are reality."[18] We're no longer expected to laugh at gaudy excess; we're supposed to cheer it on. Just as millions of Americans were facing foreclosure, Bravo was inviting us to root for massive profits for real estate speculators, as on *Flipping Out,* which started shooting its fourth season in 2010. From 2006 to 2009, viewers of *Million Dollar Listing* were encouraged to become personally invested in the triumphs and travails of "Three of Los Angeles' hottest, young, and aggressive real estate magnates in the making as they seek a fortune selling multimillion-dollar properties in the most exclusive neighborhoods—Hollywood, Malibu, and Beverly Hills." Exactly as the nation's economy was collapsing in large part due to unscrupulous real estate practices, the network's website lauded these agents' willingness to "stop at nothing to close the deal." Of course, there's never any acknowledgment that these protagonists come from some of the same industries whose practices led to overinflated property values and contributed to the collapse of the housing market.[19+]

---

* "Greed, for lack of a better word, is good," an iconic summation of 1980s economics and culture, was uttered by Gordon Gekko, Michael Douglas's ruthless character in the 1987 film *Wall Street*. But its roots weren't in fiction. The signature quote was inspired by stock speculator Ivan Boesky, who, in 1985, "drew applause and laughter" when he gave this advice to the graduating class of UC Berkeley's School of Business Administration: "Greed is all right . . . greed is healthy. You can be greedy and still feel good about yourself." Not long after, Boesky was jailed for insider trading, a symbol of the era's unethical excesses.[20]
+ Sometimes networks and reality producers are just as unethical as the real estate industry. In 2005, ABC scrapped *Welcome to the Neighborhood* under threat of housing discrimination lawsuits for violating the Fair Housing Act. On the never-aired series, a group of wealthy white families "used to a certain kind of neighbor—one who looks and thinks just like them" got to choose—based on their prejudices about race, ethnicity, religion, and sexual orientation—which family among a group of diverse contestants would be given a dream home on their suburban cul-de-sac.[21]

By no means am I saying that reality TV is responsible for the housing crisis or the larger economic instability that has us suffering from Wall Street to Main Street. What I am saying is that for many reasons—advertising and media imagery being major underlying factors—we're becoming increasingly motivated by immediate gratification. Reality TV both encourages and exalts such skewed priorities, and gives us plenty of opportunities to practice them.

Video "Shopisodes" featured on Bravo's website regularly excerpt segments from *Tim Gunn's Guide to Style* and *The Real Housewives,* directing visitors to purchase the exact Diane von Furstenberg dresses and Calvin Klein coats around which their storylines are built. From the narrator of *Say Yes to the Dress,* TLC's series-long advertisement for high-end bridal boutique Kleinfeld, we learn that concerns about financial strife should be left at the dressing room door: "When the economy is tough, the tough say let's make a deal, even if the gown costs as much as a car." And so the show highlights women purchasing $24,500 gowns by saying, "I think maybe it *should* be too much. It's my wedding day!" Once conditioned to the idea that "there is technically no budget if it was the perfect dress," viewers can then turn to TLC's website, or click on the *Say Yes to the Dress* link on Kleinfeld's website, to schedule an appointment to try on and buy any of the "Featured Gowns" advertised over the series's many seasons.

Virtually every network is in on some version of this game, with ever-updated catalogs of goods available at www.SeenOn.com, a site that's linked to many reality series' home pages.* Girls, want to buy the Chanel watch Heidi Montag wears on MTV's *The Hills,* or the Playboy Bunny–embossed Bebe stilettos worn by E!'s *The Girls Next Door?* Guys, hope Donald Trump's wealth will rub off if you buy an Armani suit seen on *The Apprentice,* or that your luck will improve if you walk a mile in *Deal or No Deal* host Howie Mandel's John Varvatos ankle boots? All you need is a high spending limit and an Internet connection.

If the fairytale romance narratives of dating shows infantilize women,

---

* SeenOn.com also sells products from scripted shows.

commercialist lifestyle shows treat all viewers like children fixated on indulgences rather than necessities, regardless of what's good for us. If a cacophony of "experts" constantly reiterate the "fact" that we won't advance professionally or be accepted socially without an expensive designer wardrobe, some of us may start to think that maxing out our credit cards at the mall is actually an investment in our future success. And throughout a decade that repeatedly pushed a version of "reality" in which average American families all seem to live in sprawling mansions like those on *Who Wants to Marry My Dad?* and *Meet My Folks,* why should it come as a surprise that predatory lenders could so easily convince us to take out larger loans on bigger, more expensive houses than we need or can afford?

Commercial Reeducation: Learning "Fashion Math"

What about those of us who prefer to save so that one day we might *actually* be able to own our own homes, pay for college, have secure futures? We're quickly taught the error of our ways.

Tim Gunn's Guide to Style offers a case study in consumerist indoctrination. We meet Arianna, who "[grew] up with a single mom who was definitely struggling to make ends meet. I remember specifically picking multifunction outfits and wearing them as long as you could. I still . . . shop in that way." During an economic downturn, Arianna's prudence should be viewed as admirable—instead, her desire to conserve is portrayed as a psychological pathology that must be cured. In aghast tones, we're told that she "looks like someone who's just *neglected* themselves!" because she's "barely been out of a $19 skirt!" Gunn, his supermodel cohost, and a cadre of "experts" from *InStyle* magazine and Banana Republic set about convincing Arianna (and those of us watching her) "that spending money [is] making an investment in yourself, in your image, and in your future." Walking her through "shoe heaven," *InStyle*'s Katrina Szish lays out this twisted algebra: "There's a concept going on here called 'fashion math,'" she explains, emphasizing the "value" of expensive, luxurious fabrics and high-quality designer attire. "You buy few items for more money, your money will go further."

Meanwhile, an on-screen caption offers the exact opposite advice needed to survive a recession:

SPEND MORE. GET LESS.*

Of course, to survive financially, most working-class women (and, increasingly, most middle-class women and men) need to get really good at stretching every dime beyond its breaking point. To keep our families fed, to keep our rent paid, to avoid foreclosure, to stay on top of medical bills, most of us need to spend *less* and get *more*. Nevertheless, Arianna proves a quick study in "fashion math": "It makes so much sense!" she nods, going on to choose new clothes regardless of what they cost. "I didn't look . . . at [the] price point!" she proclaims proudly. Gunn, overjoyed at this feat, applauds "her achievements." At the end of the episode, Gunn advises his audience, "If . . . you're on a budget" it "makes sense" to shop for high-quality fashion and "spend more."+

All of the food, dating, and real estate series discussed in this chapter attempt to reinforce just such a mentality. Never is this goal as blatant as in the fashion and makeover genre, where participants who reject the philosophy of

---

* It's galling enough that reality TV instructs viewers to "spend more" to get less. More unfortunate is the hidden fact that women actually do spend more than men for nearly every necessity of life, despite earning significantly less than men for comparable work. According to *Consumer Federation, Consumer Reports*, and Congress, women are regularly charged 32 percent more for mortgages, between 50 and 60 percent more for everything from hand soap to pain reliever, and between 22 and 50 percent more for health insurance.[22]

+ It's worth mentioning that the show's "spend more, buy less" advice can make sense for those in the position to make such an investment in the first place—but only if you actually follow the second half of that equation. If you plan to buy only a few items of clothing and wear them for many years until they are threadbare, then you'd probably be well-served purchasing a few classic, extremely well-made pieces. Such items will tend to be more expensive, but they will also generally last longer than the cheap (often sweatshop-produced), disposable fashions promoted every few weeks in glossy women's mags. But makeover shows like *Tim Gunn's Guide to Style* and *WNTW* present the act of shopping as an art, a passion, and a means of self-realization. To decide not to buy new clothing for several years would be considered not only sacrilege, but self-abuse. The goal of these shows is to get you to spend more money and shop more often.

consumer culture are aggressively scolded, shamed, and cajoled into "correcting" their wardrobes, makeup, hair-care rituals, homes, and most important, their economic priorities.

The process by which this happens reads like a Propaganda 101 manual. The longest-running practitioner of this sort of persuasion, *What Not to Wear*, debuted in 2003 and was in its seventh season in 2010. The show uses a stock template for the socioeconomic reeducation of women of all ages. Throughout the series, an ethnically and economically diverse string of women* are ridiculed for failing to conform to a single upper-middle-class, mainstream-to-conservative, traditionally feminine standard of fashion and beauty. Participants undergo an almost military-style breaking down of their individuality, after which their priorities are rebuilt in an advertiser's ideal image. Through a three-stage formula, nonconformists learn to embrace the mainstream, bargain hunters are taught to ignore price tags, and thrift store aficionados become label queens.

STAGE 1: INSTRUCTION

Each episode begins with stylists Stacy London and Clinton Kelly surprising a designated fashion victim with a $5,000 Bank of America or Visa card, then informing her that she will get to purchase a whole new wardrobe in just two days. In exchange, she must agree to model her own outfits in a 360-degree mirror (nicknamed "The Chamber of Torture") while they snarkily critique, then throw out, every item of clothing she owns. She's shown three trendy mannequins dressed according to "The Rules," a set of supposedly personalized guidelines to shop by. Though the show promises to help her "find her own individual style," these rules are remarkably similar for every woman, regardless of her age, lifestyle, or cultural identification. Whether she's a punk rock chick in her twenties or an animal trainer in her forties, a flat-chested white office worker or a curvy

---

* *WNTW* almost always focuses on women, though very occasionally, perhaps 5 percent of the time, the stylists redo a man's wardrobe.

Latina dancer, she's always told to seek out garments that will make her look "slimmer," "more feminine," and "professional." As we saw in chapter 2, slimmer always equals better in reality TV, but why a zookeeper needs to look "professional" remains unclear.

The show's rules are as much about finance as fashion. One of the first lessons is that saving money is for spoilsports. Regardless of her personal economic reality, each week a new woman is taught to stop "obsessing" over bargains and to "care about herself" enough to "buy quality things." Dumping a twenty-four-year-old's modestly priced items in the trash, Stacy barked: "What do you spend your money on? You work for a living! Where does it go!?" The young woman had a simple reply: "I eat a lot." But since being well-fed is not nearly as important as being well-dressed, fellow fashionista Clinton snapped: "Eat less, and buy clothing!" Stacy closed her tutorial with this prime directive: "It's time to go shopping. You're in your twenties. You don't have kids yet. You're not buying a house or furniture. Spend it on clothes instead of all this food!"

STAGE 2: REBELLION (TAMING OF)

Much of the show's drama lies in the tension between the women's penchant for thrift and comfort verses the stylists' desire to shoehorn them into a strict uniform of empire-waist dresses, tailored suit jackets, and pointy-toed, painfully high heels. Even with a $5K windfall, these low- and middle-income women aren't eager to embrace wanton spending—nor do they give up their favorite T-shirts, affordable jeans, and comfortable shoes without a fight. Angry at the insults hurled at her "before" wardrobe, photographer Kristen tells the camera, "That was horrific. Are they gonna see some resistance from me [while I'm shopping]? Yeah, there's gonna be resistance!"

In the face of such resistance to conformity, *WNTW*'s promises to help women embrace their individuality begin to unravel. Jessica, a frustrated office worker who misses her days in a rock band, says, "I know what I *don't* want: pointy shoes." Too bad for her. "Listen," she's informed, "you're *gonna* wear a pointy shoe." Then there's hipster Katherine, who describes her postpunk style as "really unique. It's sort of an independent thing" that lets her "reveal [my] personality." Her disapproving mother explains that "she doesn't want to follow the mainstream," but viewers are assured that her pesky "fashion rebellion needs to [and will] be tamed." When another makeover subject rejects a suggested outfit because "I'm just not feeling it. I don't like it. I don't think it's me. I don't think it's my style," Stacy literally shrieks at her: "We don't *want* you to feel like you! We don't *want* you to have your style!"

Gendered proscriptions are acute during this stage: A mechanic who doesn't feel comfortable in ruffles or frills is called "butch" and made to don "girlie" clothing and cosmetics. A professor on a casual campus who enjoys comfortable sandals because heels "hurt" is told she has no choice but "to start wearing *actual footwear.*" A lesbian biker is forced to trade her motorcycle jacket for a dress. Some of the stylists' harshest insults are reserved for women who frequent thrift stores and clothing swaps, even though it's possible to find well-made and fashionable things at consignment shops and on resale sites such as eBay.* Whether they've opted out of the retail rat race because of financial necessity, a vintage aesthetic, or an environmental ethic, they're derided as looking "insane," "homeless," and "disgusting." That's because *quality* isn't what *WNTW* wants viewers to embrace: consumption is. Carrie, who always wore the latest trends as a teenager, remembers that "it always costs a lot of money, and so it seemed like such a waste . . . when I buy a lot of clothes [I feel like] I'm kinda throwing the money away." Part of the reason "why I jumped off the fashion train to begin with [is] 'cause it was too hard to keep up with the trends," she told Clinton. "Oh no, that's not it. It's because you're cheap!" he shot back.

As cash registers ring up astronomical receipts for small piles of clothes, we watch participants freak out. "That's like my rent!" "What a scam!" and "Oh

---

* I speak from experience: As a resourceful nonprofit staffer, I've managed to collect a closet full of gorgeous, way-out-of-my-price-range Betsey Johnson dresses, Nanette Lepore jackets, and other curve-friendly designer duds via eBay and clothing swaps for just a few bucks each. My budget is intact, and I avoid financially supporting companies using sweatshop labor.

my god. There's, like, gold lining inside of them, right?" are typical responses. Single moms, college students, and others struggling to get by explain that "it's hard to spend money on one item that's like two weeks of groceries [or] to disassociate a purse from a medical bill"—only to be lectured that "low self-esteem" is what's *really* holding them back from investing in fashion. If they only "valued themselves" more they'd dress as if they "deserve respect" and "want to be taken seriously." Mothers are also told that by spending wads of cash on clothes, they will be better role models for their daughters.

STAGE 3: ASSIMILATION

At the end of every episode, the stylists and the women's families gush about how amazing they look, and the participants describe their "transformations" as "life-altering." Once offered the tools to find clothes that fit and flatter, the money to afford them, and a heaping helping of external approval, they emerge feeling beautiful and (because female value is still so connected to appearance) finally *worthwhile.* "I never felt like a pretty girl," thirty-six-year-old editor Amanda said, but after her makeover "I have more confidence in my little finger than I had in my entire body. . . . I'll command a lot more respect. I feel sexy, I feel sure of myself, and I feel pretty. When I started this journey I felt hopeless. Now . . . I feel like a sex kitten."

That's an undeniably positive result, one that's fun to watch and probably has some lasting emotional benefits for participants. But like *EM: HE*'s altruism, making women feel better about themselves is the *tactic* of *WNTW,* not its *purpose.* The big reveal at the conclusion is more ideological than visual. Protestations about frugality, comfort, and nontraditional gender presentation vanish. One stiletto-clad foot after another, these Stepford Shoppers now march to the same consumerist beat. Viewers are encouraged to emulate formerly "cheap" Carrie, who closes out her hour describing her newfound "shopping bug . . . I wanna go shopping more. Seriously, I really do." They say they plan to ask for dates— and raises—now that they "look like I deserve it." Rather than questioning why these women believe they only "deserve" romance or career advancement based on their appearances, *WNTW* codifies that idea. For example, a young woman named Jessica was nominated for the show by her boss, Dr. Lois Frankel, who offers her a postmakeover promotion. The takeaway? Don't worry about doing your job well, ladies, just worry about what you wear while you're working.*

Needless to say, these programs never discuss *actual* barriers to women's success, such as lack of childcare, pay inequity, sexual harassment, gender or race discrimination in hiring and promotion, or domestic violence.[23]

Charity, Not Change

On the other side of the reality TV spectrum are heartstrings-tugging shows that seem to glorify not capitalism, but the spirit of giving. Surely, nothing could be wrong with helping poor families or low-income students, right?

ABC's *The Scholar* gave "economically disadvantaged" but academically stellar kids—high achievers from failing inner city schools, a home schooler with four jobs, brainy immigrants—the chance to compete against privileged preppies for a full-ride scholarship to the college of their choice from an educational foundation, and partial scholarships for runners-up furnished by Wal-Mart. Many explained in heartbreaking detail that winning the show could be their only chance to receive a quality education. Sure, many of their collegiate dreams remained out of reach at the show's conclusion, but let's not let that dull the warm fuzzies of the winner's full ride, shall we?

On *Oprah's Big Give*, the talk show queen promised viewers we'd be inspired by the power of fundraising to change America. Participants were instructed to raise large sums of money (from companies like Target and celebs like Jamie Foxx) and then give it away however they thought would do the most good. Contestants bought groceries for random shoppers, passed out $2,000 worth

---

* Withheld from viewers? The fact that Jessica's participation on the show—and her promotion—were probably publicity stunts for her boss, an author and business coach who charges between $10,000 and $17,500 a pop to teach "the unspoken secrets of workplace success." Here's how Frankel promoted the episode online: "Corporate Coaching International's very own Jessica Vaughn is the 'star' of 'What Not to Wear' . . . Others in our office serve as 'supporting cast members.'"[24]

of flowers to passersby on the street, and donated instruments to a community center serving kids with Down syndrome. These were all very nice things to do, and it was lovely to watch contestants brighten people's days, pay off medical and mortgage bills, and give poor kids Christmas gifts. But by defining philanthropy so narrowly, the show reinforced the notion that what America needs is charity, not social change. Individual recipients benefited from the experience, but as Linda Diebel wrote in the *Toronto Star*, "Nothing fundamentally changed. There was no revelation that decent education and health care are rights in a developed society, not privileges to be bestowed" by those of means. Oh, and the "twist" that so often accompanies reality shows? The "biggest giver" won a million bucks from Winfrey and ABC. Because giving *isn't* the greatest reward after all—a big fat check is.[25]

A similar problem plagued *The Secret Millionaire*, Fox's even more manipulative take on wealth, poverty, and philanthropy. Each episode profiled the star's exceptionally posh lifestyle before dropping them in "the hood," where they had to "survive" on the equivalent of welfare wages for a week. Camera crews followed their "undercover" interactions with the poor at soup kitchens and battered women's shelters. At the end of the week every Richie Rich would reveal their true net worth—and distribute $100,000—to their downtrodden acquaintances. Though poverty, homelessness, and drug abuse were more of a focus here than on *Oprah's Big Give*, these national scourges were presented as individual misfortunes rather than institutional problems. In a typical encounter, Greg Ruzicka, a multimillionaire lawyer specializing in bankruptcy and foreclosures, meets a woman who lost her home due to healthcare debt. He feels sorry for her and learns that sometimes bad things happen to good people. Then he writes a few well-placed checks and feels better. You almost expected everyone to break into a chorus of "Kumbaya." Producers emphasized Greg's social awakening and (TV-show-generated) generosity, and his recipients' gratitude; viewers were not meant to question (or desire accountability from or regulation of) the mercenary industry to which he owes his millions, the same industry partly responsible for plunging that uninsured woman into homelessness. Instead, *The Secret Millionaire* buttressed the notion that some people are faultlessly poor and deserve aid. By nature, this makes invisible the economic and political causes of wide-scale inequity.*

Which brings us back to *EM: HE,* whose recipients have included Iraq war veterans, orphans whose parents were killed by gang violence, and any manner of folks portrayed as having fallen victim to a hard-knock life. See, "discrimination" is akin to a four-letter word in reality TV, rarely discussed as a factor in low-income people's lives. So when they built homes for Hurricane Katrina survivors, the show emphasized the bad luck and trauma of having lived in the flooded region rather than the poverty they experienced before the disaster. Likewise, "we do not see immigrant day-laborers struggling to meet the needs of life with cash paid under the table. . . . Nobody is a gang member underserved by the schools and living in substandard housing. We see the mother who's been laid off after years on the job, but we do not see the unemployed who have a series of low-income jobs," Shira Tarrant writes. "The unspoken message is that if these folks are not getting on the show then perhaps they are not worthy or deserving of our help."[26]

EM: HE presents itself as the ultimate in do-gooder TV, as friends, neighbors, celebrities, and advertising underwriters join in on the renovations. The Extreme Team flat-out promises "worthy" families that these new, swag-filled estates will give their lives new meaning. In response, the homeowners weep with the relieved joy of war widows whose MIA husbands have miraculously returned, as if nothing will ever go wrong again. Like all TV fiction, the cameras go dark after that happy ending, sparing us what is often a problematic

---

* A similar problem plagues CBS's 2010 postrecession *Undercover Boss,* in which rich CEOs pose as workers in their own corporations, observe mistreatment and labor abuses, feel bad, then promise their employees things will improve. Packaged as a populist fantasy in which greedy bosses finally Do The Right Thing, producers woo viewers by appealing to their job frustrations, then mollify them with the notion that since the suits at the top really mean well, everything will be okay in the end . . . no need for any pesky labor organizing. Each episode is a full-length commercial for companies such as Hooters and GSI Commerce. So when Larry O'Donnell, President and COO of Waste Management, Inc. gets emotional, promotes an administrative assistant, and promises to form a committee to address workers' concerns, viewers get a feel-good happy ending—never learning that Waste Management, Inc. has a history of union-busting. Corporate officers' *feelings* don't result in institutional change—adopting pro-labor policies does.[27]

follow-up. Exorbitant new property taxes, building code violations, and legal issues have plagued some *EM: HE* recipients, whose stories have trickled into headlines such as, "With 'Extreme Makeover' Homes, Some Get Foreclosure Instead of Happy Ending."[28]

Series that focus on charitable giving encourage some form of public service, and as such are far more positive than classically sensationalistic reality shows. However, there is danger in representing poverty, homelessness, and lack of access to education without any focus on infrastructure. Using malnutrition as an example, Joel Berg explains:

> Most Americans hold tight to the myth that neighbor-to-neighbor generosity and compassion is the best support system for those in need. But trying to end hunger with food drives is like trying to fill the Grand Canyon with a teaspoon. Because local charities cannot possibly feed 35.5 million people adequately, and because their efforts rarely enable people to become self-reliant, this belief that charity does it better than government only ensures hunger will persist in America.[29]

Such problems can only be fixed through policy solutions.[30] But corporate underwriters like Wal-Mart, Target, and Waste Management, Inc. benefit from the economic status quo, so reality TV teaches us that the world will be a better place if only more of us would give flowers to strangers.

House of Cards

Reality TV's mockery of the poor and calculated elevation of the (branded) superrich speaks to the wider dearth of opportunity in the United States at a time when education, housing, healthcare, childcare, and even adequate nutrition are becoming less and less accessible, especially for women and people of color. The trade-off for the humiliation we risk by appearing on these shows is the potential chance at financial security, in an era where the government-supported social safety net has been all but dismantled. In a culture in which young women and people of color often feel they have few options, these shows conflate self-worth with net worth. They present a starry-eyed dream of instant financial liberation via the prize package on shows like *American Idol* and *America's Next Top Model*, or the paternalistic "Prince Charming will provide for you" model of dating shows. Yet these promises of security and success are rarely more than a house of cards.

Reality TV princes always leave as soon as they're no longer contractually obligated to date their "chosen princess"; this much is clear by now. But did you know that the "million-dollar contracts" promised to winners of some of the top competition shows can be equally bogus? Adrianne Curry, winner of the first season of *Top Model,* has publicly lambasted both the show and its sponsors for stiffing her on promised pay. Four years after taking the *ANTM* crown, she still had "yet to see a dime from Revlon" for her modeling work for the cosmetics company. "We were told the winner would be an instant millionaire, that our faces would be plastered everywhere in Revlon ads. None of which turned out to be true. . . . I still haven't got paid for the work I did for them!" Curry has charged.[31] Tyra Banks often brags that all the anguish she puts the girls through is worth it because of the postseries fame and fortune that awaits her protégées. During cycle 2's postfinale episode, Banks gushed, *"America's Next Top Model* has created new lives for these women. I mean, Shandi [Sullivan] was a Walgreens clerk. And now she's gonna be a fashion model!" It didn't quite turn out that way. "Being on the show kind of hindered a lot of the jobs that I would go on. The casting directors would say to me, 'Oh, you're that girl from that model show. You should stick to TV.' At that point, I kind of just had it, and I was like, ugh, alright, I'm done," she told VH1's *Where Are They Now?: Reality Stars.* Now, instead of working the cash register at a drugstore, she answers phones at a day spa. So much for the glam life.*

---

* *America's Next Top Model* participants rarely achieve supermodel status, though plus-size model Toccara Jones's success stands out as a positive exception. The show seems to be a better stepping-stone for short-term to midlevel entertainment gigs.

Unlike *ANTM,* which has never created a modeling industry superstar, *American Idol* has a rep for launching the careers of several top-selling pop singers, including winners Kelly Clarkson and Carrie Underwood and runners-up such as Jennifer Hudson, Chris Daughtry, and Clay Aiken. But how many viewers understand that the "million-dollar recording contract" that comes with the *Idol* title doesn't actually mean a seven-figure payday for the performers? That sum is just an estimate of the combined value of the deal's promotion, production, and distribution elements, most of which the singers never see.[32]

For that matter, how many fans know that *Idol* producers have also willfully crushed kids' livelihoods? It's bad enough that the *Idol* machine takes a larger-than-industry-standard cut of winners' incomes and that winners and top-ten runners-up give producers near-complete control of their songs, images, professional engagements, and career choices. But the iron-clad *Idol* contract places similarly problematic constraints over even those contestants who never make it past the cringe-inducing audition phase.[33] Take third-season *Idol* hopeful Nicole "Scooter Girl" Tieri, an aspiring singer/actress who wheeled around the *Idol* studios on a scooter during her first tryout. Her quirky personality—and her canny use of props—earned her a ticket to the second audition stage in Hollywood. Though eliminated early, she seemed poised to turn her fifteen minutes into an actual career: Tieri was asked to endorse Razor Scooters and to play a major role in the hit Broadway musical *Rent.* But because she had signed over her professional rights to *Idol*'s stringpullers before appearing on the show, they forced her to turn down both of these rare and lucrative opportunities, despite the fact that the show wasn't paying her, or the fact that *Idol*'s production company wasn't interested in signing her for a recording deal.[34]

From *Queer Eye*'s wrinkle crèmes to *WNTW*'s pencil skirts to *EM: HE*'s furniture, reality TV tells us that advertisers' products will not only *change* our lives—they'll actually *save* our lives. A first-season *Apprentice* DVD includes a music video that repeats the phrase "You're a slave to the master" over B-roll of Donald Trump firing people.* With numerous bankruptcies under his belt, Trump's "master businessman" persona is as much a facade as Don Mueller's rented McMansion on *Who Wants to Marry My Dad?* As media literate viewers, we must topple reality TV's house of cards and recognize that hyperconsumerism is not society's cure-all, but rather the root cause of many of our deepest challenges.

* This is particularly offensive in the context of the show's treatment of African American contestant Omarosa Manigault-Stallworth, whom we'll meet in the next chapter.

Chapter Five

Erasing Ethnicity, Encoding Bigotry

Race, Pre– and Post–*Flavor of Love*

*Now the world watched as y'all made your TV debut on a show
called* Flavor of Love. *Now let me be very honest with you: The
world was not laughing with you. We were all laughing at you.
Including myself.*

—HOST MO'NIQUE, explaining the *My Fair Lady*
premise of *Flavor of Love Girls: Charm School* to the
mostly Black contestants during the series premiere.

On The Bachelor, white women get to play Cinderella. On *Flavor of Love,* Black
women get to play maids.

The mansion was vile. Unidentifiable ooze, pizza boxes, empty liquor bottles,
and mounds of trash blanketed the house and spilled into the back yard, where beer
kegs, sneakers, and garbage floated in the pool. Marble floors and countertops were
smeared with overturned drinks, rotting food . . . and feces. That's right—mounds
of shit and possibly vomit piled up on the bathroom floor and seemingly throughout the house. Miles of toilet paper dangled from a chandelier, wrapped around a
billiards table and sofa, and fell from a pot rack in the kitchen.

Tackling this mess wouldn't be glamorous . . . hell, it wouldn't even be
hygienic. But if Beautiful, Buckeey, Payshintz, Nibblz, Like Dat, and Tiger
wanted to win a date with Flavor Flav—a.k.a. "The Black-chelor"—they had to
start scrubbing. Why? Because, the former rapper announced, "I wanna know
that a girl can keep my house clean!"

The Genesis of Reality TV Racism

IN THE BEGINNING, the Network Suits said, "Let them be white," and reality TV cast members were white.

Seasons passed, and they multiplied to a mighty celluloid nation, populated by dominant men and decorative women, *Bachelors* and *Top Models*, *Apprentices* and *Swans*. We shall remember this age as "BF."*

After half a decade the Cable Suits gazed upon their Network neighbors' unscripted creations, saw the ratings bounty sexism had provided, and grew envious. Then the Cable Suits decreed that producers must layer racism atop their misogynistic bedrock, saying, "Let us remake Black people in advertising's eternal image." So producers birthed a minstrel show and called it *Flavor of Love*, and it was bad, and Kentucky Fried Chicken was happy.+ *Flavor of Love* begat *Flavor of Love Girls: Charm School* and *I Love New York*, which begat *Real Chance of Love*. And lo, people of color began to rule over their own plots of televisual land. But there was much suffering; visibility became a plague on their McMansions. Competing Cable Suits discovered Black *Housewives* in Atlanta, reformed Black and Latino men *From G's to Gents*, and taught *White Rappers* their place. And so it was, and so it still is today. We shall call this age "AF."#

To understand how reality TV has represented race generally—and women of color particularly—it's helpful to think in epochs. Before *Flavor of Love* (BF, 2000–2006), broadcast networks kept their casts predominately white, and the presence of people of color was marked by marginalization, tokenism, and typecasting. This show heralded a sea change: Reality TV racism went from subtext to text. People of color were no longer confined to the background or quickly

---

* Before *Flavor of Love*.
+ For the viewers, it was bad. For VH1, it was the biggest hit they'd ever had, as we'll soon see. And KFC? Their product placements featured prominently.
# After *Flavor of Love*.

eliminated, especially on cable. But increased visibility came with a steep price: stereotyping recalling the racist archetypes of 1800s minstrel theater, early 1900s radio, and 1950s sitcoms.

The following case studies from both eras reveal the blessings and curses that come with the initial invisibility, and eventual inclusion, of people of color in reality programming.

I. Before *Flavor of Love* (BF): Marginalization, Tokenism, and Typecasting

IT'S A NICE DAY FOR A WHITE WEDDING

In 2007, students at a Georgia high school had their first-ever integrated prom. But because some white parents and teens weren't comfortable with interracial dancing, the teens' "white prom" was also held.

Backward? Regressive? Absolutely. Yet from the beginning, unscripted dating shows have operated under the same unspoken rule: Mr. Right Must Be White . . . and so should nearly all the women who vamp for his attentions.

Producers of template-setting dating series sought to manufacture a fractured reality that looks nothing like America. The casting process started with ethnic homogeneity. The longest-running reality romance series, *The Bachelor*, has cast a white man as Prince Charming from its 2002 debut to its fourteenth season in 2010. Knockoffs such as Fox's *Joe Millionaire* and NBC's *Who Wants to Marry My Dad?* followed suit. To be sure, one or two women of color typically turn up on any given network dating show's first episode—tokens amid fifteen to twenty-five white women. Usually at least one nonwhite bachelorette squeaks by to the second round of "group dates" so that Mr. White B. Wright can avoid being labeled a racist. The few Black, Latina, or Asian women who do appear rarely get much screen time, and are generally eliminated shortly after their series

---

* In season 6, *Bachelor* producers told Byron Velvick "he made a bit of history, as the first guy to choose a black woman among the final dozen contestants." To put this in context, the "final dozen" is usually the second episode of the series.[1]

debuts.* Add the requisite limos, catfights, and "dream dates," and viewers can be forgiven if they assume ABC, NBC, and Fox generate dating show footage by sending cameras to a white prom and rolling tape.

The same whitewashing appears on the few series with many men wooing one woman. By 2010, all five queen bees of *The Bachelorette,* ABC's programmatic afterthought, were white. So was Melana Scantlin, the beauty queen NBC hoodwinked into dating a bunch of nonhunks on *Average Joe.* Intending to prove women superficial in matters of the heart, producers sought men considered "ugly" (not merely "average") by pop culture standards. Amid a mix of obese, scrawny, and sloppy white men was Tareq Kabir, a young, physically fit South Asian professor with a computer science PhD. Well-groomed and attractive (if tongue-tied around pretty women), Kabir seemed to be considered undatable by NBC mostly because of his ethnicity. Fans circulated a protest letter calling the network "particularly negligent" for "featur[ing] Asian men finally," only "to propagate the destructive stereotype of Asian men as being somehow sexually undesirable."[2]

The opposite has been true for Asian women, who've usually been fetishized rather than desexualized on network dating shows (when rarely they've appeared). Korean American lingerie model Lola Corwin was featured on *Temptation Island*—as an "exotic" "temptress" hired by Fox to seduce men away from their girlfriends. She parlayed her brush with reality TV fame into pinup work for *Playboy,* Venus swimwear, and soft-core "East West" and "ImagineAsian" nudie calendars featuring "hot Asian chicks." Corwin foreshadowed *A Shot at Love with Tila Tequila,* the only dating show ever headlined by an Asian American woman (it aired in 2007, the AF era). MTV used Tila,* *Playboy's* first "Asian Cyber Girl of the Month," to turn the premise of a bisexuality-themed search for love into a campy sleaze-fest. Contestants all slept in the same giant bed and competed in lingerie contests to win dates with the partially clothed pinup.[3]

After hundreds of prime-time hours, only one Latina defied *The Bachelor's* early elimination rut. Husband-hunter Mary Delgado brought Bob Guiney to

---

* Her real last name is Nguyen.

meet her parents on season 4's "hometown date" semifinals. Producers had no idea how to handle the language barrier between "spicy" Mary's white suitor and her Cuban American immigrant family. We saw video of the usual "what are your intentions toward my daughter?" scene as Mary's dad grilled Bob—for display only. No translator or captions were provided for his long Spanish monologue. Viewers didn't get to hear whether Papa Delgado warmly welcomed his potential future son-in-law, as per the show's unrealistic conventions, or issued some version of the classic overprotective dad's "hurt my daughter and I'll make you wish you were never born" warning. The awkward segment tacitly implied that their interracial pairing would never "fit."

After Mary was "marked consistently . . . by her Cuban ethnicity,"[4] Bob's rejection of her felt inevitable. Producers brought her back on the sixth season to compete for a ring from a white bass fisherman named Byron Velvick, but this time they downplayed her Cuban heritage. Why? Because Byron proposed to her in the end, challenging ABC's "love is for white folks" frame. By "whitening" Mary, *The Bachelor* attempted to minimize the discomfort the network assumed its audience would have with a woman of color as a "princess."

Georgia's "white prom," along with scholarly research,[5] proves we are by no means a color-blind society. But reality TV producers codify, rather than reflect, viewers' prejudices. Corporate media lag behind Americans' increasingly progressive attitudes around sex, love, and race. Just a year after Byron and Mary were lauded as a *Bachelor* "success story" on a reunion episode,* the United States elected our first Black president, Barack Obama, whose mother was white and whose father was Kenyan. Eighty-three percent of Americans approved of interracial dating in 2009, compared with 48 percent in 1987.[6] Likewise, on *Married by America,* viewers selected a Mexican American woman named Cortez as the potential arranged bride for aw-shucks Southern boy Matt, who (like every other participant) was white. But after the couples started playing house, they were the first voted off by Fox's "expert" panel.

---

* Mary was arrested for punching him and splitting his lip in 2007; they broke up in 2009.[7]

When women of color were, infrequently, allowed into BF casts, they were almost always edited to stoke classic racial stereotypes. Stock characters such as the "Black Bitch," the "Entitled Diva," the "Hootchie Mama," the "Ghetto Girl," and the "Mammy" were pioneered in reality TV by *America's Next Top Model* in 2003 and persist today on many series. The following are a few of the ways these stereotypes have played out in BF reality programming.*

THE BLACK BITCH (A.K.A. THE ENTITLED DIVA)

The "Angry Black Woman" (ABW)—also known in the reality TV universe as the "Diva with Attitude"—has been a staple throughout various subgenres, from competition to lifestyle to dating and domesticity series. She made her network debut on *Top Model,* as we'll see in chapter 6, but quickly took up shop in many unscripted series. On *Wife Swap,* the first thing we learn about "pampered" African American hairdresser D'eva Robinson is that "I consider myself a diva so much that I am legally changing my name to D'eva." (AF, this bitchy bogeywoman trope thrives on *The Real Housewives of Atlanta,* where Black women's backstabbing, verbal sparring, and physical fights draw boffo ratings for Bravo.)

The ABW is an updated version of the Sapphire trope of Black women as "rude, loud, malicious, stubborn, and overbearing," which later originated with a character of the same name in the 1928 radio show *Amos & Andy,* which later aired as a sitcom on CBS through 1966. The Sapphire has "irrational states of anger and indignation—prone to being mean-spirited and abusive [with] venom for anyone who insults or disrespects her."[8]

Reality TV's most polarizing ABW dates back to 2004, when the world met *The Apprentice*'s Omarosa Manigault-Stallworth, the most famous nonwhite personality ever to emerge from network reality television.

Make that infamous. The breakout star of NBC's series, Omarosa was

---

* The ethnic homogeneity of *The Bachelor* and other network dating shows, like the stock racial characters on *The Apprentice* and other series described below, created the mold from which women of color would be represented on network reality television. All the shows I'm discussing as BF debuted before *Flavor of Love* first aired, but some of the examples given below are from their later seasons, as well as from AF cable series such as *Charm School* and *I Love New York.*

statuesque, tough-talking, and accomplished. Her resume was as hefty as her midriff-baring clothes* were skimpy. A doctoral candidate at Howard University, she had worked in the Clinton White House. Once Donald Trump and Mark Burnett were done with her, she added another title to her CV: "the most reviled person in reality TV history."

That's how *TV Guide* described her, ranking her number one on their list of all-time "Top Ten Reality TV Villains." A *Mahogany* magazine cover story attributed her supposedly diabolical behavior to genetics: "Natural Born Villain," their headline read. Print, broadcast, and online journalists—not to mention bloggers and TV fans—described her as an "evil sistah," a "moral cretin," and a "she-devil."[9]

To what did Omarosa owe her "Black villainess diva" reputation?[10]

It wasn't her behavior. She played the *Apprentice* game like an egotistical schemer, but no more so than most contestants on cutthroat competition shows. She was verbally vicious, slacked off sometimes, and never backed down from a fight: again, par for the course. So, what "high cultural treason" did she commit to make *Entertainment Weekly* say that "every single black woman . . . wanted to punch her" because "she was taking down all sisters with her"?[11]

Omarosa's sin: She dared to talk about race on national TV. When her competitors disliked her, she said it was because they were intimidated by a strong Black woman (she was the only woman of color among the cast). She was motivated by the show's $250K prize money, not political purpose—she seemed to use accusations of racism as a strategy to throw white competitors off kilter. When a tipsy white woman said "that's like calling the kettle black," Omarosa snapped back, "There you go with your racist terms . . . try to contain your prejudice, okay?"+

---

* A penchant for provocative attire seemed to be a job requirement for most of the women selected to compete for The Donald's professional attentions.

+ That's all we saw, though in postshow interviews Omarosa told reporters that she reacted so strongly because she'd been called the "N-word" off-camera. Producers denied the slur was used. Without access to Mark Burnett Productions' proprietary tapes, it's impossible to know which side was lying. But the press had a field day, insisting she "played the race card" and issued "false accusations" to cover for her professional inferiority. Some outlets used the incident as an excuse to trot out the corporate media truism that naming racism is as bad—or worse—than experiencing it.[12]

That comment opened the floodgates for racial typecasting. Producers spent the rest of the season framing her as manipulative, untrustworthy, and lazy. Her fellow contestants constantly attacked her, screaming in her face while she remained calm, yet editors branded Omarosa the "angry bitch" of *The Apprentice*. When she insisted on taking time off to see a doctor after concrete fell on her head at a construction challenge, she was said to lack a work ethic. The Donald called her "rude," "vicious," and "repulsive." In her final episode, she burst into his boardroom uninvited to defend herself and was fired. Viewers didn't know that she only went into the room because producers told her to, a classic bait-and-switch that solidified her status as an entitled, unprofessional diva. In a typical editorial response, a *Chicago Sun Times* columnist wrote that this "prime-time 'Angry Black Woman'" gave America "a view of a stereotypical black woman in over her head."[13]

Most reality show contestants quickly exhaust their fifteen minutes. Not Omarosa. In 2005, she spoke at a congressional forum called "Me, Inc.," which aimed to "empower participants to better market themselves by creating their own personal brand." No one knows how to do that better than Omarosa, who built a lucrative career based on the ABW persona assigned to her by reality TV producers. In 2008, she made the talk show rounds to promote her book, *The Bitch Switch: Knowing How to Turn It On and Off.* She turned it on that same year when she became the only former *Apprentice* candidate to appear on *The Celebrity Apprentice.* And Trump couldn't have thought she was so "repulsive" after all, since he teamed up with TV One and Comcast in 2009 to create *Omarosa's Ultimate Merger,* based on the premise that "it is time for this strong-willed and wily schemer to settle down and find a husband." In keeping with the classic "domineering, aggressive, and emasculating" Sapphire stereotype, a TV One press release promised that "successful, egotistical" men will "fight back" against their "difficult" star, to "tame this shrew." The network claims the series will be not only "a guilty pleasure" but also a "compelling take on universal aspects of the black experience."[14]

Omarosa has capitalized on a virulent stereotype about Black women, a path *Apprentice* producers laid out for her. "When I was a good girl, there were no cameras on," she told *Time*. "The minute I started arguing, there was a camera shooting me from every angle." So she played the game, and she was turned into a national punching bag. This should come as no surprise: The Jim Crow Museum of Racist Memorabilia explains that the classic Sapphire stereotype has functioned as "a social control mechanism that is employed to punish Black women who violate the societal norms that encourage Black women to be passive, servile, nonthreatening, and unseen."[15]

THE MAMMY:
"IF THEY'RE NOT HAPPY, I'M NOT HAPPY."

Unlike the race-conscious dialogue surrounding Omarosa, most BF racial typecasting played out under the surface. Take the "Military Mammy" who appeared on *Profiles from the Front Line*, a heavy-handed propaganda series following U.S. troops in Afghanistan during the country's initial response to the September 11 attacks.

Aired by ABC in February 2003 at the same time as corporate journalists were beating the drums for war in Iraq, the show cynically attempted to exploit post-9/11 fear and patriotism for ratings, and to increase support for the impending U.S. invasion.* Produced by Jerry Bruckheimer (known for war blockbusters like *Black Hawk Down* and *Pearl Harbor*) with full cooperation from the Pentagon, *Profiles* employed all the bells and whistles Hollywood could muster to gin up anti-Arab, anti-Muslim sentiment. Action unfolded through tension-building night-vision cameras. With faux-documentary overtones, episodes opened with a

---

* *Profiles* contributed to viewers' confusion about the differences between Afghanistan, where the "show" was set, and Iraq. This confusion was already instigated by op-ed writers, broadcast news anchors, pundits, and policy wonks who falsely claimed that Iraq held weapons of mass destruction, supported al Qaeda, and was responsible for 9/11. The more TV news Americans watched, the more likely they were to incorrectly believe such inaccuracies, according to a 2003 study from the Program on International Policy Attitudes (PIPA). Holding such misperceptions was directly correlated to a person's likelihood to support the war, meaning that corporate media bears major responsibility for U.S. involvement in Iraq.[16]

narrator announcing that "U.S. Special Operations Forces . . . highly skilled in unconventional warfare, communications, intelligence, and diplomacy" were leading "Operation Enduring Freedom in Afghanistan. . . . These are their stories."

In numerous breath-holding scenes, Brave Men in Uniform Did Their Duty to Keep You Safe, searching for weapons, interrogating combatants, and performing lifesaving surgery. The Great American Hope *Profiles* presented was not just a buff boy in uniform; he was, largely, a buff *white* boy. While Afghan people were given screen time to build Bruckheimer's narrative, military personnel of color were largely overlooked, giving the impression that Americans are white and our enemies are not. These tales of heroism were also highly gendered. Men did the saving and women provided support, in keeping with Susan Faludi's *The Terror Dream,* which details how "media, entertainment, and advertising declared the post-9/11 age an era of neofifties . . . redomesticated femininity, and reconstituted Cold Warrior manhood."[17] Hence, a ponytailed blond medic who worked on a transport plane enthused that her job offered "a weight loss plan for women over thirty: 'Pump your bags every other day, extreme heat, and no food!'"* Images of male strength and bravado were juxtaposed with tearjerker home-front interviews with grieving white war widows and moms saying their husbands and sons were risking life and limb to protect America and "fight evil." (Of course, the role of evil was uniformly cast with Afghan men, whose speech was often untranslated and whose mere presence in a scene was enough to indicate "enemy," even when they were working for the troops.)

When race and gender intersected, the *Profile* wasn't pretty. While they featured courageous white Special Forces dudes and stoic white widows and moms and reduced a dedicated servicewoman to "Army Barbie," they also introduced us to Sargeant First Class Danette Jones. An African American woman who oversaw food services in Bagram, she had a role that was captioned on-screen: "Mission: Breakfast for 3500." Here's what we learned about the only woman of color profiled on the episode: "My job is to supervise the kitchen, ensure that everything

---

* I can see the recruitment poster now: "Uncle Same Wants You . . . to trim those thighs, tubby!"

is getting done properly by the book, and the soldiers are happy. I feed everybody in this tent." As cameras panned over Jones dishing grub, she narrated, "We got steak, eggs, hash browns. . . . Keep the line goin'—put steak *and* bacon on that plate!" She lamented that "these soldiers work so hard it's pathetic, and they don't get no thank-yous, no morale boost," but at least when they eat her food she knows she's "doing a good job—these soldiers are enjoying what they're getting!" But as per Hollywood's usual script about women of color, you wouldn't like her when she's angry: "I scare people. I'm called 'The Intimidator,'" she said, brandishing a large knife. "To be truthfully honest, I be a bitch in the kitchen."

The many guys quoted on *Profiles* expressed pride in their roles as defenders of God and Country—Jones was just proud to serve her boys: "I try to keep everyone happy out here. If I make 'em happy, I'm happy. If they're not happy, I'm not happy."

Black people make up 13.2 percent, and women make up 11.3 percent, of service members deployed in the U.S. wars in Afghanistan and Iraq.[18] Thousands of Black servicewomen hold a wide range of positions in Afghanistan and Iraq. They provide crucial support such as food prep, translation, and strategic information analysis. They also face danger head-on: They drive trucks in bomb-filled areas, serve as tank gunners, raid houses, guard prisoners, and rescue the wounded in battle. But those women were ignored by *Profiles from the Front Line,* just like the news media virtually ignored the heroism of Army Specialist Shoshana Johnson, the first Black woman ever to be held as a prisoner of war in 2003.*

Sgt. Danette Jones served her country honorably and well by supervising food services in Bagram. Yet by choosing to focus only on her KP job while excluding other women of color in the service, Bruckheimer turned her into a caricature: Military Mammy.

The "mammy" archetype, in which Black women play fawning domestic

---

* Shoshana Johnson was shot and held as a POW in Iraq in 2003, during the same famous ambush in which pretty, blond Private Jessica Lynch was captured. While Johnson's story went mostly untold in corporate media, a falsified version of Lynch's rescue was plastered all over print and broadcast headlines. Lynch later said she believed she was used as a propaganda tool by the press and the Pentagon.[19]

servants, cooks, and surrogate mothers for white people, originated in minstrel theater but has haunted Black women in American media. In late 1800s advertising, Aunt Jemima breakfast products were marketed with the image of a heavyset, grinning, kerchief-wearing Black woman described in original ads as a former slave. Aunt Jemima is one of the most enduring and famous ad campaigns, partly because she taps into what author M. M. Manring has called nostalgic "perceptions of the South as a culture of white leisure and black labor. Aunt Jemima's ready-mixed products offered middle-class housewives the next best thing to a black servant: a 'slave in a box' that conjured up romantic images of not only the food but also the social hierarchy of the plantation South."[20]

Mammy made her way from advertising to television in 1950–1953, when ABC began airing *The Beulah Show,* the first American sitcom to revolve around an African American star. Called the "queen of the kitchen," the title character was a middle-aged Black domestic servant for a white family. Though *Beulah* was a comedy, the NAACP didn't find it funny: At their 1951 convention, the civil rights organization condemned the series for perpetuating prejudices "that Negroes and other minorities are inferior, lazy, dumb and dishonest."[21] In the 1980s, Nell Carter "revived the archetype of mammy" as a loud but loving housekeeper for a white family on NBC's *Gimme a Break!*[22] And the image popped up again on a 2004 episode of ABC's *Wife Swap,* in the form of a mammy cookie jar and a mammy children's doll in the home of a white Southern family. For pointing out that these items are part of the legacy of slavery, Shelley Elliott, the Black "swapee" mom from Maryland, was framed as "inappropriate" and oversensitive. "Drop it!" the white teen daughter screamed at her.

At least *Wife Swap* gave Shelley the space to protest mammy imagery and clarify its history. That's more than Bruckheimer allowed Sgt. Danette Jones. Exactly fifty years after ABC canceled *Beulah,* the same network chose to reduce Black military women to a single, antiquated stereotype: a "bitch in the kitchen" who cheerfully slings hash to keep others happy.

SILENT NATIVES, NOISY GONGS

Cultural appropriation has been persistent across many reality subgenres.

In FX's *Black. White.*, a Black family from Atlanta (Brian, Renee, and son Nick) and a white family from Santa Monica (Carmen, daughter Rose, and Carmen's boyfriend, Bruno), used studio-quality full-body makeup to "trade races."* Producers promoted the show as a progressive exposé of hidden racism. "This series is an example of how television can be an extremely powerful and useful medium," they told reporters, promising it would "force people to challenge themselves and really examine where we stand in terms of race in this country." To hear FX tell it, their "docu-series" would be like a modern update to *Black Like Me,* which chronicled a white journalist's experience passing as Black in the civil-rights-era South. Many media outlets bought into the bogus framing, calling it a "provocative exploration of race relations," and a "documentary" answering the age-old question, "What's it like to live in someone else's skin?"[23]

Yet *Black. White.* had little in common with ethical documentary. Instead, producers used every trick in the reality TV arsenal proven to generate melodrama. They cast people they knew would clash, forced them to live in the same house, then edited the show to reinforce stereotypes. In blackface, Bruno denied the existence of racism and said he was looking forward to strangers calling him "nigger." In whiteface, Brian was depicted as an Angry Black Man who jumped at any possible opportunity to "cry racism." In an attempt to be a convincing Black woman, Carmen bought an African-print dashiki and greeted Renee with "Yo, bitch!" The teens learned that etiquette classes represent white culture, while poetry slams and "gangsta rap" represent black culture. All this was set to the tune of "Race Card," the theme song by coproducer Ice Cube.

The premise that "race relations" only apply to African Americans and Caucasians was problematic enough.⁺ But *Black. White.* wanted us to believe two

---

* *ANTM* has also used blackface and other ethnic props (Native American headdresses, grass skirts for Polynesians, etc.) to make models "become another race" in photo shoots.
⁺ Black women have been far more present within reality TV than Latinas and Asian women, while Native American and Arabic women have been virtually invisible.

deeper mythologies. First, that ethnic identity is only skin-deep and second, that racism is about individual attitudes, not societal structures. As journalist Sheerly Avni wrote, this hides the fact that "we can't [eradicate] racial conflict without dismantling the institutions that help perpetuate it," such as "failing educational systems; welfare reform; [and] measures like the Rockefeller Drug Laws."[24]

Where *Black. White.* pretended that a lifetime of racist barriers or privileged opportunity could be experienced—or sloughed off—with a quick trip to a makeup salon, other shows have co-opted entire countries through clichéd cultural reduction. This kind of fetishization is standard practice on *ANTM,* especially during "destination" episodes. Lion dancers pranced, martial artists played with swords, and gongs blared when Tyra Banks told her models they were going to China. In Brazil, they got styled like Carmen Miranda (explained as the Chiquita Banana lady) for a photo shoot in a São Paulo favela (slum). Glam cams used poor children playing on garbage-strewn streets to lend gritty authenticity to the pictures, while judges swept their poverty under the rug, complaining that some contestants didn't look joyful enough since "there's a lot of happiness in favela."*

Survivor pushes cultural appropriation to its limits, often presenting a colonialist vision of Westerners in "foreign" lands—especially true on *Survivor: Africa,* where voiceless locals and their customs were portrayed as primitive and shocking. As scholar H. Leslie Steeves notes, "One of the two appearances by Kenyans is a Samburu blood-drinking challenge . . . their role is to bring in the cows, wear traditional clothes, retrieve the blood, and serve as props. They never speak." Steeves sees similar representations on *The Amazing Race* "at almost every location in Africa. . . . Additionally, a colorfully (sometimes scantily) dressed native stands next to host Phil Keoghan at every location and greets teams as they arrive at finish lines . . . the locals at the end became almost entirely decorative, with no more than one scripted line, for instance,

---

* *ANTM* practices similar co-optation within America: A photo shoot at a homeless shelter used actual homeless youth as background props in contestants' pictures.

'Welcome to Burkina Faso.'" In this way, reality TV's tourism competitions mirror classic adventure tourism advertising, "by emphasizing differences over similarities between visitors and visited."[25]

Though *Survivor* and *The Amazing Race* engage in cultural appropriation, there's a mammoth difference between the two CBS shows. *Survivor* lacks diversity and glories in gross-out contests and petty dramas; *TAR* features inclusive casting and unusually conscientious editing. While they often show Americans behaving badly abroad—yelling at herbalists in Thailand, harassing cab drivers in India—*TAR* producers frame entitled, ignorant snits as unacceptable. "Such Ugly American behavior elicits bad-guy music on the soundtrack and dirty looks from passersby," travel writer Bob Harris notes. And unlike other reality shows, we're allowed to see participants express remorse when they've been hostile or bigoted: After being rude to a taxi driver, gay Christian activist Mel White, who competed with his actor son, Mike, told the cameras, "This race certainly isn't important enough to dehumanize someone by yelling and screaming at them. So I'm going to feel bad about that for the rest of the day." *TAR* is unique in bringing viewers something they rarely see in the corporate media landscape: a constantly updated queue of insights into the lives and cultures of communities across the globe. They visit Kuwaiti souks, Ukrainian concert halls, and Mongolian monasteries. Traditions are often condensed or staged to the point of misrepresentation, but this trivialization is balanced by *TAR*'s potential educational benefit to audiences, who learn that "the world outside our borders is filled with creative and resilient people." Asks Harris, "When do American television audiences ever even see Estonia, Madagascar, or Burkina Faso on a map, much less watch fellow Americans engaging in any way with their customs?"[26]

Like VH1's race- and gender-conscious *The Cho Show* (which aired only seven episodes), *TAR*'s sixteen-and-counting seasons illustrate that reality television has the potential to be engaging and edifying without being exploitative. It's too bad it's such an exception.

BEAUTY "CORRECTION"

While marginalized in most other subgenres, women of color have always shown up in large numbers on network and cable makeover, modeling, and beauty-based competition series.

Producers have granted a sketchy "equality" in incorporating Black, Latina, and East and South Asian women into these casts (though Native Americans and Arab Americans are still mostly invisible in this subgenre). But proportional equity becomes a double-edged sword once the judges start critiquing, the surgeons start slicing, and the video editors start cherry-picking for attacks on any deviation from media-approved beauty standards. Once racial beauty biases are added to the genre's already bitterly sexist brew, the resulting representations can be damaging to cultural perceptions (and internalized self-impressions) of women and girls of color.

Some series teach us that ethnic features must be "fixed," by drastic means if necessary. Plastic surgeons with questionable ethics give insecure women of all ethnicities boob jobs, liposuction, and face-lifts on shows such as *Extreme Makeover*, *The Swan*, and *Dr. 90210*, ignoring medical risks and reinforcing problematic ideas about women's worth. Yet they don't make white surgical candidates feel like their cultural identity should also be on the chopping block—or that they'd be so much more attractive and fulfilled if only they didn't look so . . . Caucasian. In contrast, TV docs' scalpels reduce or remove racial markers on patients of color. Black women's noses and lips are made smaller. In an increasingly common procedure targeting Asian women, creases are added to Asian women's eyelids. And while white women's surgery is "never figured as having racial meaning" on shows like *Extreme Makeover:*

> the "concerns of ethnic cosmetic surgery" are discussed and dismissed by introducing a Black surgeon, who explains that, of course, all of his patients want to retain their distinctive ethnic appearance, but also aspire to make their features more "proportionate," or suitable for their individual face . . .

in a show that relies on the language of authenticity, the specter of "passing"
is never more palpable than when race is at stake.[27]

By attempting to surgically erase or "correct" visual traits that connect women of color to their ancestry, these shows perpetrate a symbolic form of ethnic cleansing. That this is justified via the language of individuality and appropriateness—under the guise of helping women "retain their distinctive ethnic appearance"—makes it all the more insidious.

A similar (though less invasive) narrative exists on talent programs. A classic example is what I like to call "The Homogenator," the *American Idol* style machine. For *Idol*'s female singers, non-Western features are often treated as a liability. White girls who look like Britney Spears circa " . . . Baby One More Time" have squeaked by with faulty pitch and minimal vocal range, a luxury not afforded to Black, Latina, and biracial female contestants. Instead, their curly, kinky, and dark hair is nearly always straightened and/or lightened, with makeup and fashion carefully selected to mask full lips and curvy behinds. "This is an image business," judge Simon Cowell has rationalized. "Image" was the euphemism he used on season 2 when he told African American contestant Kimberley Locke that her rich, sultry singing voice was wonderful, but it couldn't compensate for her plus-size body and her "weird" hair. That was his coded admission that as a music producer and pop star puppet master, he considers natural Black hair unattractive and unmarketable. Cowell didn't stop haranguing her until she emerged from The Homogenator, a process chronicled in a segment on a live *Idol* results show. In front of a massive studio audience, a photo of Kim auditioning with kinky hair was blown up on a giant screen:

HOST RYAN SEACREST: And the hair. The hair is different.

KIMBERLEY LOCKE: The hair is different. I love to wear my hair straight
     but it takes a looong time.

RYAN: To get your hair straight?

KIM: Like two hours! And then I got highlights so it took like four hours. So I was like, "This is *so not* worth it."

As troubling and should-have-been unnecessary as those four hours were, they changed Kimberley's fate on the show. As *Idol*'s most influential voice during the first nine seasons, Cowell often helped determine which singers viewers voted to keep in the competition. After she acquiesced to The Homogenator, here's how Cowell responded to her vocal performance: "Ever since you got rid of that *weird hair*, you got better. No, seriously! Because you look cute now! You do!" Once given silky, lightened hair that looked more like white women's locks, he finally saw Locke as a singer he could sell—crucial on a show built around embedded advertisers.*

How relaxer and dye changed the sound of Locke's voice remains a mystery.

On second thought, someone should lend Simon a copy of *Hair Story: Untangling the Roots of Black Hair in America,* by Ayana Byrd and Lori Tharps, for an education on the social, cultural, and economic implications of what he so crudely called "weird hair." Cowell has taken his place in a century's worth of media makers and marketers to reinforce the notion that "good hair" (white or, sometimes, Asian hair) is key to women's social and professional success, while "bad hair" (Black, often Latina, and sometimes Jewish hair) is naturally ugly and "low-class."

For that matter, someone should sit Tyra Banks down for some education on the subject. For all her "girls of color are beautiful!" rhetoric she almost never allows African American models to compete with their hair kinky, curly, nappy, or otherwise natural. Yes, all women get dramatic makeovers on *Top Model*—but shortening a redhead's long tresses or making a brunet go blond doesn't bear the sociological significance of policing Black hair with weaves and often-painful chemical treatments. In "Why Hair Is Political," Susannah Walker writes:

---

* Compare this to his comments to Carmen, a pretty blond teen, during that same season. A bright-eyed Britney-in-training, she sang off-key often enough to make an average listener cringe. Yet after one such pitch-poor performance, the usually critical Cowell remarked, "Carmen, I don't think that you are the best female singer in this competition. But, I think you are the most commercial of the girls left. And I thought that was one of your better performances. I liked it." She was "commercial" because of her pop star package— light skin, blond hair, thin figure, youthful glow. Whether she could actually *sing?* Irrelevant.

African American hair has historically symbolized and continues to reflect struggles over race and gender in the United States. This . . . has been demonstrated in news stories about black women being fired from their jobs, or girls being sent home from school, for wearing braids, dreadlocks, or other hairstyles deemed "extreme" by employers and principals.[28]

Hair wars are just the beginning of *ANTM*'s racial beauty biases, as you'll see in the next chapter.

II. After Flavor of Love (AF): Modern-Day Minstrel Shows

In some ways, it is safer to be invisible when being visible means being harmed.

—MALKIA CYRIL, executive director, Center for Media Justice*

The mansion was awash in spandex and anticipation. Twenty buxom young women (mostly African Americans, plus a handful of Latinas, Asians, and whites) were waiting to meet the man of—well, not exactly their dreams, but of their contractual obligations.

Outside, their suitor, a Black man twice their age, sported an oversized hot pink suit, a glittery bow tie, and a black top hat, with a giant clock on a chain around his neck. When he grabbed the doorknob to enter the manor, the camera zoomed in on his short, white gloves, the sort worn by servants and minstrels. Seeing his groupies for the first time, he danced toward them with footwork that might as well have been soft-shoe. "Yeaaaaah, girls!" he screamed. "Wasssup, baby? Yeaaaaah!"

Flavor Flav had arrived.

By the time *Flavor of Love* debuted in 2006, eight seasons of *The Bachelor*

---

* Malkia Cyril made this statement during a keynote about the risks butch lesbians take when choosing to live openly in a hostile culture. Yet her point can very much apply to representation of "othered" communities within corporate media.[29]

had taught viewers what to expect from dating shows: pretty white people, faux sincerity, and the trappings of "fairytale love." VH1 drastically changed that formula, and not just through diverse casting. Structural differences were built in from the get-go. Instead of a handsome, sophisticated Prince Charming, *FoL* starred a man whose face was haggard from nearly fifty years of partying and drugs, who had famously done jail time for violent offenses and was arrested for shirking child support. A cheesy, Barry White–sounding narrator introduced us to Flav in an opening montage that coached us to see the aging rapper as an ignorant clown. He wore a dual-horned Viking helmet, played basketball in cheetah-print pajamas, described hideous paintings of himself as "rare, valuable works of art," and said that despite fame and fortune, "None of these things means nurthin' without a woman to spend it with." Hence, his quest to find a recipient for a symbol of his momentary affections: not a diamond ring for her finger, but a gold-plated grille for her teeth.

That's where the "Flavorettes" came in. Unlike ABC's perky Stepford Wives in training, VH1 seemed to go out of its way to cast women who had worked in strip clubs, porn, and other sex industry jobs—only to frame them as promiscuous, vulgar train wrecks. Producers portrayed these bachelorettes of color as prone to poor grammar, tacky fashion sense, and outbursts of profanity and violence. By season 2, they were even literally pooping on a staircase. In the press, VH1 programming execs called them "refreshingly real"—but the narrative message we were meant to receive was that these weren't wholesome, genuine girls next door—they were "low-class" Jezebel whores from the wrong side of the tracks.[30]

Producers made sure viewers understood that race was the reason why this show was so different from anything we'd seen before. From the archetypical reality TV limousine during the series premiere, Flav screamed, "I know y'all heard of that show called *The Bachelor*. Flavor Flav is the Black-chelorrrrrrrrrr . . . orrrrrrrrrrr. . . . "* Lest that prove too subtle, he yelled, "I'm the pimp behind

---

* BTW, that's the exact number of Rs used when his quote was captioned on screen to hammer this racial distinction.

the wheels!" He certainly acted the part, demanding "the girls" perform actual or implied sexual favors or get kicked out of the house.

Viewers were never expected to suspend their disbelief to root for the goofy and physically grotesque Flav to find "true love" with any of three seasons' worth of nubile fame seekers. Producers wanted us to do something else: laugh our asses off. Using the campy conventions of the blaxploitation film genre, *Flavor of Love* set out to mock people of color for our collective enjoyment. Intrinsic to *The Bachelor*'s earnest packaging is the pretense that Mr. White B. Wright lets his growing feelings of "connection" determine which women he takes on helicopter rides or whisks off to sun-drenched islands. But on this "ghetto-fabulous" knock-off,* Flav didn't choose his dates—producers did. Women got "alone time" by winning competitions designed to minimize dignity and maximize stereotypes. Some contests involved servitude: The Flavorettes had to compete to be the best maid (in the "clean my shit-filled mansion!" challenge described at the beginning of this chapter), the most diligent fast food joint staffer ("Yo' man Flavor Flav was puttin' their ass to work, dog!" he smirked), or to "[cook] the best fried chicken." Other contests emphasized another set of assets, with Flav judging naughty-nurse challenges, calendar-girl photo shoots, and booty-dance-offs (his instructions: "I want them asses shaking!"). Challenge winners would be rewarded with "romantic dates" to places like Kentucky Fried Chicken(!), whose brand was integrated into numerous episodes.

There were endless excuses for on-command lap dances, lingerie, and slow-mo, sexytime camera work while Flav chomped on KFC drumsticks. Flavorettes were often filmed only as disparate body parts: The screen would fill with shots of one woman's giant, surgically enhanced breasts or another's ample ass. Flav regularly used dehumanizing language, bragged about dating "all of these beautiful, gorgeous, sexy items." That paled compared with the show's ultimate objectification: The women were stripped of their identities, forced to assume nicknames

---

* Seriously, that's the phrase media outlets from *The New York Times* to *Entertainment Weekly* used to describe the show.[31]

Flav chose and then gropingly affixed to their chests and butts via nametags. "Branded! USDA!" he yelled after christening his playthings. During *FoL* and in subsequent media interviews and VH1 spinoffs, these modern-day Jezebels were always referred to only by these nicknames, such as "Nibblz" (who had prominent nipples), Deelishis (whose big booty was a series fixation), and "Bootz" (because seeing her, Flav said, made him "wanna knock boots!").*

Decades before *Flavor of Love,* Flavor Flav played a radical role in pop culture. As hype man for socially conscious hip-hop group Public Enemy, he helped to popularize songs like "Fight the Power," "Don't Believe the Hype," "911 (Is a Joke)," and "Fear of a Black Planet," shining a spotlight on systemic racism, police brutality, and white supremacy. In the 1980s and '90s, Flav's crazy costumes, hyperactive energy, and gold teeth were the sugar that made rapper Chuck D's serious political medicine palatable to mainstream audiences. He'd scream "Yeah, Boooyyyyy!" and "Flava Flaaaaaaav!" and crowds would go wild, while Chuck D railed against racial and economic injustice.

As Public Enemy's comic foil, Flav clowned for a cause. His group "made hip-hop that was more than entertainment. They inspired a lot of people who believed that you can effect change through music," *Rolling Stone* declared, naming them one of the "Greatest Artists of All Time."[32] In contrast, *Flavor of Love* played like the fantasies of the worst of corporate hip-hip videos, with twenty lusty "bitches" and "hos" throwing themselves at one arrogant rapper.⁺ Politically neutralized without Chuck D by his side, VH1 reduced Flav to a shucking-and-jiving fool. (At one point, he proudly wears a jester's crown.) In return, they received the highest ratings in their network's history, when nearly 6 million viewers tuned in to *FoL*'s first finale. VH1 broke their own record later that year,

---

* Non-Black contestants were often given nicknames that othered them, such as "Miss Latin" for a Latina, or "Red Oyster" for an East Asian.
⁺ Such descriptions of women of color were extremely common on *FoL,* and throughout its legion of spinoffs. In *Hip Hop: Beyond Beats and Rhymes,* filmmaker Byron Hurt notes that the misogyny and violence in mainstream hip-hop is due to the corporate takeover of the musical genre. Before the corporate music industry bought up indie labels and chose to emphasize gangsta rap and video vixens, hip-hop was an organic voice of Black musicians who rapped about racial injustice and community power.

when 7.5 million people made season 2's finale the number one nonsports telecast on basic cable in 2006. Additionally, *FoL 2* was number one in its time slot on cable and broadcast television among eighteen- to forty-nine-year-old African Americans. (VH1 honcho Michael Hirschorn used these ratings to dodge reporters' questions about "whether the show was exploiting racial stereotypes.") And though plenty of progressive critics decried the show's bigotry, *Entertainment Weekly* included it on a list of "20 Best Reality-TV Shows Ever," calling it "undeniably mesmerizing—as is the skankertainment genre it spawned."[33]

With *Flavor of Love,* reality TV used an icon of Black-positive pop culture to bring the minstrel show back to contemporary television. As *St. Petersburg Times* columnist Eric Deggans noted, Flav colluded with VH1 to bring about this devolution: "One of rap's most militantly pro-black groups has produced one of TV's biggest black buffoons. . . . Looks like someone decided that fighting the power wasn't as profitable as joining it. And we all may be the worse for his choice." But Black people's complicity in performing the racist roles producers set out for them is in keeping with the history of American minstrel theater in the 1800s, early-twentieth-century film (such as *Mammy* and *Steamboat Round the Bend*) and midcentury radio and TV (such as *Amos & Andy*). In all these media, Blacks have acted alongside blackface-wearing whites to portray derogatory African American archetypes such as "mammy," "wench," "old darky," "coon," and slave characters who loved pleasing their masters or, after being freed, longed to return to bondage. (The "dandy"—whose attempts at mixing with white society were meant as comical reminders of his inferiority—wore white gloves similar to those Flav donned on the first episode of *FoL.*) In minstrelsy, African Americans were seen as dehumanized caricatures with huge eyeballs and lips that hung open farcically. They were often described in animalistic terms: Their children were called "darky cubs," and they had "wool," not hair. Black men were depicted as stupid and lazy, while Black women were hypersexual provocateurs or subservient caretakers. Biracial women were particularly exoticized as titillating and wanton.[34] This minstrel legacy echoed throughout *Flavor of Love*'s three seasons and its many spinoffs.

Flavor Flav (and three seasons of Flavorettes) allowed VH1 to profit from the revival of these anti-Black stereotypes, just like Stepin Fetchit in the 1930s. Short for "Step 'n fetch it," that was the stage name of Lincoln Theodore Monroe Andrew Perry, the first Black Hollywood millionaire. Perry became a superstar by playing film's most famous "lazy, slow-witted, jive-talkin' 'coon"—also known in his act as "The Laziest Man in the World."[35] Perry's characterization of African Americans was the subject of ongoing protest by the NAACP, which considered Stepin Fetchit detrimental to the ability of Blacks to be accepted as equal to whites. Seventy-some years later, VH1, Flavor Flav, and his castoffs-turned-D-list-celebs are the ones being called out by culture critics. In *Essence,* columnist Debra Dickerson pointedly equated the treatment of women of color on *Flavor of Love* with imagery dating back to slavery:

> *Where have we seen this before, the forced extraction of a subjugated class's names to be replaced by demeaning ones; the refinement of the crabs-in-a-barrel gambit in which the oppressed are taught to fight one another; the refusal to allow victims a sense of personhood or privacy by entering their (mass) bedrooms unannounced. . . .* [36]

Turn Off Channel Zero, a film collaboration by media activists, artists, and musicians, went further, targeting Viacom (parent company of VH1, as well as MTV and BET) for "showing the whole world who they think we are" through programs like *Flavor of Love* and "using our culture to destroy us." Professor Griff, another member of Public Enemy, appeared in the film to urge people of color *"to control our own images."*[37]

Cocreator Mark Cronin (Mindless Entertainment) insists *FoL* wasn't demeaning because Flav "just behaves the way he wants to behave." Chuck D dismantled this disingenuous claim on PBS. "I blame Viacom and maybe the VH1 station. Flavor is Flavor—he's been the same dude forever," he told Tavis Smiley. "But they saw some DNA in there where they said, 'Wow, we can go into that and we can just mass produce it and just repeat it over and over again.'"

He's absolutely right. Though Cronin claims that he and coproducer Cris Abrego (51 Pictures) "don't have a political agenda. We don't have an exploitation agenda," they made an intentional choice to give *this particular man* a dating show specifically because he'd reliably act the fool—and then they cast, edited, and framed women of color in ways that intentionally played off deep-seated racial stereotypes. Like most reality producers, Cronin reverts to a standard media copout: It's not racist if people enjoy it. "I feel if we do a show that wasn't controversial or outrageous, then why bother? It's entertainment. It's meant to be fun," he told *The Washington Post*.[38]

Translation: We wanted to piss people off, because controversy generates ratings. *FoL*'s large African American audience complicates viewership reception and impact, but doesn't change the fact that Cronin and Abrego intended (consciously or not) to *make racism fun again* in the minds of millions of viewers—just as white and Black minstrel show producers did a century ago.

JEZEBELS, PIMPS, AND THUGS

Flavor of Love heralded a reality TV renaissance in the latter half of the decade. The invisibility, tokenism, and typecasting that marked BF unscripted programming was largely replaced by African Americans headlining cable dating shows *(I Love New York, Real Chance of Love, For the Love of Ray J)*, lifestyle series *(The Real Housewives of Atlanta, Let's Talk About Pep, Fantasia For Real)*, and faux-"rehab" programs *(Charm School, From G's to Gents, T.I.'s Road to Redemption)*. Additionally, one dating series centered on an Asian American *(A Shot at Love with Tila Tequila)*. Long-standing series increasingly used racial conflicts as promo tools: In 2008, *The Real World* heavily hyped a Southern white woman screaming that a cast member shouldn't "get ghetto" even if she's from "inner-city . . . Blackville."[39]*

---

* *FoL*'s influence was felt on network TV, too, with previously whitewashed shows recruiting more people of color—sometimes with problematic results, as when *Survivor*'s thirteenth season divided competitors into segregated Black, White, Hispanic, and Asian "tribes." Still, some producers continue Herculean efforts to maintain ethnic homogeneity. Take MTV's *Maui Fever*. Census data documents that Maui residents are 31 percent Asian, 10 percent Native Hawaiian, and 22 percent mixed race. Whites, just 33 percent of the local population, were 100 percent of *Maui Fever*'s horny, hard-partying cast. Locals protested that the show "gives viewers a skewed impression of their island," and a petition circulated.[40]

With *FoL* as the bedrock that spurred these new shows (and with producers like Cronin and Abrego behind many of them), reality TV's increased racial
inclusivity may be more a curse than a blessing. Entire series are now devoted to
minstrel archetypes reborn in the name of "reality." Bravo aired three seasons of
The Real Housewives of Orange County and one season of *The Real Housewives of
New York City*—both of which followed only white women—before debuting
The Real Housewives of Atlanta in 2007. Focusing on "Black elites," *RHOA* shared
the "rich women = superficial bitches" frame of *RHOC* and *RHNY.* That's where
the similarities end. More than just self-centered and snooty, *RHOA*'s women
were often portrayed as verbally and physically violent. Producers centered race
as the unspoken cause for their "low-class," "ghetto" behavior. The old minstrel
"dandy" in a newly gendered context, *RHOA* implied that all the money in the
world couldn't make rich Black women civilized. And when season 1 castmate
DeShawn Snow couldn't be shoehorned as a dandy or an Angry Black Woman,
she was promptly fired.*

The most prevalent (and profitable) example of post-*FoL* racial typecasting
is the Jezebel. According to this age-old trope, an African American woman is a
"seductive temptress with an insatiable and animalistic appetite for sex. Beguil-
ing, voluptuous, lewd and lustful." During slavery, Black women's supposed
sexual voraciousness was used to rationalize raping female slaves.⁺ Vast moral,
legal, and constitutional progress has been made in the intervening years, yet the
mediated image of Black women as Jezebels has persisted from the 1915 movie
Birth of a Nation to 1970s blaxploitation films such as *Black Hooker* and *Sweet
Sweetback's Baadasssss Song*—and finally in contemporary reality television. *FoL*
introduced this caricature to a new generation of viewers, and she has been a
staple of both VH1 and MTV programming ever since. While virtually all Black
bachelorettes on cable dating shows have been portrayed as "opportunistic, one-

---

* Snow was the head of a girls' self-esteem foundation, a divinity grad student, and a Baptist minister, but viewers didn't know that because she wasn't filmed studying, preaching, or mentoring girls.

⁺ Masters needed no *legal* justification: Since slave women were considered property, there was no law against sexually assaulting them.

dimensional and sexually deviant," no one has been so more cartoonishly than *I Love New York* star Tiffany "New York" Pollard.[41]

VH1 gave the rarely fully clothed New York a mansion full of suitors to preside over after she sexed up—and was dumped by—Flavor Flav on *FoL's* first and second seasons. As self-proclaimed "Head Bitch in Charge" she divided her time between erotic teasing and emotional torment. Not one *I ♡ NY* episode went by without New York rubbing up against, stripping for, and making out with numerous guys, whom she alternately seduced, manipulated, and emasculated. In *"I Love New York:* Does New York Love Me?" a team of scholars noted that Pollard's "lustful appearance, promiscuous demeanor and manipulative behavior make her the perfect Jezebel for the 21st century," as everything about her was "a profound exaggeration, from her lengthy highlighted hair weave and thick protracted false eyelashes to the four inch stiletto shoes she dons." We heard her moan breathily one minute and rant in irate, Sapphire-esque tirades the next, always in getups that revealed as much of her breast implants as allowed on basic cable.[42]

In Pollard, Cronin and Abrego found not only the ultimate Jezebel, but someone they could position as embodying every trope discussed in chapter 3. In multiple seasons of *FoL, I Love New York, New York Goes to Hollywood,* and *New York Goes to Work,* VH1 framed her as:

- a bitchy, backstabbing Angry Black Woman who flies off the handle with little to no provocation;
- a gold digger who'd willingly get into a man's pants if that's what it took to get into his wallet; and
- an incompetent idiot who can't properly pronounce common words, much less hold down a job.*

Just like Flavor Flav, Pollard's "bad Black girl" routine was a cash cow for VH1. With 4.4 million viewers, *I ♡ NY's* 2007 debut was their most watched

---

* In *New York Goes to Work,* viewers voted for Pollard to attempt different jobs each week. They selected work that would maximize her humiliation, including pig inseminator, nudist resort employee, and—in a particularly meta media moment for VH1's favorite Black female jester—circus clown.

series premiere ever, and the highest-rated show on all of cable on the day it launched.[43] After basing a lucrative franchise on racist mockery of Pollard and fellow Flavorettes, Cronin and Abrego wanted us to believe they *really cared* about helping women of color improve their lives. So when Pollard's hormone-soaked dating show wrapped production, they began filming a different kind of series in the mansion they'd rented for her entourage.

Enter *Flavor of Love Girls: Charm School,* an "etiquette boot camp" for Flav's disgraced daters. VH1 billed the series as a "real life 'My Fair Lady,' [in which] these women will be given the opportunity to transform from a flavor of the month to the ultimate standard in class and sophistication." Each week the least improved contestant would be voted off the show; the last woman standing would win $50K. Comedian and host Mo'Nique explained the premise in an opening montage:

> *Once upon a time there were thirteen girls who needed a little help. You see, all of these ladies made the very same, very big mistake: They showed their unruly behavior to the entire world on a little show called* Flavor of Love*. . . . Some of them won't admit it, but they need to change their ways. . . . They also needed a mentor to guide them on a path towards self-respect and prosperity . . . these ladies need my help. So I came up with a plan [to] send the* Flavor of Love *girls to charm school. They're gonna be taught everything, from how to make a good first impression, proper etiquette, style, and last but not least, how to have healthy relationships.*

Under this guise of benevolent "rehabilitation," the first installment of *Charm School* reinforced a hideous parade of isms. Viewers learned that women in general are stupid bitches; Black and Latina women are "slutacious" divas with neck-bobbing, finger-snapping attitude always one bad mood away from beating the shit out of white girls; low-income women are ignorant and "ghetto"; overweight women are disgusting and lazy; and Asian women will "love you long time." (They also all come from the same place. In one episode, Filipina "student" Leilene was alluded to by her fellow housemates as Japanese, Chinese, and Korean.) Oh, and we also learned that women of color are little better than animals: "Another rule, and it's a shame you gotta say this. There are seven bathrooms in this house. Seven. Don't nobody shit on my floor," Mo'Nique commanded.

The Grande Dame of this hypocrisy fest, "Headmistress" Mo'Nique spoke of how *Charm School* would teach Black women in particular to "gain our respect back" by becoming "cultured" and "classy ladies."* The former Flavorettes had to redeem their tarnished reputations not just for their own benefit, she said, but as representatives of their entire race: "They watching us. They watching us," she admonished. "Let us make that woman named Harriet Tubman—let's make her proud. Let's make that woman named Dorothy Dandridge proud. Let's make your mother proud. Let's make your grandmother proud."

By blaming these women for acting out the roles they were selected to play, *Charm School* shrewdly deflected responsibility from VH1, Cronin, and Abrego, who carefully crafted these shows to make sport of our culture's most disturbing beliefs about women of color. In one telling example, Mo'Nique berated the women for their "disgusting nicknames" and, in an elaborate reverse-naming ceremony, threw each woman's nickname tag into a fireplace. The scene had the air of a cleansing ritual to it, with fake gospel music played in the background as she spouted sanctimonious words about their being "willing to free themselves." The cynicism that fueled the production of this scene is breathtaking. "Those horrible nicknames" Mo'Nique railed against were *the cost of entry into FoL's cast*—it was entirely Flav's and the producers' decision to refer to them as childish, sexualized

---

* Producers didn't want them to display *too* much self-respect: As DeShawn Snow learned on *RHOA*, *Charm School* students who didn't perform diva antics—like Courtney, an intelligent aspiring comic—were sent packing.

+ Should the women have walked off *FoL's* set when the nicknames were first proposed, backing out of their signed contracts? Perhaps—but it's more relevant to ask why producers assigned them in the first place. What purpose did those nicknames serve, and why have nicknames become mandatory on subsequent VH1 and MTV shows? Women's willingness to do degrading things on reality TV shows is often used to justify the biases built into content. Why people choose to play by reality TV's rules is an interesting sociological question, but if we care about media's role in shaping social and political discourse in America, we should keep our analytical focus on the ways reality TV is structured, the messages these shows send, and the industries that produce and profit from them.

personas rather than actual people. The Flavorettes had no choice in the matter, unless they wanted to quit the show en masse.*

Each week focused on a different "lesson," whose stated goal of empowerment was undermined by subtextual messages. A tutorial supposedly about business acumen involved women using their bodies to sell products. Mo'Nique said a fashion challenge would help them learn how to dress in a dignified way, yet the takeaway was that fat women look "like a bunch of sausages stuffed into a bag" in dresses. Public relations training was just a pretext to bring in New York to insult the "students" in the most hateful ways she could muster—as when she asked a domestic violence survivor "How did you feel after you got your ass beaten? Was it wild animal sex afterwards? Like, what happened after this beat down?"

Speaking of unhealthy relationships, one particularly destructive bit of "education" codified reductive stereotypes about men of color under the guise of teaching contestants how to find higher-caliber men than Flavor Flav. The "teacher" was Tariq Nasheed, author of *The Art of Mackin'* and *The Art of Gold Digging*,* who cautioned the women to avoid four types of men: "the players, professionals, pushovers, and parolees." Pushovers are "92 percent sensitive" and "all about doing whatever you say, catering to your every need," he explained—as if treating women well is actually a demerit. Parolees are "the thugs, the gangtas, the hustlers. These guys know how to handle themselves in the bedroom; that's an excitement to women." Instead of dating any of "the 4Ps," Nasheed instructed, they should look for the "Urban Renaissance" men who "have swagger, but they're about their education . . . can be somewhat sensitive but they still got little gangsta in 'em . . . are suave and mentally stimulating like a player, and they know how to satisfy you sexually like a parolee. These are the exceptional men." They're also exceptionally elusive, we were told.

If even one viewer's perception of men, women, or relationships was

---

* It's no coincidence that VH1 would turn to Nasheed to teach the women "Relationship 101." He wrote *The Art of Mackin'* to help men score, based on "what he learned from older hustlers he had encountered on the streets of Los Angeles." The book made him a nationally recognized "game advisor," and "laid the foundation for the modern 'seduction' industry."[44]

affected by this twisted definition of what women want and who men are, that would be one too many. The idea that men of color are gangstas—or that gangstas are the only ones who know what they're doing in the sack—is a time-tested media trope, from the "Super Predator" myths in inaccurate '80s and '90s crime journalism to the music industry's co-optation of hip-hop. For decades, corporate media have pumped out fetishized images of the supposedly Violent Black Male to sell everything from public policies pathologizing youth to sneakers, cars, and Courvoisier.

After Nasheed's racialized theory of masculinity appeared on *Charm School,* MTV rolled out two shows dedicated to the notion that Black and Latino men (and low-income white men) are criminals, thugs, and pimps who can only be reformed through the aid of magnanimous reality producers. In 2008 and 2009, *From G's to Gents* promised to help gangstas "leave their thug lives behind" and become sophisticated gentlemen, through a *Charm School*–style format. On the premiere, a Latino "thug" framed the "G" lifestyle for the audience: "Of course I've been arrested! Who hasn't been arrested? I'm from the hood!" A Black finalist in the second season was an *actual* pimp, whose "job" was selling women—including his girlfriend. The series offered some positive surface messages, as when a former prisoner's effort to make a new life for himself was commended, or when low-income men were encouraged not to let their economic status damage their pride or confidence. A frank condemnation of homophobia during season 2 had actual cultural and educational merit. But just like *Charm School,* the show's structure and master narrative reinforced more racist archetypes than it exposed. "Eloquence" lessons played to classic stereotypes of men of color as inarticulate coons, while "etiquette" classes evoked the dandy whose ethnicity disqualifies him from upper-crust acceptance. The significance of such messages was ignored by "Gentlemen's Club" leader/host Fonzworth Bentley, a musician and former assistant to Sean "P. Diddy" Combs. On the season 1 reunion, Bentley described *From G's to Gents* as more than "just a TV show," but a force that transformed the men and "changed the lives of everyone that's watching." Similarly high-minded claims were attached to 2009's *T.I.'s Road to Redemption,* in which African American rapper T.I., convicted on felony gun charges, spends his last forty-five days before sentencing telling youth (again, mostly of color) to avoid a life of crime.*

Beware reality shows promising self-improvement and cultural change— especially those produced by the same teams that traffic in minstrel mayhem and "skankertainment." When Mo'Nique mused about her high hopes for "her sisters" to "take the spirit of *Charm School*" and improve their daily lives, viewers got to feel all warm and fuzzy. And sure, just like *FGs2Gs,* a few positive ideas did come through. Yet if VH1 had truly intended to combat the bold bigotry and misogyny of *FoL* and *I ♡ NY,* they wouldn't have reassembled the *Charm School* brood in a reunion show that resembled *The Jerry Springer Show,* with a live audience cheering as the women cursed and fought. "It breaks my heart," Mo'Nique said sternly, "to see . . . beautiful Black women sit up here and degrade and demean and disrespect each other as if you're animals."

Right, because demeaning beautiful Black women is VH1's job.

The reunion played a key role in upholding the channel's dominant narrative: that women—especially women of color—are irredeemable, untamable sluts. And those nicknames Mo'Nique "freed" them from? When *Charm School* "graduates" starred in future VH1 series such as *I Love Money,* producers reverted to calling them by their Flav-given names. Ah, respect: how fleeting on reality TV.

THE "LARGE CONTEXT"

Like most reality producers and programming execs, Cronin insists that "We don't produce our shows in a large context. We produce shows to be entertaining."[45]

---

* *T.I.'s Road to Redemption* didn't rely on a game show format but attempted to portray a sense of gritty realism. There's nothing wrong with showing mentors coaching youth to strive for healthy possibilities for their careers and their lives. Still, it's important to ask why an "inspirational" show for youth of color should star a convicted Black man and frame his history as a drug dealer as A) the result only of his own poor choices with no consideration of institutional factors such as education, poverty, law, or public policy and B) a cautionary tale for kids of color, who were assumed to all be potential delinquents. Michael Hirschorn's Ish Entertainment could have created an "inspirational" project following activists fighting to improve their communities, or youth of color achieving great successes in music, education, business, and political leadership. But that's not the kind of *ish* Hirschorn's interested in.

Sorry, that just doesn't fly. No matter how hard Cronin and his cronies flee accountability, entertainment *always* exists in a larger cultural and commercial context. As Mark Anthony Neal, author of *Soul Babies: Black Popular Culture and the Post-Soul Aesthetic* told *The Washington Post,* "The problem isn't Flavor Flav. . . . The problem is Flavor Flav becomes the stand-in for the one or two black people you see on TV," and therefore "takes on more importance than he should."[46]

With networks reducing scripted programming to make room for cheaper reality fare, far fewer roles exist for actors of color now than a decade ago, when twenty-six new shows in ABC, CBS, NBC, and Fox's 1999–2000 lineup didn't feature even one character of color in a leading role. The NAACP threatened to boycott the broadcasters over this "massive whiteout." Flash forward to December 2008, when a follow-up NAACP study found that the number of actors of color in regular or recurring roles on scripted series actually *decreased* on CBS, NBC, and Fox, with only ABC making progress toward more diverse casting. During the 2008–2009 season, when *Entertainment Weekly* called the broadcast nets' fourteen new shows "alarmingly pale," noting that "the only minority character anchoring a new series on the Big Five networks" was Cleveland Brown, a Black cartoon figure voiced by a white actor.* Blacks, Latinos, Asians, and Native Americans were significantly underrepresented across all scripted programming, a trend that worsened with the recent cancellation of minority-led series such as *Ugly Betty, Girlfriends,* and *Everybody Hates Chris.* Available roles for women are also shrinking, and actresses of color continue to be cast mostly as maids, hookers, drug addicts, assault victims, and "sassy" token friends.[47]

This "whiteout" persists when viewers flip from scripted to news programming. As *Extra!* magazine has repeatedly documented, people of color are disproportionately underrepresented as experts and subjects of broadcast journalism—while being overrepresented in crime reporting. Women, more than half the population, are also drastically marginalized as newsmakers, composing just 14 percent of guests on the broadcast networks' influential

---

* The CW completes the "Big Five" broadcast nets.

Sunday morning debate shows and 17 percent of hosts and cohosts of nighttime news programs on CNN, MSNBC, and Fox.[48]

Behind the scenes, as we'll see in chapter 8, white men remain the vast majority of writers, creators, directors, and producers of media content and decision-making executives and owners of media companies. With just a small handful of women and minorities—and even fewer women of color—in clout positions within the media industry, those whose communities are most affected by offensive or inaccurate news and entertainment have little influence over its production and scant power to green-light more positive, diverse, and compelling programming.

This is the larger context within which viewers have to make sense of reality TV's images of women and men of color, which are presented—in Cronin's words—as "real people doing real things."[49]

Just as the Jezebel mythology had dire consequences for the lives and safety of Black women during and following slavery, such depictions in contemporary reality television have social consequences. As reality shows are some of the only places viewers regularly see people of color on TV, their imagery takes on greater significance. When the primary televised narratives about race and gender are Jezebels, Mammies, and Sapphires, "spicy" Latinas and "exotic" (or passive) Asians, our collective cultural understanding of who women of color "are"— what they're capable of intellectually and professionally and how they should be treated socially and sexually—becomes poisoned. Likewise when men of color appear mostly as buffoons, thugs, and criminals.

Pop culture portrayals can influence self-perceptions, public perceptions, and even legislation about people of color, as K. Sue Jewell argues in *From Mammy to Miss America and Beyond: Cultural Images and the Shaping of U.S. Social Policy.*[50] Women of color are still paid less than all other (legal) workers, face continued discrimination in business and politics, and suffer dramatic rates of sexual assault and domestic violence, while men of color are disproportionately targeted by the criminal justice and prison systems.[51] Dehumanization within reality television only serves to exacerbate these social problems by reinforcing notions of people of color as inarticulate, immoral, lazy, and violent.

Representation in media is often key to our ability to feel valued and to believe that the world holds positive possibilities for people who look like us and share similar backgrounds and identities. Yet when a community's main media presence consists of mockery, misrepresentation, or demonization, invisibility may be preferable.

Chapter Six

Ghetto Bitches, China Dolls, and Cha Cha Divas

Race, Beauty, and the Tyranny of Tyra Banks

It's my number one passion in my life to stretch the definition of beauty. I listen to many heartbreaking stories of women who thought they would be happier if they looked different. I want every girl to appreciate the skin she's in.

—TYRA BANKS, apologizing for making
girls don blackface on *America's Next Top Model*.[1]

As executive producer, Tyra Banks claims *America's Next Top Model* aims to expand beauty standards, as she herself did as the first Black solo cover model for *GQ, Victoria's Secret,* and *Sports Illustrated*'s swimsuit edition. Chapter 2 documented how she fails at this lofty goal regarding weight, size, and eating disorders. Does she do any better at exploding race-based beauty biases?

Sometimes, yes. She exhorts *ANTM* contestants to be confident and love themselves, flaws and all. Her methods may be devised to break most models' spirits for our viewing pleasure, but there's something to be said for casting diverse young women and at least telling them that they're gorgeous. In a TV landscape that has typically depicted girls of color as ugly when not ignoring them entirely, sometimes a slightly positive mixed message is as good as it gets. Better yet, every once in a while a truly subversive, dare I say *feminist,* moment can be found among *ANTM*'s emotional and cultural wreckage. Model Anchal

Joseph, who emigrated to the United States from New Delhi when she was six years old, wore blue contacts to her cycle 7 audition. When the judges asked her why, she said she'd always wanted different colored eyes:

> TYRA: Do you think there's something culturally in America or even in your own country that is telling you that a lighter eye is prettier?*
>
> ANCHAL: In India they do believe that lighter skin and lighter eyes are prettier. I actually want to beat that. Be like, "Hey, I'm dark, I'm beautiful, and I'm Indian, so I don't have to have light skin or have light-colored eyes to be beautiful."

After Anchal's baby browns were photographed au natural, the judges said she was so gorgeous she could be Miss World. Asked how she felt looking at her picture without the contacts, she replied:

> ANCHAL: It makes me feel pretty.
>
> TYRA: It does? Why's that?
>
> ANCHAL: Because in a way I think I was hiding behind them. I'm glad. [At this, she broke down in tears of self-acceptance—and we got to watch her psychological breakthrough.]
>
> TYRA [to judge Nigel Barker]: Nigel, you being Indian, how do you respond to that?⁺
>
> NIGEL: You are beautiful the way you are. We are all unique in our own ways, and it's that uniqueness that makes people beautiful.

---

* Asking Anchal to discuss beauty standards in the United States versus those from her "own country" is typical of ANTM. The show both normalizes and others immigrants, portraying them as an unmistakable part of the beauty that is America, while constantly implying that they are less authentically American than those born here.

⁺ Close, but no cigar. Fashion photographer and *ANTM* judge Nigel Barker (who passes for white) isn't Indian, he's British and Sri Lankan. Just another instance of *Top Model* playing the all-Asians-are-alike game, as many other reality shows do.

I'll never accuse Tyra Banks of having a tenth of Toni Morrison's wisdom. Still, I was impressed by the editing of Anchal's initial longing for societal affirmation, à la *The Bluest Eye,* followed by her eventual realization that her dark skin and brown eyes simply make her more authentically stunning.

China Dolls, Dragon Ladies, and Spicy Latinas

Such moments are exceptions on *ANTM,* which, as previously discussed, set many of the templates for racial typecasting on network reality TV.

Of the 170 contestants cast by cycle 13, only five besides Anchal have been East or South Asian. The first, April Wilkner, half-Japanese and half-white, said that before she decided to model, "I never really thought about my ethnicity." *ANTM* made sure viewers could think of little else. They framed her as uncomfortable with her cultural identity, while confusing that identity by adorning her with symbols from a country unconnected to her heritage (Chinese lanterns placed on her head, a dragon painted on her chest).

Cut to the cycle 6 audition of Korean contestant Gina Choe, who said, "I think there's just not enough Asian models out there. I feel that I can break down that barrier, and I think it's my responsibility." Nice! You'd almost think the casting directors finally sought out an Asian American woman who was proud of her racial background.

Sadly, no. A moment later, she told us, "I'm not into Asian guys." From then until her elimination five weeks later, Gina was edited as if she was struggling with "an identity crisis," and stereotyped as an "exotic" fading flower who couldn't stand up for herself when attacked by her competitors. She was vilified on the show, on fan sites, and by culture critics as being a poor representative of her race for making statements such as "As a Korean person and as an American person, I'm just a little bit of both, and I don't know which one I am more of." What went unexplored was why *Top Model* thought it appropriate to make Gina feel she had to choose whether she was "more" tied to her ethnicity or her nationality—the subtext of which implies that a Korean American is not a "real" American, just as Anchal was asked about attitudes in her "own country."

Top Model has mixed and matched from various long-held stereotypes about Asian women in American movies, described in *The Asian Mystique* as including the cold and calculating "Dragon Lady" (traits assigned to ambivalent April) and the submissive "Lotus Flower . . . China Doll" (docile Gina).[2] Cycle 11 finally cast a truly proud Asian American woman . . . then promptly reduced her to the clichéd "Vixen/Sex Nymph." When we were first introduced to Sheena Sakai, a half-Japanese, half-Korean go-go dancer with a large rack and an even bigger swagger, she announced, "I'm gonna show you, America. You ain't ready for this yellow fever. One time for the Asians!" Sheena was recruited by a casting director who saw her working as a stuntwoman for the movie *Tropic Thunder*— but as is often the case on reality television, producers revealed only those details that reinforced the frame they'd chosen for her character. Since they wanted her as that season's resident "hootchie," her stunt work wasn't discussed on the show or mentioned on her CW bio. Instead, she was criticized as too sexy in every episode. Early on a judge sneered, "You look like Victoria's Secretions." Later, during a challenge in Amsterdam's red light district, where prostitutes pose in storefronts to entice customers, she was told she looked like she should be selling herself in that window, rather than modeling clothes.

Latina *Top Model* hopefuls have been consistently typecast as promiscuous sluts, "naturally" good dancers, or bursting with machisma and ready to throw down. Semifinalist Angelea didn't make cycle 12's final cut after she got into a fight and was written off as hot-tempered, "ghettofied," and easily provoked to violence.

Cycle 8 winner Jaslene "Cha Cha Diva" Gonzalez, who spoke Spanish in her CoverGirl commercial, was called "spicy" and portrayed as a cross between a "drag queen" and Carmen Miranda. High school dropout Felicia "Fo" Porter, half-Mexican and half-Black, was used to reinforce the "Latinos are lazy" trope: The unemployed model said she auditioned for the show to save herself "the busy hassle of putting your pictures out to agencies and hoping to get a call back."

Other Latina models throughout the series have been called "fiery" as a compliment and "hootchie" as an insult. Second-cycle winner Yoanna House, named one of *Latina* magazine's "It Girls," notably avoided such typecasting. Since she is fair-skinned enough to pass for white, the show chose to erase her ethnicity, playing into the standard Hollywood convention that positions Caucasians as the "default" American. Most viewers were unaware that she was half-Mexican. Instead, media outlets from NPR and *Time Out Chicago* to *International Cosmetic News* refer to Jaslene as "the first Latina" to win the series, an assumption echoed by *ANTM*'s fans.[3]

Entitled Divas and Ghetto Bitches

African Americans are pigeonholed into similar categories on *ANTM,* which introduced the Angry Black Woman to reality TV before Omarosa was a glint in the eye of *The Apprentice* producer Mark Burnett. Season 1 brought us self-indulgent, catty Camille, the Black model everyone loved to hate. By season 3, Tyra took to pretending she's not an executive producer who casts for type. She warned eventual winner "Eva the Diva" to act sweet, because "I don't want to cast another Black bitch." But of course she did cast and edit Eva as the bitch du jour—until week 8, when two white image consultants instructed her to doff the diva label by "showing your best possible manners."*

The Violent Ghetto Girl (or as one model was described, the "ghetto Black Barbie") also looms large. During her third-season tryout, low-income single mom Tiffany Richardson, who got kicked out of high school for acting like "the Devil," said she wanted to be on *ANTM* to "soften up" because "I don't want to fight no mo." Uh-oh. The semifinalists went out to a bar, where a local "skank" poured a drink over Tiffany's head. She freaked out, yelled, "Bitch poured beer on my weave!" and hurled a glass at her. Bottles started flying, and they hightailed it

---

* Lighter-skinned African American and biracial girls such as cycle 4 winner Naima Mora and second-season finalist Mercedes Yvette have often escaped this frame. In this way, the show plays to intraracial beauty hierarchies in media, advertising, and political history positing that the darker a woman's complexion, the nastier her personality. Such hierarchies continue to cause pain within communities of color.[4]

out of there. A white model condemned violence; Tiffany retorted, "That's great, Martin Luther King. But I'm with Malcolm." Violence is "all I know," she said, because "nobody ever taught me to handle my problems without fighting."

Though she was "trying to change for the better," she got sent home to "the hood" by the end of the episode, calling herself a failure. But because she *always* wants to feature "another Black bitch"—especially of the ratings-generating "ghetto" variety—Banks brought Tiffany back for the fourth season, after she'd been through anger management classes.* She made it to the seventh episode, where she couldn't read from a teleprompter, grumbled, "This is humiliating more and more each week," and was eliminated. This time, instead of calling herself a failure, she smiled, hugged the other models, and told them she'd be okay. This didn't sit well with Tyra, who prefers self-flagellation and depression from rejectees, especially when they're poor and Black. So, she took it upon herself to remind the girl of her place: "This should be serious to you!" Tiffany replied that looks can be deceiving, but she was "sick of crying about stuff that I cannot change. I'm sick of being disappointed, I'm sick of all of it." Now apparently clairvoyant, Tyra yelled that Tiffany wasn't really sick of disappointment, because if she were, "you would stand up and take control of your destiny!"

Tyra continued to criticize her "defeatist attitude" until Tiffany got choked up, saying, "I don't have a bad attitude. Maybe I am angry inside, I've been through stuff, so I'm angry, but—" But she couldn't finish, because Tyra cut her off with a neck-rolling, finger-pointing, top-of-her-lungs tirade:

> Be quiet, Tiffany! BE QUIET! STOP IT! I have never in my life yelled at a girl like this! When my mother yells like this it's because she loves me. I was

---

* Tiffany never really had a chance of winning *ANTM*, lacking the "girl next door" image demanded by program sponsors CoverGirl and *Seventeen*, which use the winner in their ads. Producers raised her hopes for nothing; they only had her return because they knew she'd be a ratings draw. She was one of the most talked-about contestants on the third season, even though she lasted only one episode. "Bitch poured beer on my weave!" became an iconic quote, repeated on hundreds of fan sites and used as a *Vanity Fair* headline.[5]

rooting for you, we were all rooting for you! How dare you! Learn something from this! When you go to bed at night, you lay there and you take responsibility for yourself, because nobody's going to take responsibility for you. You rollin' your eyes and you act like it's because you've heard it all before—you've heard it all before—you don't know where the hell I come from, you have no idea what I've been through. But I'm not a victim. I grow from it and I learn. Take responsibility for yourself!*

And with that, Tiffany was turned into *ANTM*'s symbol of the irresponsible ghetto chick who isn't willing to work hard to care for herself or her child. Such pop culture imagery builds on decades of inaccurate, scapegoating news reports dating back to the 1980s, which blamed so-called "welfare queens" (a phrase that became code for poor women of color, often young mothers) for the poverty, educational inequity, and violence that plagued their communities. According to this media mantra, these weren't systemic problems requiring institutional solutions, they simply stemmed from laziness, greed, and lack of discipline inherent among poor youth of color. (Black and Latina girls bore the added burden of being branded promiscuous and immoral, while young men of color were pathologized as "Super Predators").⁺ Tyra's hissy fit about Tiffany's supposed "victim" mental-

---

* Seems Tyra needed Tiffany's anger management course more than the model did. Faced with the privileged judge screaming in her face, Tiffany remained calm and in control. With an even voice, she told the cameras, "I'm not gonna break down for you or nobody else. You ain't did shit for me but bring me here and put me through hell." As the credits rolled, we heard her say she's glad that Tyra cares about her, and that will inspire her to be a better person. Two years later, Tiffany finally revealed her honest reaction to the incident on an *E! True Hollywood Story* exposé about *ANTM*. "Before, in all of my interviews . . . I would always tell people, 'Oh, Tyra loves me. I feel like the reason that she yelled at me was because she loved me.' That was bull. So let me tell you how I really felt. I feel like if she loved me, she wouldn't have showed it the way she showed it. Like my grandmother said, 'If you love someone, you won't humiliate them.'"

⁺ To convince the public to roll back the social safety net for the poor, 1980s and 1990s conservatives waged a war in the media against poor women. In addition to the derogatory "welfare queen" said to be "popping out babies for checks," African Americans and Latinas in particular were labeled "immoral" "brood mares," and even called "public enemy number one" by ABC's Diane Sawyer. *Newsweek* senior editor Jonathan Alter went further, insisting that "every threat to the fabric of this country—from poverty to crime to homelessness—is connected to out-of-wedlock teen pregnancy." Riddled with inaccuracies, these reports nevertheless helped turn the tide of public opinion, enabling Democratic President Bill Clinton to pass a punitive welfare reform package in 1996 that resulted in hundreds of thousands of women and children falling deeper into poverty.⁶

ity and "defeatist attitude" was a revival of that sorry script. That she issued this verbal beatdown in the name of "love"—and treated the twenty-two-year-old as "ungrateful" for the chance to be used and shamed on national television—is deeply manipulative. That *Top Model* affects viewers' perceptions of young women of color is even worse. Parroting Tyra's rhetoric, a Television Without Pity commenter wrote, "Tiff *and others like her* can't be bothered to pick up a book? Read. Learn. Get good grades . . . Tyra was right. Get off your ass Tiff and accept responsibility for yourself. Her granmama put a roof over her head and food on the table and yet Tiff can't be bothered to study and get good grades and pull herself out of poverty? Slackers disgust me" (emphasis mine).[7]

Uppity Black Girls Need Humble Pie

Faced with a strong Black woman who couldn't be shoehorned as an ignorant, angry, ghetto bitch, Tyra had only one more card to play: "Bourgie Snob." Meet Yaya DaCosta, cycle 3's Ivy League runner-up. An African Studies and International Relations student at Brown University, she spoke Portuguese and French, auditioned with her hair in braids, and intended "to represent a beauty that is Black." She was elegant, intelligent, and poised. Tyra was initially "impressed" with Yaya's education and "her Afro-centric vibe," which may be why she was one of the only girls in *ANTM*'s history to be allowed to wear her hair in a natural 'fro, saying it showed her pride as a strong Black woman.

Alas, the sisterlove was short lived. Yaya looked like a stunning "chocolate Barbarella" in photos, but Tyra said she didn't seem "modelesque" in person. "Think . . . glamour, as opposed to natural," she instructed. A white stylist was brought on to tell her that her "Earth Mother" look would turn off advertisers: "If you go into a toothpaste ad, are you gonna go in a dashiki?" she sneered. "They'll see the big hair and they'll see the African print and it's like, oh my God!" Later, during judging, the stylist disparaged her "intensity to prove your sort of Africanness . . . it's overbearing. It's just too much. It's sort of a layer on top of a layer." To her credit, the camera caught Tyra glaring, clearly pissed off.

In contrast, Yaya wasn't allowed to be upset at this obviously racist swipe.* When she protested being stereotyped and turned into "a cliché," Tyra reprimanded her for "being very defensive, and it's not attractive," and made her apologize to a kente cloth hat. During evaluation, Tyra reiterated that "Yaya brings [a] superiority, condescending attitude" that is "so ugly."

From then on, they had their frame. Through the magic of editing, Yaya's education and elegance became pretentiousness; her eloquence was characterized as showing off. She took dazzling photographs and shined on the catwalk, yet for the rest of the competition Yaya was represented as an arrogant, Blacker-than-thou snob. She was chosen as fashion designers' favorite at client meetings, yet the judges condemned her as so stuck-up and hypersensitive that "no one will want to work with you." She made it to the finale, but lost because the judges didn't consider her "likable" enough.

Viewers tend to believe that the caricatures they've seen on reality TV match (or at least resemble) participants' real-life personalities, regardless of the truth or falseness of that person's portrayal. Yaya is a case in point. The image foisted on her by *ANTM*'s producers clung to her for five years and numerous film and TV jobs later. In 2009, when *Entertainment Weekly* reported that she landed a role on ABC's *Ugly Betty*, readers said they "hate Yaya with a passion," called her "arrogant," "pretentious," and "nasty," and wrote that "she needs a big piece of humble pie!" When a smart, self-possessed African American woman is said to "need humble pie," the message is that this "uppity" Black person just doesn't know her place.[8]

Curious George, Work It Out!

Some of the above tropes, like Tyra's tirade against Tiffany, require some unpacking to realize how they connect to a long history of attacks on women of color

---

* Banks has regularly encouraged Black models to put up with blatant bigotry she herself would never stand for. For example, on an episode in Spain, a male model disparaged African American contestant Jaeda Young, saying he didn't like Black women and didn't want to kiss her in a commercial they had to film for Secret deodorant. Editing emphasized how shaken she was by his racism, which could have led to a denunciation of bias in the industry by the judges. Instead, they eliminated Jaeda for making "excuses" and having poor chemistry in her ad.

in politics and the media. But deep-seated beauty biases were all too clear in the representation of Kelle, an affluent African American gallery owner who called herself "a white girl with a really good tan." She came into the competition exuding confidence to the point of conceit, but a few weeks in Tyra's den of self-doubt changed all that.

Over numerous episodes, viewers were treated to multiple scenes in which Kelle sadly inspected herself in a mirror, pondering newly perceived flaws and telling the camera that she'd grown to believe the judges' appraisal of her. "I just see myself and I'm like, *Oh my God, I'm hideous!*" she sobbed. "I can't look at myself in the mirror anymore. . . . Every time I look in the mirror I'm crying." As one of her competitors explained, "Kelle came in this competition and she was like, 'Oh, oh, I'm beautiful!' and the judges have totally broke her!" After being told repeatedly that her face, and particularly her mouth, were not photogenic, she broke down in a fit of internalized racism. While Tyra made each girl reveal her deepest body insecurity, Kelle complained that she hated her profile. "It's like I have a protruding mouth. You know what I mean? I almost feel like I have a monkey mouth. I guess [it] can look like really, I don't know, primitive."

It's telling that the show chose to air that comment rather than leaving it on the cutting room floor with hundreds of not-ready-for-prime-time hours of tape. Yet such a statement could have been used as a teaching moment, to raise awareness of the historic dehumanization of Black women starting with imagery during slavery and progressing to contemporary ads that depict Black women as exotic, primal animals. So, did Tyra "I'm a proud, beautiful Black woman" Banks break it down for Kelle, and for the millions of young viewers who idolize the former Victoria's Secret supermodel? Did she tell Kelle to do some emotional work to reject the external messages she's gotten from a culture that tells Black women that they are low, ugly creatures? Or did she even spout one of her clichéd "Girl, your mouth is fierce!" Tyra-isms?

Fat chance. Rebuking racist imagery doesn't fly in advertiser-driven reality TV, and Banks's role as producer took precedence over any sense of social responsibility or ethnic solidarity. "We're gonna have to do some profile shots and analyze that. . . . I'd be like, 'Go, Curious George, work it out!'" *Top Model*'s diva-in-chief replied. "I'm glad you guys are so honest, you know what I mean? That's what it's about, that everybody understands that you're not perfect. And that this is a business of smoke and mirrors, and fooling people into thinking you look like something else."

Let's unpack, shall we? A Black teenager thinks she's hot until *ANTM*'s judges convince her she's an ugly ape. To make her feel better, Tyra calls her Curious George,* but assures her that with the "smoke and mirrors" of makeup, lighting, and camera angles she can "fool people" into thinking she's not so primitive after all. Kelle revealed what *ANTM* taught her in an episode titled, "The Girl Who Cries When She Looks in the Mirror":

> *I've realized what it was. It's this part of my mouth. It's like an extra layer of fat or something. So it's like a snout. . . . I was in denial about my snout. And now I know, and so it's just hard to work . . . [it makes me] very limited.*

Black Models Gone "Wild"

Here's a phrase I wish I didn't have to say: At least Tyra didn't order Kelle to wear a monkey suit.

Remember the "sexy little animals" ad *ANTM* shot for Lubriderm as soon as they arrived in Cape Town, South Africa, mentioned in chapter 2? That shoot—like Kelle's "Curious George" instruction—fits into a lengthy and shameful history of racist imagery in advertising, media, and American politics.

The depiction of African Americans as animals and/or savages dates back to preabolition newspapers and magazines, where political cartoons and crude artwork accompanied editorial copy justifying the ownership of, and denial of basic

---

* Curious George, the inquisitive monkey of children's book and PBS Kids fame, has been interpreted by literacy and culture scholars as a slave narrative. In the original story, The Man with the Big Yellow Hat kidnaps George from the African jungle and brings him to America, where he gets thrown in jail, escapes, and ends up behind bars in a zoo.[9]

human rights for, "the Negro race." At the same time, print ads sold all manner of products using such imagery to mock and dehumanize Black men, women, and children. Historically such media images functioned as visual propaganda, working to convince whites that Black people were not quite human—laying the groundwork for rationalizing slavery before abolition, segregation during Jim Crow, and contemporary proeugenics arguments.[10]

Such imagery is no longer considered appropriate in most mainstream news outlets.* But just as modern beauty advertisers discovered more sophisticated ways to package the same messages found in those early-twentieth-century Camay Soap and skin-whitening ads discussed in chapter 2, the advertising industry continues to employ these themes, especially with female subjects.

Women's bodies have borne the brunt of this vile ideology in contemporary advertising, which continues to portray Black women as provocatively clothed, snarling-mouthed animals, in jungles, deserts, and safaris. "Tame and timid? That goes against my instincts," says a Black woman smoking a Virginia Slims cigarette in skintight leopard-print pants and matching halter top. "The hunting's always good at Daffy's," reads the caption of an ad featuring a Black model crouched on a beach next to a lion, her leg tucked under her in the same position as the cat's. "Gather your ammunition (cash, check, Mastercard or Visa) and aim straight for Daffy's. It's the best hunting with the best bargains around." Are we hunting the feline, or the human? The ad draws no distinction—they're both wildcats.[11] In a September 2009 *Harper's Bazaar* spread headlined "Wild Things," supermodel Naomi Campbell skips rope with monkeys, rides an elephant and an alligator, and races a cheetah while her own spotted dress trails like a tail in the wind.⁺

Like *ANTM*'s "sexy little animals" photo shoot, Daffy's ad and *Harper's* spread tread old ground. In 1985, supermodel Iman was photographed next to a

---

* This is not to say it doesn't exist: During and after the 2008 election, media outlets such as Fox News, along with conservative news sites and blogs, circulated artwork, political cartoons, and protest imagery of President Barack Obama photoshopped as an African witch doctor with a bone through his nose, wearing a tribal headdress.[12]

⁺ According to journalist Claire Sulmers, "The black-woman-in-the-African-wild theme . . . has been in vogue since the press pegged Somalian-born model Iman as a goat herder discovered in the jungle. She was, in fact, a university graduate and the daughter of a gynecologist and a diplomat."[13]

cheetah, her head tilted in the same position as the animal, her body turned in a catlike contortion, and her hair wrapped in cheetah-print scarf. That same year, Iman stalked down a Thierry Mugler runway in safari garb with a live monkey hanging on her shoulder(!), while two buff Black men in loincloths trailed behind her carrying a giant umbrella.

Such images in advertising and fashion code women of color as "primitive," with untamed sexuality both fearful and seductive. Taken to its (il)logical conclusion, this fetishized depiction culminates in images of Black women as dangerous creatures who must be literally deprived of their freedom. Naomi Campbell's "Wild Things" pictorial was shot by world-famous fashion photographer Jean-Paul Goude. Nearly thirty years ago, Goude produced an infamous image of singer Grace Jones on all fours, naked, oiled up, and snarling inside a cage, surrounded by raw meat. Above her head, a zoolike plaque cautioned: Do Not Feed the Animal. (A similar caged photo of Jones graced the cover of Goude's 1981 book, *Jungle Fever*.) Locking her up is the only way to prevent her dangerous sexuality from overwhelming everyone in her wake, the picture suggests. This and several other now-iconic images of Jones posing behind bars, in chains, and with whips were replicated by biracial (Cape Verdian and Italian) model Amber Rose in the September 2009 issue of *Complex* magazine. As journalist Claire Sulmers notes, "Though the photos were taken decades apart, the message is the same. These women are so wild they must be caged—they're sultry, snarling sex beasts."[14]

By dressing a group of models up as "sexy" "native" creatures for a beauty ad as soon as they arrived in South Africa, *ANTM* wasn't engaging in a harmless homage to the land they were visiting. The Lubriderm photo shoot illustrates how the advertising industry's long-held racial essentialism influences the depiction of people of color in product-placement-driven reality TV.

I'm sure some may question whether the episode was actually racist, since white models were also featured as wildlife in the Lubriderm challenge. Yes, it was. The shoot built on a preestablished ad-industry precedent in which the mere *concept* of Africa and Black Africans are conjured to "represent white humans' own more primitive past," writes scholar Lisa Wade, on *Sociological Images*. Wade was describing a 2008–09 ad campaign by "Wild Africa Cream" liqueur, packaged in a leopard-print bottle with *ubuntu* beads around the neck. In the ads, a seductively clothed Black woman has grown a leopard's arm; another sports a cheetah's tail. White women and men in other ads in the series also have nonhuman features. The tagline? "Unleash your wild side." Each ad featured a smoldering male or female model, Black or white, each with a leopard's ear, hand, or arm. In an accompanying radio spot, a man speaks of following a sexy woman, wondering, "Did a leopard escape from the zoo?" while a female voice purrs that the liqueur can help everyone find "a little wild in them."[15]

Since fashion and beauty advertisers have worked with *ANTM*'s producers to build the show's content around their products (and ideas), it's no surprise that *ANTM*'s South African animals shoot shares the "Africa connects us to our animal natures" reasoning of Wild Africa Cream's marketing gambit. It's also why the show would see no problem devoting several episodes to the process of convincing a beautiful (and formerly confident) Black teenager that her "monkey" "snout" makes her ugly.

Dehumanizing African American women in advertising and media carries very real consequences for the self-esteem of Black girls and women, as well as for larger society. When an entire class of people are seen as animals, it becomes harder to prevent violence against them and easier to justify denying them equal social, economic, and political rights. If only Tyra Banks were equipped to realize the impact her programming choices can have.

Tyra Banks: Fashion Victim Turned Fashion Perpetrator

Tyra is a favorite punch line of *The Soup's* Joel McHale and *The Dish's* Danielle Fishel, who mock her increasingly cringe-worthy acting and odd insistence on inserting photos of herself into every episode. Culture analysts have wondered why a powerful Black model who seems to really want the best for young women of color would subject them to such demeaning double standards. "On camera, many of the black *ANTM* contestants talk about how thrilled they are to be in Tyra's presence; how her success as a black supermodel inspired them, helping them see themselves as beautiful for the first time," *Slate*'s J. E. Dahl writes, "but how does she repay their adoration? By trying to eradicate ethnic idiosyncrasies in their personality and appearance."[16]

Comics call her crazy, critics dismiss her as an opportunist, and her young fans fiercely defend her as the benevolent granter of young women's dreams. I have a different theory: I believe she has grown up mentally colonized by fashion and beauty advertisers, leaving her with something akin to Stockholm syndrome.*

Tyra Banks is many things. She's someone who believes she's an advocate for girls, especially girls of color. Four years before *ANTM* debuted she founded T-Zone, a summer camp program focused on self-esteem and leadership skills. Yet, she's also the ultimate capitalist beauty industry success story. She grew up without money, but used her nearly naked body, and an incredible parade of wigs, to become a media mogul. In addition to serving as host and executive producer of *ANTM,* she filled both those roles on her daytime chatfest, *The Tyra Show,* for five seasons. This helped her earn an estimated $30 million in 2009 alone, more money than any other woman on prime-time TV. Her increasing fiscal power has drawn comparisons to Oprah Winfrey, despite the intellectual chasm between them.[17]

Most of the rest of us learn to navigate the everyday struggles of adolescence—body image insecurities, emerging sexuality, interpersonal relationships, and personal identity—from our friends, family, and community, at the same time as we are influenced by the media images surrounding us. But those images, and their makers, *were* Tyra's dominant community. From age fifteen on, Banks was raised by the fashion and beauty industry and its advertisers. In loco parentis, they gave her fame and fortune beyond her wildest dreams—but

---

* Stockholm syndrome is popularly defined as a psychological condition in which kidnap or abuse victims form attachments to and identify with their captors.

always while pitting her against other women, requiring her to hide her natural hair, and reminding her that her value depended on being young and thin.*

And so the cycle continues. As a curvy Black model who achieved many firsts, Banks fought against unfair race and gender barriers throughout her career. But like so many dysfunctional patterns, Tyra grew up to become the ultimate perpetrator of the ideology of the fashion and beauty advertisers who stunted her intellectual development and shaped her self-image, psychology, and values. In that context, why is anyone surprised that she is simultaneously

- hilariously narcissistic, as well as compassionate;
- wracked with internalized racism and sexism, while renouncing the concept of discrimination; and
- concerned with girls' self-esteem, while profiting from a show that reinforces unhealthy body standards and racial stereotypes?

When she quit *The Tyra Banks Show* in 2010, she announced that her intention was to focus her Bankable Productions company on films that "can promote positive images of women."+ I don't doubt Tyra's sincerity. But as *ANTM* illustrates, victims of advertiser-based Stockholm syndrome have an extremely skewed definition of what "positive" media imagery is and what it isn't.

The truth is, the best thing Tyra could do to help "more women and young girls" to "feel as fierce as we truly are" would be to take *ANTM* off the air—or drastically remodel its format.[18]

---

* Banks quit high fashion for Victoria's Secret fame when she realized that curvy adulthood isn't welcome on couture catwalks.

+ She also signed a three-book deal to write a YA fantasy series about girls at a magic model school—sort of a *Harry Potter*-meets-*Top Model* franchize—to start being released in the summer of 2011.

Chapter Seven

Beautiful Corpses, Abusive Princes

Violence against Women as Glamorous, Romantic Reality

Picture this, for a moment: You're wandering, lost, in a foreign country. You don't speak the language, you're trying to get to a business meeting, and a random man approaches you on the street, clutches your leg, and tries to shove his hand up your skirt. Though you're traveling with an entourage, not one person makes any effort to come to your aid as you attempt to fend him off.

Now, imagine that when you finally get to your gig (having been delayed by the attempted sexual assault), your bosses berate you as irresponsible for being late, rather than offering to call the police, get you a counselor, or even give you the afternoon off to compose yourself.

Wow, what a fairytale.

This pleasant little scenario was caught on tape during the first season of *America's Next Top Model*. When Adrianne Curry—the working-class wild child eventually crowned best walking billboard of all—was accosted in France on her way to a "go-see" (fashion industry speak for a meeting with designers), the camera crew trailing her simply filmed the groper's attack rather than intervening on her behalf, making the show complicit in this attempted crime. Worse, *Top Model* chose to run the footage on-air without any critical context, never once calling the incident an assault. In fact, the entire event was never even discussed beyond one brief comment from the shaken model, who missed one of her four required go-sees because "I was really upset—I was right there by the agency, but I couldn't go in."

Yet instead of giving Adrianne any space to process the impact of being accosted—or even acknowledging that it happened at all—the show used the incident against her in a twist on classic victim-blaming: Come evaluation time, one judge after another rebuked her for being tardy, warning that they wouldn't tolerate any "excuses" for her lateness.

In the end, *Top Model* depicted attempted sexual assault as nothing more than a trivial, unremarkable annoyance. (What? Some creep tried to forcibly grab your crotch? Quit your bitching! Missing a meeting—now *that's* unacceptable.)

Such is life in reality TV, where manufactured drama reigns, but bona fide reality—like the dangerous prevalence of unwanted sexual harassment and assault—is a little too messy, a little too ugly, and a little too, well, *real* to deal with.

These Are the "Most Eligible Bachelors in America"?

Ironically, even when producers have full control over casting, the crown princes of reality TV are often no better than Adrianne's street harasser.

A veritable lineup of criminals and ex-cons have been installed as eligible bachelors on dating and mating shows. Take California criminal Ulrick Kevin White, sentenced to eight years in prison for rape and kidnapping, who was found by police only when his victim identified him after seeing him on TV . . . on an episode of *Blind Date!*[1]

At least White was caught. On the fourteenth season of MTV's *The Real World: San Diego,* which aired in 2004, a male friend of cast member Randy Barry picked up a twenty-two-year-old woman at a bar, drugged her, and brought her back to the *Real World* house. Then, while she was unconscious, the man— only IDed as "Justin" in the press—allegedly raped her in the bathroom, the only area not under surveillance. "I just hit that," Justin was overheard saying as he sauntered out of the bathroom, where the woman was found naked and passed out on the floor.[2] Though this never made it to air, the cameras were rolling when the disoriented young woman was woken up and told—with a team of videographers in her face—that she might have been raped the night before, so the victim now has that shocking, dehumanizing revelation caught on tape for posterity. Police investigated and believed the rape had indeed occurred, but Bunim/Murray Productions, creators of the show, didn't immediately cooperate with law enforcement and initially prevented them from viewing the film from the day of the rape. A search warrant was eventually obtained, but no arrest was ever made. Though the case became a headline-generating scandal in print news and the entertainment press, a month of footage from that period of time was omitted from the show, as if it never happened. Producers never addressed it on air during the series' run—which, according to Nielsen ratings, was the top-rated series on basic cable among viewers ages twelve to thirty-four, seen by approximately 3.7 million people during that TV season.[3]

The *Real World* rape controversy is by far the most egregious case of violence against women to (allegedly) take place during the filming of a reality TV show, but the genre has featured more than its share of abusive characters and sketchy situations. One classic example was *For Love or Money* stud Rob Campos, who, while presiding over a room full of romantic strivers, got drunk and demanded that his playthings line up to remove his boots for him, as if they were his personal geishas. As the first woman to do so got down on her knees facing him and tugged, she got a nasty whiff of his feet while he enjoyed peering at her cleavage down her low-cut shirt. Not content with some semifrontal, he instructed a second woman to pull his boots off backward, which entailed her bending over, taking his leg between her knees, and yanking on his heel while he positioned his other foot squarely against her ass and then kicked her. "While it was happening, I don't think anyone was really realizing that that might be a little degrading, or not a cool thing to do," the woman with the bruised behind mused to the cameras.

Um, really? 'Cause I can't think of a clearer illustration of misogyny than making women line up to be kicked in the ass. Yet NBC could have predicted such inappropriate behavior from the crass Campos: Prior to landing the part of Prince Charming, he had been booted from the Marine Corps Judge Advocate General (JAG) unit for sexually assaulting a female officer.

According to TheSmokingGun.com—which researched Marine Corps records and conducted first-person interviews with the victim and others familiar with the incident—Campos derailed his once-promising military career by getting drunk, barging into a Navy officer's room in the women's dormitory, and grabbing her breasts. He advanced on her, but the officer fought back, knocking him out with a knee to the groin and bolting out the door.* She didn't report the incident, but when word got out around the base, "she was approached and interviewed by Naval Criminal Investigative Service (NCIS) agents," who yanked him out of the JAG program. He received a formal "non-judicial punishment" from the Marines, which shipped him off to a tax-filing unit and ordered him to enroll in a substance abuse treatment program.[4]

If a small website could expose such damning information in just a couple of days, surely NBC, with their vast resources, could have uncovered Campos's dark past and ruled him out before duping fifteen women into believing he was happily-ever-after material. But *For Love or Money* didn't bother to do such rudimentary legwork because the safety of their female cast members doesn't seem to be much of a motivating factor to the people who put these programs on the air. (At the least, when you consider the technically competent visual components of these shows, producers appear to prioritize women's well-being somewhere beneath wardrobe, lighting, and the constant free-flow of liquor.)

Too bad the contestants don't seem to be in on that open secret. The women who appear on reality TV dating shows often say that they were motivated to compete for some stranger's affection because they believe that the producers are offering up leading men with spotless legal, medical, and moral pedigrees.

---

* Incidentally, if the officer Campos groped hadn't practiced self-defense, the laws of probability make it likely that a far more serious crime would have transpired, since most aggressive, drunken sexual assailants don't stop midassault unless they're physically prevented from doing so. As self-defense instructors often say, "Behind every headline about an 'attempted rape' thwarted is a woman who did something to get away."

Explaining why she thought it was safer to let ABC arrange a boyfriend for her than to meet one on her own, Heather Cranford, a second-season castoff of *The Bachelor,* told *TV Guide* that the show offered a great way to avoid the "trust issues" she'd have meeting someone in a bar: "They do the FBI background checks and the drug testing and blood tests for diseases. They also do his college transcript and credit reports—so he's screened through and through, and you know what you're getting out of this guy."[5]

Unfortunately, that's just a crock. Despite perfunctory background checks, reality TV men have often had violent histories, just like that first false prince, *Who Wants to Marry a Multi-Millionaire*'s restraining-order-tainted Rick Rockwell, who (as mentioned in this book's introduction) allegedly slapped, hit, and threw around a former girlfriend, threatened to kill her, vandalized her car, and broke into her home. In 2007, after *America's Most Smartest Model* runner-up Andre Birleanu was arrested for harassment and sexual abuse charges, it was revealed that he had served several prison terms for assault, harassment, criminal contempt, criminal mischief, and trespassing *before* being cast on the VH1 show. Did producers 51 Minds learn their lesson and employ more thorough screenings to keep dangerous criminals off future shows?[6]

Sadly, no.

Two years later, Ryan Jenkins—who had a prior assault conviction and had been charged with "battery constituting domestic violence" against model Jasmine Fiore—was a semifinalist on VH1's *Megan Wants a Millionaire*. He and Fiore got married in Vegas after Megan sent him packing. Then, three days after Jenkins picked up his check for appearing on *I Love Money,* a previously filmed 51 Minds show, Fiore's body was found mutilated and stuffed in a suitcase. Her fingers and teeth were yanked out; she could only be identified by the serial numbers on her breast implants. Jenkins was charged with Fiore's murder; he killed himself before he could be convicted. The network blamed "clerical errors" for their failure to uncover his criminal history not just once, but twice.[7]

In the weeks following this gruesome crime, numerous reporters called to ask me permutations of the same misguided question: "Had reality TV created a monster?" No, I responded, Jenkins was a monster long before he was cast on VH1. He may stand out as the most brutal, but he's just one of a long line of abusive men who have appeared on reality TV dating shows and other unscripted programs where strangers live together.

Adam Shapiro, executive producer of CBS's *Big Brother,* claims that if "somebody has restraining orders against them or has violent incidents in their background, no matter how good a candidate might be, they don't get on the show. That's something that we just don't fool around with." If only that were true. In 2001, Justin Sebik put a knife to fellow *Big Brother 2* housemate Krista Stegall's throat while kissing her and asked, "Would you get mad if I just killed you?" Six months after being kicked off the show, Sebik was arrested for attacking his girlfriend—just the most recent charge on a rap sheet that included five prior arrests for assault and theft. Stegall sued CBS for putting her in danger; the suit was settled out of court.[8]

Most of these criminal histories come to light only after trouble arises during or after a reality show. Not so with former Public Enemy hype man Flavor Flav, whose stints in prison for crack cocaine and burglary in the 1980s and '90s are hardly a well-kept secret. But few *Flavor of Love* fans likely remember that fifteen years before VH1 anointed Flav to head their twenty-first-century minstrel revival, the star was locked up for domestic violence. In 1991, he pleaded guilty to assaulting his then-girlfriend, Karen Ross, served thirty days in jail, and lost custody of his kids. Or that in 1993, he spent another ninety days in jail for shooting at his neighbor; more domestic violence charges followed. None of this bothered Cris Abrego and Mark Cronin, creators and executive producers of *The Surreal Life* and *Flavor of Love,* who discovered Flav for VH1 less than a year after his last stint at Rikers Island. "We knew he had a history," Cronin told *Entertainment Weekly.* "It's almost expected when you've gotten to be an elder statesman of rock or hip-hop. There's not a lot of clean living in music. The requirement for us is that you be in a positive place in your life." (Translation from the original Producer Speak: If you can bring profits for our production company, our network partners, and their advertisers, you're in a "positive place in your life." We don't care that you're prone to beating your romantic partners, or that you've been in and out of prison for violent assault—we'll give you your own dating show anyway. *What could go wrong?* Besides, "clean living"—not beating women, not doing time—isn't big with "elder statesmen of hip-hop." Come on, you expect us to find a Black man who hasn't done any of those things? You think we're Houdini or something?)[9]

Nothing as dramatic can be found in the past of *Age of Love* star Mark Philippoussis, a thirty-year-old tennis champ who set up the show's smarmy "cougars versus kittens" premise by confessing that he's only attracted to younger women and that his last serious girlfriend was just twenty years old. What he didn't mention on air was that, as show host Mark Consuelos told *TV Guide,* Philippoussis was not long before engaged to an eighteen-year-old.[10] It's pretty easy to do *that* math: Unless he met, began dating, and proposed to this girl all in the same year, NBC's legal department either made some very charitable assumptions about their chastity until she turned eighteen . . . or they simply were willing to overlook that the guy they described as "the most eligible bachelor in America"[11] could have been brought up on statutory rape charges in many states for having sex with a minor.*

Standards for entry into reality casts are so low because background checks aren't intended to ensure contestants' safety. Instead, they're conducted primarily to absolve producers and networks of legal liability. If they throw a few bucks at

---

* Let me be clear here: I'm not accusing Mark Philippoussis of rape. Nor am I saying that a sixteen- or seventeen-year-old girl doesn't have the right to consent to sex—while I believe every act of forcible or coercive sex should be treated as criminal abuse, I find statutory rape laws extremely problematic when applied as an attempt to police teen girls' consensual sexual behavior. But my own beliefs are not the point—in many states, an adult in his late twenties who has sex with a minor under any circumstances is considered guilty of statutory rape. Considering these legal realities, NBC's show runners had fertile ground to at least investigate the potentially thorny implications of their star's relationship history before calling him a prince among men. Yet there's no indication that this question was ever even considered by anyone associated with *Age of Love.*[12]

some less-than-thorough security firm to screen potential participants, they'll be less likely to be held financially accountable if the next version of Ryan Jenkins doesn't wait until he's kicked off a dating show to kill someone. In fact, casting directors often seek out participants who are prone to violence—including alcoholics, drug addicts, and emotionally unstable people—the better to ensure fights, tears, and that oh-so-important "drama." One anonymous producer admitted as much to *Entertainment Weekly:* "The fact is, those shows work only because of the irresponsible casting. If you force people to cast upstanding citizens without criminal records, you're not going to get the same show."[13]

Liposuction and Silicone as Antiviolence Building Blocks

Still, despite the presence of batterers, rapists, and sexual assault perps on shows like *Who Wants to Marry a Multi-Millionaire? Blind Date,* and *For Love or Money,* actual on-air violence has been rare (24-7 video surveillance makes people a bit less likely to act out felonious instincts on camera, after all). Yet even when acts of physical abuse *do* make it to the screen, they're not treated as seriously inappropriate—they're simply used as a promotional device. At least Campos lost his prestigious JAG job and got forced into rehab when he groped a woman against her will on a military base. In contrast, NBC didn't dethrone the former Marine as head-of-harem after his inebriated ass-kicking incident; instead, they hyped his beer-fueled buffoonery in tune-in-next-week teaser ads tinged with a salacious, "you won't *believe* this boys-will-be-boys moment!" tone.

It's not just dating shows that trivialize abuse of women as a ploy for ratings: *America's Next Top Model* regularly plumbs contestants' sad stories of incest, rape, and even female genital mutilation as a cheap ploy to induce those all-important tears they promise to deliver each episode. Perhaps the single most vulgar example of women's real life trauma being exploited for ratings appeared on Fox's depressing cosmetic surgery/beauty pageant series *The Swan,* which introduced us to one contestant, a domestic violence survivor, via this video confessional:

My name is Belinda. I'm twenty-eight years old. I used to have the perfect
body, and I used to be pretty, and I used to be able to walk down the street
and have guys chasing me. And not having that now, it makes me feel horrible.
Growing up I was so tall and so skinny, I heard from everybody, "You should be
a model." And so I thought, well I'll try it—and it was great and I loved it. And
unfortunately I ended up with the wrong guy. I've been married two times. I
wouldn't want to talk to any of the men in my past, because they're not good
people. I just kind of ended up in several abusive relationships. Alcoholics,
drug users, something along those lines. My dream for myself is to learn to
know that I deserve someone to treat me good.

Anyone with a remedial knowledge of domestic violence could have
inferred that Belinda might have been vulnerable to abusive relationships
because she seems to measure her self-worth entirely by her physical measurements and by external male validation via possessive behavior such as street
harassment. Defined by Holla Back NYC as "a form of sexual harassment that
takes place in public spaces," street harassment functions from and reinforces
"a power dynamic that constantly reminds historically subordinated groups
(women and LGBTQ folks, for example) of their vulnerability to assault in
public spaces. Further, it reinforces the ubiquitous sexual objectification of
these groups in everyday life."[14]

After such a meaty introduction, did the show's team of "medical
experts"—including one described on air as "life coach" Nely Galán and another
as therapist Dr. Lynn Ianni—discuss specific ways they might probe the psychology that led Belinda into a series of hazardous relationships or, hopefully, reorient
her thinking in ways that might help her develop a healthier sense of self? Fat
chance, considering that *The Swan*'s supposed dynamic duo of mental health
were not qualified to counsel anyone about anything. As discussed in chapter
2, Galán was actually the series creator and executive producer, *not* a life coach,
while the "doctor" got her degree from an unaccredited diploma mill. Instead,

show host Amanda Byram posed this question to Galán, Ianni, and a gaggle of plastic surgeons: "She reminisces about having the guys chase her. Do you think we can have the guys chasing her up the street again?" The reply came unanimously, without a hint of irony: "Absolutely!"

Yet periodically throughout the hour, Byram repeatedly promised that *The Swan* would also help Belinda "break the cycle of violence," "leav[e] her past behind," and "break her cycle of abusive relationships." How would they make good on this high-minded pledge? By putting her on a twelve-hundred-calorie-per-day diet and giving her, as Byram rattled off in rapid succession: a brow lift, a midface lift, fat transfer to her lips, lower eye and cheek fat removal, several visits to a dermatologist, Lasik eye surgery, breast reduction and lift, liposuction in six different areas, dental procedures including zoom bleaching, a bridge for her front teeth, da Vinci Veneers (™), gum tissue recontouring, cleaning, and a root canal, all of which the show's panel of "experts" claimed she "needed" to feel better about herself.

Tagged on at the end of this ludicrously long litany of plastic surgery, almost as an afterthought, Byram added, "she will also undergo weekly therapy and coaching to improve her sense of self-worth and end her cycle of abusive relationships."

The sum total viewers saw of any of this "counseling"? Over the course of the hour—in between numerous disparaging discussions about her appearance and several lengthy, explicit shots of Belinda going under the knife—viewers were treated to just one forty-five-second segment in which Galán sends Belinda to a gym to kickbox a punching bag plastered with photos of "all these men that have done you wrong," and a seven-second snippet of Belinda telling "Dr." Ianni that "I've been slapped, punched, kicked, and I'm ready to meet a decent, loving, caring man," with the faux therapist telling her to end the sentence with the phrase, "And I deserve it."

So, to recap: A battered woman tells *The Swan*'s producers that her "dream for myself is to learn to know that I deserve someone to treat me good" and that *"the main thing I want to fix* is my inability to pick a decent man. I always end up with men who are abusive and mean and wrong, and I don't want to be in that situation again," and they respond by informing her that she's not feminine enough and that "she needs" a complete cosmetic overhaul to "correct" her many physical flaws and get men to chase her down the street again. (Verbal abuse and possible stalking by strangers, good. Physical abuse by loved ones, bad. Got it. Check.) According to reality TV, twenty surgical and dental procedures, seven seconds of "therapy," and a role-playing exercise that would be far more useful for aerobic health than mental health are all that's necessary to "break the cycle of violence." Too bad the show itself reinforces it.

"Slap-Happy" Plot Devices

When violence against women isn't being pumped for ratings-generating pathos, it's being played for laughs. One of the most talked-about episodes in the history of MTV's long-running *The Real World* franchise involved a male housemate from 1998's Seattle season slapping a young woman in the face. The scene has been shown in numerous slo-mo "Let's see that again!" highlight reels and clip shows, coming in at number nine on VH1's two-hour special, "40 Greatest Reality TV Moments." In response, rather than raising concerns about the cultural implications of such scenes, the corporate entertainment press treats moments like these as a source of endless amusement, as when this "bitch-slap" (so named by VH1) landed the number two spot in an *Entertainment Weekly* article listing the "5 BEST REALITY MOMENTS" ever for providing "the ultimate Starbucks spit take." *EW*'s caption? "A very slap-happy 'Real World.'"[15]

Because, clearly, hitting women is a laugh riot.

The slapping scene was tops among thousands of hours of reality television, *EW* explained, because it showed "What happens when people stop being polite and start being real." And so corporate media that follow, feed on, and fuel pop culture (from bottom-feeder VH1 clip shows to the often-critical *EW*) are complicit in perpetuating the notion that violence against women is not only the stuff "good TV" is made of, but the kind of supposedly amusing behavior women and men should just consider normal in day-to-day life, unless they're stuffy, uptight, and too "polite" for the "real world."

Eleven years later MTV was still milking laughs from violence against women, but this time with more than a slap. When the network was launching its first season of *Jersey Shore*—marketed as a cross between *The Hills* and *"Flavor of Love* for Italians"—they released a promo clip of some drunk dude with a boxer's arm punching a woman nicknamed Snookie in the face so hard that her head flew back several feet. The scene of this "guidette" getting viciously cold-cocked quickly went viral, with replays on popular entertainment news sites and thousands of YouTube page views. Bloggers anticipated the full episode would "go down as one of the greatest moments in the history of television," replaying looped video of the sucker punch on pages headlined, "The Countdown to Snookie Getting Punched in the Face Is On!"[16] After the clip had done its buzz-generating job, MTV announced plans to pull the scene, feigning concern that the violence was taken "out of context" online. Conveniently, they failed to acknowledge that they chose to release the contextless clip to get people talking about the new series. Compounding the exploitation, syndicated infotainment programs such as *The Insider* reported on MTV's decision not to air the assault—by running footage of the punch five times in an eighteen-second segment.[17]

Where these sorts of "slap-happy" moments appear infrequently, abusive language is ever present. In classic fairytales, heroines are mistreated by wicked stepmothers and evil stepsisters, but in reality TV, would-be princesses are regularly degraded by none other than the handsome prince himself, who can usually be counted on to use a regular stream of gendered slurs like "bitch," "slut," "ho," "whore," and "feminazi" to describe the women around him. Additionally, run-of-the-mill insults like "vindictive," "stupid," "insane," "psycho," "gold digger," and "loser" are hurled at female participants so often on these shows—by men and women alike—that they start to blend into the vernacular background, as if treating women with this level of disrespect is just a normal part of everyday speech. Crude appraisals from Mr. Right are common: Viewers tune in specifically to hear Flavor Flav call women "sexy items" and yell "I want them asses shaking!" during booty-dance-offs. But even one of the "nice guys" on NBC's *Average Joe* called the supermodel he was wooing a "beaver" behind her back. ("I did use a word describing Larissa: It starts with a B, ends with an R, it's an animal that builds dams, and there's a show, *Leave It to*—It's a slang term meaning a very beautiful, hot, sexy girl.")* Way to class up the joint.

When behavioral and verbal abuse isn't offered up by the bachelors themselves, producers turn to one of their favorite tools—humiliation—to keep women in their place, with scenarios carefully crafted to make them feel like crap—quite literally. For example, *Joe Millionaire*'s concubines were instructed to dress up for a glamorous, elegant date only to arrive at a horse farm, where they learned that they were expected to muck out shit-filled stables in their fancy duds before they could "earn" the privilege of going riding with Liar McFakebucks. Meanwhile, the object of their questionable affections was mocking their discomfort in one of those ubiquitous confessionals to the camera. Similar scenes have become a staple. During a "stinky barn challenge" on VH1's *Real Chance of Love,* brothers Ahmad and Kamal Givens laugh from a sweet-smelling distance as the women scramble to clean up horse, sheep, pig, and goose droppings . . . which was only moderately less disgusting than the episode of the CW's *Farmer Wants a Wife* in which "big city girls" have to prove themselves worthy of dating a hunky country boy by sticking their arms up a cow's ass to check whether it was pregnant. (Quick, someone call PETA!)

Sometimes humiliation takes the form of complete subjugation of female identity. On *Flavor of Love,* identical twins Trisha and Tresha were only referred to by Flav, by other daters, *and even by themselves* as "Thing 1" and "Thing 2." Pioneered on *Flavor of Love,* it is now standard practice for women on many cable dating shows to have their real names replaced with infantilized or sexualized nicknames assigned to them by men.

---

* Actually, that's not what "beaver" means . . . but a proper grasp of vocabulary is the least of this guy's problems, so let's not quibble.

Beyond the threat posed to female contestants' safety by producers' lack of real scrutiny into their male stars' violent histories, the dangerous messages being sent to the viewing public are even more significant. By presenting an array of physically, verbally, and emotionally abusive men as the "princes" that "all girls dream of"—and by presenting women as only lovable if they are willing to give up their identities and their ability to make self-defined choices—reality television is reinforcing dangerous power dynamics that lie at the heart of violent relationships. This genre is telling women that as long as a guy is rich enough or hot enough, we should simply overlook it if he knocks us around a little, puts us down, treats us like dirt. Meanwhile male viewers, young and old, are learning that they can get away with this kind of behavior—that women will even consider it a turn-on—as long as they can bring enough bling to a relationship. No one wins when men and women are defined in such debasing ways.

It's tempting to dismiss this as "just television," just escapist farce; tempting to believe that this sort of storytelling has no impact. But that's not so easy in a country in which a woman is battered every fifteen seconds, usually by her intimate partner, and an average of three women are murdered by their husbands or boyfriends every day. According to the Department of Justice's National Crime Victimization Survey, someone is sexually assaulted in America every two minutes—that's 272,350 sexual assaults per year, a figure that doesn't even include victims who are twelve years old or younger (meaning the numbers become even more extreme when child molestation and incest are taken into account). Three-quarters of these attacks are committed by intimate partners, relatives, friends, or acquaintances.[18] As harsh as these sorts of statistics are, they only begin to paint the picture of what the reality of violence against women and girls looks like in the United States, the consequences of which never make it into the sanitized, advertiser-defined version of reality promoted by the shows discussed in this book.

Media images don't directly cause this violence, but they certainly contribute to a culture that promotes it. Which, in turn, helps to maintain the kind of gender-based power differentials that allow such abuse to thrive. By glossing over, tacitly accepting, and sometimes even mocking verbal and physical violence and humiliation of women by men who claim to care about them—and doing so in the name of "reality"—this genre attempts to inure viewers to the impact and even the existence of *real* violence against women and girls, and to make the results of such violence seem less extreme, less damaging, and less objectionable than they really are.

In the late 1970s and through the 1980s, influenced by the women's movement and by new ways of understanding gendered violence and abuses of power within intimate relationships, Hollywood began to produce provocative, engaging programming that entertained viewers while still challenging them to question their preconceived beliefs about date rape, sexual harassment, spousal abuse, and more. It's not like the television landscape of twenty and thirty years ago was a bastion of feminist ideology (not by a long shot, with female characters falling in love with their rapists on soap operas like *General Hospital*). But at least when these issues came up on "very special episodes" of sitcoms like *All in the Family, The Facts of Life, Diff'rent Strokes,* and *Good Times,* or in made-for-TV movies like *The Burning Bed,* they weren't presented as a joke. Victims weren't generally mocked, and degrading conduct didn't tend to be explicitly condoned. The idea (well-intentioned though perhaps a bit naive) was that if popular media raised awareness about the nature of violence and treated these issues with the seriousness they deserved, entertainment could help our culture progress to a point where we might see a dramatic drop in the prevalence of rape and domestic violence and an end to the gender inequity such abuse perpetuates.

In contrast, reality TV is conditioning contemporary viewers to tolerate destructive language, manipulative situations, and actual physical abuse in their own relationships, even to consider this kind of treatment romantic. Responsible media representations—especially programming that claims to be about real people's actual experiences—would lead us to perceive these kinds of behaviors as inappropriate, sometimes even criminal conduct to be rejected and rebelled against. Instead, too often, reality TV romances subtly reinforce some of our culture's darkest (and, one would hope, most outdated) notions of love, in which male partners can mistreat women's bodies, minds, and hearts with impunity, while women are expected to shut up and take it, even beg for it.

"House of Pain"

Of course, since shows like *The Bachelor, Joe Millionaire,* and *Who Wants to Marry My Dad?* are built around "happily ever after" mythology, producers can't risk openly interrupting their fairytale narratives by *explicitly* telling women to expect physical, verbal, or emotional violence from the men who claim to love them. Instead, they sell that message through subtext and implication. In scene after scene and series after series, dating, mating, and marriage shows subtly reinforce regressive stereotypes about the dreck women should accept by presenting abusive language and behavior as normal, inoffensive, even loving.

Where do these implicit messages become explicit? For *overt* glorification of these same concepts, just flip your remote to beauty-based and product-placement-driven modeling shows, whose imagery and ideology are about as subtle as a 1970s slasher flick. And sometimes just as gory.

Of the hundreds of reality shows to litter our celluloid wasteland since *Who Wants to Marry a Multi-Millionaire?* and *Survivor*'s debuts sparked a new genre in 2000, one series stands out among the throng as the ultimate in wish-fulfillment television for the fashion and beauty industry: *America's Next Top Model.*

For decades, the advertising industry's deep hostility toward women has manifested in a fetishization of images of beautifully bruised, beaten, raped, drugged, amputated, and murdered femmes. But until *ANTM* debuted in 2003, beauty and clothing companies had to rely on thirty-second broadcast spots and static print ads to beseech us to buy the mascara running down the bruised, tear-stained cheeks of models made up to resemble battered women in cosmetics and perfume commercials; sigh over the stilettos worn by women dangling heel-first from nooses or hanging out of the back of a car trunk as a man with a shovel digs a grave nearby in ads for Foot Petals and Jimmy Choo shoes; and covet the couture adorning lovely lasses locked in cages, glass-eyed victims of gang-rape, and corpselike waifs in death-themed fashion spreads for designers like Bebe, Dolce & Gabbana, and Marc Jacobs.[19]

The arrival of *America's Next Top Model* has been a game changer, spawning numerous copycat modeling- and makeover-themed shows, from Bravo's *Make Me a Supermodel,* Oxygen's *The Janice Dickinson Modeling Agency,* and VH1's *America's Most Smartest Model* to ABC's *Extreme Makeover* and Fox's *The Swan.* Now, beauty and fashion advertisers are able to work with reality producers to weave violent images—and the hateful beliefs that lie beneath them—into not only a TV show's initial premise but also numerous episodes' competitions, prizes, plot points, and dialogue plugs. In the case of *Top Model,* that's meant one full hour of advertiser-crafted TV content per week, thirteen episodes per season (except for seasons 1, 2, and 14, which filmed nine, eleven, and twelve episodes respectively), for fourteen seasons and counting as of the spring of 2010—meaning that by the time this book went to press, fashion and beauty advertisers were presented with approximately 175 hours of prime-time network programming to play with . . . not to mention ad nauseam reruns on cable, where channels such as Oxygen regularly run "Top Model Obsessed" marathons. (And that's just within the United States; thanks to corporate media imperialism, the series has spun off more than forty international versions—and generated more than ninety seasons—in Spain, Italy, France, and even such unlikely fashion outposts as Afghanistan, Kazakhstan, and Croatia.) Networks rake in record ratings among the eighteen- to thirty-four-year-old viewers beauty and fashion advertisers covet.[20] The biggest win for marketers? These hundreds of brand-rich programming hours can get to us on a deeper level than traditional ads, because most viewers are unaware that their favorite reality shows are simply series-long infomercials, repackaged in the name of "reality."

For seven years and counting, *America's Next Top Model*'s infomercials have hyped an industry that has long gotten rich promulgating the kinds of "sexy torture" ads discussed above, making it a perfect case study of the way violent imagery plays out in the reality TV landscape. Where *ANTM* was quick to gloss over an actually unscripted (read: impossible to control) attempt at violence by Adrianne's street harasser during the show's first season,* the series has pioneered a whole new standard of placing women in danger, sometimes imaginary and sometimes all too real.

Sadism has been a recurring theme. Right from the get-go, *ANTM*'s producers began manufacturing moments that would inevitably result in pain or injury to the girls. In May 2003, when "unscripted programming" still seemed like a bad phase networks would grow out of, the very first episode of *Top Model* featured an extended scene in which ten uncomfortable young women were forced to get Brazilian bikini waxes. Cameras flitted back and forth from their pained facial expressions to their nearly nude legs spread wide in the air, while the audio lingered at length on the models' blood-curdling screams as hot wax was spread over their genitals and their pubic hair was ripped off.

As the series progressed, pain became not only a by-product but a basis upon which the girls were judged, in contests requiring the women to repeatedly fall from platforms and crash onto barely padded surfaces, recline in bikinis on ice sculptures in frigid rooms, and so on. In one particularly nasty sixth-cycle challenge, models were made to strut around in impossibly difficult ten-inch heels, while the judges mocked them as they twisted their ankles, grimaced in pain, and fell down. Their biggest belly laugh was reserved for a model named Danielle Evans, whose shoes sent her tumbling to the floor and literally crawling off set, gasping, "Ow! Ow! Ow! Ow!" She ended up with a sprained toe and had to finish the episode on crutches. As luck would have it, Dani's was the only injury, and no one broke any bones that night.

Speaking of luck, *ANTM* aspirants had better have it in spades. If fourteen seasons' worth of footage of models being treated by medics or rushed to hospitals in ambulances tells us anything, it's that luck is all these girls can count on

---

* My sense is that the producers' real problem wasn't with Mr. Grabby's actions, it was simply that he wasn't part of their planned story arc.

to protect their safety on a show that plays fast and loose with women's health and well-being. By cycle 7, four seriously skinny finalists were made to pose for an extended amount of time in a pool filled with freezing water. With the models having next to zero body fat for insulation, viewers got to voyeuristically peer at close-ups of their shivering lips, shaking limbs, and chattering teeth as they winced through the photo shoot. When one shuddering contestant complained about the extreme temperature, judge and series creator Tyra Banks taunted her: "CariDee, you're from Fargo! Come on! This is real, real modeling, guys, being cold as heck!" We watched her beg for a short break as the cameras zoomed in on the moment her body began to shut down, convulsing from the cold, the color draining out of her face despite all the CoverGirl products slathered on her cheeks and mouth. Next thing we knew, the Fargo native was huddled under a blanket and judge Jay Manuel was assuring the cameras that she, not the show, had irresponsibly endangered her own health: "As a model, you need to tell people when you're past your limit. It wasn't just that she was cold; it wasn't just that her teeth were chattering. She had reached the moment of hypothermia," he groused.

Then, maybe as a sop to the network's lawyers, *Top Model*'s executive producer attempted to cover her ass. Having previously ignored CariDee's complaints and egged her on even while she was visibly quaking, Tyra reproached her with faux concern: "You have to listen to your body, and you have to tell us, okay? Because all we know is go-go-go-go-go, go-go-go-go-go, but you have to tell us no." Yet come evaluation time *Top Model* flipped that script to play the other side of the victim blame game. Just like the judges scolded Adrianne after she was grabbed by a stranger on the street, CariDee's hypothermia was framed as self-indulgence, rather than as a natural biological response to extreme physical conditions unnecessarily imposed on her by drama-seeking producers. (The pool couldn't have been heated? Set dressers or show techs couldn't have found a few heat lamps? Come on.) The hypothermic hottie was "high maintenance" and "needs a lot of attention," judge Nigel Barker griped, while fellow judge J. Alexander sniped, "With CariDee it's all about me, me, me, me, me, me, me."

After pushing this underweight beauty's body past its breaking point and then telling her it was her fault for not quitting sooner, Tyra Queen-of-the-Mixed-Message Banks banished her to the dreaded "bottom two" as punishment for "her weakness" in the pool. The model narrowly escaped elimination; viewers couldn't escape the message that women in pain bring it on themselves.[21]

When *Top Model* producers aren't making sadistic sport of *literally* hurting women, they're concocting photo shoot challenges in which pain is supposed to be the models' motivation, terror and violence the backstory, and the image of a woman in jeopardy an advertiser's ultimate "money shot."

In an episode titled "House of Pain," Mama Tyra offered cycle 10 contenders this bit of wisdom she picked up after decades as an advertiser's muse: "The biggest modeling secret trick/tip that you can get," she told the girls, is to "pose with pain . . . when you're stuck and you don't know what to do and [a photographer] is yelling at you . . . think pain, but beauty."

Sure, because as anyone who's ever thumbed through *Vogue* is supposed to believe, the more agony a woman's in, the more attractive she is.

To demonstrate how stunning suffering can be, Victoria's Secret's former meal ticket led a little tutorial, clutching at various parts of her body and moaning, "Ow! It hurts so bad! It hurts so bad!" Then came a pain-themed "pose-off," with Tyra instructing each model to embody a different variety of physical anguish: menstrual cramps, migraine, chest pain, sprained ankle, fingers slammed in a door, and even, for a contestant named Claire, an ache that came with this helpful backstory: "You did a movie and you had to do a scene with a man who strangled you, and your neck hurts."

But pain isn't women's only route to beauty: According to *Top Model,* fear is fierce, too. "You're scared! Something's chasing you! Something's coming to get you!" judge Jay Manuel coaches the models in cycle 5, who had to play "fashion victims" fleeing from some threatening force that would later be digitally inserted into their pictures. "You can't believe this is happening to you! . . . You're running for your life!" Echoing every creepy cultural equation of female beauty with helplessness and danger, Manuel repeatedly reminded the girls of their primary goal: to look "scared and pretty . . . pretty, but still scared." Tyra offered that same phrase—"You're scared but still pretty. That's hard to do!"—to model Jayla Rubinelli as her highest mark of praise during that week's judging. On another episode, Tyra told cycle 11 winner Brittany "McKey" Sullivan that her "signature pose" should be to look like "the girl that's getting punched."

"Death Becomes You, Young Lady"

Like many high-fashion advertising spreads, *ANTM*'s many seasons have unfolded like a serialized thriller, with women's (symbolic) pain and fear leading to their abuse, torture, and eventually, their death. So it came as no surprise when a cycle 4 photo shoot involved lowering the models into coffins at the bottom of a shallow grave in a cemetery, while various onlookers gushed about how hot they looked in their caskets. Guest photographer Johann Wolf wasn't immediately impressed, though. When one of the judges asked him if he thought the models were pretty, the shutterbug replied, "Well, they all look too alive."

That wouldn't be a problem by the show's eighth season, when *Top Model*— taking their cues from the likes of Jimmy Choo and Marc Jacobs—did their best to convince viewers that there ain't nothin' hotter than a dead girl.

That was the takeaway message of what I like to call the "beautiful corpses" episode, which featured ten posers as the mutilated, mangled, and murdered epitome of beauty. Ordered to convey the most convincing corpses in a "crime scene victims" photo shoot challenge, the lithe lot of 'em were arrayed in awkward, broken poses, splayed out in cold concrete corridors, their bloody, lifeless limbs positioned provocatively, *just so,* at the bottom of staircases, bathtubs, and back alleys, mimicking their demise via stabbing, shooting, electrocution, drowning, poisoning, strangulation, decapitation, and organ theft(!), while following stage direction such as "It looks like you're taking a nap. We need it to look like you were brutally killed."

For their attempts to look fatally attractive in skimpy undies and ripped cocktail dresses, the girls were rewarded by rave reviews from the judges: "Gorgeous!" "Amazing!" "Absolutely beautiful!" they gushed. My favorite accolade of the episode? "Death becomes you, young lady!"

Top Model's pretty-as-a-picture crime-scene challenge epitomized the worst of an insidious advertising trend that, ahem, just won't die. But this episode was especially ugly even for a series that traffics in bottom-feeder humiliation, objectification, and degradation of women in the name of fashion, fun, and beauty for the deep profit of integrated marketers such as CoverGirl cosmetics, *Seventeen* magazine, and Wal-Mart. At last, producer Tyra Banks's disinguous claim to care deeply about girls' empowerment was exposed as crassly as the lacy lingerie adorning the dead sexpots. The necrophiliac shoot laid bare *Top Model*'s blatant nexus of ad industry misogyny and corporate media's pursuit of the almighty dollar.

ANTM and its many copycats have created a reality subgenre that allows advertisers to advance their backward notions in 3-D, with dangerous ramifications for girls and women. I'm certainly not the first to contend that images like this help to desensitize viewers to violence against women. Media critics such as pioneering advertising theorist Jean Kilbourne (in books such as *Can't Buy My Love: How Advertising Changes the Way We Think and Feel* and films such as the influential Killing Us Softly series) have long argued that ad imagery equating gruesome violence against women with beauty and glamour works to dehumanize women, making such acts in real life appear not only more palatable and less shocking, but even aspirational. In our media-saturated culture, thong underwear and "Slut!"-emblazoned T-shirts are marketed to eleven-year-olds, and photos of women with puffy, black eyes for that "just-punched" look are used to sell everything from shoes to sports cars. Media and advertising combine to teach girls that they will be valued, desired, loved, and successful only if they enact a commercialized, often traumatized, version of beauty. And if that ideal du jour happens to be grossly violent? Well, then violence must not be so ugly after all.

But where entire academic departments and social science research teams are now devoted to deconstructing the glorification of violence against women in print ads and TV commercials, so far reality TV has mostly escaped this kind of intellectual rigor and sociological scrutiny.[22] Scholars and analysts (not to mention parents, responsible journalists, ethical media-makers, and anyone who might appreciate living in a more humane society) should pay closer attention. Unlike traditional ads, whose commercial and ideological implications many of us now have the tools to consciously consider and resist, the glammed-up depictions of violence against women shilled within this TV genre are presented in the name of reality—as if actual women experience physical and psychological abuse as sexy, as a means toward power, and suffer no ill effects from the pain and violence represented by these images.

Substantive media literacy education can help us to counter or complicate these insidious messages as we develop our own self-perceptions. But without the tools needed to critically unpack these representations, any image labeled "beautiful"—regardless of the context or cost—can become positioned as something for girls and women to emulate (and, perhaps more frighteningly) for boys and men to desire.

During media literacy workshops I've facilitated about reality TV with high school and college students since *The Bachelor* first began passing out roses, I have observed the deep level of identification many younger viewers attach to shows like *America's Next Top Model*. This personalization became evident when a critique of the "beautiful corpses" episode on WIMN's Voices, the media-monitoring group blog of Women In Media & News[23] prompted scores of impassionate comments, many from girls like fifteen-year-old Katarina, who vehemently defended the show's presentation of bloody, beaten, bruised, and broken babes. "I don't quite understand why so many people are finding this photo shoot inappropriate or appalling," Katarina wrote. The "crime scene victims" challenge

> *isn't a big deal, and I will continue to watch ANTM, a show that empowers women and gives aspiring models a chance at their dream and young teenage girls the notion that they too can achieve their goals . . . I fully support the*

show, and, unfortunately I do find seeing all these pretty girls taking beautiful

photographs very entertaining.

Unfortunately, indeed. After decades of feminist activism, girls and women are still being told that their primary access point to power is through their bodies, and that the amount of power they can wield will be directly proportional to how much they weigh, how much of themselves they're willing to wax, how Western they look, how provocatively they can preen and pose. So deeply do some girls buy into *Top Model*'s false promise of fame, fortune, and mass adulation—so profoundly do they fantasize that they are the girls being feted as fiercely, fabulously, powerfully beautiful—that Katarina and several of her peers interpret criticism of the show's content and thematic messages as a direct, personal attack on themselves and on young women everywhere. "This 'dead model' photo shoot is not spreading any negative images . . . [and] the show does not affect my decisions or opinions about . . . topics such as self-confidence" Katarina insisted, because "teenage girls also aren't impressionable/stupid enough" to be impacted by these sorts of representations of women on television. Other teens who commented on the blog agreed. Mandoline, a seventeen-year-old who said she watched ANTM after coming home from fencing practice, assured us that "a TV show has very little effect on my identity as a strong confident person/ girl/woman/whatever," while sixteen-year-old Veronica accused our blog of "fully underestimating young girls. We're not as ignorant as you seem to think we are" because we ascribed political and cultural relevance to *Top Model*'s beautiful corpses spread. "It's entertainment, people. It does not affect me."

And isn't that, to some degree, what we all think? As an intelligent and competent person, you probably feel similarly unaffected by advertising and television, don't you?

That's how advertisers want you to feel. Advertising banks on the idea that we (all of us, not just youth) believe we are not affected by the images we see in ads—and now, so does the product-placement-generated reality TV genre that has resulted in hour-long commercials masquerading as entertainment programming. The smarter we are and the less we think marketing affects us, the less likely we are to bring an active critical lens to the images they're spending more than $200 billion annually to create—and the easier it becomes for advertisers to break down our defenses and weave their messages into our psyches. Plainly put, advertising doesn't work *despite* our belief that we are above it—it works precisely *because* of that belief. As Jean Kilbourne writes in *Can't Buy My Love: How Advertising Changes the Way We Think and Feel*:

> In spite of the fact that we are surrounded by more advertising than ever before, most of us still ridicule the idea that we might be personally influenced by it. The ridicule is often simplistic. The argument essentially is: "I'm no robot marching down to the store to do advertising's bidding and therefore advertising doesn't affect me at all." . . . Of course, most of us feel far superior to the kind of person who would be affected by advertising. We are not influenced, after all.[24]

Playing on this belief allows advertisers to then "co-opt our cynicism and our irony just as they have co-opted our rock music, our revolutions and movements for liberation, and our concern for the environment," Kilbourne argues.[25] So, as it turns out, the very girls going to the mat defending *Top Model*'s sexy dead spread in online chat rooms and sorority houses because they believe the show has zero impact on them are, by nature, among the viewers most vulnerable to internalizing the dangerous ideology the show is selling alongside their many plugs for CoverGirl Long Lash Mascara or the latest $200 pair of La Perla panties.

The persuasive art of marketing works on a subconscious level—and not just on youth. As the editor-in-chief of *Advertising Age* once said, "Only eight percent of an ad's message is received by the conscious mind; the rest is worked and reworked deep within the recesses of the brain, where a product's positioning and repositioning takes shape."[26] In reality TV, advertisers don't only sponsor programming but work in tandem with producers to position and reposition our core perceptions about ourselves, our place in society, and our culture in general right alongside the Steve Madden stilettos and Heatherette dresses showcased by *Top Model*'s living mannequins.*

This is the context through which we need to understand the implications of allowing advertisers—especially fashion and beauty industry advertisers—to create an entire genre of entertainment infused with their historically misogynist and bigoted philosophies. The "crime scene victims" challenge—like the many episodes of *ANTM* centered around female pain, terror, and torture—serves as a sharp reminder that what millions of reality TV viewers believe is harmless fluff . . . is anything but. *Top Model* is less a "guilty pleasure," as *TV Guide* and infotainment shows have called it, than it is a cynical cash cow guilty of making product placers, and producers like Tyra Banks, rich at the expense of not only the self-esteem of the few hungry (in every sense) young models appearing in the competition but of the millions of girls and women, boys and men, who learn from the show that unhealthily underweight, Brazilian-waxed waifs can only achieve the ultimate in beauty when they appear to be erotically pained, provocatively maimed, self-abusive⁺ corpses. These butchered-for-beauty gore fests are the ultimate silencers of women—dead girls don't talk back, after all.

The mainstreaming of violence against women and girls as a normal part of "real" life is the seamy underbelly of the "romantic fairytale" reality show producers are selling. From the implicit acceptance of physical and verbal abuse on

---

* When I describe *Top Model* contestants as living mannequins, that's not just snark. In one cycle 3 challenge, the girls were instructed to "look alluring . . . look interesting, but [not] cheap and slutty" while posing in the teeny-tiniest of overpriced La Perla bras, thongs, and G-strings in the high-end lingerie designer's New York store window. While passersby gawked and sleazy onlookers snapped cell phone photos, ad-copy-esque voice-overs from the girls informed viewers that "Everybody knows La Perla is *it* in lingerie. It's just [makes kissy noise] *mwah*—beautiful!"

⁺ To rationalize their gruesome = gorgeous themes, *Top Model* sometimes concocts backstories in which women are supposedly the culprits committing the abusive behavior, either against one another (in the "beautiful corpses" episode, for example, each of the women was said to be fictitiously killed by another model) or via self-abuse (for example, in photos where they pose as bulimics midpurge or junkies midfix). The implication is that these shows are not actually promoting violence against women because men aren't always the fictional perps. It's a shallow argument: Violence is violence no matter who commits it, and the psychological and sociological impact of *Top Model* pumping out gory-as-glam images of women in pain, in jeopardy, and in "eternal rest" is the same regardless of such rationalizations.

dating shows with leading men of questionable legal repute to the over-the-top worship of images of female fear, pain, torture, and death on modeling shows more grotesque than gorgeous, reality television is spoon-feeding a generation of viewers decidedly unhealthy ideas about gender and power, love and sex, beauty and body—ideas that threaten the physical and emotional safety of girls and women and harm the psyches, reputations, and relationships of boys and men. This is the subtextual thorn on *The Bachelor*'s rose. And just like *The Bachelor* . . . the flower's pretty packaging might just be masking a dangerous prick.

Chapter Eight

"I Would Be a Servant to Him"

New Millenium, Same Old Backlash

But surely, it's only television, isn't it? Most people realize that the real world is different, don't they? Well, yes and no . . . the line between the TV world and the world beyond the screen has, for most people, become exceedingly hazy. . . . We know that [TV characters] are not real, yet we continually think about them as if they were. We are seduced by television's fictions to believe partly that this is how the world is but mostly to believe that this is how it could be. We learn to live in the dreams sold by network executives.

—SUT JHALLY AND JUSTIN M. LEWIS, *Enlightened Racism*[1]

Step right up, folks, it's time for everyone's favorite guessing game, Regress-o-Rama. Can you trace this quote to its source?

I will make the best wife for Bob because I will be a servant to him. And if he comes home from a long day at the office, I'll just rub his feet, and have dinner ready for him, and just [giggle] love on him!

Was it:

A. Nicole Kidman as a subservient cyborg in the 2004 remake of *The Stepford Wives;*

B. a devout attendee at the Southern Baptists' 1998 Convention, heeding her clergy's call for wives to "cheerfully submit" to their husbands;

C. Christine, a bubbly twenty-four-year-old administrative assistant on *The Bachelor*, explaining why she should win a marriage proposal from some guy she'd never met.

If you guessed C, congratulations—you win! Christine's quote came during *The Bachelor*'s season 4 premiere—before she'd ever met the man.

On second thought, we all lose.

In *Backlash: The Undeclared War Against American Women*, journalist Susan Faludi documented how attacks on women's rights periodically flare up in journalism, pop culture, and advertising as a reaction to "the perception—accurate or not—that women are making great strides" to improve their collective status. Threatened by signs that women might be on the verge of achieving great progress, media respond by condemning not only their ability to succeed in education, sports, business, and politics, but also the notion that they should want to do so at all. "In other words," Faludi argued:

> antifeminist backlash has been set off not by women's achievement of full equality but by the increased possibility that they might win it. It is a preemptive strike that stops women long before they reach the finish line . . . these codes and cajolings, these whispers and threats and myths, move overwhelmingly in one direction: they try to push women back into their "acceptable" roles—whether as Daddy's girl or fluttery romantic, active nester or passive love object.[2]

I began actively monitoring unscripted programming when *The Bachelor* debuted, sensing a new resurgence of this time-tested media tactic. Since that time, reality television has emerged as America's most vivid example of pop cultural backlash against women's rights and social progress.

A cursory look at a timeline of this supposedly reality-based genre is telling:

2000: Condoleezza Rice is named the first African American national security advisor. Fox airs *Who Wants to Marry a Multi-Millionaire?* based on the notion that women can only achieve success by proxy, as arm candy to rich husbands.

2002: *The New York Times* finally updates their wedding announcements policy to include same-sex nuptials. ABC debuts *The Bachelor* to remind us that romance and marriage are the sole domain of wealthy white men and pretty white women.

2003: Athletes including Michelle Kwan, Mia Hamm, Serena Williams, Martina Navratilova, Regina Jacobs, and Stacy Dragila score record-breaking wins in figure skating, soccer, tennis, swimming, and pole vaulting, respectively, while nearly three thousand girls play high school football as kickers, wide receivers, and linebackers.[3] UPN unveils *America's Next Top Model,* teaching young women that their bodies are valuable only as decorative props for advertisers—the skinnier and weaker the better.

2004: Cindy Sheehan, mother of a soldier killed in Iraq, meets with President George W. Bush along with other military families. She soon becomes one of America's most vocal antiwar activists, organizing peace actions in the name of her son. ABC introduces *Wife Swap* and *Supernanny,* which generally portray women as bad wives and mothers if they pursue professional or political interests outside the home.

2006: Representative Nancy Pelosi is elected the first female speaker of the house. CBS's Katie Couric becomes the first solo female anchor of a network nightly newscast. VH1 rolls out *Flavor of Love,* depicting women—especially women of color—as nothing more than ignorant, violent, gold-digging sluts.*

---

* Four other first-woman-leader barriers were broken in 2006: Ellen Sirleaf-Johnson became president of Liberia, Michelle Bachelet was elected president of Chile, Portia Simpson Miller was elected Jamaica's prime minister, and Han Myeong-Sook became prime minister of South Korea.

2007: Drew Gilpin Faust becomes Harvard's first female president, and Dr. Peggy Whitson is the first woman to command the International Space Station. TLC premieres *Say Yes to the Dress*, where women find complete fulfillment in thousands of dollars' worth of beading and tulle, and the CW embarks on *The Pussycat Dolls Present: The Search for the Next Doll*, where pole-dancing prowess is the key to success.

2008: Senator Hillary Rodham Clinton is the Democratic front runner for president, eventually losing the nomination to Senator Barack Obama. Sarah Palin becomes the Republican nominee for vice president. Bravo's new series *The Millionaire Matchmaker*, *The Real Housewives of New York City*, and *The Real Housewives of Atlanta* showcase women who aspire mostly to lives of leisure.

2009: The median age of first marriage for women rises to an all-time high of 25.9; *Singled Out* author Bella DePaulo notes this as a sign that women are increasingly embracing and enjoying single life.[4] VH1 offers *Tough Love* via matchmaker Steve Ward, who opens every episode saying, "Nobody knows single women like I do. They're lonely. They're clueless. They're needy." Stylized illustrations of dapper dudes rejecting lovelorn ladies accompany this intro, rendering The Single American Female a symbol of misery.

As the above illustrates, American women have made great strides over the last decade in every professional field. Yet in the world of reality TV, women are not concerned with politics, law, athletics, activism, or even careers in general (unless they're competing for the supermodel/starlet/rock star jobs that populate ten-year-olds' daydreams). Instead, reality TV producers, casting directors, and story editors have collaborated to paint American women as romantically desperate, matrimonially obsessed, and hypertraditionalist in their views about the proper role for wives and mothers, husbands and fathers.

When dating show hotties say, "I would give it all up for [bachelor-I-barely-know]!" the first "it" they mean is their jobs, which are painted as inconsequential in comparison to the promise of "fairytale love." While contestants usually do work, casting directors seem to prefer women with jobs that were acceptable in prefeminist days: models, flight attendants, secretaries, pro sports cheerleaders. The few women with lives outside of 1950s conventions find their careers held against them or turned into cautionary tales: A rocket scientist was called "intimidating" and promptly sent packing on *More to Love,* while a medical grad student was depicted as cold and stuck-up, even though her season's *Bachelor* was a doctor himself.

Having fallen "completely in love" with Jake, *Bachelor* number fourteen, bubbly twenty-five-year-old Ali learned that she'd be fired from her position as an advertising manager at Facebook if she didn't immediately return to work. Jake couldn't promise that he wouldn't dump her for three other women, so after endless on-screen sobbing, she made the only rational choice: She left the show to keep her "dream job," instead of joining nearly 15 million people unemployed in early 2010.[5] This act of independence was unprecedented: For the first time in the franchise's nine-year run, a woman decided that her real life was more valuable than the show's faux-fairytale fakery. Naturally, producers couldn't leave it at that. One week later, they sent a camera crew to her house to film her bemoaning her "mistake" and begging Jake to let her come back to play her 25 percent shot at being with him. Her career meant nothing without "someone to share it with," she pleaded, falling apart when he wasn't interested. "I'm completely heartbroken . . . I made the wrong choice," she sobbed. "I will forever regret this decision." On the "Women Tell All" episode, Ali confessed that although it would have meant losing her apartment and her livelihood, she "would choose love over work" if she could do it again. "Don't get me wrong, I am the biggest advocate of women going out there and having careers. One thing I know, though, is that when I'm on my deathbed I don't want to look back and say I didn't love enough," she said, promising to "put love first" from then on. Now cured of her pesky self-reliance, the newly retro-tastic Ali quit her job to become the sixth *Bachelorette.*

Dating show women must also be willing to leave their friends, families, and hometowns behind to be with men they've only just met. Whomever the network-approved stud chooses, it is understood that she will relocate for him, and that their life will unfold on his terms. "You can lead," doe-eyed divorcée Tenley whispered as she danced with fourteenth-season *Bachelor* Jake. "You can lead me in life. And that's what I want."

If there's no potential boyfriend to kowtow to, producers often have women submit to the nearest male authority figure. Tina, a project manager nicknamed "Miss Career Obsessed" by *Tough Love*'s relationship drill sergeant Steve Ward, lamented, "I put work first. At the end of the day you're still sad and alone at home. . . . What's wrong with me? This is one of my last options because I feel like I'm on the path to not find someone. *I'm ready for Steve to control my fate.*" VH1's promotional materials tell viewers that Kanisha, "Miss Gold-Digger," joined the show because "I have a bad habit of being picky with the men I date," but "I believe that Steve Ward can put me in my place."* That's certainly how Ward sees his role. Through insults, paternalism, and universal statements about "the male mind," he commands women to follow his "boot camp" rules or be alone forever. It's all or nothing, he barks, because if he can't "train" this cast of "slutty," "dumb," "soul-sucking" "losers," they'll never be able to land "Mr. Right."

Female submissiveness is still imposed as a major theme even when the roles are supposedly reversed on shows like *The Bachelorette,* where many men pursue one woman. "For the first time in TV history," the host declared during the spinoff's first season, "a woman has *all* the *power!*" The majority of *The Bachelor*'s stars have been plucked from obscurity to sit on the proverbial throne and choose among twenty-five women. In contrast, each star of *The Bachelorette* was previously humiliated and dumped by one of *The Bachelor* boys. This assures that their pathetic bona fides—and their bikinied bods—are known

---

* Tina and Kanisha were the only Black women on *Tough Love* season 2. Extra creepy points to VH1 for presenting African American women as subservient to a patriarchal white man asked to "control" their fates.

commodities to any man who auditioned to date them, not to mention viewers.* Instead of flipping the script, *The Bachelorette* reinforces the same old gender stereotypes as its counterpart. Trista, a former Miami Heat dancer, became the first and most famous *Bachelorette* in 2003. She spoke in grating baby talk, cried whenever she rejected suitors, and moved to Colorado, where Ryan, the man she selected, worked as a fireman. Producers pursued the same framing all the way through 2009, when interior designer Jillian, the fifth *Bachelorette,* said she was tired of making important decisions and preferred to sit back and let her man determine where and how they would live.

Dating show dudes, meanwhile, are assumed to have careers, homes, and social ties too important to alter just for some woman. While *The Bachelor* draws its female competitors as overly emotional backstabbers who'll do anything for an engagement ring, guys vying for smooches from *The Bachelorette* are usually shown palling around with one another, chugging beer and male-bonding over *The Bachelorette*'s hot bod.⁺ Producers stress this sort of camaraderie among brothers because, at heart, they don't want to give the impression that men are deeply invested in the romantic outcome of the show, other than as exceptions that prove a macho rule. The audience is meant to understand that these aspiring actors and models are in it for career advancement, and the larger TV landscape underscores that point: Rather than badgering *Bachelorette* runner-up Charlie Maher with hurtful questions about how devastated he must feel after being dumped at the faux altar, as they do with booted *Bachelor* babes, the infotainment show *Extra* hired him as a correspondent. And while *The Bachelor* bumps to commercial asking, "Who will get sent home brokenhearted?" over footage of weeping women, *The Bachelorette*'s narrator teases, "Who will make the cut?" and "Who will have his ego shattered?" (both questions that connote the woman as commodity and the show as a game) or

---

* Show runner Mike Fleiss initially hesitated to give a woman the appearance of romantic control in a spinoff. He eventually relented, but the franchise has remained heavily weighted away from queen bees. By March 2010, ABC had aired fourteen seasons of *The Bachelor* and only five of *The Bachelorette.*
⁺ Punctuated, of course, by enough testosterone-fueled brawls that viewers remember that they're *real men.*

simply, "Who will get sent home?" No need for any adjective or qualifier, since we assumed they hardly cared in the first place.

Sexual double standards are also pervasive. With a wink-wink and a nudge-nudge, *The Bachelor* has encouraged its fourteen male stars to get as far as they can—with as many women as possible—in hot tubs, mud baths, and "fantasy suites." But while *The Bachelorette's* leering cameras offer a series-long ogle-fest, zooming in on their stars' breasts, asses, and legs whenever possible, their female stars are harshly judged for behaving half as wantonly as any of the randy *Bachelors*. Host Chris Harrison actually sat Trista down and asked her to explain to uncomfortable viewers why she kissed more than one prospective fiancé during her season. She jumped at the chance to tell the audience that she's a good girl and not a tramp, but she had to kiss several men to make sure she had chemistry with her future life partner. Likewise, Harrison made Jillian justify a steamy hot tub makeout session with former *Bachelor* Jason Mesnick before he dumped her. (To Jillian's credit, she was the first *Bachelorette* to refuse to apologize for her sexuality. She was a normal, healthy adult, she said firmly, and if she wanted to pursue sexual attraction with a consenting partner, she saw nothing wrong with that.) This sort of slut-shaming has traveled from the prime-time series to the media spectacle that surrounds it, with bloggers calling the women whores and even CNN's Anderson Cooper casting aspersions about their supposed promiscuity. Guest-hosting Live with Regis & Kelly, Cooper demanded Jillian tell him, "How many [guys] did you actually hook up with? How many did you actually sleep with?" Flustered, she answered, "I kissed ten guys, but only four with tongue."[6]

"Equal Society? I'm Sick of It!"

Power imbalances in heterosexual relationships are codified and glorified in relationship shows. How-to-land-a-man series like *Tough Love* give women ideological makeovers, with advice ripped from 1950s finishing school manuals: Laugh at men's jokes even if they're not funny. "Act interested even though you're not." "When it comes to sexual partners, for women it should be like a golf score. The lower the better." *Don't* be opinionated, *do* be "uncomplicated."

The Millionaire Matchmaker's Patti Stanger spells out gendered proscriptions point-blank: "It is so important for women to be women and men to be men, and to keep those roles intact. It's worked for millions of years." But what does it mean for "women to be women" and "men to be men?" Simple, Stanger instructs: On a date, "women should listen. You're not the leader in this situation. You let the man lead. . . . You gotta, like, be the actress in the movie, not the director." The condemnation of female leadership and celebration of the dominant "hunter-gatherer male" have been through-lines over three seasons of *The Millionaire Matchmaker*. Women who make more money than men or who make the first move sexually or socially are "aggressive" and "masculine," therefore emasculating and undesirable. Women must keep themselves thin, gorgeous, and agreeable at all times, but accept dates with schlubby chauvinists ten to twenty years their senior.* Men "want Madonna in the bedroom, Martha Stewart in the kitchen, and Mary Poppins in the nursery," Stanger explains, so if a woman wants love, she'd do better to hide her ambition and reveal her cleavage.

But what of men who want partners, not servants? *The Millionaire Matchmaker* sets out to show them the error of their ways. When charismatic ex-NFL star (and rare African American participant) Matt "Hatch" Hatchett said that "chivalry is dead" and he wanted a relationship with an "ambitious" "career woman," Stanger flipped out. Hatch "needs to shut his mouth and open his mind," she told the cameras. "He's got a chip on his shoulder. He's pissed off that women get their dinners and their drinks paid for. Women get their car doors opened. He wants it to be equal society here . . . I'm really getting sick of this!" To correct Hatch's enlightened sensibilities she sent him to "chivalry boot camp," where Naomi, an "expert" his grandmother's age, insisted that when he takes a woman out to dinner he shouldn't allow her to speak to

---

* Though she reprimands male clients for seeking women young enough to be their daughters and pays lip service to how much she "hates ageists," Stanger tells viewers that it is "age appropriate" for a fifty-year-old to date women in their late thirties. When a redhead in her early to midthirties said that a fifty-year-old millionaire is "too old" for her, Stanger screamed that she'll be single forever because of her bad attitude.

the waiter, ordering for her instead. When he pointed out that women of his generation like to make their own decisions, this simple idea flew over the heads of Stanger and her "expert," so Hatch suggested they role-play the scenario:

> STANGER (playing "the guy"): "What would you like to drink?"
> HATCH (playing "the girl"): "I'll order it when [the waiter] comes."
> STANGER: "Well, why don't you let me order it 'cause I'm gonna order for the table."
> HATCH: "Because I'm an adult, and I'm grown, and I make my own money, so I'm gonna order my own drink."
> STANGER: "Then that's not a girl you should be dating!"

Annoyed, Hatch asked, "If that's my girlfriend for six months and she likes ordering my food for me, what's wrong with letting her do that?" Naomi's reply: "If you don't mind being with a shrew who's going to take over your life!"

Now, consider: Hatch didn't suggest that his girlfriend asked him to do 50 percent of their housework, or fend for himself while she worked late, or march with her at an antirape rally. All he said was that he doesn't want to control women's choices at dinner (or, by implication, in life). But just that glimmer of male respect for female independence and equal partnership, so rare on reality relationship shows, was enough to elicit condemnations against "shrews" and dire warnings: "He's gonna be alone for the rest of this life," Stanger told viewers.

Far more typical was Jason, an overweight, seemingly stoned heir to the 20th Century Fox fortune, who wanted *The Millionaire Matchmaker* to locate his dream woman: "I want hot blond, big tits. Definitely funny. Kind of like a Stepford Wife." Potential Stepford wives are Stanger's specialty, so she set him up with a trophy bride hopeful who looked like a pinup, giggled at his lame jokes, and didn't object when he demanded that she fetch his dinner because, "You're the woman, you're supposed to serve."

Women who would recoil at their presumed subservience either are not cast, or are edited to appear ditzier than they are, or find their objections left on the cutting room floor. As a result, the "self-loathing single gal" joins chapter 3's bitches, incompetents, and gold diggers as a dominant dating, mating, and marriage show archetype. "I'm a loser . . . what is so wrong with me that someone cannot love me for who I am?" wept Heather, offering the ubiquitous, tear-stained money shot that follows every *Bachelor* elimination ceremony. On *Tough Love,* sexy simpleton Liz chirped that she has trouble concentrating because "I'm usually thinking about kittens or sunshine or something." Ward described her as "so desperate to get married she's ready to settle for anything with a pulse." The pretty young thing confirmed: "I would love to be a housewife. . . . The fact that I'm not married right now at twenty-four years old makes me feel like a *failure!* Walking down the aisle would finally make my life complete."

With few exceptions,* relationship and lifestyle shows have framed women as unaware that there is anything more to life than tossing back martinis, lounging in hot tubs, and as bachelorette Christine suggested, meeting their husbands at the door with dinner and a foot rub at the ready.

Between 2000 and 2010, American couples redefined relationships in countless ways. Women postponed marriage longer than ever before. More stay-at-home dads took primary responsibility for childcare. More long-term heterosexual partners with kids began living together without legally formalizing their unions, while lesbian and gay couples continued to fight for—and increasingly won—the right to legally marry. Reality producers wanted none of that, showcasing mostly a narrow, nostalgic interpretation of marriage in which all single women are pathetic, all couples are straight, parenting and housecleaning are exclusively women's work, and families can get by on just the income of a male provider. Off-screen, low-income women were working multiple jobs to keep food on their tables and roofs over their kids' heads, feminists were advocating family leave and childcare policies

---

* Some of Bravo's *Real Housewives* have jobs. Many of their husbands are presented as afterthoughts (itself problematic). More positive is the MTV series *Run's House,* which profiles pioneering hip-hop artist Rev Run (Joseph Simmons, formerly of Run-D.M.C.), his wife, and their kids. Justine and the Rev are portrayed as having a mostly egalitarian marriage, making joint decisions and treating one another with respect.

to allow women and men to more sustainably balance work and family obligations, and middle- and upper-middle-class women continued to break barriers in top-tier businesses and elected office. The babes of reality TV? They dreamed only of suburban domesticity and cheerful dependence.

"Most definitely I see Aaron as my husband," declared Heather, a thirty-one-year-old flight attendant on season 2 of *The Bachelor,* "I can see everything. I see the house. I see the white picket fence. I see the wife. I see the mother. I see the children. I see him coaching the soccer team." In this hazy vision, all the problems of the world magically melt away when Daddy walks through the door. Fourth-season *Bachelor* contestant Kristi, a twenty-four-year-old loan processor, mused, "I see myself in the future as the mommy. You know, I'm trying to get everything together. And the phone's ringing and the stuff's boiling over and the kids are screaming, and I'm like, 'Ahhh!' All of a sudden . . . the door opens, there's Bob. 'Honey I'm, home!' And he comes up behind me, puts his arms around me, and gives me a kiss, and at that moment everything's okay. You know? Just *perfect.*"

If the message isn't clear: *"Every little girl* grows up dreaming, you know, about the big wedding and children and the white picket fence with 2.5 kids and a dog," twenty-five-year-old schoolteacher Lee-Ann insisted. Producers marshal such quotes in editing to reinforce the stereotype that these unbridled bridal fixations are universal . . . and, by implication, if anyone in the audience can't relate, she must be a freak.

And why is this message so important and consistent? As we learned in chapters 1 and 4, the product placement trappings are what matter, not the bloke who pops the question with the name-brand diamond. Attempting to convince women that starring as the princess of a huge, ostentatious wedding is the most important thing they will ever accomplish, dating shows as well as programs like *Say Yes to the Dress* and *Platinum Weddings* are the mouthpiece of what Chrys Ingraham, author of *White Weddings: Romancing Heterosexuality in Popular Culture,* calls "the wedding-industrial complex." By 2006, the wedding industry was generating a whopping $80 billion annually for companies hawking rings, bridal apparel, invitations, flowers, receptions, catering, destination weddings, honeymoon travel, gifts such as household furnishings, appliances, consumer electronics, and even wedding insurance.[7] That astronomical figure doesn't even include the profits of media companies and advertisers via these programs.

"I'm Going to Die Alone."

Some apologists claim that reality TV is not sexist because no one forces women to sign on. That's beside the point. The genre's real impact isn't on the handful of women who willingly appear on these programs, but in the narrative messages sent to millions of viewers tuned in to the vicious spectacles of *The Swan* and *Joe Millionaire,* or the millions of young girls for whom *America's Next Top Model* is aspirational. We may talk back to our screens, we may think we're above it, but the more we watch, the more we learn that only the most gorgeous, least independent women with the lowest-carb diets and the highest thresholds for humiliation will be rewarded with love, financial security, and the ultimate prize: being selected by some guy—*any* guy—because nothing is as important as male validation.

Despite how frivolous reality TV may seem or how much producers say it's all in good fun, the psychological browbeating these shows engage in has political ramifications. These programs reinforce insecurities bred into women by years of factually inaccurate news media reports of supposed "man shortages" and broken-down biological clocks. They play on the same fears as the infamously inaccurate but wildly influential 1986 *Newsweek* cover story that claimed single women had a better chance of being *killed by a terrorist* than finding a husband after forty. The statistic *Newsweek* quoted—only 2.6 percent will wed and the rest will die alone—was debunked at the time by journalists like Susan Faludi, and by *Newsweek* itself in a 2006 anniversary mea culpa (as it turns out, 23 to 40 percent of women aged forty and up will marry). But never mind the facts; the notion that women "past their prime" are doomed to a life of loneliness spread like a bad rash through newspapers, magazines, TV, and film, so pervasively that the "killed by a terrorist" meme has became one of those pop culture "facts" that reporters, fictional characters, and people on grocery store lines quote as pseudo-scientific "proof" that women looking for love really shouldn't be too picky.[8]

It's the same message reinforced in a recent tidal wave of cautionary-tale news reports, op-eds, and conservative-think-tank-produced books that (as Caryl Rivers documents in *Selling Anxiety: How the News Media Scare Women*) predict that women who don't "opt out" of the workplace, who instead prefer to wait until they're emotionally and financially ready to marry and have children, are bound to wake up barren and full of regret in their thirties and older. But where news media usually rely on misrepresentative statistics and flawed studies to manufacture their misleading case against women's independence, reality TV producers cherry-pick through thousands of hours of videotape to highlight the fears and yearnings of specific women like Heather, the lovelorn woman who called herself "a loser" when *The Bachelor* sent her packing. On *The Bachelor: Where Are They Now*, the host told viewers that "Heather is now back in Dallas, continuing her quest for an engagement ring," over B-roll of the solitary gal sadly searching the city for her other half. Filmed in her kitchen *(the spinster!)*, she explained that her "goal right now is to get married. You always hear those *horror stories*. You know, 'forty and single!' . . . I'm always nervous that Mr. Right is not going to come along."

"A backlash against women's rights succeeds to the degree that it appears not to be political, that it appears not to be a struggle at all," Susan Faludi explains. "It is most powerful when it goes private, when it lodges inside a woman's mind and turns her vision inward, until she imagines the pressure is all in her head, until she begins to enforce the backlash, too—on herself."[9] As we've seen, much of the representational power of unscripted programming comes from the overwhelming presence of women who have internalized backlash ideology (or who are willing to pretend as much in trade for airtime), coupled with the invisibility and demonization of women with more progressive values. *Of course* a successful executive is described on VH1's website as being loveless and crushed by regret because she mistakenly prioritized a career. "After over a decade of working her way to the top of her business [she] quit her job" to appear on *Tough Love,* because she realized "at the age of thirty-seven" that "she doesn't want to live a life of loneliness." That's not incidental to the series—it's arguably the program's primary point.

Ultimately, though we usually understand that reality shows are not fully real, female contestants' desperation, sadness, and questionable self-esteem all seem so authentic that this "fact" of female desperation (even among gorgeous twenty-four-year-olds) becomes to viewers in 2010 what that *Newsweek* killed-by-a-terrorist story was in the '80s and '90s. When a dejected forty-year-old businesswoman says "I'm going to die alone!" on *The Millionaire Matchmaker,* we believe her . . . and we file it away in the back of our minds, more "proof" that liberation leads only to heartache.

Working hand in hand with print media hit-pieces on women's achievement and highly hyped books like Lori Gottlieb's *Marry Him: The Case for Settling for Mr. Good Enough* (sample chapter title: "How Feminism Fucked Up My Love Life"), reality TV dating and mating shows prey on women's insecurities to convince us that we're doomed to unhappiness unless we rid ourselves of all traces of individuality, ambition, or—heaven forbid—feminist thought. The scare-tactic message sent to self-sufficient, independent women is that we need to do whatever we can to make ourselves as thin, attractive, and nonthreatening as possible before it's . . . daa daah dummm . . . *too late!* Once we've gotten our *Extreme Makeovers* and figured out *What Not to Wear,* we need to lower our standards and settle for any *Bachelor* who'll have us—ASAP! If we demand respect, intelligence, kindness, honesty, or actual love, these shows insist, we'll wake up to find that Mr. Right has been snatched up by one of twenty-four other cuter and more compliant chicks waiting in the wings. And then we'll be left alone, unloved, childless (or an overburdened single parent), and miserable.

The result is deeply political. What these shows are ultimately trying to drag us back to is a time when women were told that no other emotional, professional, political, or academic accomplishment could compare with the goal of becoming "Mrs. Something." That's the exact phrase used by Christy Fichtner, chosen as Miss USA 1986 over runner-up Halle Berry (!) when she was asked why she wanted to compete for a stranger's heart on *Who Wants to Marry My Dad?* "I want to be 'Mrs. Something,'" she told NBC's bald, suburban Adonis, "I don't want to be 'Miss' forever." Even *Miss USA* is worthless if she doesn't transform into a Mrs. Somebody, and soon.

Life's a Bitch and Then You Marry One

Depressingly, the depth of reality TV contempt for women runs so deep that even those who buy into the genre's retrograde June Cleaver worship are met with the equivalent of a televised bitch-slap. Those who actually pursue the consumerist version of the diamond-encrusted, name-brand-approved, sugar-daddy wedding portrayed as the ideal are eventually vilified for wanting their "special day" to be as "perfect" as the ones on *My Fair Wedding*. "Eight of America's most demanding brides-to-be have let us into their lives for a peek behind the veil. Meet the *Bridezillas,* and let the madness begin!" an alarmist announcer told viewers of *Bridezillas,* a Fox special that was spun into a WE network series. "There's three kinds of *Bridezillas* stalking the streets of America. The Princess Bride, the Neurotic Bride, and most frighteningly of all, the Obsessive Bride," the narrator classified. Graphics of shattered glass were thrown up on-screen in between each segment with captions such as, "LIFE'S A BITCH AND THEN YOU MARRY ONE."

On the WE series, "out of control" stress cases of all ages have screaming hissy fits over place settings and dress fittings, verbally abuse loved ones and "hired help," and behave like entitled, irrational bitches. The show layers racial prejudice into their backlash toolkit when the bride isn't white. Perhaps no *Bridezilla* was portrayed as more despicable than "Queen Melissa," a full-figured African American mom depicted as a violent thief. She wielded a handgun and threatened to shoot anyone who'd dare spoil her trip to the altar. She stole her fiancé's ATM card and withdrew hundreds of dollars, plunging his account into a negative balance, then lied about it. Worse, she called her ex-husband, a soldier stationed in Iraq who didn't know she was remarrying, and told him to wire $600 by the afternoon, to fix some fabricated emergency for their children. Amused, she told the cameras that in between his military duties he had sent more than $4,000 "on top of the child support he has been sending. . . . I've been saying it's going towards the kids, bills—he doesn't know it'd been going towards my wedding." Just as grave a sin, we learn from the narrator, she "refused to take her husband's last name."

Women rarely come off any better after they're married with children. ABC's *Wife Swap* and Fox's *Trading Spouses* stoke animosity between women with opposing value systems, encouraging each to disparage the way the other runs her home, raises her kids, treats her husband, and lives her life. Stay-at-home moms berate women with careers as "selfish" mothers and "bad" wives for not "obeying" their husbands, while women who value—gasp!—egalitarian division of household chores and childrearing condemn traditional homemakers as ignorant doormats. "The woman who doesn't listen enough to her husband is chastised. The woman with an unclean home is berated. The woman who doesn't get sole satisfaction from her family is told she should," Shira Tarrant writes.[10] Whether they conform to or reject traditional models of marriage and motherhood, all women are presented as domestic failures on these shows, which, along with *Supernanny* and *Nanny 911,* function as reality TV's answer to the news media's trumped-up "Mommy Wars."[11] Meanwhile, men who rule their homes with an iron fist and control every aspect of their wives' behavior, appearance, and daily routine are a staple on these shows. Though they're often called jerks,* they're rarely rebuked for displaying a level of dominance often exhibited by batterers. (One *Supernanny* episode offered a rare

---

* *Wife Swap's* most famous misogynist is Richard Heene, a bizarre storm-chaser who spent the hour cursing at and castigating his "new wife" as "a stand for every man in America." If Heene's name sounds familiar, you were probably one of millions worldwide who watched news reports about a missing six-year-old boy, Falcon Heene, who supposedly floated away in his family's homemade balloon. Worried that he fell to his death, the National Guard and local police conducted an expensive, high-profile manhunt, only to find Falcon hiding in his attic. As it turned out, Richard Heene orchestrated the "Balloon Boy" hoax in attempt to get his own reality show. Instead, he got a ninety-day jail sentence.

exception, making a verbally abusive husband and father get counseling.) On the other hand, when the occasional progressive-minded man or nurturing, stay-at-home dad shows up on shows like *Wife Swap*, he's branded a "sissy" and a "loser," told he's being a bad role model to his kids, and encouraged to assume his rightful place as his family's breadwinner, "ruler," or "master."

This is conservative gender war ideology disguising a counterattack on women's rights with soft-focus lighting, string quartets, and Cinderella ball gowns. All this compulsory domesticity, this negating of individuality and will, rests on the underlying notion that women should think like June Cleaver, fuck like Jenna Jameson, and look like Miss USA. It's Donna Reed meets Pamela Anderson, and it ain't pretty.

These narratives also deeply underestimate men's intelligence, their ability to love, and their basic decency. Where women are considered perfect 10s simply for being pretty, pathetic, and passive, reality TV tells us that all men need to be Mr. Right is wealth—their own, or an illusion borrowed from producers. Kind, sweet, funny, smart, dignified, and loving men who respect women *really do exist* in the world—but they're all but invisible in the world of reality TV, where Mr. Right is less likely to be a decent human being than he is to be a lying *(Joe Millionaire)*, cheating *(Tool Academy)*, insincere *(Age of Love)*, frat boy *(Meet My Folks)* who crushes beer cans on his forehead *(The Bachelorette)*, tricks women into bed *(The Pickup Artist)*, objectifies them *(Flavor of Love)*, verbally abuses them *(Average Joe)*, and even kicks them in the ass *(For Love or Money)*. Women deserve better from their lovers—and boys and men deserve better pictures of themselves than these limited interpretations of masculinity.

Sex: It's Only Okay if She Doesn't Really Want It

The morning of the America's Regal Gems pageant had arrived, and Morghan was pumped and ready.

She'd spent hours getting her game face on. Rosy blush over flaw-concealing foundation lent her skin a dewy glow. She batted fake eyelashes under carefully plucked eyebrows. Piercing blue eyes with dramatic black mascara completed that perfect smoky eye look. Her voluminous blond hair was pin-curled in a sophisticated updo. While her full-body spray tan didn't exactly seem natural (how could it, after four consecutive applications?), it certainly looked expensive. She pursed her glossy pink lips, practiced her best come-hither look, and rehearsed the coy, over-the-shoulder shimmy/smile combo she hoped would wow the judges during both the swimsuit competition and her dance talent portion.

Oh, one more thing: Morghan, a contestant on *Toddlers & Tiaras,* is seven years old. She started her dance in a trench coat with her back to the judges. All of a sudden—bam!—she stripped it off to reveal short-shorts, boots, and a fringed, midriff-baring halter top, turned around, and began pumping her hips to club music. Her performance resembled a cross between burlesque and a Dallas Cowboy Cheerleaders routine.

Toddlers & Tiaras and *Little Miss Perfect* get my vote for most exploitative reality shows of the decade.* Girls as young as five and six years old are hypersexualized before they can possibly understand or consent to the implications. It's a pedophile's dream come true: Why risk renting illegal kiddie porn when you can watch little kids mimicking the sultry stares, flirty winks, and booty-shaking moves of exotic dancers on TLC and WeTV? There's a reason the term "prostitots" was coined for the early introduction to raunch culture media give girls not yet old enough to cross the street by themselves.[12]

These baby beauty pageant shows play like Intro to Misogyny for the preschool set. Girls are taught that their bodies are to be always on display, that it's normal to be graded on how pretty your eyes, smile, and hair are, and that it's *really, really important* to be more beautiful than other girls. In short, they learn how to perform femininity. "It looks like a twenty-year-old face on a

---

* *The Swan,* which gave unnecessary surgeries and quasi-abusive "therapy" to unstable depressives, was the most sadistic.

five-year-old, seven-year-old's body," one pageant dad told *Toddlers'* cameras, a bit uncomfortably. "It's just different to see kids that way."*

Toddlers functions as a training ground for female sexual performance, preparing little girls to cultivate and relish objectification. (I can fast-forward past a discussion of "the male gaze," right?) They're told to "never stop smiling," even if they're unhappy. They're instructed to use their nascent "feminine wiles" to impress judges (especially "boy judges"). And they're trained to strive for physical perfection in constant competition with female peers.⁺

In this sense, four-year-olds on *Toddlers & Tiaras* aren't much different from twenty-four-year-olds on E!'s *The Girls Next Door*, where *Playboy* playmates prance around in thong panties and flash their surgically enhanced double-Ds to tease pervy octogenarian Hugh Hefner. They're cast on the show and live in Hef's mansion solely as eye candy. But unlike on *The Bachelor* and similarly contrived "love stories," producers are straightforward about the fact that women's bodies are commodities, women's sexuality performative. Problematic? Sure. Yet this lack of artifice—or, more accurately, the transparency of this transaction—makes E!'s portrayal of Hef's multiple centerfold "girlfriends" less insidious than the ways women are treated on *Flavor of Love* or *The Bachelorette*. We're encouraged to watch *The Girls Next Door* with a winking understanding that these nubile young things are acting a role; it's doubtful anyone believes for a minute that they're sleeping with the eighty-four-year-old soft-porn scion. What's more, we're meant to understand that they like sex and, unusual in the reality landscape, we're not supposed to scorn them for it.

For a genre overflowing with casual sex, reality TV is surprisingly opposed to women's desire. Looking the part of femme fatale is expected; *acting* the part will earn them a scarlet letter. We learn that women should be continually sexually available . . . so long as it is for a man's pleasure, not their own. Ever since season 1's

---

* It's especially offensive to lure viewers with the promise of seeing kids "that way" when we consider that 27 percent of women and 16 percent of men report being sexually abused as children.[13]

⁺ Can you think of a more certain recipe for eating disorders, therapy, or a future seat on the stage of the *Maury Povich Show*?

Bachelor chose the voluptuous and unabashedly sexual Amanda and was lambasted for that choice, dating shows have sent the message that women who actively seek sex for pure physical enjoyment are contemptible whores. Women can be "good girls" if they are seduced after copious amounts of booze, coerced into making out because they fear rejection if they don't go along with it, or if they use sex as a bargaining chip to trap a man or as an act of desperation to prove their love. But if they give in too quickly or (heaven forbid!) make the first move just because they're turned on, we're supposed to consider them promiscuous, immoral, and downright filthy.* And Lord help the girl who doesn't need a man to satisfy her desires: When a bored dater quipped that she wished her *Bachelor* castmates would leave so she could have some time alone to take care of her needs, her little masturbation joke ended up getting her labeled disgusting and inappropriate.

Producers paint women of color—especially African Americans and Latinas—as particularly hypersexual on shows like *Flavor of Love* and *Real Chance of Love*. Built into these shows' structure is the requirement that they pole dance, lap dance, wear fetish costumes, and perform sexual favors to "win" dates or avoid elimination, for which they're then demonized. This is a typical argument from *Flavor of Love:*

WOMAN A: "Are you proud to be stripping on a pole, bitch?"

WOMAN B: "You're a whore!"

WOMAN C: "And to me, you're still a slut!"

More irate rants were followed by moralizing condemnation from *Flavor of Love Girls: Charm School* host Mo'Nique, who told viewers that the cast arrived "look[ing] like hookers. Some of the skirts was up their ass. Some of the heels looked like they'd come off a pole."

---

* On *The Millionaire Matchmaker,* Stanger's #1 rule is "no sex before monogamy." Women who disobey are called "cheap," "not virtuous," and told they'll "pay the piper." Once they've got a guy on lock-down, though, Stanger instructs them to use sex to keep him happy, not experience it for their own enjoyment: "A good BJ goes a long way, baby. *You can actually watch television and do it at the same time,*" she told viewers.

If reality TV makes women out to be whores (sometimes right in the title, as in *Lady or a Tramp?*, a series Donald Trump once planned), then the networks themselves are the pimps. They provide an endless array of needy sexpots to buff dudes with six-pack abs and hope like hell they'll paw each other on film to rake in ratings and ad dollars, à la *Temptation Island*, where sexy singles (including porn stars) were hired by Fox to attempt to break up committed relationships. All this gyrating, tempting, and teasing does double duty when cobbled together in cable specials such as E!'s *True Hollywood Story: The Bad Girls of Reality TV* and the pay-per-view offering *Reality TV's Sexiest Vixens*.

And then there's HBO's *Cathouse* series, filmed at the infamous Bunny Ranch brothel in Las Vegas, where sex workers nonchalantly rattle off price points for various erotic services and johns haggle over the cost of blow jobs and threesomes. If you missed an episode, never fear—HBO's official website for the show is there to help: "Can't tell the johns from the dicks? *Need to ID a ho?* Consult our episode guide!" (emphasis mine).

Prime-time prostitution? Really?

Don't be surprised. *Cathouse* is not only the logical progression of the genre—it's also one of the more honest reality shows of the decade. The terms are clear at the Bunny Ranch: When the women sell their bodies they set their own prices, clearly articulate their limits, and don't pretend to be in love with guys they've just met, weeping about how worthless their lives will be if they don't find a man whose coattails they can ride. They just take their money, feign attraction, and help their clients get off. This isn't the ideal form of sexual agency,* but it may be preferable to the majority of dating shows where ladies in waiting have no sexual agency at all. For all the reasons some feminists might object to prostitution (selling sex is a valid economic choice for many people, but it's hardly liberatory), at least *Cathouse* doesn't glory in breaking women's hearts and crushing their spirits.

---

* When it comes to sex work, choice is a loaded concept in a country in which women are disproportionately poor but the sex industry is always hiring.

Certainly, *Cathouse* was more honest than *Joe Millionaire,* whose most notorious scene strongly implied that one of the contestants, "bad girl" Sarah Kozer, hooked up with Liar McFakebucks in the woods just to get her hands on his great big . . . billfold. When they snuck off into the woods away from the cameras, producers transformed what could have been an exceptionally boring extended still shot of a grove of trees into a soft-porn spectacle, through the propagandistic power of editing and sound effects. They pumped in some "chicka-chicka-pow-wow" mood music, spliced in out-of-context dialogue from a different day to make the couple's conversation seem incriminatingly randy, and threw the words "Shhh . . . " "Ummm . . . " "Slurp . . . " and "Gulp . . . " in captions on-screen, all of which appeared to be damning evidence that she performed oral sex. She didn't—but reality hardly mattered.* Excerpts from that "slurp, gulp" scene spread like news of a Lindsay Lohan car crash through the infotainment cycle. Shows like *Access Hollywood* and *Entertainment Tonight* depicted Kozer as a mercenary skank. She was trashed in newspapers, magazines, and blogs, and by viewers on fan sites. As one commenter put it on FoxReality .com, "There's no question that SARAH is a BIG gold digging, money hungry ho who's willing to take any Dude into the woods at night to get some $$$ Hehe!"

The Gender Binary: Reality TV's Definition of "Normal"

As we've established, reality TV has defined "Woman" nearly universally as heterosexual, domestically inclined, obsessed with thinness and beauty, and desperate to be married. The genre's "almost relentless heteronormative impulse," culture scholar Shira Tarrant writes, "reproduce(s) powerful and repressive ideological messages about the politics of identity."[14] This plays out in the tropes we've explored about women as stupid, bitchy, gold-digging girlie-girls, and in the underrepresentation—and hypersexualization—of lesbians and bisexuals.

---

* Both Kozer and McFakebucks himself, Evan Marriott, confirmed to media after the fact that the scene was "staged."

We've seen the Predatory Dyke out to seduce and "turn" straight women: An early example was *America's Next Top Model*'s Kim Stoltz—a lesbian often criticized by judges as looking "too masculine"—who joked about a straight blond competitor's crush on her after they kissed in a limo and made out in bed. *A Shot at Love with Tila Tequila* and *A Double Shot at Love with the Ikki Twins* treated us to bi-for-boys'-viewing-pleasure fantasies, where lingerie-clad femmes with long fingernails felt each other up as male onlookers hoped to join in. Producers milked Sapphic lust for ratings, but undercut notions of authentic lesbian desire by ensuring that men always "won" the dubiously bisexual dating series— affirming the second-class nature of same-sex relationships. Tila Tequila wrote on Twitter that "MTV made me pick Bobby," despite her "crying and begging" producers to let her choose a woman named Dani at the end of the first season. In interviews, she said she nixed a third season because they wouldn't "let me choose who I want" and only did season 2 because of contractual obligation.*

On the plus side, some nonhetero reality TV participants have managed to escape such typecasting. *Top Model* has included a significant number of lesbian and bi contestants over fourteen seasons, confirming that beauty isn't only the domain of straight girls. Bravo has allowed a couple of open lesbians to headline shows based on their professions: Hairdresser Tabatha Coffey rules *Tabatha's Salon Takeover*, while fitness trainer Jackie Warner is ass-kicker-in-charge on *Work Out*. The tenth season of CBS's *The Amazing Race* featured their first lesbian contestant, twenty-seven-year-old speech pathologist Lauren Marcoccio, and Duke, her formerly homophobic father.[15] Not only did viewers see Lauren as an able competitor, they observed familial love conquering prejudice. Duke had rejected his daughter when she first came out, but later realized the error of his ways. He encouraged parents of LGBT kids to "deal with it, cope with it, accept it, and move on. Life is too short. . . . "

---

* Since she's an unstable tabloid-chaser, it's never quite clear how much of what Tila says is embellished. Yet her claim that *A Shot at Love* was rigged maps closely to the way the show's content was framed. Her description of producers' behind-the-scenes machinations would also explain why straight women pretending to be bisexual were cast on both Tila's and the Ikki Twins' seasons.[16]

The rare presence of women like Coffey, Warner, Marcoccio, and Stoltz—and their girlfriends, wives, and families—on lifestyle, competition, and modeling shows has allowed Americans a positive opportunity to see televised images of queer women working, dating, and generally living and thinking just like anyone else. Regrettably, this has been more the exception than the rule.

More typically, women who flout conventional ideas about "proper" sexual behavior are marginalized. Reality TV hews to what scholars and culture analysts refer to as the "gender binary," in which socially constructed gender roles are considered "natural" and only two recognized genders are considered valid—male or female. Within this system of thought, to be considered "normal" people must look and behave in traditionally "masculine" or "feminine" ways based on the genitals and secondary sex characteristics they had at birth.* In contemporary society, this deeply ingrained idea that there are only two "normal" genders has led to misunderstandings, mockery, and violence against people who are transgender (those who feel uncomfortable with or disconnected from their birth gender) and intersex (individuals whose biological sex cannot be classified as simply male or female).

Within the reality TV universe, the gender binary punishes even straight, "cisgender" women* who don't conform to the strictest social constructions of femininity. If they wear flat shoes, boxy pants, and little to no makeup, makeover shows like TLC's *What Not to Wear* brand them "butch" and "manly." Male adjectives are hurled as high insults, intended as "tough love" encouragement to coerce them to embrace stilettos, cosmetics, and curve-hugging dresses. Fox's *The Swan* went further, surgically altering women to "correct" their "ugly," "masculine" features, employing silicone implants, liposuction, and collagen lip injections to make them "look feminine." These artificial,

---

* Much has been written on the differences between sex and gender, though they are too often confused in both the media and the public imagination. Simply put, sex refers to biology or physicality (for example, genetics and genitals), while gender is a social construct that prescribes standard, static ways to "be a man" or "be a woman."

† Coined in recent years, the term *cisgender* refers to people content with their birth gender.

high-femme transformations were portrayed as the only possible route "mannish" women had toward being beautiful—and, therefore, being loved.

Reality TV's adherence to the gender binary has resulted in near-total invisibility for transgender women. I can remember *only four transgender women* on a decade of broadcast and major cable reality shows. The most talked-about of these, African American model Isis King, was recruited in 2008 for cycle 11 of *America's Next Top Model,* after she and other homeless women were used as background props in a cycle 10 photo shoot. Predictably, *ANTM* played up some competitors' antagonistic insistence that there's no place for a "he-she" in a "real" woman's modeling contest ("Reality is, she's a man!"). But the show balanced attacks and jokes with sensitive scenes in which Isis's beauty—and gender identity—were accepted and her bravery admired. The judges applauded when she said, "This is not something I chose. This is who I've always been." Lounging in a pool in a bikini top, she explained without apology that she was taking female hormones because she was "born in the wrong body," and that transitioning felt like going through puberty all over again. When Isis mentioned that she was "developing," a fellow model replied, "Like a butterfly." Others called her "brave" and even gave her moral support during her hormone injections. Sometimes she was referred to as a "sexy," "gorgeous," "beautiful girl," other times as an imposter with "manly" hands, feet, waist, and another conspicuous part.

These mixed messages were trumped when Isis earned a stamp of "Fierce!" approval from über-model Tyra Banks, whose opinion holds powerful influence among many young women. Still, acceptance had its limits. In Isis's audition, Tyra asked what her presence on the show would do for the LGBT community. The self-confident twenty-two-year-old answered that she was proud to represent, but her "eyes are on the prize" and she only cared about winning. "I like that Isis does not have an agenda, she really just wants to be a model," a judge replied. A trans body may have been appreciated on the show, but activist intentions? Wanting to be a visible agent of social change, rather than just posing in sponsors' ads? Now *that* would be unacceptable.

Also in 2008, transgender activist and performer Laverne Cox was cast on VH1's *I Want to Work for Diddy*, an *Apprentice*-style knockoff replacing real estate tycoon Donald Trump with hip-hop mogul Sean Combs. While some of Laverne's competitors respected her as a worthy adversary, others called her a "joke" and a "spectacle." At one point, her teammates even instructed her to "tranny it up" in a challenge involving on-camera interviews with Diddy's former assistants. ("She's gonna use her trannyness! And you can just laugh at that, period," a male teammate giggled. Though reluctant, Laverne gave in, vamping and giving a beefy dude a lap dance.) Still, the show generally emphasized her poise, competence, and dignity, helping to buck stereotypes within the hip-hop community and earning an award from GLAAD (the Gay & Lesbian Alliance Against Defamation).*

The next year brought two additional transgender women to MTV: Kate-lynn Cusanelli, a computer geek who enjoyed walking around in her underwear on *The Real World*, and Leiomy Maldonado, a member of Vogue Evolution, one of the groups competing in *America's Best Dance Crew*. Like Isis and Laverne, Kate-lynn's and Leiomy's character arcs were edited to create narratives that fluctuated between reinforcing transphobia and rejecting it. Though imperfect, this dual-ity could still be considered a positive antidote to media coverage that typically treats trans people as laughable freaks, deceptive sex workers, or pathetic crime victims. Overall these four shows emphasized the humanity of their transgender cast members more than their difference. In doing so, these few exceptions illus-trated that reality television has the potential to tell compelling stories in ways that enlighten audiences, subvert conventions, and defy expectations—much like *The Real World* used to do in the early 1990s.

If only producers and networks challenged themselves more frequently to fulfill that potential, and not just with regard to storylines involving LGBT people.

---

* LOGO's *Transamerican Love Story* tied with *I Want to Work for Diddy* for the GLAAD award. *TransAmerican Love Story* Star Calpernia Addams, an activist and actress who prioritizes media education about trans-gender issues, accepted alongside Laverne. Her viral videos run the gamut from snarky monologues to patient, academic explanations.[17]

Twenty-First Century Backlash: Your Handy-Dandy Annotated Guide

After "giving gold diggers their comeuppance" on *Joe Millionaire*, breaking would-be brides' hearts on *Married by America*, and ogling bikinis on *Temptation Island*, Rocket Science Laboratories wondered if women with "axes to grind" can "effectively rule society." Enter *When Women Rule the World*, a Fox reality series planned in 2007, described as follows by the network's "evil genius" of unscripted programming, Mike Darnell:

> You take 12 attractive women who feel like it's still a man's world and who think they've hit a glass ceiling, and you give them their own society to run," complete with "12 macho, chauvinistic guys [who become] literally manservants. . . . They'll have to obey every command from the women."[18]

According to Fox Entertainment's Peter Liguori, "What it's doing, in a very Fox-like fashion, is testing social mores. . . . We decided, why not create this Petri dish of a society and see what happens." Darnell was sure *When Women Rule the World* would be a smash hit, because "The biggest reality shows we've done, other than 'Idol,' have been social ideas."[19]*

Where most reality series hide their antifeminist backlash under a saccharine, fairytale gloss, Fox's promotional release—excerpted and translated below for your enjoyment—offered an unvarnished glimpse at how reality producers and network executives perceive gender politics in America. It is extremely telling that Darnell and his Rocket Science buddies Chris Cowan, Jean-Michel Michenaud, and Charles Duncombe consider women's protests about sexism as simply "personal axes to grind." It would be laughable if it weren't so pathetic.

Darnell & co. interpret women's demands for respect in the personal sphere

---

* In the end, *When Women Rule* was scrapped around the time when the Writers Guild strike caused widespread programming upheaval. A version of the series later ran on the U.K.'s Channel 4, promising "Backstabbing, bitching, [and] all-out physical violence" when men have to learn how it feels "being the weaker sex."

WOMEN BEHIND
THE SCENES

• Women are only 25 percent of all creators, executive producers, directors, writers, editors, and photography directors on reality shows, sitcoms, and dramas on ABC, CBS, NBC, Fox, and the CW.[20]

• This marginalization is even more stark in the leadership of Fortune 1000 media and telecommunications companies, where women are just 12 percent of corporate board members and 15 percent of executives.[21]

• Female executives hold a paltry 3 percent of the "clout titles" that wield real decision-making power in these media and telecom companies, from executive vice president to chair and CEO.[22]

• Women owned 28 percent (and minorities 18 percent) of all nonfarm businesses in 2002, but by 2006 owned less than 5 percent and 3 percent of commercial broadcast TV stations, respectively.[23]

Human rights shouldn't be such a confusing concept. Yet when women talk about correcting injustice, media powerbrokers tend to think of a "gender war" in which the winning side dominates and the other submits—and they deploy programming accordingly.

If the men who occupy media boardrooms and key executive suites are hostile to feminism, hardly any women exist in their power-peer group with the ability to sway them—or, for that matter, to veto their choices and set different corporate priorities for what we get to watch. The fact that women are only 3 percent of top-level decision-making media and telecom executives has broader impact than average employment discrimination. "The people who tell the stories in our culture ultimately control that culture and have a lot of power over how we see groups of people [and] events," notes Dr. Martha M. Lauzen, executive director of the Center for Study of Women in TV and Film. "That remains a mostly male activity."[24]

With so little equality at the top, perhaps the gender bias in ten years of reality programming can hardly be seen as a surprise.

and an end to discrimination in public life as a power grab by rampaging fembots who want to control the world and turn men into their slaves. So accustomed have male media leaders become to the wealth and decision-making power they command (see sidebar) they just can't parse the notion of *equality* between the sexes. They have never understood the world feminists actually envision, in which women and men share equal educational, economic, and professional opportunities, live free of abuse, can be fully sexual without judgment or coercion, and where girls and boys alike can embrace their authentic selves because no one will be told that strength, tenderness, confidence, empathy, or aggression is "inappropriate" for their gender—a society in which power and dignity are not rationed based on gender, ethnicity, sexual orientation, or physical ability.

Reading Between the Lines

Now that we've unraveled reality TV's twisted fairytales and examined how advertiser ideology influences depictions of women, people of color, and class and consumerism, my hope is that you'll be better armed against the subtle indoctrination these shows engage in. This requires active, critical viewership—the opposite of irony, our usual shield when we watch kitschy, over-the-top shows like *Flavor of Love, Tool Academy,* or *When Women Rule the World.* As Susan Douglas writes in *Enlightened Sexism,* "irony means that you can look as if you are absolutely not seduced by the mass media, while then being seduced by the media, wearing a knowing smirk."[26]

The more you hone your media criticism instincts, the less affected you will be by sexist, racist, hyperconsumerist representations—and the more easily you can predict whether new reality shows are likely to offer harmless entertainment or antagonistic attacks.

As a sample of the fun you can have with media literacy, try predicting what future reality shows will be like by annotating press releases from production houses bragging about new programs. For example, the following phrases come from Fox's "Fall Preview 07" release for *When Women Rule the World,** decoded via my handy-dandy "Reality TV Speak to Plain English" translation guide:

" . . . a group of strong, educated, independent women . . .
each with a personal axe to grind . . . "

> = Women will be portrayed as castrating bitchqueens; however, the female cast members won't actually be feminists.

---

* Read the full release here: http://www.fox.com/fallpreview/new/whenwomenrule.htm

" . . . *unsuspecting men used to calling the shots . . .* "

> = Men will be cast specifically because they are prone toward domineering, controlling, possibly abusive behavior, and are likely to say regressive, patronizing things about women.

" . . . *a world where women are in charge and men are subservient . . .* "

> = Feminism (the idea of eliminating barriers to women's equality) automatically involves denigration and submission of men.

" . . . *each gender's ability to adapt to a new social order will be put to the test . . .* "

> = Traditional gender roles are innate; by messing with biological destiny, this "social experiment" will result in total chaos, proving that feminism is futile.

" . . . *a remote, primitive location . . .* "

> = Flashback to Bill Maher being boiled in a cauldron by hot, cruel babes in *Cannibal Women in the Avocado Jungle of Death*. Women will wear revealing island outfits provided by producers.

" . . . *build a newly formed society—one where there is no glass ceiling and no dressing to impress . . .* "

> = Fashion and the glass ceiling are the only two forms of oppression women face. Rape, poverty, state attempts to control reproduction, racist targeting of women of color, marginalization of female leadership in politics, sports, business, and media . . . simply don't exist.

"For the men, their worlds of power and prestige are turned inside-out and upside-down"
= Up is down, night is day, cats and dogs living together—total anarchy! It's unnatural, I tell you—unnatural!

"for these women, turnabout is fair play! . . . women command and men obey."
= Let the ballbusting begin!

"How will the women treat the men?"
= Like dogs . . . which is why women shouldn't be given leadership roles in the real world.

"Will this new society be a Utopia or a hell on earth?"
= That's an easy one. . . .

"Who will be man enough to succeed in the new social order"
= A man, *naturally!*

In the end, *When Women Rule the World* wasn't a Petri dish, it was a cesspool. Hardly "testing social mores" in a hands-off "experiment," as Luguori claimed, Rocket Science and Fox manufactured a manipulative premise based on a bastardization of "women's rights," all to burn straw feminists in an island campfire.

These are the sorts of "social ideas" around which Mike Darnell has built a decade of unscripted programming: Women's leadership is laughable, men's rightful place is in charge, and women really belong—as *The Millionaire Matchmaker* put it explicitly—in the bedroom, the kitchen, and the nursery. As we've seen throughout this book, as much as Darnell claims that he and other reality programmers are just "giving people what they want, pushing the envelope to match tastes," the opposite is true. In fact, they're doing their best to *alter* our tastes, in an attempt to convince us that at the dawn of the twenty-first century, Americans do not see women and men—or our soci-ety in general—much differently than we did before the women's rights, civil rights, and gay rights movements. Though full-fledged equality still awaits, the advancement of women and people of color in nearly every aspect of pub-lic life stands counter to producers' attempts to redact several generations of social progress. Yet reality TV producers, advertisers, and media owners have done what the most ardent fundamentalists have never been able to achieve: They've created a universe in which women not only *have* no real choices, but don't even *want* any.

I encourage you to take to heart this antidote for such backlash fare, offered by author Susan Douglas:

> producers insist that mass media are simply mirrors, reflecting reality, what-ever that is, back to the public. . . . Whenever you hear this mirror metaphor, I urge you to smash it. Because if the media are mirrors, they are funhouse mirrors . . . [that] "set the agenda for what we are to think about, what kinds of people deserve our admiration, respect and envy, and what kinds don't."[26]

No matter how often reality TV's funhouse mirrors replay nearly identi-cal images, it's important to note that there's no conspiracy of rich, chauvinist WASPS locked away in a media boardroom, asking each other between cigar puffs, "Okay, boys, how do we keep the chicks and uppity minorities down?" Anachronistic, yes—orchestrated, no.

Still . . . who needs a conspiracy when the impact of corporate media con-solidation has led to the same results? Today, as a result of fifteen years of media deregulation, almost three-quarters of all broadcast and cable channels are owned by six conglomerates, soon to be five if an impending Comcast/NBC merger goes through (more on this in the next chapter). Reality programmers are landscape-shaping agents in the backlash, consciously or not, but they play just one part in a much larger institutional problem.

Market-based priorities have dumbed down network entertainment, corrupted mainstream journalism, and allowed media companies to lag way behind most other major industries in the percentage of women and people of color in leadership. In the following chapter, I dig into one aspect of media economics—how product placement led to the rise of reality TV, and what this means for media content in the future. I hope that by the time you get to the media activism conclusion, you'll be ready to start working to change the system responsible for backlash programming.

Chapter Nine

The World According to CoverGirl

Advertiser Ideology Goes 3-D

During a recent challenge on America's Next Top Model, *the contestants were asked to step into the limelight with CoverGirl® beauty products at Wal-Mart®. . . . You may not be trying to wow any judges, but that doesn't mean you can't use these products to create your own runway-worthy look. Start at the same place the* America's Next Top Model *contestants went to fill their makeup bags—Wal-Mart.*

—"In Stores Now" section on Wal-Mart.com

A neon Wal-Mart sign glows conspicuously behind *America's Next Top Model* judge Nigel Barker and his wife, CoverGirl spokeswoman Chrissy Barker. Ten lithe young women are gathered outside the megastore, the set for this episode's competition. "You are going to be racing through the One-Stop-Shop CoverGirl Challenge," Chrissy announces. "You'll have to race through different departments within Wal-Mart to create that model basic look," Nigel explains. "You're gonna hit clothes, you're gonna hit shoes, you're gonna hit makeup," he narrates, as *ANTM's* cameras pan through Wal-Mart aisles and rest on in-store ads, rollback sale signs, and constant close-ups of sponsors' apparel and cosmetics. "The girl who puts her look together best of all will win."

What, exactly, will be her reward? After urging the models to "enhance[e] your natural beauty" by "working with CoverGirl Lash Blast Length"* Chrissy

---

* Chrissy Barker's ad-spewing monologues were lengthier than her lashes. Under the guise of offering contest rules, she told viewers that "of course" CoverGirl mascara will "help you stand out by stretching your lashes to extreme lengths that last without flaking or breaking," chirps: "The winner is going to receive a photo on CoverGirl's page of WalMart .com, and also a $1,000 Walmart gift card provided by CoverGirl.[1]

Ah, the chance to *work for free* and have two giant corporations profit from your unpaid labor—the ideal prize in the World According to CoverGirl.*

The Reality of Media Economics

To truly understand images of women in reality TV (as in the media in general) we need to look at the financial big picture.

The primary purpose of contemporary television is not to entertain, engage, or inform us. Today, the driving factor for all corporate media production is to turn tidy profits for the tiny handful of megamerged corporations that own the vast majority of media outlets and control the bulk of what we are given to watch, see, and hear on TV and radio, in movies, video games, and more. The suits in charge of deciding what shows, songs, films, and news programs we get to choose from care only about their companies' bottom line—and see their media products as virtually indistinguishable from sneakers, Snuggies, or any other doodad to be bought and sold.

In this climate, what viewers want will always take a back seat to what multinationals such as the Big Six media owners (Disney, News Corp, Time Warner, General Electric, Viacom, and CBS) can convince us to watch.⁺ TV shows live or die in today's media market based not on pure-and-simple ratings, but on demographics (*which* viewers are watching, in relation to age, race, gender, and income

---

* If young women viewers longed to be as glamorous as their favorite *ANTM* contestants, they could turn to the "In Stores Now" page of Wal-Mart's website. There, they'd find the winner's picture, and learn that "Only one can be *America's Next Top Model* but you can have what's in her makeup bag." The site urges shoppers to use "CoverGirl essentials to create the clean, fresh, natural CoverGirl look" that will make any girl "runway-worthy. . . . Start at the same place the *America's Next Top Model* contestants went to fill their makeup bags—Wal-Mart."

⁺ National Amusements, Inc., which owns and operates approximately fifteen hundred movie screens in the United States, U.K., South America, and Russia, has voting control of Viacom and CBS through NAI's founder, chairman, and controlling shareholder, Sumner M. Redstone. And as this book goes to press, cable giant Comcast is angling to acquire NBC Universal from General Electric, in an attempt to control media across all distribution platforms, from broadcast to Internet to cable. While corporate news media are reporting the merger as a done deal, the Department of Justice announced in January 2010 that it would lead a review of the deal to evaluate it within the context of antitrust laws. By June 2010, media justice activists were still pressuring the FCC and the Obama administration to reject Comcast's bid as an antitrust violation.[2]

bracket, not just how many overall) and broader economic factors, including the cost to produce a program versus the amount of profit it generates.

The key to media profits is advertising, a $200 billion annual industry.[3] In the last decade, TV companies' ad revenue has come not only from traditional commercials between, but increasingly from product placements within, the content of our favorite shows. Embedded sponsorship has been a particular windfall for cable, which operates under a subscription model and is therefore seen as an "ad-free" medium.*

Forgive this geek moment, but to paraphrase *Spider-Man:* with great cash comes great influence.

Corporate sponsors have long lorded their lucre over TV networks to promote programs that advance their values, and regularly withhold ad buys to squelch content they deem controversial (or material geared toward the non-white, low-income, or aging demographics they consider undesirable).[4] This has been partly responsible for the ongoing whitewashing of prime-time network television. Back when sitcoms and dramas ruled, *Extra!* magazine's Janine Jackson documented the way advertisers' racial prejudice resulted in the sidelining of actors of color in 1990s scripted programs. "Advertisers pay less for programs that garner non-white audiences, in a widely acknowledged policy called 'discounting.' Some flatly refuse to buy ads on stations or shows that reach primarily non-white audiences, the so-called 'no urban/no Spanish dictate,'" Jackson wrote.† Ten years later, advertisers' bias against multiracial casting continues to play out in the reality genre, as the lily-white *Bachelor/Bachelorette* franchise attests.

---

* Consider that the next time Bravo's Tim Gunn tells you that you can buy a winning *Project Runway* design on Bluefly.com.

† Comparing four shows on the same network, Jackson found that, "The WB's *Felicity* draws similar numbers of 18- to 49-year-olds as the net's two highest-rated black series, the *Steve Harvey Show* and the *Jamie Foxx Show*. But last season, *Felicity* commanded more than twice as much money per 30-second commercial than either show ($80,000 vs. less than $40,000). In the first week of the new season, *The Steve Harvey Show* pulled in 500,000 more viewers than *Dawson's Creek;* but *Dawson's Creek* gets $63,000 more for a 30-second. . . . How can that be simple ratings?"[5] Simple: It's not. *Felicity* and *Dawson's Creek* focused on angsty white students and were watched by young viewers who looked like them, while *Harvey* and *Foxx* featured Black people and drew a more diverse audience—one devalued by advertisers because of its racial makeup.

Standard commercials are still an important revenue stream for network TV. When the people and the homes on reality shows resemble wealthy, white gated communities, chalk it up to advertisers like Toyota, whose marketing manager explained in 2003 that they were buying time during *The Bachelor* and *The Bachelorette* because "We're definitely looking for upper middle-class content— more like *The Bachelor.*" That same year, McDonald's, Visa, Pfizer, the U.S. Army, and at least ten other advertisers spent an average of $210,000 each for thirty-second spots during the first month's episodes of *Joe Millionaire.* Many of these major corporations were telling journalists that they wouldn't advertise on programs such as *Fear Factor,* because they considered "contestants eating 'horse rectum'" offensive. They had no problem running their ads on shows that treated women like subservient losers and greedy gold diggers, though—apparently that was just considered good business practice.[6]

Where traditional commercials allowed advertisers to sway program content through veiled financial blackmail, the new economic model of reality television handed them the holy grail. Today, to combat cable-channel proliferation and technologies like DVRs, media companies wooing ad dollars are encouraging a rapid disintegration of borders between marketing and editorial. With "brand integration," advertisers no longer have to rely on threats—or even program breaks—to make their desired impact. Instead, they are weaving their products directly into the fabric of popular unscripted shows, where not even the most careful TiVo jockey can fast-forward through them. Sometimes marketers pay millions for the privilege; other times they simply deliver goods and services (like luxury resort accommodations on dating shows) gratis. Either way, companies get their brands displayed while prop managers, costumers, set designers, and travel coordinators get free supplies, reducing overall production costs. And then there's cross-promotion: Advertisers attempt to cash in on the entertainment vehicle's cachet by using its celebrities, clips, and themes in marketing campaigns for their own products, and they use their own ad budgets to hype the show. This value-added promotion expands both advertisers' sales and ratings success for networks.

Product placement used to be mostly limited to subtle (or blatant) dressing of characters and scenery with recognizable brands. And sure, shots of sponsors' goods are ubiquitous on almost all reality shows, from *The Bachelor*'s fridge full of Pepsi and the GE appliances on *Top Chef* to the close-ups of name-brand picture phones used by aspiring *American Idols* and *Biggest Losers*. CoverGirl, Steve Madden, La Perla, and Ethan Allen have had deals to dress the faces, the feet, the boobs, and the sets of *America's Next Top Model*, where young women are berated for being too fat, too skinny, too short, too tall, too aggressive, too timid, too prudish, too "hootchie," too "ghetto," and my personal favorite, for sounding too smart when they speak. Offensive? Yep . . . but entirely typical of the way fashion and beauty advertisers have always portrayed women.

This starts early. Eight "young black elite" friends in Manhattan "swish Listerine, treat their allergies with Zyrtec, and sweeten their coffee with Splenda" on *Harlem Heights,* the result of a partnership between BET and Johnson & Johnson.[7] Long before filming began, participants were surveyed about their health and wellness habits, so that it would seem like the company's mouthwash, medical products, and sweeteners, along with their Ambi skin creams and Purell hand sanitizer, were just "part of their daily process."* Producers told *The New York Times* that "we would come on the set with boxes and we would place things within the scenes, while trying to make it as organic as possible." Other times, visual endorsements are so jarring that they can disrupt the momentum of a show's (and I use this word lightly) storytelling. When women in their forties on NBC's *Age of Love* are shown using Downy Simple Pleasures Fabric Softener to do their laundry (because that's what "cougars" do when they're tired of chasing beefcake prey, right?), the camera zooms in on a detergent bottle placed next to a stove. The very next second

---

* For now, it's allergy meds on *Harlem Heights*. How long until future reality series are created to push Prozac, Zoloft, or other antidepressants? After all, *Bachelor* producer Mike Fleiss has professed his love of "getting girls to cry" on his shows. As culturally corrosive as reality TV has been, how much more dangerous could it be if women sob about their bodies on *The Swan*, their love lives on *The Bachelor*, and their addictions on *Sex Rehab with Dr. Drew*, only to emerge the picture of health and contentment after popping some strategically placed happy pills? I'm not joking. Since reality TV allows embedded advertisers to avoid regulations governing traditional medical marketing—and flout industry standards around advertising in general—this is a serious potential concern.

a woman is shown opening a washing machine door in an entirely different room. Oopsy . . . shilling is a little more important than "reality," ain't it?

Conspicuously brand-conscious camera work is just the first layer. The second is dialogue. As we've seen, advertisers infiltrate climactic reality moments. *Bachelors* propose by telling their *Bachelorettes* "that this Tacori diamond ring symbolizes forever." Fashion adviser Tim Gunn tells *Project Runway* contestants to "use the Banana Republic [later Bluefly.com] accessory wall" and "go down to the L'Oréal hair and makeup studio" right before they hit the runway. *Top Model* ingenues mouth advertisers' slogans every episode—sometimes while nude. (Psst! Wanna see someone's side-boob again? Pinup pics are available in the "CoverGirl Close Up" gallery on the CW's website.) Such sound bites are hardly natural. When a runway challenge was staged at a Kmart store rather than at some high-fashion locale, *ANTM*'s contestants were confused and annoyed. Their distaste was edited out. The Writers Guild reports, "Kmart only allowed a comment like, 'What are we doing at Kmart?' if it was followed up by 'That's OK, I shop here all the time.'"[8]

The third level of integration: plot. Every season of *ANTM* includes one or more episodes in which contestants must act in a CoverGirl commercial; just one of these can feature forty verbal and twenty-two visual endorsements. We listen as they rehearse lines about the many merits of "LashBlast Mascara" and "Eye Enhancer Blast Collection Shadows" and watch them perform as spokesmodels in would-be TV ads. Then we see those ads again, as judges evaluate which girl "sold it" best. When they finally bump to an official commercial break, actual CoverGirl ads appear, featuring previous *ANTM* winners telling us that they feel "Easy. Breezy. Beautiful."[9]

Easy, breezy? I feel a little queasy. *ANTM* viewers are marketing hostages; there is no respite. The only thing that distinguishes those "My Life As a Cover-Girl" commercial breaks from program content is higher-quality film.

Advertisers have paid NBC as much as $2.5 million for integration into *The Apprentice*, where products such as "Chrysler vehicles [are] involved from the start, as central 'characters.'" The financials are even steeper at Fox, which reaps millions each season by making *American Idol* hopefuls literally do backflips over corporate logos spray painted on the floor, fake orgasms while getting "totally organic" Herbal Essences shampoos, and drive Ford Focuses in exceptionally cheesy mini music videos that viewers are encouraged to download online. By 2003, Ford and AT&T were paying $20 million for the privilege, while Coca-Cola now reportedly pays upward of $26 million annually for the Coke cups on *American Idol* judges' desks, Coke-red walls, and Coke-bottle-shaped interview couch with its signature white ribbon across the back, which permeate an estimated 60 percent of the show's airtime.[10]

Queer Eye for the Straight Guy's Fab Five primped with Neutrogena tanner, Norelco nose-hair trimmers, Redken pomade, and other beauty, fashion, and interior-design products, all aggressively promoted in "shopping guides" on Bravo's website. A *What Not to Wear* special blew $50K on about a dozen outfits from high-end designers like Gucci and Armani. The sales staff of bridal behemoth Kleinfeld tell *Say Yes to the Dress* viewers that their weddings can only be perfect with this $12K Pnina Tornai ball gown or that $17K J'Aton Couture creation. Spending a year's salary on clothes and styling products is portrayed as a "fairytale" come true. With reality TV offering that kind of bang for their buck, advertisers assess, who needs *Vogue?*

Even fashion mags themselves now see reality TV as the ultimate pitching platform. On MTV's *Miss Seventeen,* girls vied for an internship and a coveted spot on the teen mag's cover (oh, and an afterthought scholarship). *Seventeen* editor Atoosa Rubenstein served as host. "Every editor in chief's dream is to have a television show," she told *The New York Times.* "The modern editor in chief has to see themselves as the editor in chief of a brand, with the publication one part of that brand." That line of thought led to what the *Times* called "a match made in demographic heaven." Two issues of the magazine devoted covers and editorial to MTV's stars, while ten half-hour episodes of *Miss Seventeen* ran on the network, as did commercials for the publication—with revenue from the show shared between the two media properties. *Seventeen*'s publisher was salivating. "We're going to have our brand exposed on MTV for two months, every day. . . . Everywhere you turn, you will see Seventeen." Fox's Mike Darnell may like to pretend that reality TV shows appear because "We're giving people what they want," but Rubenstein was far more honest: "At the end of the day, this is about branding, this is about marketing, and this is about getting to as many eyeballs as possible."[11]*

"A Commercial Vehicle as Much as a TV Drama"

If you watch reality TV you've probably noticed some of these plugs—they're not exactly understated. What you may not know is the level of control sponsors have over which reality shows get made in the first place, and what happens on any given episode. As *Miss Seventeen* illustrates, advertisers are now creating entire unscripted series whose primary purpose is to push their brands.

When ABC's *Extreme Makeover: Home Edition* premiered in 2003, a group of designers were given a week to remodel the house of a suburban, middle-class family whose rosy-cheeked little daughter survived leukemia. Cameras captured the clan cavorting at Disney World while the team, led by toolmaster Ty Pennington, renovated their home with Craftsman tools, stocked their kitchen with Kenmore appliances, and filled their living room with electronics from Toshiba, Panasonic, and Sony—all of which were available for purchase from a Sears-sponsored, link-filled "As Featured On" section of ABC.com (which viewers were prompted to visit at the end of the program). The sentimental climax came when the adorable cancer survivor gasped with glee at the life-size dollhouse Pennington had built for her. The happiness on that brave little girl's face, Pennington mused, is what this was all about.

Well . . . not quite. *EM: HE* is about what most reality TV series are about: manufacturing entertainment around sponsors' goods. When it debuted, *EM:*

---

* *Miss Seventeen* was indeed all about branding, marketing, and eyeballs—it just wasn't remotely interesting. The show spanned one season in the winter of 2005, after which *Seventeen* abandoned cable to integrate themselves into an already-proven hit among their target young female demographic: *America's Next Top Model.* Since then, for seven seasons and counting *ANTM* challenges have revolved around *Seventeen* photo shoots, and every *ANTM* winner has appeared on the cover of the magazine.

HE was the most lucrative branded-entertainment deal ABC had ever inked, with Sears paying more than $1 million for narrative integration in each of six episodes, plus purchasing commercials during each hour.

Many people believe that we're currently seeing so much product placement on television because the reality format opened the floodgates.* As *Advertising Age* editor Scott Donaton writes, "Product integration could never have risen to such prominence so rapidly if TV schedules were still dominated by sitcoms and hour-long dramas . . . rather than brash reality shows with short lives and an anything goes sensibility. They make a perfect Petri dish for advertisers."[12]

What most people don't understand is that the flip side is also true: The genre of reality TV would not exist as we know it today without embedded advertising.

MTV's *The Real World,* and *Cops,* a syndicated scare-fest of racial stereotypes, have been around since the 1990s. But those shows were marginal, not powerhouses. Reality TV now has its own Emmy category and, as the sidebar "Prime-Time Programming Lineup by Network" illustrates, a significant percentage of every major network's primetime lineup is dedicated to unscripted fare, with Fox devoting nearly half its roster to reality. (CBS seems more dedicated to fiction than the other nets: Aside from *Survivor,* they air nearly all their other unscripted hours during the summer.) This change occurred because networks were willing to offer a new format to sponsors, who consider brand integration a "more intrusive," "more aggressive" way of weaseling into your psyche.⁺

It all started with *Survivor,* which instigated reality's shift from cable to network TV in the summer of 2000. Now in its twentieth season, the series was a hard sell. "Skittish programmers balked" at a premise that sounded like *Gilligan's Island* with the Skipper and Mary Ann eating bugs. CBS only green-lit the project after producer Mark Burnett explained that instead of paying high-priced actors and a

---

* In 2008, the top ten broadcast network programs with product placement activity featured a combined 29,823 embedded ads. Only one scripted show, CW teen drama *One Tree Hill,* made the list. *The Biggest Loser* led with 6,248 placements, while *American Idol* had 4,636, *EM: HE* had 3,371, and *Top Model* had 2,241.[13]

⁺ "We will use a diverse array of entertainment assets to break into people's hearts and minds. In that order. For this is the way to their wallets," Coca-Cola's CEO announced at an advertising conference in 2003, shortly after they began embedding their brand in *American Idol.*[14]

PRIME-TIME PROGRAMMING LINEUP BY NETWORK: SCRIPTED VERSUS REALITY PROGRAMMING

	UNSCRIPTED	SCRIPTED	MISCELLANEOUS
Fox, 2009	41%	59%	—
Fox, 2008	48%	52%	—
NBC, Fall 2009 season[15]	9.1% Reality 22.7% *Jay Leno Show* (comedy chat show format)	45.5%	4.5% Newsmagazine 18.2 % Sports
NBC, 2008–2009 broadcast year	24.8%	58.2%	8% Newsmagazine 6.1% Sports 3% Specials
CBS, 2009–2010 broadcast year, projected	14%	77%	9% Newsmagazine
CBS, 2008–2009 broadcast year	10.3%	79.1%	10.6% Newsmagazine
CW, 2009	17%	83%	—
CW, 2008	27%	65%	10.6% Sports

team of union writers, *advertisers would pay the network* for a starring role. Burnett "envision[ed] 'Survivor' as a commercial vehicle as much as a TV drama," *Advertising Age* noted. The adventure theme is simply a pretext for contestants to interact with brands such as Doritos, Mountain Dew, Bud Light, Saturn, and Target to the tune of more than $3.7 million each for the initial series and $12 million for the second installment. The price tag has risen exponentially each season.[16]

That may seem pricey, but as CBS's sales president told *Advertising Age,* it was "one of the best bargains in TV history." It's not every day that advertisers get offered "many opportunities to have *products play meaningful roles in surviving."* (Emphasis mine.) In addition to getting months of prime-time exposure to viewers, advertisers use *Survivor* imagery in their marketing campaigns and get added exposure from countless clips played on news and infotainment shows.[17]

Burnett told *The Hollywood Reporter* that brand integration in reality TV is "a very good business move" because "it's a great opportunity for sponsors to have more control and networks to have less risk."[18] The philosophy was even more unabashed on another early Mark Burnett Productions series, NBC's *The Restaurant,* which followed celebrity chef Rocco DiSpirito in 2003. Ben Silverman, the self-described "media synergist" responsible for ABC's product-laced *Who Wants to Be a Millionaire,** conceived the show. It was coproduced by Silverman's production company, Reveille, along with Magna Global Entertainment, a branded-entertainment development wing of media giant Interpublic "dedicated to the creation of original television programming that is funded by and serves the needs of Interpublic's clients."

In this case, Magna clients Coors, American Express, and Mitsubishi paid between $4 and $6 million in development and advertising for story-driving presence in the food-themed reality show. *NBC didn't have to pay one dime to make or air the series*—all the network had to do was save half the commercial time for the sponsors and reap cross-promotional benefits from AmEx ads starring DiSpirito. Opening credits featured an AmEx OPEN sign on the door, along with customers charging meals to their AmEx cards. DiSpirito talked shop in his Mitsubishi Endeavor, invited the bouncy Coors Twins to the restaurant's opening, and issued stilted commands to his employees—some reportedly dubbed in by producers—such as "Don't come back without Coors for all these people." Looking back on his experience, Albert Davis, the restaurant's espresso maker, said, "I will forever be trained to hold a Coors Light bottle by the neck with the label facing outwards."[19]

Media scholars Robert W. McChesney and John Bellamy Foster have noted that by 2003, 80 percent of U.S. ad spending was funneled through the eight largest advertising corporations, giving companies like Interpublic "considerable

---

* In 2007, Silverman became cochairman of NBC Universal's entertainment division, promising to force "the creative community" to kowtow to embedded sponsors. "If you're making broadcast television, you better get the joke: We get financed by advertising," he told *TV Guide.* Silverman personally supported replacing five prime-time programming hours with *The Jay Leno Show* at 10:00 p.m. The former *Tonight Show* host got Silverman's joke, making his new show the number one user of product placement in prime time for 2009—but was a programmatic failure in every other respect, helping to drive the ailing fourth-place network further into the ground.[20]

ability to name their tune with corporate media firms more than willing to play ball." For example, during a series of top-level meetings held in 2000 by USA Network, major advertisers were invited to "tell the network what type of programming content they wanted."[21]

This should give us pause.

Silverman told reporters that the networks "had these huge doubts" about *The Restaurant,* like *Survivor* before it, but warmed up once the advertisers were brought in. "This couldn't have happened without them," he said. "If not for us, it's very possible the show would not have gotten on the air."[22]

The question is, would anyone have missed it? More than a scripted show we could have enjoyed instead? Likewise, would MTV viewers have been worse off if they'd never been able to watch *The Gamekillers,* a series based on an Axe ad campaign and developed by Unilever PLC's ad agency, in which Axe deodorant helped men "keep their cool" while trying to score with women? TV fans are still angry nine and five years after the cancellations of *Firefly* and *Arrested Development,* blogging about how much they wish the zany space Western and the biting comedy were still on the air. No one seems to remember the Coors-guzzling *Restaurant,* or the body-spray-touting *Gamekillers.*[23]

"It's Not at All about Making Better Television"

According to Magna's Robert Riesenberg, "'*The Restaurant*' represents a bold new era in television." Burnett agrees, calling such shows "the next evolution of storytelling."[24]

In this "bold new era," well-written TV fiction is more the exception *(Mad Men, 30 Rock)* than the rule. Chasing *Survivor*-style ratings, networks give scripted series very little time to cultivate audiences, making it hard for new shows to survive. ABC yanked Sally Field's drama *The Court,* about a female Supreme Court justice, after only three episodes; they let Geena Davis serve as *Commander in Chief* for only one season. Networks are not only decreasing the number of slots available for quality scripted programs (which, unlike reality series, offer union writers, crew, and actors fair pay and health insurance), they're also slashing their budgets. Once *Idol* was on the air for a couple of seasons, Fox tasked veteran sitcom producer Bruce Helford to create a sitcom for comedian Wanda Sykes—but, he said, only with "the lowest budget I've ever worked with to launch a show." Discussing the greed that governs such programming decisions, *Bernie Mac* producer (and later *The Daily Show* contributor) Larry Wilmore told *Entertainment Weekly* that despite winning an Emmy and a spate of other awards in its first season, *Mac* was regularly preempted by Fox in favor of ratings draws like *Joe Millionaire*. "Now, this is an award-winning, groundbreaking show. Let alone, when was the last time a black show has been in that position?" Wilmore asked. "They don't care. . . . They'll pull us for whatever reality show brings that 30 share." But as Wilmore aptly says, it's "an unfair argument about scripted shows versus reality—it's like asking, Why does the *National Enquirer* sell more copies than *Scientific American?*"[25]

Beware storytellers concerned only with commerce, who care little about art, intellect, creativity, or culture. Once in a while they may stumble on a formula that is truly engaging and even edifying, like *Project Runway* or *The Amazing Race*—but more often than not, they aren't even *attempting* to entertain us. "We're trying to create marketing platforms through television for our clients," Riesenberg has said. "*It's not at all about making better television*. We don't profess to be able to do it better. It's really about finding that right fit, and then integrating them into that fit" (emphasis mine).[26]

This explains why reality TV shows position products as literally intrinsic to our survival, whether it's a Target tent sheltering *Survivor* castaways from the elements or Sears giving new homes to natural disaster victims on *Extreme Makeover: Home Edition*. Stealth advertising co-opts our emotional connections to stories, and we respond like we do to most savvy marketing gambits: by opening up our wallets. A survey by PR firm Jericho Communications found that "men were five times more likely than women to go shopping" on a Wednesday after a new *Queer Eye* episode aired, and respondents said they'd be most likely to purchase products endorsed by Carson Kressley, *QE*'s fashion expert, than any other celebrity. *The Apprentice* "greatly exceeded our expectations in terms of response from consumers and retailers," a Crest spokesperson said, after the show generated 3 million visits and 20 million page views to the toothpaste giant's website. Beyond just prompting viewers to buy Crest Whitestrips, the show motivated big-ticket spending decisions. In an online tie-in, more than one thousand viewers preordered the Pontiac Solstice *sight unseen* within forty-one minutes of GM launching the car on a segment of *The Apprentice.*[*27]

Brilliant from a business standpoint, this model has serious implications for programming, and for our culture. Advertising is profoundly manipulative at its core. Its imagery strives to deprive us of realistic ideas about love, sex, beauty, health, money, work, and life itself, in an attempt to convince us that only products can bring us true joy. Its practitioners are trained in psychology, sociology, argumentation, poetry, and design. These are powerful tools in the art of persuasion, more so when deployed by a multibillion-dollar industry. Decades of research by analysts such as Jean Kilbourne, Robin Andersen, Anne Elizabeth Moore, and Sut Jhally have documented how advertising sees everything women have—our bodies, our minds, our fears, our dreams—as fodder to be traded, mutilated, and sold back to us for profit. As noted in chapter 2, studies show that the more ads we view, the worse we feel about ourselves.[+] This is hardly coincidental. Advertisers—especially those who target women—intentionally undermine our self-esteem to position their brands as the solution to the insecurities they've piqued. "Subtle manipulations can temporarily 'shake' one's self-view confidence, resulting in an increased propensity of choosing self-view-bolstering products in a subsequent choice task," advises a 2009 study in the *Journal of Consumer Research,* an industry trade publication.[28]

---

[*] At the time, the Solstice had a base price of $19,995 plus a $575 destination charge. That would put the value of those first one thousand *Apprentice*-generated orders at $20,570,000. According to *Automotive News*, the results were "spectacular," with thirty-six thousand additional web visitors expressing interest in purchasing the vehicle.

[+] If just a few minutes of reading ad-heavy fashion magazines increases girls' and women's body hatred, what impact might fourteen seasons of *America's Next Top Model* have on viewers?

This psychological exploitation becomes all the more insidious when woven directly into our narratives, as is happening in reality TV. The stronger the foothold advertisers gain over entertainment, the more power they have to define our collective values, and the more poisonous media images of women and people of color become. Reality TV's racial typecasting, infantilizing fairytales, and hyperconsumerism—indeed, all the issues explored in *Reality Bites Back*—are a testament to what happens when advertisers expand the stories they tell from static print ads and thirty-second commercial breaks to feature-length programming. Using real people as their props, marketers have worked with producers to cultivate entire faux worlds based on sexist, racist ideologies. Worse, they have pretended the results are just reflecting—rather than attempting to shape— American life.

So, what do we learn about "reality" when we allow advertisers to tell us who we are and what we want?

America's Next Top Model's racial typecasting, glamorization of female pain and fear, and body dysmorphia are Madison Avenue staples. In the world according to CoverGirl (and Wal-Mart, Kmart, *Seventeen,* and a host of other sponsors), women are always on display for the gratification of others, but are not afforded control of their own sexuality or pleasure. Beauty is the key to women's worth, but even the most gorgeous girls are fundamentally flawed. Young women are commodities, posed in La Perla panties as living mannequins in store windows. The symbolism is exceptionally clear: mannequins have no voice, no choice, no agency, no personality (and no asses—ever see those teeny plastic bods undressed? Scary!). In this universe, we're encouraged to buy *America's Next Top Model*–branded "fashion-forward clothing, bags, hats, fragrances, and room decor" exclusively at Wal-Mart, but never to question the big box chain's reliance on sweatshop labor, its record of employment discrimination and environmental pollution, or the strain it causes to local economies.[29]

Embedded advertising in reality TV has sociopolitical significance beyond representations of women. In the world according to Kentucky Fried Chicken, whose fast food was regularly featured on *Flavor of Love,* Black men are callous clowns who objectify, control, and mock Black and Latina "bitches" and "hos" while chomping on chicken wings. And in the world according to GM, Visa, and the dozens of others who've spent millions to make their brands "central characters" on *The Apprentice,* sexual harassment is fun, professionalism is optional, and business ethics are a joke. The quality of a person's work doesn't determine *Apprentice* challenge winners, the financial bottom line does, sending the message that the only thing that matters on the job is how much money you make—even if you have to lie, cheat, or commit fraud for every buck. It's appointment TV for the likes of Ponzi schemer Bernie Madoff.

This medium seeks to channel our every desire into consumer behavior. If we long for adventure, we can book a trip with *Amazing Race* sponsor Travelocity. If we buy into *The Bachelor*'s princess mythology, a "fairytale wedding" at Disney World is just a drained bank account away. And if we want to lose weight, we can stock up on *The Biggest Loser*–brand protein supplements, panini makers, and other goods of questionable health value.

But here's the kicker: It's not just advertisers who influence unscripted programming. In today's multimerged media environment, TV networks, film studios, newspapers, and magazines are just a small sample of parent companies' cross-holdings. Big Media corporations are also invested in industries such as travel and theme parks, insurance and financial services, sports teams and stadiums, medical technology, and aircraft, weapons, and nuclear manufacturing, to name just a few. In practical terms, this means that some reality TV content is crafted to serve the financial and ideological agendas of the owners of the networks airing the shows.

This can manifest in unscripted programming that promotes some points of view and squelches or demonizes others. Remember *Profiles from the Front Line,* which, as discussed in chapter 5, presented men as leaders and women in support roles and depicted Black military women in particular as mammies? It's no coincidence that *Profiles* ran on Disney-owned ABC. By the time it aired in February 2003, Disney had already spent more than a year deploying ABC, ESPN, the Disney Channel, and Disney Radio to capitalize on Americans' grief and fear after 9/11. Less than two weeks after the September 11 attacks, Michael Eisner, then Disney's chairman and CEO, told the *Orlando Sentinel* that he planned an "extensive marketing campaign" that would help Americans "get back to normal" and boost his bottom line, all at the same time. "We're going to use our own media companies to make sure the word gets out that it's a good idea to have a good time after a period of mourning—to come to our parks, movies and buy Snow White on DVD," Eisner said.[30]

In the media biz, that's what's called "synergy." In Disney's case, synergy goes a long way toward explaining why ABC News was so hawkish throughout the wars in Afghanistan and Iraq—and why the network's entertainment programmers thought it was appropriate for Jerry Bruckheimer to partner with the Pentagon to produce *Profiles from the Front Line.*

It also helps to explain the 2005 *Wife Swap* episode that framed a mom from a military family as "pro-Bush, prowar, pro-U.S.A.," while a peace activist mom who opposed the Iraq invasion was called "antimilitary, anti-Bush, antiwar" by the narrator. Got that? On ABC's *Wife Swap,* prowar *equals* "pro-U.S.A.," while peace activists are, by default, anti-American. Producers lied about the antiwar family's religion, calling them atheists in an attempt to further demonize them in comparison with the Christian promilitary family. Mina Leierwood, the antiwar mom, corrected this misrepresentation on her family's website, writing, "It is not a crime to be an atheist, and it is good for our democracy to be able to debate issues in a civil way," but "our family is not agnostic or atheist, we are Quakers." This was no small oversight on the show's part: Peace and nonviolence are core principles for Quakers, and the Leierwoods' faith is a key component of their identity, one producers had to actively work to ignore. And just as *Profiles* (like ABC News) attempted to confuse viewers into erroneously believing that Iraq was responsible for the September 11 attacks, so did *Wife Swap.* At a peace vigil Leierwood organized for her new conservative family, her new neighbors supported the Iraq war by saying, "Do you think it was right for *those people* to come over and blow up the World Trade Center?" and "9/11 scared the hell out of me. If we have to go to war to get rid of people like Saddam Hussein, then by God, let's go!" *Wife Swap* producers emphasized such comments to make it appear that Leierwood alone questioned U.S. involvement in Iraq. Hidden from viewers was the participation of members of Veterans for Peace, who "added tremendously to the depth of the discussion." We didn't hear from them because antiwar vets would have interrupted *Wife Swap*'s preferred narrative, that of Leierwood as a misguided idealist working against America's best interests.[31]

Manipulating perceptions about the Leierwoods is a lark, compared to the biggest victory for corporate media synergy: convincing us we demanded reality television in the first place.

Creating the Illusion of Public Demand

Let's go back to former VH1 programmer Michael Hirschorn's claim that "if women didn't want these shows, they wouldn't get made." This gender-specific variant on Darnell's "giving people what they want" mantra ignores a central truth: Marketing plays a mammoth role in generating the illusion of populist demand.

Without *Survivor,* the reality genre may not have become a network mainstay. But behind *Survivor*'s long-term, landscape-shifting impact was the relentless promotion of the series by Viacom, which had recently merged with CBS and Infinity Broadcasting. *Survivor* wasn't only a new format for network TV, it was also a test case for the power of the new TV/radio/billboard conglomerate. Instead of the standard one publicist per show, *Survivor* had six PR staffers.[32] To generate buzz before the series ever aired, more than a hundred affiliate radio stations ran segments, including dozens of drive-time interviews with Burnett (which folks could listen to while driving past Viacom-owned billboards previewing the show). Sixteen of CBS's TV stations plus Viacom's MTV and VH1 covered *Survivor*'s ins and outs as if everything about the show was news. When the series started airing, *Entertainment Tonight* and a slew of other infotainment programs jumped on the bandwagon, interviewing booted contestants (after they had appeared on CBS's *Early Show,* of course), a practice that has become de rigueur for broadcast tabloids and respected news outlets alike.*

If you participated in nearly any aspect of pop culture during *Survivor*'s first summer—even if you simply kept your eyes open while driving past billboards—it would have been very easy to believe that you were *the only one* who hadn't seen *Survivor,* and that you'd be left out if you didn't tune in. For several months leading up to and through its debut season, your clock radio shock jocks could wake you up joking about the hot babes in bikinis eating bugs on some upcoming TV show. At breakfast, you could watch the *CBS Morning News* or *The Early Show* discuss an exotic-sounding series where people trapped on a remote island compete for a million bucks. Then you could drive to school or work listening to a news radio host interviewing the producer of that show. At lunch, your friends might mention this new phenomenon "everyone's talking about" and ask you if you'd seen it, or planned to watch. If you turned on the TV when you got home you might catch a segment of *Access Hollywood* or *Entertainment Tonight* playing dramatic clips with lots of mind games, drama, and (naturally) bikinis, while an enthusiastic correspondent would describe *Survivor* as a unique new series *everyone's* talking about. When night fell, you could hear about the show yet again on *CBS Evening News, 60 Minutes, 60 Minutes II,* or *The Late Show with David Letterman.*

Thing is, "everyone" wasn't talking about *Survivor*—a cacophony of Viacom/CBS/Infinity employees were. Their PR blitzkrieg made it appear as though there was overwhelming yet spontaneous popular interest in this series, and made it seem *important.* It worked: 15.51 million viewers checked out the premiere to see what all the fuss was about. Many viewers found it honestly entertaining, but

---

* When would-be brides get jilted by *The Bachelor* and fleet-footed celebs are voted off of *Dancing with the Stars,* you can tune in to ABC's *Good Morning America* for their postgame interviews. Similarly, when *The Biggest Losers* lose their spots in their casts and *Apprentices* get fired, they show up on NBC's *The Today Show* the next morning. During the height of *Joe Millionaire*'s ratings extravaganza, a Fox news affiliate in New York hired the show's British butler to do a puff piece on the women known to have dated Mayor Mike Bloomberg—or "Mike Billionaire," as he was dubbed in the segment.

the audience grew largely because the endless, from-all-corners buzz made viewership seem almost like a cultural imperative. That winning formula drew 51.69 million viewers to the first season's finale—by far the most watched episode of any of *Survivor*'s twenty seasons to date.*[33]

Most of the biggest reality series, such as *American Idol*, have achieved their spectacular popularity by replicating *Survivor*'s strategy of multiplatform media attention, public relations, and product integration. A tectonic shift occurred once the networks realized they could generate boffo ratings among their preferred demos by running cheaply produced shows with lucrative back-end endorsement deals. It's undeniable that millions of fans now adore shows like *Idol, Survivor,* and *Amazing Race* season after season. But even ignoring the chicken-and-egg question about where that interest came from, most reality shows do not perform to skyrocketing numbers. The truth is, unscripted programming carries so little financial risk that networks now often prefer likely ratings flops like Fox's creepy, Electra-complex adoption show *Who's Your Daddy,* or ABC's (just as gross as it sounds) *Conveyor Belt of Love* over nurturing more-expensive scripted fare, regardless of viewers' inclinations.

Idol is now network TV's eight-hundred-pound gorilla, but its lesser-known precursor, *Popstars,* came first. The 2001 program revolved around Eden's Crush, a marketing scheme–turned–WB show–turned–girl group created to test the power of the newly merged AOL Time Warner empire. Girls at home were encouraged to identify with the hundreds of contestants competing to become Spice Girls clones, as they were whittled down to five over several prime-time episodes. Though the show also pushed Salon Selectives hair care products, the performers themselves were the ultimate product placement. "You can't buy that kind of advertising," producer David Foster told the *St. Petersburg Times,* not acknowledging that the entire series was one long ad. Warner Music Group

---

* I'll come clean: It worked on me, too. By the week before that first season's finale, I'd never seen an episode of *Survivor,* yet I knew the names of competitors Richard Hatch and Susan Hawk because I read newspapers and watched TV news. So I gave in and watched the finale, knowing so many people I knew would be talking about it the next day.

chairman Roger Ames saw it slightly differently, calling the WB tie-in "a huge running start" for future record sales and a "dream come true," because "even if you could buy all the advertising in the world, there's the difference between advertising and editorial, and this is editorial."*[34]

The value of the media time given to the yet-unformed group was estimated to be at least $20 million. Because of the built-in fan base they imagined would result from so many hours of "editorial" exposure on the WB, Warner's London/ Sire Records inked a recording contract before the band had a name—or even singers. Not until the songs were written, the show placed in the prime-time lineup, and the pre- and postproduction planned were the artists plugged in, like an afterthought. Once selected, Eden's Crush appeared on WB affiliate news stations in New York and Chicago, guest-starred on the WB's *Sabrina, the Teenage Witch,* were featured on the Warner Brothers–syndicated infotainment show *Extra,* and conducted live chats on AOL. The group's first single sold 219,000 copies right out of the gate. Whether or not the girls in the group had any talent was irrelevant. Since the reality-show-to-mass-market formula hadn't been perfected yet, Eden's Crush album sales stagnated once *Popstars* was off the air and the girls were no longer benefiting from the illusion of popularity bestowed upon them by corporate synergy. The group folded shortly thereafter. To add insult to injury, the members of Eden's Crush had signed away all their rights as a standard reality TV prerequisite, so they weren't able to reap any of the profits from their short-lived success. When former *Popstar* Nicole Scherzinger was asked, "What did you learn from Eden's Crush?" she replied, "After I worked my balls off for two years and didn't make a dime?"[35]

Scherzinger was the group's only success story, plucked like a nearly naked phoenix from *Popstars'* ashes and positioned as the lead stripp—er, lead *sing*er— of the Pussycat Dolls, a burlesque troupe cannily recast as pop starlets known

---

* Translation: reality TV provides viewers with the appearance of "editorial" integrity, which does not actually exist in the genre. This is one reason why embedded marketers prefer unscripted programming: because its practices are allowed by networks to bypass FCC regulations for advertising, as the Writers Guild of America, Commercial Alert, and FIT Media have noted.[36]

mostly for the lingerie-draped video for "Don't Cha [wish your girlfriend was hot like me]." Like a rider on an endless celluloid merry-go-round, Scherzinger ended up back on reality TV in 2007 on the CW's *The Search for the Next Pussycat Doll,* where nine fishnetted babes vamped against stripper poles to display their . . . voices . . . for the chance to perform with the musical hotties and score a place on their second album. But contrary to the CW's implication that the winner was actually going to get a lucrative music contract out of the deal, that was not to be. The show was a joint production of Ken Mok's 10x10 Entertainment (one of the producers of *America's Next Top Model*), and Interscope A&M Records, the label that owns the Pussycat Dolls. Under a unique arrangement, each performer is a salaried (and thereby completely interchangeable) employee of Interscope, allowing the company total control over the Dolls' income, their image, and every financial and creative move they make, including CD sales, videos, websites, touring, and merchandise (like the Pussycats' own line of "bustiers are for babies, too!" dolls by Hasbro for their tween fans). From *Popstars* in 2001 to *The Search for the Next Pussycat Doll* in 2007, these shows pretended their talent competition prizes were guaranteed windfalls. The truth is that reality TV music and modeling franchises function much like the sex industry. Like most sex workers, the *Dolls* get a tiny fraction of the cash their bodies generate, while their pimps—the former WB, Interscope, 10x10 Entertainment, the CW network, and embedded sponsors like Secret deodorant—control the profits generated by their gyrations. The workers are undervalued and treated as interchangeable.

Though *Popstars* fizzled (as did the CW's *Pussycat* copycat) it provided, along with *Survivor,* a marketing template Fox built upon to completely dominate TV for the bulk of the '00s. By the time Fox rolled out the more compelling *American Idol* in 2002, the infotainment circuit was primed by several seasons of reality hype. *Idol* gossip, ear-curdling audition outtakes, and mean-spirited judges' rebukes ran seemingly at every hour, for months—and not only on Fox. Hundreds of kids were humiliated, insta-celebrity was bestowed upon several nominally talented contestants, and millions of home viewers subscribed to

AT&T Wireless to vote for their favorite singer. Eventual winner Kelly Clarkson, an aw-shucks girl with a powerhouse voice, appeared pretty much everywhere. All that cross-promotion guaranteed ratings gold for Fox and an astonishing debut for Clarkson's single, which broke the Beatles' record for fastest-ever rise to number one on the *Billboard* charts. "I was like, 'How did that happen?'" Clarkson exclaimed, a bit dazed, on an *Idol* reunion show.*

Gee, I wonder.

Ad Creep Just Gets Creepier . . .

Few other issues pose as serious a threat to our notion of entertainment—and to our understanding of ourselves and of our society—as the increased commercialization of contemporary corporate media. Yet both stealth advertising and sexist, racist reality programming too often fetch a ho-hum response. Why should we care about product-hawking, stereotype-heavy reality TV, we wonder, when television in general has become so risk-free and hackneyed that a sitcom like *According to Jim* could last for eight years on ABC, and rape-of-the-week procedural crime dramas dominate NBC and CBS? It's an understandable reaction to media that have consistently frustrated, bored, or disappointed us. It's also a bit misguided: network TV content has degenerated as quality has increasingly taken a back seat to media companies' and sponsors' quest for astronomical profits. Advertisers already have too much control over what we watch, hear, and read. We should identify brand integration—and the reality genre that brought it back to TV—as a threatening progression of that structural problem. If we care about independent thought, artistic integrity, and cultural diversity, we must demand that programming *improve,* not accept its erosion with a yawn.

Through sheer repetition, reality shows are training us to shrug all this off as inevitable. Advertisers are banking on our apathy. In 2003, a product

---

* Fox may earn more than $60 million annually from embedded advertisers, but just as with *Popstars,* the contestants themselves are product placements for *American Idol* CDs, videos, concert tickets, and merchandise sales. The show does make some young performers famous, but the draconian contracts discussed in chapter 4 ensure that the bulk of the profits from their careers go directly to the producers, not the performers.

integration specialist predicted to *The Boston Globe* that "viewers will grow accustomed to receiving commercial messages" before, during, and after their favorite shows—even when "tacky" and "annoy[ing]"—because "it's a matter of time. . . . What may seem intrusive today will likely be normal five years from now."[37]

It didn't take five years. Numbed by advertiser-created or supported reality shows like *Survivor* and *The Restaurant,* we began to overlook such intrusions in scripted programming as well. By 2007, viewers of *The Starter Wife* didn't think twice when they watched Molly, a divorcée played by Debra Messing, use Ponds "Age DefEYE" and "Time Rewind" creams to quell her fears of wrinkle-induced lovelessness. In exchange for sponsorship of the USA Network miniseries, Ponds got a seat in the writer's room, ensuring them "1) a hand in shaping the story and character arcs; 2) some standard product placement; and 3) a few key 'signature moments' in which an on-screen interaction with the Pond's brand triggers a thought or motivation in a character." No wonder we were treated to campy, noiresque fantasy sequences in which detectives grill Molly about what an old, unattractive loser she is. Is it too much to ask, she cries, for someone to return the romantic effort she puts out there? "With those bags under your eyes?!" one private dick snaps, while his buddy shines the bad-guy spotlight in her grimacing face. Molly snaps out of the fantasy and obsessively pats her puffy eyes with Ponds crème to help forestall rejection for another day.[38]

Even writers of successful, widely respected series have been ordered to change story arcs to accommodate integrated sponsors, as NBC forced *The Office* to do for Staples, Sandals Resorts, HP, Apple, Cisco Systems, Gateway, and Hooters, among others. This is a major thorn in the side of the Writers Guild of America, which has filed comments with the FCC protesting the impediment product placement imposes on their jobs.*

If such trends continue unabated, entertainment crafted around commer-

---

* As part of their ongoing attempts to unionize reality workers and protest product placement, the WGA once hired the *Upright Citizens Brigade,* Amy Poehler's improv comedy troupe, to perform guerrilla theater outside an *Advertising Age* conference. Spoofing *The Apprentice's* excessive product placement, the comics impersonated hosts Donald Trump and Martha Stewart, designating various parts of their bodies as advertising space.[39]

cial messages could largely replace traditional narrative. Media insiders say the future of scripted television is an immediate, interactive model in which viewers will be able to instantly purchase products they see on their favorite shows. Eric Yaverbaum, president of the firm that conducted the *Queer Eye* shopping survey, told me that he predicts "a scrolling ticker at the bottom of every show. It'll be like this: You like the bed Frasier's sleeping in? Buy it at X furniture store."[40]

We've seen what "reality" looks like in the world according to CoverGirl, Coke, and KFC. Now imagine *everything* we watch on TV conforming to these regressive, hypercommercialist values. What little diversity exists in media will only decrease. One-look-fits-all casting will worsen, as will the homogeneity and vapidity of storylines. Considering how steadfastly fashion advertisers cling to young anorexics as the female ideal, average-size and older actresses will find it even harder to score roles once shows are literally designed to sell clothes off characters' backs. Let's say Pottery Barn creates a family drama that revolves around a set full of their furniture: What are the chances that abortion or racial profiling would be discussed by characters whose main function is to showcase a trendy couch? Dozens of years and mergers ago, television occasionally gave difficult social issues the dramatic treatment they deserved.* But a groundbreaking miniseries like *Roots* wouldn't happen in the TV future Yaverbaum imagines, since advertisers aren't interested in the horror of slave owners branding human beings—they're only interested in positive branding opportunities.

As advertisers seek more direct control over media content than they had even in 1930s radio and 1950s TV (when soap operas actually sold soap to housewives and a character on *Fibber McGee and Molly* was an S.C. Johnson Wax salesman), product placement apologists claim critics are misguided Chicken Littles, fearing falling sky where no real danger exists. Today's real-life Don Drapers+ say we needn't worry our pretty little heads about ads populating our

---

* From the 1970s to the 1990s, for example, *M*A*S*H**, *All In the Family*, *Maude*, and *Roseanne* weaved uncompromising messages about war, racism, feminism, and poverty into their comedies. While some contemporary cable series like HBO's *The Wire* and AMC's *Mad Men* tackle tough political topics head-on in nonexploitative ways, it is now almost unheard of for network shows to do so.

+ Ad man Don Draper is *Mad Men's* slick, sexy central character.

programs because TV is simply returning to media's golden age. Since branded entertainment wasn't so bad back then, they ask, what real harm could it possibly pose today?

Though seductive, this argument is factually specious and historically unsophisticated. Take tobacco advertising, which contributed to widespread health problems among the TV-watching and moviegoing population during those "simpler days" when the Marlboro Man was a trusted friend. Eventually, this issue came to be seen as a threat to media and democracy.* "Following the quiz show scandals of 1959, Congressional and FCC hearings revealed sponsor-control of TV content verging on censorship," writes FIT Media Coalition organizer Nancy Marsden. "Networks evicted advertising from program content and held the ethical line for more than three decades. *That* was the *real* Golden Age of television."[41]

Advertiser-controlled content is more threatening today than at any prior point because of the sheer breadth and inescapable power of our modern mediated landscape. Yesteryear's viewers could turn off "their stories" if they were annoyed by silly soap jingles. Today, it's nearly impossible to tune out the commercials woven into not just reality TV shows, but also blockbuster films, music and talk-radio programs, magazine and newspaper "advertorials," VNRs (public relations videos packaged and aired as impartial journalism) on TV news, websites, social media networks, video games, children's classrooms,+ and outdoor ads that pervade public spaces.[42]

Women bear an undue burden from this mercenary approach, especially in reality television. Fox's Mike Darnell wasn't kidding when he told *Entertain-*

---

* As recently as the 1980s and '90s, TV networks self-regulated this threat. In a letter to the FCC, Korby Siamis, one of the original writers of *The Cosby Show* and executive producer of *Murphy Brown*, wrote: "During my career, there was a clear distinction between art and advertising. On occasions that we used a product name, we would receive notices from the network Standards and Practices department. If the reference were necessary for the joke, it would stay. Otherwise we would take it out. And under no circumstances would a product be named if the network knew that there was a commercial for that product scheduled to run during the airing of the episode." The idea of being forced to embed products into content would have been seen as "beyond ludicrous" and "the worst kind of assault on our creative process."[43]

+ Channel One beams advertiser-influenced "news" (plus commercials) into middle and high schools across the United States, wasting teaching time while indoctrinating the next generation of consumers.[44]

ment Weekly that he'd love to do a reality show with female prisoners in a beauty pageant. Something similar aired in Lithuania, he said, and he thought it would do gangbusters in America: "You give them a chance to get a makeover, and it's a 40-share special!"[45] Since nothing is too mercenary in the media era Darnell has helped to usher in, any number of brand integration opportunities could be written into that sort of exploitative stunt. Corporations that replace salaried workers with captive prison labor could reposition their brands as socially responsible businesses, rehabilitating criminals via telemarketing and product assembly skills.[46] Can you picture it? Connie Convict, an unkempt inmate who spends her day booking American Airlines reservations and bagging Starbucks espresso beans for pennies per hour, could emerge as a beauty queen . . . with a little help from some benevolent cosmetics company. I hear it now: "Maybe she found it behind bars—maybe it's Maybelline."

Indeed, this is exactly the sort of thing we should expect from what Mark Burnett calls "the next evolution of storytelling." Unless we get serious about product placement and reality TV—collectively, and quickly*—we shouldn't be shocked if "Miss San Quentin" sashays her way to prime time.

---

* See chapter 11 for many ways you can take action!

Chapter Ten

Fun with Media Literacy!

Drinking Games, Deconstruction Guides, and Other Critical Thinking Tools

As a sophisticated media consumer, you probably already know this, but it bears repeating: Our democracy cannot thrive without critical, independent journalism; our culture cannot expand without creative, thought-provoking art. Currently, our profit-driven media climate fails to meet these basic needs.

If you're tempted to get all Debbie Downer right now . . . don't.

Yes, reality TV can be toxic for women.* And, yes, this would all be really depressing if there were nothing you could do about it. Luckily, there's a lot we can do individually and collectively to transform the way we experience media—and the institutions that create, produce, and distribute it. A vibrant, multifaceted media justice movement is emerging as a powerful force in America: In the next chapter I'll suggest plenty of ways you can get involved in local and national efforts for systemic change.

But before you roll up your sleeves and get to work for healthier entertainment and news media, the first step is to become an active, critical media consumer. The tools in this chapter are geared toward reality TV viewership specifically, though they can be applied to scripted entertainment in general. Yet being an educated media consumer also requires bringing critical media literacy skills to the news we read and watch; the music, videos, and movies we hear and see; the video games we play; and the print ads, commercials, and billboards that

---

* And for men, and people of color, and the economy, and love, and sex . . . and while we're at it, the genre ain't so great for sheer common sense, either.

surround us. That process can be intense, but it can also be fun. The activities, games, puzzles, and resources below are designed to help you develop crucial media literacy skills and awaken the same in those around you. They can also help educators bring media literacy discussions into the classroom, so if you teach, feel free to adapt these tools to suit your students' needs.*

Backlash Bingo:
Media Literacy Meets MST3K

I've just spent an entire book critiquing the damaging ideological and commercial biases of reality television, so I'll forgive you if you don't believe me when I say: I love pop culture. I swear, I do. Especially TV. I was one of those much-fretted-about '80s "latchkey kids" who spent about as much time with *Roseanne* at dinner as I did with my own mom. Think you can name more characters from *A Different World* or *Murphy Brown* than I can? I'll take that bet.⁺

By the time I got to college, my friends and I had a blast shouting one-liners over intolerably bad B movies during *Mystery Science Theater 3000* parties. (If you've never seen *MST3K,* get the DVDs. Really. You'll thank me.) A '90s-era Comedy Central-turned-Sci-Fi Channel show, *MST3K* was 20 percent media criticism, 80 percent lunacy. Mad scientists trap a comedian in space and force him and his robot buddies to watch the most craptacular flicks of all time. Viewers get to listen in as they mercilessly mock the likes of *Sampson vs. the Vampire Women* and *The Incredibly Strange Creatures Who Stopped Living and Became Mixed-Up Zombies.* The show was pure hilarity, and adding our own jokes to their running commentary made it even more fun.

I developed Backlash Bingo to bring the wacky energy of *MST3K* to the seri-

---

* FAIR's "What's Wrong with the News" (www.fair.org/index.php?page=101) provides an overview of systemic problems that inhibit journalism, and WIMN's "Media Justice: A Women's Issue" (www.wimnonline.org/reform/media_justice.html) highlights how these issues impact women specifically. The Media Literacy Project (www.medialiteracyproject.org) offers a variety of online tools that can help you deconstruct various forms of media messages.

⁺ Don't mean to imply that's all in the past. I can sing almost every lyric to the *Buffy: The Vampire Slayer* musical episode by heart, and I hope Amy Poehler's idealistic public servant Leslie Knope lives on for many more seasons of *Parks and Recreation.*

ous business of deconstructing misogyny, racism, and commercial biases in reality television. If you've ever complained about how vapid female characters are in chick flicks only to be told, "Oh, relax, *it's just a movie . . .* " or been called a party pooper for not thinking that the racism in a *Flavor of Love*–style reality show is "hilarious," then you know what media educators are up against. For many people, resistance is a knee-jerk response when first introduced to media criticism. Fortunately, you already have one of the most important tools you need to break through that reluctance: humor.

I've conducted versions of this game in media literacy workshops for high school and college students, and for youth organizations*—but it works just as well or better during lively TV and movie nights at home, in dorms, or at family gatherings. Photocopy the blank bingo card on page 305 and use it as a way of spreading the gospel of media literacy among your friends, relatives, classmates, colleagues, and community. Have fun!

Backlash Bingo

A MEDIA LITERACY GAME
FROM WOMEN IN MEDIA & NEWS

Appropriate for all ages.

Does your family watch *American Idol* or *Project Runway* together and judge from the couch? Is *America's Next Top Model* appointment TV for your sorority sisters? Do you and your friends gather around to laugh at whatever hot mess VH1 is pumping out this season or discuss, Facebook, and Tweet about the latest catfights on *The Real Housewives of* . . . anywhere?

Are you a mom, dad, older sibling, or teacher uncomfortable that kids you care about watch these series uncritically, but you don't know how to have a productive conversation with them about the messages they're receiving from their favorite shows?

If you watch reality television with your friends, a rousing game of BACKLASH BINGO can add some extra fun to your group TV nights. This game can also be an enjoyable and engaging way to get kids identifying and talking about the ideas their favorite shows are selling them. (And, bonus: They won't look at you like you're wearing a ratty bathrobe, waving your fist, and shouting "You kids stay away from my flat-screen!")

HERE'S HOW YOU PLAY:

STEP 1: On a night when you'd usually get together to watch a particular reality show, have a party at least an hour before airtime. Ask your friends, siblings, classmates, or kids—whoever normally watches TV—to list the reality shows they see regularly. Talk about what usually happens on those shows, especially the one you're about to watch together.

STEP 2: Ask yourselves questions such as:

• Who are the stereotypical characters who tend to appear each season? (For example: "The Weeping Woman," "The Bitch," "The Skank," the "Ghetto Girl," etc.)

• What specific quotes and phrases pop up repeatedly, even though the shows are "unscripted"? (For example: "I'm not here to make friends!" or "The claws were *bound* to come out. . . . ")

• What kinds of situations regularly occur that wouldn't usually happen in real life? (For example, everyone seems to think it's completely normal to sob about how desperately you want to marry someone you've only known for twelve days. Or, the only women of color in an entire community are exotic dancers, porn actresses, or violent divas itching for a fight. Or, in the middle of a conversation about something else entirely, one of your friends suddenly holds up or points to a specific eyeliner, cell phone, soda can, or laundry bottle, and starts spouting talking points about how it improves her life.)

STEP 3: Photocopy the blank Backlash Bingo card on page 305, or DIY your own. Have enough cards for everyone in the group. Fill in the bingo squares with your answers to questions such as those above, and any others that come up as you brainstorm together. Write your answers in different squares; no one's card should be exactly alike.

STEP 4: Game play begins when you flip on the remote and settle in to watch your favorite reality show. As you watch, identify quotes, characters, and scenarios similar to the things you've predicted on your bingo card. As soon as you see something on your card, call it out so everyone knows you've X'd off a square. You'll be creating your own *MST3K*-style commentary, except instead of singling out B-movie plot holes, you'll be identifying problematic reality TV messages. Every "Single woman called 'loser'!" or "Model in blackface!" or "Blatant product placement!" that matches your card brings you closer to victory.

STEP 5: The winner is the first person to find enough reality TV tropes to cross off every square on your card. If no one completes the entire card, the victor is the person who IDs the most squares.

The level of discussion is up to your group. You can go deep into subtext, attempting to identify behind-the-scenes manipulations via casting, editing, production tricks, manipulative soundtracks, and the like. Or, you can keep it simple and discuss just what you see on-screen, what aspects of the shows you enjoy, and what, if anything, may make you uncomfortable or annoyed. Adapt the game as you wish, and use it as a jumping-off point for conversations about what we're getting from media, what we like, and what we'd prefer to see.

Contact WIMN:

• to schedule a Reality TV Bingo media literacy workshop

• to bring WIMN's full multimedia presentation on representations of gender, race, and class in reality TV to your campus or community group

• or for more information on women and the media

WOMEN IN MEDIA & NEWS   www.WIMNonline.org   Info@WIMNonline.org

Reality TV Drinking Games

"Backlash Bingo" can be great if you have a group of folks who don't mind spending a few minutes talking about the TV they're about to watch before they actually watch it. But what if you don't have a pen . . . but you do have an ID that proves you're over twenty-one?

Well, then, my friends, that's where reality TV drinking games come in. Ideally, your rules would aim to identify the same sorts of issues that you'd call out during a game of Backlash Bingo, just with less writing. Watch to expose and laugh at (and drink when you see) stereotypes or biases—but not to reinforce unhealthy images.* Create rules specific to whatever program your group of friends enjoys watching. A few examples:

DURING *AMERICA'S NEXT TOP MODEL,* TAKE A SIP WHEN:

- a very thin girl is called fat, calls herself ugly, or says she needs to eat less

- a Black or Latina model is told not to look too sexy, slutty, or "hootchie" (Take a shot if "ethnic" music or imagery—i.e., hip-hop for Black women, Latin clothing or music for Latinas, sounds of gongs or East or South Asian garb for Asians—is used to distinguish models of color from white models.)

- the girls say "Easy, breezy, beautiful. CoverGirl," or repeat ad copy for a show sponsor as if it were a normal part of the day's events

- a country's culture is appropriated (African tribal dance, Japanese tea rituals, etc.)

- Tyra Banks does something batshit crazy

---

* I've heard of drinking games where people take a shot whenever "the bitch they hate gets eliminated." That's the opposite of media literacy, in that players are buying into these shows' manipulative framing and editing, rather than questioning it. As most comedians know, there is a fine line between humor that shines light on injustice and jokes that simply prey on the weak and bolster the powerful. You'll have more fun, and a more edifying experience, if you choose rules that debunk rather than reinforce bias.

DURING *FLAVOR OF LOVE*, *FOR THE LOVE OF RAY*, OR ANY VH1 OR MTV DATING SHOW WITH MEN OF COLOR AS BACHELORS, TAKE A SIP WHEN:

* women are called hos, bitches, or baby mamas
* a Black or Latino man behaves or is talked about as if he is a buffoon, thug, pimp, or criminal
* an Asian woman is described as exotic or portrayed as subservient
* a Black or Latina woman is judged only in relation to her body parts (Take a shot when her ass is the subject of extended conversation or video close-ups.)
* a dark-skinned woman of color is portrayed as an entitled diva, while a lighter-skinned woman is treated as comparatively sweeter, more beautiful, or more sophisticated

DURING *THE BACHELOR*, *MORE TO LOVE*, *TOUGH LOVE*, OR ANY DATING SHOW PACKAGED AS AN EARNEST QUEST FOR ROMANCE, TAKE A SIP WHEN:

* a voice-over from the narrator promises that someone "will get sent home brokenhearted," "hearts will be broken," or "the claws will come out!"
* women are portrayed as overly emotional, unstable, and desperate
* someone says she wants to be treated "like a princess," is "looking for Prince Charming," or gets a "fairytale" date (Take a shot if someone is dressed in a Cinderella-style gown, rides in a pumpkin-style carriage, wears a tiara, or visits a castle.)
* a man is considered more attractive based on the gifts, trips, or jewelry he provides; a woman is considered more attractive the thinner, younger, or more Western she looks

- someone describes the show as her "only hope" or "last chance" for love; marriage and motherhood are described as the only possible way a woman can be happy

DURING *THE HILLS*, *KEEPING UP WITH THE KARDASHIANS*, *THE RACHEL ZOE PROJECT*, OR *THE REAL HOUSEWIVES*, TAKE A SIP WHEN:

- social or professional outings seem fake or scripted
- heart-to-hearts, fights, or crises seem rehearsed
- someone plugs his or her new book, album, DVD, perfume, or fashion or product line
- a woman is portrayed as stupid, stares blankly at the camera, or says something completely nonsensical (Take a shot if a woman is especially clueless about money.)
- someone uses a dog, a child, or a gay person as an accessory

I've kept these intentionally short as a jumping-off point; add to them as you wish.* The possibilities are endless—make your own games for whatever show you watch.

NOTE: Even if you're legal and you don't have a drinking problem, you should really play these with water, juice, or soda. Considering an average reality TV episode, if you play with booze you'll be putting yourself at risk for alcohol poisoning by the second commercial break!

---

* A twenty-point *Top Model* drinking game on Racialicious, a critical pop culture blog, would have you sloshed five minutes into any given episode.[1]

Media Literacy:
Fun for the Whole Family

From cable news to Dr. Phil, we're regularly bombarded with scare-tactic stories about how *The Media Are Hopelessly Corrupting Our Impressionable Youth!!!* While media do have an undeniable impact on all of us—kids as well as adults—this narrative often underestimates the intelligence of young people and denies their ability to question, interpret, and resist problematic messages in news and pop culture.

Media literacy strategies can help kids do just that. As parents, siblings, teachers, and friends, we have to get beyond condescending or judging the media that girls and boys identify with and enjoy. Instead, it's up to us to pay attention to the TV they're watching, the social media they're interacting with, the video games they're playing, and the music they're listening to. Interact, play, listen, and watch with them. Talk with them about what they're learning from these forms of media, how they feel about their favorite musicians, actors, TV shows, movies, magazines, and websites, and how they feel about themselves when (and after) they engage with these media.

For these ongoing conversations to be met with anything other than an eye roll, they should be both fun and youth-led. Create a safe space that allows kids to investigate and decode media for themselves. Don't lecture; listen and ask questions. You may be the expert in life experience, but kids are the experts in the media that surround them.*

Any of the games in this chapter can be adapted for younger kids. With access to a VCR, a DVR, or online video, they can make their own Mad Libs based on recorded episodes of their favorite shows. Reality TV drinking games can be kid-friendly if you ditch the liquor and have the kids come up with the game rules: Maybe instead of taking a drink, they jump up and do a silly dance,

---

* I don't believe parents should forbid their kids from watching all TV. Not only will that make them want to watch it more when you're not around, it also leaves them vulnerable to deception and bias in advertising and media. It is much healthier to watch with them and talk with them about what they're seeing—on a regular basis. That said, limiting the number of hours of media consumption per day is a healthy practice—and television may not be appropriate for extremely young children who have not gone through the developmental stages necessary to decipher truth from fiction, reality from representation.

or they choose a treat of some kind. During Backlash Bingo games, every time kids check off a square on their card, they get a prize—for example, a piece of sidewalk chalk. At the end of the game (and the show), they can draw a mural responding to what they've just seen.

Or, take an example from family TV nights at Dr. Natalie Wilson's house. A women's studies professor, she plays "reality TV charades" with her son and daughter: "As we watch *American Idol* or *So You Think You Can Dance*, we observe the inane comments of the judges (particularly in relation to any sexist, anti-fat, racist, etc.)" and then act out role-playing scenes "mocking the closed-mindedness of the judges." After her daughter coined the term "boob crack" to refer to cleavage, they came up with "The Boob-Crack and Six-Pack Game": each player makes a "list of overt displays of cleavage and six packs" that appear on a show they're watching. "This game leads to useful discussions of how female bodies are far more likely to appear less clothed and why," Wilson notes. They also keep a running score of how often nonwhite, nonheterosexual contestants win competition series. "We have noticed that people who are disabled, fat, or do not accord to normative gender standards are most likely to NOT win. Thus, whenever we see such contestants, we cheer them on and celebrate with some candy, popcorn, or loud cheers."

Be creative, be open, and help foster an environment in which critical thinking isn't a buzzkill, but a natural instinct.

Critical Thinking:
The Building Blocks of Media Literacy

Media literacy is our strongest weapon against propaganda and manipulation in today's profit-driven media culture.

Advertisers and media producers want us to watch their offerings passively, to zone out and let their messages wash over us uncritically. Playing games like Backlash Bingo or making Mad Libs out of the most outrageous or inappropriate reality show content can help you retrain yourself into active viewership. We need to change how we've been conditioned to receive media messages. Smart, empowered viewers take active notice of the ideas being sent through the dialogue and action of reality shows, examine the meaning embedded in their narratives, and note the production tricks used to convey those messages.

I'm not here to tell you to stop watching reality TV. If you admire the fashions on *Project Runway* or enjoy laughing at *Tool Academy*'s alpha males, go right ahead. On the other hand, if *Flavor of Love* or *Wife Swap* gives you hives, by all means turn off your TV. Voting with your remote is one way to punish those networks and advertisers who bring us insulting, bottom-feeder schlock, especially if you back up that action with letters, calls, and emails explaining exactly why you're saying no to their programming. You might even find your free time and your self-esteem increase as a result.* But ignoring bad TV is a limited strategy: Simply tuning out won't help you defend your psyche against equally problematic media messages coming at you from other directions. Nor will it give you the tools you need to help members of your community identify and challenge media representations that degrade women, demonize the poor, stereotype people of color, or marginalize LGBT people, the disabled, and immigrants.

You don't need to divorce yourselves from *The Real Housewives,* shoot down *The Pick-Up Artist,* or cancel your cable. Over the long haul, it's far more important to learn *how* to watch: that is, how to resist the lure of passive viewership and turn your critical filters on high. *Banish the phrase "mindless entertainment" from your vocabulary.* The games in this chapter are enjoyable conversation starters, but you don't have to rely on such prompts to engage your critical faculties. This can become second nature, if you keep some basic questions in mind whenever you engage with any form of media. The following

---

* "Seriously, you need to turn that shit off." In *Lessons from the Fat-o-Sphere: Quit Dieting and Declare a Truce with Your Body,*[2] Kate Harding and Marianne Kirby advise readers to "stop watching television, or at least seriously reduce [y]our TV consumption" because televised images of women's bodies are so consistently unhealthy and demeaning that they can't help but affect our self-perceptions. "While you're at it," they suggest, "lock your women's magazines away," too. While I believe it is more empowering to learn how to actively deconstruct disturbing media than to reject it completely, I understand and respect their "media diet—the only kind of diet we recommend," as it can be psychologically freeing.

template from the Media Literacy Project (MLP) can help youth and adults deconstruct many forms of media, from TV, movies, and music videos to commercials for everything from cosmetics to politicians:

Deconstruction Questions

1. Whose message is this? Who created or paid for it? Why?

2. Who is the "target audience"? What is their age, ethnicity, class, profession, interests, etc.? What words, images, or sounds suggest this?

3. What is the "text" of the message? (What we actually see and/or hear: written or spoken words, photos, drawings, logos, design, music, sounds, etc.)

4. What is the "subtext" of the message? (What do you think is the hidden or unstated meaning?)

5. What kind of lifestyle is presented? Is it glamorized? How?

6. What values are expressed?

7. What "tools of persuasion" are used?

8. What positive messages are presented? What negative messages are presented?

9. What groups of people does this message empower? What groups does it disempower? How does this serve the media maker's interests?

10. What part of the story is not being told? How and where could you get more information about the untold stories?

By the Media Literacy Project. See www.medialiteracyproject.org for more, including a "Deconstruction Gallery," a "Tools of Persuasion" overview, and a guide to creating counterads.

As you can see, the key to becoming media literate is learning to decipher not only what is being said and shown on-screen (the "text" of an episode of *America's Next Top Model,* for example), but also the nature and meaning of the show's underlying messages (the "subtext"). *Top Model,* for example, imparts many lessons about what types of bodies—and what kinds of women—are valuable and, in contrast, who among us are ugly, pitiful, worthless.

MLP's excellent sample questions can be applied to many forms of print and broadcast media. With respect to reality TV, several genre-specific areas deserve further inquiry. Unscripted programming claims to explore how "real people" feel about beauty, romance, marriage, money, ethnicity, sexuality, and more. Each series has a specific premise, and in support of that premise producers cherry-pick through hundreds of hours of videotape to choose each moment you see on air. When you're watching a dating, makeover, lifestyle, or competition show, consider the following:

- FRAMING: What narrative messages did the show's producers decide are central to the series? How is each episode framed to support that master narrative? What do the producers (and the show's embedded sponsors) want you to believe about women and men, people of color and white people, wealthy and low-income people, heterosexuals and lesbian, gay, bisexual, and transgender people? What ideas are being normalized?

- CASTING, CREATING CHARACTERS: Though participants are, increasingly, professional or aspiring actors, most reality shows are still packaged as being about "real people." Why did producers select each individual to join the show? Which stereotypes do those stock characters reinforce? Do you believe you know who a person is, based on how you've seen them behave on TV?

- EXCLUSION: Consider the age, gender, ethnicity, appearance, sexual orientation, profession, physical ability/health status, nationality, and expressed ideology of the cast members. Who is excluded from participating on the show? Would the master narrative shift if a broader set of participants were allowed to be involved? If yes, how so? If not, why not?

- **METHODOLOGY:** What storytelling devices are used to get you to buy into the show's master narrative? Consider casting, drama-inducing contests and plot devices, editing, voice-overs, narrators' and hosts' descriptions, music, screen captions, direction, cinematography, how much alcohol is present throughout the series, and "Frankenbites." (For example, if the camera cuts away from someone while they are in the middle of making a statement, but you continue to hear their voice and their volume or tone is slightly different, the first and second part of the quote were most likely edited together from two or more distinct conversations, to alter the meaning of their comments.)

- **ADVERTISING:** Who profits from the framing, editing, and direction of this show? Are products integrated into the show's scenery, dialogue, contests, or plot development? Are elements of the "content" similar to the commercials in between the show? How might casting choices, show premises, and master narratives differ if the show weren't built to be a "complimentary environment" for showcasing certain products?

- **IMPACT:** When you watch the show, how do you feel about yourself? About others? What impact might the narrative have on viewers? On communities? On culture? On public policy? How might that impact shift depending on viewers' gender, race, class, age, sexual orientation, immigration status, or physical ability?

Make Your Own Media

One of my favorite media justice mantras is a simple call to action: "Don't like the media? Be the media!" Once you've become media literate, you're in a perfect position to create the kinds of media options you want to see, that you aren't getting from corporate sources. If you're frustrated by reality TV, or think you can do it better, there are plenty of new media tools that make it extremely easy to write, produce, record, film, and distribute your own alternatives.

If you have access to a cheap video camera, microphone, and/or the Internet, you can:*

---

* The digital divide is a major concern, as many low-income people, especially of color, have no Internet or cable TV access at home. (This is one of the many reasons why "net neutrality" provisions are crucial.) If you don't have a computer or can't get online at home, chances are good that you can do so either at school, at work, or at your local library, community center, or cable access center.

- create counterads to parody the messages and manipulation of commercials, product placements, print advertising, and billboards;

- start your own blog, online magazine, or social networking community;

- record interviews and commentaries via podcasts and video blogs;

- start a pirate radio station or produce your own cable access show; and

- distribute your blogs, podcasts, and videos through social media sites such as YouTube, Twitter, Facebook, MySpace, SheWrites, or whatever the next big online scene is by the time you read this book.

Some of the most effective media protest is also the most fun. Creating biting satire, video mashups, and political remixes will allow you to flex your creative muscles to subvert dominant media messages and tell different stories, using existing movies, TV shows, and music videos as inspiration.*

As a highly edited—i.e., already remixed—presentation of people and events, reality television is ripe for such spoofs. Take *The Queer Housewives of NYC*, two video remixes of *The Real Housewives of New York City* by feminist remix artist and hacktivist Elisa Kreisinger. The focus of the mashups is Bethenny Frankel, whose singledom was the subject of much drama on the series (until her spinoff, *Bethenny's Getting Married?*). Weaving together snippets from various out-of-context conversations, Kreisinger makes it appear as if Bethenny has come out of the closet and fallen for fellow *Housewife* LuAnn de Lesseps. "I have never gone out with a man in my life. It's not that I don't like men, it's just not typically a priority of mine. I want to come out," Bethenny says in the first video. Merging sound bites from different sentences in multiple scenes, Kreisinger serves up a patently misleading—but editorially convincing—story. "My whole life was defined by men. I mean, it was always defined by men. This is real. This is not just dialogue, this isn't just something I'm saying, this is real. I want to come out. No more bullshit." In the second installment, Bethenny and LuAnn, a heterosexual

---

* Many of the organizations and websites listed in the resource guide can help you make your own media.

married mother of two, are alone at a restaurant together. As edited by Kreis-inger, their conversation unfolds as a lesbian soap opera:

> BETHENNY: I wanted to let her know. This is who I am. And I don't act like I'm something else on a date or otherwise.
>
> LUANN: It takes her a while to warm up to people. So it was a bit of a challenge to kinda get her into it.
>
> BETHENNY: And it felt great.
>
> LUANN: I didn't expect her to like jump on me like that.

With the complexity of lesbian, gay, bisexual, and transgender people's lives still largely invisible in reality TV (no, Tila Tequila's bikini foam parties don't count), remixes like this one provide a subversive retelling of the genre's tales of compulsory heterosexual domesticity. An equally useful benefit of Kre-isinger's work is its stark illustration of how easy it is for reality TV producers to fictionalize the personalities and identities of real people. She proves that selective editing can create caricatures out of whole cloth ("This is real! I want to come out!"), something we should all keep in mind when we evaluate which reality stars we consider villains and which we find sympathetic.*

According to video remix artist Jonathan McIntosh (@rebelliouspixels on You-Tube), "political remix video [is] created by re-cutting and re-framing fragments of pop culture media to construct a new re-imagined narrative." McIntosh's work offers feminist media makers a great case study in the possibilities this political art form presents for challenging sexist media. In July 2009, McIntosh gained instant notori-ety for answering the question "What Would Buffy Do?" by using "new media tools to allow one of the strongest female television characters of our generation" to kill an undead tween heartthrob. McIntosh and his partner, media literacy advocate Anita

---

* "The queering of on-screen relationships is especially important for LGBTQ fans who have so few options of characters to identify with in mass media," Kreisinger writes. You can watch *The Queer Housewives of NYC* at Pop Culture Pirate: http://elisakreisinger.wordpress.com/, and see the next chapter for Kreisinger's quick-tips guide to making remix videos.

Sarkeesian,[3] were disturbed by the creepy-stalker-as-dreamy-boyfriend positioning of the vampire lead in the movie *Twilight*. So, he cut and edited clips from the tween hit and combined them with excerpts from the strong-girl-saves-the-world TV series *Buffy: The Vampire Slayer*, in what he calls "a humorous visualization of the metaphorical battle between two opposing visions of gender roles in the 21st century." He titled the six-minute mashup *Buffy vs Edward* and posted it on YouTube.

Funny and provocative, the video became a viral sensation. Volunteers translated it into twenty-seven languages. It was reviewed in major media outlets from the *Los Angeles Times* and *Entertainment Weekly* to high-traffic websites such as Jezebel.com and Perez Hilton's blog. More than 2 million people have seen the video. Many thousands more read about McIntosh's political and artistic motivations via an article he wrote for the media analysis blog WIMN's Voices. The remix has been assigned in media studies curricula (as have Kreisinger's *Queer Housewives* mashups). Half a year after its creation, *Buffy vs Edward* is still being used by kids and adults as a springboard to talk about the meaning of media portrayals of girls and boys, dating and violence, romance and power.*

If you'd prefer creating completely new content to editing preexisting video, you can write, perform, produce, and distribute original parody projects. Global Action Project (GAP): Youth Make Media spoofed the *Top Model* format to explore race, gender, economics, labor, and the politics of immigration. In October 2008 GAP created *America's Next Top Immigrant*, a short film that "follows seven immigrants as they battle it out for the American Dream. A satire on reality TV, this piece brings to light what the Dream means" to young immigrants from the Philippines, China, Dominican Republic, the United Kingdom, Russia, and Liberia. Originally posted on YouTube, GAP's ten-minute film screened at the prestigious "Our City, My Story" event at the 2009 Tribeca Film Festival.⁺

---

* Watch *Buffy vs Edward,* and read McIntosh's WIMN's Voices July 1, 2009, blog post, at www.wimnonline .org/WIMNsVoicesBlog/?p=1272. Or watch *So You Think You Can Be President?* McIntosh's reimagined reality TV show where candidates compete for American votes, at www.rebelliouspixels.com.

⁺ Watch *America's Next Top Immigrant* at RaceWire, ColorLines' blog: www.racewire.org/archives/2008/11/ americas_next_top_immigrant_1.html.

Similarly, *America's Next Top Dork,* created by teens in the girls' media training program Reel Grrls, wonders what a reality show might look like if contestants competed to be named the most intelligent, independent, altruistic young woman in the country.* And in May 2008, a group of students from The College of New Jersey staged their own satirical reality TV dating show called *The Bachelor: Tool Edition.*[4]

Not into video production or blogging, vlogging, or podcasting? Well, there's nothing like making your own books or zines. Called "the founding documents of third-wave feminist political culture,"[5] zines are a creative, low-budget, hands-on way to self-publish. As Anne Elizabeth Moore, who has taught zine-making to young women in Cambodia, writes:

> *Making your own book or zine is the only way to exercise true freedom of the press, which is something everyone should experience at least once. Hand-stitch or use a sewing machine to bind paper onto cardboard or a thicker paper surface. You can also drill through paper and tie cord through the drill holes to bind a book, if you can get your hands on a drill. Experiment! . . . Be sure to keep a copy for yourself and donate a few to your local zine library.*[6]

Your talents and interests will draw you to the formats that are right for you. Whatever you choose, print, video, audio, or online media, just remember: You have as much right to tell stories as Fox, VH1, and *Cosmo.* Now, get cracking!

Raise Your Voice, Change the Debate

Making independent media is crucial, but so is holding corporate media accountable for their content. Throughout this book we've heard lots of hollow justifications from network execs and producers like Mike Darnell, Mike Fleiss, and Michael Hirschorn. They're not sexist, they're not bigots, they've told us—they're just plying us with cheap, sensationalistic reality shows because that's what we want.

---

* Reel Grrls staffer Maile Martinez discusses how you can make your own films—or encourage young people you know to do so—in the following chapter.

We know that's just not true. Even on cable, could a scripted one-hour show draw only 673,000 viewers to its premiere, max out with a 1.3 rating among eighteen- to forty-nine-year-olds as a series high, yet still get green-lit for a second season? Um . . . no. Yet despite those paltry numbers, VH1 picked up *The Pickup Artist* for a second go-round, giving "Mystery" another nine weeks of prime time to teach men how to trick hot babes into bed by crushing their self-esteem.

This isn't what we want, and it's not what the majority of American TV viewers want, either. It's time to burst corporate media executives' bubble: Tell them that the public they're always talking down to deserves—and demands—better. And while you're at it, tell them what types of shows you *do* want to see.

After reading about cosmetic surgery shows jeopardizing women's health, dating shows treating single women as pathetic losers, and various cable sub-genres portraying men of color like criminals and thugs, you'd probably like to give the networks an earful. I say, go for it! The following tips will help you effectively communicate with media owners, execs, producers, and if you choose, embedded sponsors of reality programming. You can find most media addresses online. You can also use this as a guide to craft successful, publishable letters to the editor. Print may be a dying medium, but millions of people still read newspapers and magazines every day, and it's an important medium through which to change the public debate.

How to Write a Protest Letter

BE FIRM BUT POLITE:

Make your case without insults, rants, or excessive profanity. Nothing makes it easier for editors and producers to dismiss your argument than name-calling.

GOOD IDEA: "It's ridiculous that forty years after the birth of the women's movement, shows like *The Bachelor, More to Love,* and *Bridezillas* are trying to convince us that American women have zero ambition and zero self-respect. This isn't 'reality,' it's just *Mad Men* without the cool clothes, furniture, or SAG actors."

BAD IDEA: "Who the hell green-lit *The Bachelor, More to Love,* and *Bridezillas?* Those are some of the most fucking worthless pieces of shit to ever appear on TV. Go to hell, you woman-hating douchebags!"

GOOD IDEA: "America has progressed so far as a nation since the days of slavery, Jim Crow, and minstrel shows. Yet the same year our country elects our first African American president, *America's Next Top Model* puts contestants in blackface, and VH1 and MTV portray young Black and Latino men predominately as criminals, thugs, and buffoons. Your viewers deserve better."

BAD IDEA: "Everyone involved with *Flavor of Love, Real Chance of Love,* and *From G's to Gents* might as well join the KKK, you racist jackass bigots!"

BE REALISTIC BUT OPTIMISTIC:
DON'T expect networks to change their entire business model overnight based on one letter. DO explain why you find certain programming problematic and request more creative, engaging entertainment options.

Demanding that Fox, ABC, and VH1 never air another reality show will get you nowhere. You'll be taken more seriously if you protest specific reality series that you find offensive, or that insult your intelligence—and explain why those shows do viewers a disservice. Remind the networks that creative, intelligent sitcoms and dramas are beloved by large audiences: *Lost, The West Wing, Glee, Buffy the Vampire Slayer,* and new media programming such as *Dr. Horrible's Sing-Along Blog*—all of these shows had unique premises or unusual formats and became either smash hits or cult favorites. List some current or canceled scripted series you found funny, compelling, and well-written, and ask for more quality programs in that vein.

PRACTICE POSITIVE REINFORCEMENT:
Be constructive if possible.

Explain that you don't have a problem with the concept of unscripted entertainment, just the way most reality shows beat us over the head with damaging stereotypes and blatant product plugs. Highlight elements of any reality programs you may consider positive, such as *Project Runway's* focus on talent, or comedian Margaret Cho's funny and upbeat *The Cho Show*. Encourage more programming that emphasizes humor and skill, rather than humiliation and sensationalism.

CHOOSE YOUR BATTLES:
Identify areas where advocacy can make a difference.

While we'd all like to see television programming that is completely free of commercial influence, demanding that the networks reject all advertising will just give them a good giggle. However, if you favor transparency over propaganda and want media companies to maintain clear distinctions between content and advertising, support efforts to demand full disclosure of brand integration in entertainment and news content.

EXPOSE THE PROFIT MOTIVE:
Let corporate media owners know that you understand reality TV is created to meet advertisers' needs, not our desires.

Tell the networks you're not buying what they're selling. Monitor the ratings for yourself (Neilsen numbers aren't hard to find); tell the networks and the entertainment press that you notice when they're keeping salacious reality shows on air because they're cheap, even though they're ratings flops. Ask how much money their product placement sponsors have paid to integrate their brands into these programs, and expose how viewers lose out when profit is the only consideration behind the development of media content.

AVOID OVERGENERALIZATION.

Don't complain that ABC, NBC, CBS, and FOX "never" include people of color in their reality series, or "always" ignore lesbian, gay, and bisexual participants. Yes, broadcast network reality shows are overwhelmingly white and hetero (unlike some diverse casts on VH1, MTV, or Bravo). But tokenism and marginalization aren't the same as complete invisibility. Language like "all" and "none" gives executives an easy out—they can point to one transgender housemate on one season each of *America's Next Top Model* or *The Real World,* or a few Black, Latina, or Asian women quickly eliminated on *The Bachelor,* to "prove" that your complaint doesn't apply to their network.

KEEP IT CONCISE AND INFORMATIVE.

If your goal is publication in a print or online news outlet's letters page, a well-documented paragraph or two will always be better received than an emotional three-page manifesto. Sticking to one or two main points will get a busy editor to read through to the end.

IMAGINE BETTER POSSIBILITIES.

Can you imagine reality shows that aren't exploitative, but fun, engaging, even positive? Well, don't just critique: Play amateur producer. Think people would watch *Greening America,* a game show in which towns race to make their homes, schools, public buildings, and offices the most environmentally friendly in the country, or *Heart Smart,* a lifestyle series following the dating lives of an ethnically and physically diverse group of comedians, professors, artists, and others with above-average intelligence and humor? How about *Miss American Dream:* Women compete to find creative, innovative solutions to pressing social problems; no one gets voted off, and each week the show's sponsors invest in a different winner's project? There's plenty of drama, emotion, and laughs to be plumbed from actual reality—we've just been conditioned to believe that "drama" means manufactured fights, manipulation, and humiliation of the weak or oppressed. Along with your complaints about the way reality TV has played out so far, pitch positive alternatives.

PROOFREAD!

Nothing peeves an editor faster than typos and bad grammar.*

For a version of this tip sheet focused on letters to news editors, see my journalism-oriented article in the Spring 2003 issue of *Bitch* magazine, "How to Write a Protest Letter," from which this is adapted.

FINALLY ...

. . . this greeting card is ready to be sent from Reality Bites Back readers to any networks whose programming you think deserves improvement.

Dear Hollywood Suits:

We are your fans, your eyeballs, your coveted demographic.

So, let's make a deal:

You stop treating us like sheep and give us diverse, creative entertainment options, and we'll keep watching TV.*

Surprise me,

XOXO _____

* But if you keep insulting our intelligence, your coveted 18- to 49-year-old demographic
will abandon you to make our own media on YouTube, Vimeo, Blip.TV, blogs, podcasts, pirate radio, cable access, zines . . .

For more media literacy games, Reality TV Mad Libs, and resources, visit
us at RealityBitesBackBook.com.

Chapter Eleven

What Are You Going to Do?

How *You* Can Transform the Media—Starting Today

I'm not one to depress and run.

I know how frustrating it is when books, lectures, and documentaries get me all fired up about poverty, violence, misogyny, bigotry, or impending environmental doom, yet leave me without any realistic solutions to those problems.

I won't do that to you.

If anything in this book made you angry, I want you to find ways to channel that frustration into effective action—and so do the independent media producers, educators, and activists you'll hear from below.

As I said in the introduction, I wrote *Reality Bites Back* because we need to take an honest look at how reality TV's backlash against women's rights and social progress is affecting our beliefs, our behavior, and our culture. I hope that you will use the previous chapter's media literacy tools to resist the seductive sexism of *The Bachelor*, the hateful racism of *Flavor of Love*, the ugly torment of *America's Next Top Model*. And though I may need to wash my brain out with soap, all those hours transcribing VH1 marathons will have been worth it if this book prompts dinner table conversations, classroom discussions, op-eds, academic scholarship, blogging, and satire.

Still, becoming critical media consumers isn't enough. We can't afford to see media literacy as the means to an intellectual end. Instead, let's use it to prepare us to take on Goliath (for example, the "Big Six" media owners: Disney, News Corp, Time Warner, General Electric, Viacom, and CBS). Structural changes are needed to achieve the creative, diverse, challenging media we all deserve, and we're going to have to fight for such shifts. But what does that kind of activism even look like? How can we envision the change we hope to see, and what do we need to do to achieve it?

I'll level with you: We're facing an uphill battle. Reality TV's ideological and commercial biases stem from a combination of institutional factors, including

- financial and political agendas of megamerged media monopolies;

- Big Media networks and producers pandering to advertisers' and owners' profit motives without regard for the impact of their entertainment (and news) programming on viewers or our larger culture;

- limited access of women, people of color, low-income people, LGBT people, and other marginalized communities to the means of media production, distribution, and information communication technology;

- marginalization of women and people of color from positions of decision-making power within media companies; and

- funding restrictions that limit independent media alternatives.

Seems overwhelming, doesn't it? Never fear. A vibrant, multifaceted media justice movement is working for change on all of those levels, and there are plenty of ways you can plug in. If you truly want media that entertains, engages, and informs rather than harms, there has never been a better time to become a media activist, or more ways to make a difference.

The following women and men are doing crucial work at various points across the media justice spectrum. I've asked them to answer one question: What are you doing—and what can *Reality Bites Back* readers do—to positively transform the media?

There's an issue area for nearly any interest and a strategy suited to every temperament. You don't have to do it all . . . just choose something that feels important, roll up your sleeves, and dig in. Together, we can make media justice a reality.

I'll get you started with a form of activism directly related to the problems outlined throughout this book:

Regulate Product Placement and Deceptive Marketing

Did you know that there is a legal framework through which you can take action to curb embedded advertising in media content?

People are "entitled to know by whom they are being persuaded."[1] This longstanding legal principle gets to the heart of media ethics and consumer rights. Under federal law and Federal Communications Commission rules, TV and radio broadcasters must disclose the source of any message embedded in a program in exchange for a payment.[2]

Problem is, disclosures are buried in the credits—too small, too fleeting, and too confusing ("promotional consideration provided by") to be effective, when they take place at all. Worse, there are no disclosure rules for most cable and satellite programs, no codified rules to protect children from embedded TV ads, and no rules requiring disclosure of paid brand integrations in movies, songs, music videos, video games, or novels.

HERE ARE SIX WAYS YOU CAN TAKE ACTION:

ONE: Be informed, get involved: Keep up with developments and legislation through groups such as Fairness and Integrity in Telecommunications Media Coalition (FIT Media), Commercial Alert, the Writers Guild of America, the Campaign for a Commercial-Free Childhood, Free Press, and the Benton Foundation. Join and support these and other organizations fighting for policy changes to protect the public.*

TWO: Talk, blog, and/or report about product placement. Until Americans become aware of the scope and impact of embedded advertising,

---

* See the resource guide for contact information.

public officials will have little incentive to curb corporations that profit from deceptive or harmful marketing practices.

THREE: Fight to regulate stealth advertising: Pressure Congress to regulate product placement and embedded advertising in reality TV storylines built around brands, and in movies, video games, books, "adversongs," and VNRs (video news releases from advertisers packaged to look like journalism). File comments to the FCC and the FTC (Federal Trade Commission).*

FOUR: Stop manipulative marketers from targeting children and adolescents: Banning product placement in children's TV shows will not protect youth during prime time (for example, twelve-year-olds who watch CoverGirl commercials masked as content on *America's Next Top Model* or Coke and Ford branding on *American Idol*). Many child advocates are calling for a ban on embedded ads in prime-time shows. Others want the FCC to provide a ratings system for commercials and product placements, so parents can protect their kids.+

FIVE: Lobby to ban embedded ads for harmful or addictive substances: Health advocates such as the Marin Institute are calling for a ban on product placements for alcohol, tobacco, pharmaceutical drugs, gambling, and weapons.

SIX: Use your consumer power: Write or email sponsors who use deceptive or harmful marketing tactics, and tell them you will not purchase products advertised in this manner. Turn off shows laden with product

---

* In response to citizen and consumer advocacy groups' demands, a petition by Commercial Alert, filings from the National Writers Guild, and bipartisan pressure from key members of Congress, the FCC proposed rule amendments in 2008 that would: 1) specify the size, duration, and placement of Sponsorship Identification notices to ensure that they are salient to the audience; 2) extend disclosure rules to cable and satellite programming; and 3) ban product placement in programs for children under twelve. As of this writing, the docket is open and pending. And in 2009, facing increasing public pressure, the FTC (which monitors deceptive advertising both on TV and in media that fall outside FCC rules and jurisdiction, such as movies, songs, music videos, video games, and novels) revised its Truth in Advertising Guidelines and for the first time extended the rules to require disclosure of paid endorsements in blogs and other Internet sites.[3]

+ See the resource guide for the Campaign for a Commercial-Free Childhood and other groups working on these issues.

placements. Tell broadcast and cable networks that you will not watch programs that are, in fact, paid infomercials.

Loving—and Improving—Pop Culture

BY ANDI ZEISLER,
editorial director, Bitch Media, which publishes

Bitch: Feminist Response to Pop Culture magazine

Love/hate relationships aren't always ideal, but as the cofounder and editorial director of Bitch Media, a multimedia organization devoted to feminist media and pop culture criticism, I base my activism on my love/hate relationship with television, movies, advertisements, and more. At *Bitch*—we're best known for publishing the magazine of the same name—we truly believe that you can love pop culture, but also want to make it better: smarter, less sexist, and healthier for women. We see pop products like TV shows and blogs as a great jumping-off point for feminist change making.

How does that work? One important step is to *demystify the process*. A lot of *Bitch* readers don't know that most women's magazines exist to sell readers to their advertisers. We educate our readers about the ad-driven model of most magazines—explaining, for instance, that it's no coincidence that a magazine with thirty cosmetics ads in each issue isn't going to urge you to eighty-six your pressed-powder foundation. Likewise, blogs like Jezebel.com delight in revealing the way women's magazine cover subjects are airbrushed into improbable versions of womanity. *Don't be shy about speaking up.* It's easy to get resigned to the idea that media and culture can't change—that we just have to get used to it. (Or have to, as so many advise us, "get a sense of humor" about sexism in the media.)

Bitch urges readers to believe that even one person speaking up can make a difference. And readers have shared with us their triumphs—"girlcotts" of Abercrombie & Fitch and their offensive T-shirts, letters of apology from corporations who really didn't get just how offensive their billboards were until a critical mass of protest letters arrived. Finally, *have fun with activism* by finding actions and events that speak to you.

Pop Culture and Community Engagement

BY PATRICIA JERIDO,
executive director, GoLeft.org

TV, film, music, and video games can be solitary experiences, or they can help us bond with friends and family. But as much pleasure as they can provide, engaging with pop culture often requires compromises of the highest order: dancing to songs that promote abuse, playing video games where you're killing "foreign" enemies, watching movies or reality shows that denigrate entire communities. We have many reasons (it was the only thing on; I just need to relax after a hard day at work/school; that song has a killer beat!), but the bottom line is that we all make choices about which pop cultural mediums we consume. Those decisions, and their meanings, offer a great opportunity for social engagement.

At GoLeft.org, a community of progressive-minded media junkies, we use pop culture to inform, inspire, and move people to action. We host movie nights discussing what we learn and how we can use positive (or respond to negative) images, ideas, and narrative themes in our political organizing. For example, a viewing of the *Sex and the City* movie opened up space for activists, parents, and teens to discuss the consumption and production of fashion. How can women resist manipulative commercial messages, and what opportunities exist to pull women together as a sisterhood that mirrors the close bonds of Carrie, Samantha, Miranda, and Charlotte? When screening films in a group setting where enjoyment and critical thought are encouraged, we can indulge in the comfort of entertainment, but limit our detachment from reality. The key is not to denigrate or critique, but to connect our realities with media messages.

It's easy and usually inexpensive to organize movie or TV nights in your home, or in your local school, café, bar, or independent bookstore. Create spaces to share your feelings and reactions to media with others. It's a fun, enriching way to become a more conscious and engaged media consumer.

Monitoring Media and Demanding Accountability

BY JULIE HOLLAR,

managing editor, *Extra!*, the magazine of Fairness & Accuracy In Reporting

Challenge corporate media to be accountable for what they put on their airwaves. Freedom of speech belongs not just to corporate media—you have the right to speak out against bias and inaccuracy. The simple act of documenting and publicly protesting media sexism and bigotry can have a huge impact. It shows others out there that those views are *not* mainstream and *not* harmless, despite the fact that they've been given a prominent media platform. Putting your muscle behind media monitoring can ultimately help to shift cultural standards for what has a place in our media.

For example, FAIR has documented shock jock Don Imus's hateful rhetoric for years, so when Imus took heat in 2007 for calling the largely African American Rutgers women's basketball team "nappy-headed hos," we had plenty of other examples to show it wasn't an aberration. Imus called African American journalist Gwen Ifill "a cleaning lady," tennis player Amelie Mauresmo "a big old lesbo," *Washington Post* reporter Howard Kurtz a "boner-nosed . . . beanie-wearing Jewboy," and an Indian men's tennis duo "Gunga Din and Sambo." FAIR, Women In Media & News, the Women's Coalition for Dignity and Diversity In Media, and other activists pressured MSNBC, which simulcast Imus's morning radio show, to explain how his record of hateful rhetoric jibed with company policies. The network dropped Imus, citing the negative impact such derogatory language has on young women of color. Though Fox Business Network hired him in 2009, Imus is on record apologizing for his words.[4]

That's the true victory: shifting the standards of what's considered worthy and responsible media. If you don't step up and speak out, inaccurate and biased content will continue unchecked. You have the power to demand change.

Advocating for Media Literacy Programs in Local K–12 Schools

BY ANDREA QUIJADA, executive director, and
CHRISTIE MCAULEY, community education coordinator,
Media Literacy Project (MLP)

The ability to critically consume and create media is an essential skill in today's world. Here are several ways you can make media literacy (ML) available in your local K–12 schools.

Legislation: Work to create and pass legislation to mandate that ML is taught in your state's schools. Support funding for technical equipment, professional development, and staff salaries for schools that teach ML. Hold an ML day during legislative sessions. Write or visit legislators, and encourage students/young people to do so.

Professional Development: Provide ML trainings for all teachers in a school or district to get them interested. Offer support to the individual teachers who choose to infuse ML into their classrooms.

Build Community Interest & Support: Organize ML trainings for your local school board. Talk with district administrators and board members about ML. Provide ML trainings for PTAs so parents and teachers can collectively strategize to integrate ML into their school.

Assist Teachers: Offer curricula that are in line with the teaching standards of the state (for example, see MLP's DVD-ROMs). This step means that teachers won't have to justify teaching ML. Providing curricula with media examples means less prep time for teachers. Raise funds to purchase technical equipment for schools.

Use Educational Standards: Ensure that teachers and administrators understand that ML aligns with teaching standards for various departments (for example, Health, Consumer Ed., Language Arts, Social Studies, Library Sciences, Media & Digital Ed.) and does not need to be its own class. Learn if district standards have ML components or requirements (not all districts do). Create ML standards for your district, or push for stronger language in current standards.

Involve Higher Education: Demand that more universities and colleges have ML classes in their education departments for preservice and returning teachers.

Remember Librarians: School librarians and media specialists can help you get your foot in the door. They are often supportive of ML curricula and tools and have ideas on how to implement them into the classroom.

Use Research: Create fact sheets and reference publications to demonstrate the strong influence of media. Kaiser Family Foundation has several reports about media and young people, including how media impacts children from a health perspective. Create your own research by pre- and post-testing students who take ML classes in your district. Share research about ML and successes in the classroom. More resources are available at www.medialiteracyproject.org and in this book's resource guide.

Fighting for Healthier Media Policy

BY JONATHAN LAWSON,
executive director, Reclaim the Media

A free, fair, and just media is as important a part of our democracy as Congress or the courts. Journalism is the only business deemed so crucial that it was specifically protected in the Constitution.

But TV, films, radio, newspapers, and magazines aren't produced on a level playing field, designed to give access to all viewpoints and voices. Instead, the current system privileges a handful of giant communications companies. This is not a naturally occurring phenomenon, like the weather. It's the result of a history of policy decisions. When it comes to what we see, read, and hear in the media, how important are these companies' financial and political interests, versus the public interest?

To understand how the American media landscape came to be the way it is, we need to know something about the governmental and corporate policies that slant the playing field. As media activists (since you're reading this book, that means you, too!), it is part of our job to help reveal those policies, and to figure out where our media could benefit from a little extra democracy.

So, how can we effectively improve the media? First, discuss how media problems affect your community (your neighborhood, your friends or colleagues, your organization), then reflect on what media structures or policy decisions may have contributed to these conditions. Effective media policy campaigns can begin with questions like these:

- Who decided that there should be so many sexist reality shows?

- Why are there so few local DJs on commercial radio in my town?

- Why are so few commercial TV or radio stations owned or run by people of color or women?

- Why does so much public TV and radio programming seem designed for upper-class, white audiences?

- Why is broadband Internet slower, less available, and more expensive here than in some other countries?

Next, take action—and understand where to push. At the federal level, Congress makes laws that have long-term effects on media ownership, distribution, and diversity. They set rules on how broadcasters use and share the public airwaves, provide support for public broadcasting, and check the power of large media companies. The FCC is the most prominent among several agencies that deal with media policy.

State and local governments have less to do with media policy than the feds but are also involved in broadband deployment and digital inclusion efforts,* negotiating local cable franchise agreements, and establishing media literacy education standards. Find out who else in your community is involved with media activism, and join them, or get your own organization to take an interest in media issues that affect you.

---

* Digital inclusion initiatives seek to enable all people to become expert in the use of electronic communications tools for enhancing social, economic, and political power. Digital inclusion has three aspects: universal, affordable broadband access; digital literacy; and a participatory Internet, providing culturally relevant information to all people as well as the means to produce and distribute one's own content.

Grassroots community activism for fair media policy has exploded over the last decade, and a growing number of national and regional organizations can help you learn about ways to hold media accountable to values of fairness and justice. Visit ReclaimTheMedia.org, Center for Media Justice, the Media Justice League, or MAG-Net.org (the Media Action Grassroots Network) for information on current media issues and ways to get involved.

Building and Supporting Independent Media

BY TRACY VAN SLYKE,
project director, The Media Consortium

1. Be your own journalist: What subjects fascinate you? What information, voices, and reporting do you think are missing from the media? Ask yourself what unique niche you can fill in the media environment. Through independent newspapers and magazines, video production, blogging, podcasting, and more, tell the stories that need to be heard. Don't be afraid to have fun and be playful, but if you're relaying information and facts, always make sure to have reliable sources and check for accuracy. Audiences are attracted to strong voices and information they can trust.

But being my own journalist is too much work/takes too much time, what else can I do?
Here are three options:

- Do you have friends or colleagues interested in the same topic area? Share the load with them. Create a group blog or website.

- Many popular sites, from Open Salon to Feministing, provide space for users to add their own content. Such platforms allow you to contribute whenever you want and have a built-in audience, so you don't have to manage your own site.

- Work with already established independent media organizations that are looking for help with research, media production, commentary, etc. More and more independent media organizations such as The Uptake (tagline: "Will journalism be done by you or to you?") are engaging their communities to be part of the editorial process.

2. Become an independent media evangelist: Help increase the impact of the media you love on the public debate. Read and support independent magazines and websites such as *Bitch, ColorLines, Teen Voices, Mother Jones*, RH Reality Check, and WIMN's Voices. Watch and listen to indie TV and radio shows, such as *GRITtv with Laura Flanders, Paper Tiger TV,* Democracy Now!, UpRisingRadio, and CounterSpin. Check out listings of more great independent media outlets at www.themediaconsortium.org/our-members/. Introduce these independent media outlets to new audiences. As I discuss in the book *Beyond the Echo Chamber*[5] and on BeyondTheEcho.net, you are a key part in breaking the corporate media stranglehold. Now more than ever, everyday people have the opportunity to spread critical information through their networks, whether it be Facebook, MySpace, Twitter, Digg, email, texts, and more. Explain what independent media outlets mean to you and what you think your friends, family, and colleagues can get from them.

3. Donate: If it's $5 or $5,000, most independent media outlets are underfunded and struggle to stay afloat. Every dollar helps. It takes a lot of time and money to produce quality journalism, analysis, and more. If you want it, help them produce it.

Cable Access and Localism: Representing Ourselves

BY BETTY YU,
community organizer and media activist,
former staffer, Manhattan Neighborhood Network

Are you tired of the mainstream corporate media's portrayal of women, people of color, immigrants, and other traditionally marginalized groups? Do you want the opportunity to control how your community is represented? Public access TV can be the answer. Public, Educational and Governmental (PEG) Access television, also known as Community Media Centers (CMCs) provide an "electronic greenspace" that gives local residents and nonprofits control over some means of media production. They foster self-determination, allowing local communities to tell their own stories on their own terms.

There are nearly three thousand PEGs in the country, possibly one in your town. These centers produce ten thousand hours of programming a week, more than all the major networks combined. Today's CMCs serve core principles of public access, social justice, and media democracy. Public Access is the only forum on television where residents can create and find local programming on issues that directly affect them. Today CMCs are taking advantage of "digital convergence" and have integrated the full range of Internet distribution and web 2.0 tools into their centers. Public Access centers are shifting from being just channel operators to becoming community multimedia centers that provide access to various forms of electronic media.

The introduction of broadband Internet services has blurred the line between Internet, phone, and cable TV services. Phone companies seeking to maximize their profits are spending millions of lobbying dollars pressuring states to pass state-wide legislation to replace local franchising—the major funding stream for PEGs. As a result, dozens of centers have shut down or reduced their services.

Community media advocates and public access supporters are mounting grassroots opposition to these changes. If you want to produce TV yourself, or want to ensure that historically marginalized communities have the opportunity to do so, join efforts to protect PEG Access. The Alliance for Community Media (ACM), the national organization that represents U.S. PEG Access Centers, is working with other media activist organizations to protect PEG and communication rights and

- end discriminatory treatment of PEG channels;
- direct the FCC to study and report on the negative effects of recent states' video franchising legislation on PEG access; and
- close the loophole that telecommunication corporations use to avoid paying adequate franchise fees to PEGs.

Find out where your nearest PEG Access Center is located, and learn ways you can get involved.

Freeing the Radio Airwaves

BY SAKURA SAUNDERS, regulatory research coordinator, and
BRANDY DOYLE, regulatory director, Prometheus Radio Project

You don't own a radio station or a television studio. What right do you have to say what goes on the air? Actually, broadcasters use a valuable national treasure—the airwaves— that is owned by us, the public. The FCC leases out chunks of the spectrum—an invisible natural resource that is worth more than Bill Gates, the U.S. military budget, and McDonalds combined. They are entrusted to do this on our behalf.

Yet just a few companies control all our media, limiting the range of political debate and views that we can access and music we can hear. Only 6 percent of the full-power radio stations in the United States are owned by women, and only 8 percent are owned by people of color. A powerful few have taken advantage of the complicated bureaucracy of media regulation. They are rich, powerful, and— not surprisingly—they aren't covered by the news.

At the Prometheus Radio Project, we demystify media policy and technology so that more people can make their voices heard. In the struggle for local, participatory radio, we helped organize more people to file FCC comments than had ever commented on any other issue. We won, and the FCC created the low-power radio service, opening the airwaves to noncommercial community groups such as unions, neighborhood associations, churches, and schools. Next, we teamed up with the Media Access Project to win a federal lawsuit to roll back media consolidation, while helping to build radio stations nationwide to reflect real community needs and values.

We have a long way to go to reach a brighter media future, but a national movement of grassroots groups is reclaiming the airwaves. We need your help for media to realize its full potential as a tool for social justice and community expression. Write comments at the FCC, engage Congress . . . you can even organize to start your own radio station! If the broadcasters aren't serving the public interest, we can take the airwaves back and do it ourselves. Get involved at Prometheusradio.org/take_action.

Documentary Films and Social Change

BY CYNTHIA LOPEZ,
vice president, American Documentary/POV, PBS

How can we use documentaries to tackle tough issues? At POV our films illuminate stories at the heartbeat of American society: obstacles facing young girls, the life of a white supremacist, mothers who have lost sons to police brutality, gay and lesbian issues, adoption, political corruption, family crises, healthcare, living wages, religion, immigration, the Iraq war, and more.

Like all good cinema, documentaries should take you on a journey, make you ask questions. One recent example is *Made in L.A.*, directed by Almudena Carracedo and Robert Behar. The film follows three Latina women in Los Angeles's garment factories as they wage a three-year battle against clothing retailer Forever 21 to get to the bargaining table. The film portrays the "other" California, where immigrants are paid subminimum wages for many long hours of work.

POV is not just a broadcaster; we create national public-awareness campaigns, and did extensive outreach for *Made in L.A.* We shared the goals of the filmmakers, to capture the attention of labor, policy makers, and economists and encourage discourse. We held fifty-five screenings in twenty-three states and forty-six cities and worked with filmmakers to coordinate a Capitol Hill event for labor and Latino policy makers. The film and its organizing kit are still being used as educational tools to change labor practices at sweatshops. We developed a dual promotional strategy to garner English and Spanish press, resulting in over 7,000 media placements, including 179 print articles, 13 radio programs, 17 TV news programs including CNN en Espanol, Primer Impacto, Univision, Fox News, and MSNBC, and created a wide-ranging online campaign.

Made in L.A. went on to win an Emmy and reach over 1.1 million viewers, most of whom learned something new about undocumented workers in America. Most important, documentaries are a reflection of life, and in this case the garment workers—the outsiders—were finally let inside, to the people who form public opinion and legislation. This film played an important role in a continuing effort to ensure that the rights of immigrants are respected. It's a powerful example of the potential for public-service media to have a real impact on public policy.

Making Political Remix Videos: A Quick-Tips Guide

BY ELISA KREISINGER,
Pop Culture Pirate, http://elisakreisinger.wordpress.com

Want to try your hand at mashing up the media landscape, reinterpreting narratives, and blurring the line between passive audience and active creator? These steps will get you started:

1. Gather source materials: Record commercials off TV, pull TV, film, or music video clips from online video sharing sites, or download from file sharing sites such as Bit Torrent. Because you are transforming this copyrighted material to make a new work that comments, critiques, or satirizes original content, your remix video will be highly eligible to make a Fair Use of copyrighted material, protecting you from infringement.*

2. Convert file formats: Some of your source materials might be in different formats, or may not communicate with your editing software. Programs such as MPEG Streamclip allow clips to be converted to and from any format (for example, an .AVI file, an .MOV file, etc.).

3. Make your statement: Here's the fun part. What are you trying to say? A political remix video works best when it articulates an argument and visually supports that argument with clips from appropriate media texts. Keep it short, simple, and effective. While not everyone will understand or like what you have to say, your critique is a valid contribution to participatory culture and media literacy.

---

* Fair Use is one feature of copyright law that, under certain conditions, permits quotation from copyrighted works without permission from or payment to the copyright holder. Remixes are highly eligible to be considered a Fair Use due to the transformative nature of the work, but what constitutes a Fair Use and what is considered copyright infringement is a case-by-case judgment call. Remixers can help make their case based on the Center for Social Media's Best Practices for Fair Use in Online Video.

4. Export: Once you've completed your remix, export your file and compress it for the web. The best formats for this compression are H.264 or MPEG-2.

5. Distribute: Make sure to look for the Fair Use clause on each site to which you plan to distribute your remix. (If they don't have one, ask!) For example, Blip.tv has a Fair Use clause; YouTube does not. Unfortunately, asking about Fair Use may trigger the removal of your material, due to identification systems that scan for copyrighted content. Don't let this stop you if you believe your work qualifies as Fair Use. Check out the Chilling Effects Clearinghouse, a joint project of the Electronic Frontier Foundation and seven law schools, for legal help with the dispute process. Try your best to upload your work to multiple sites.

Improving Representation of Transgender People: Tips for Media Makers

BY JULIA SERANO,
author, *Whipping Girl: A Transsexual Woman on Sexism and the Scapegoating of Femininity*

There are a number of things that reporters and media producers can do to improve coverage of transgender people and issues. The most basic of these is to use pronouns and language respectful of the gender trans people currently live and identify as, rather than the one they were assigned at birth. Depictions that are needlessly objectifying or sexualizing should be avoided, including those that:

- focus on trans people's physical transitions (e.g., surgeries and other medical procedures);
- rely on before/after photos and shots of trans individuals putting on clothing and cosmetics;
- place undue attention on trans people's sexualities;
- purposefully employ trans characters as a device to elicit sexual anxiety in other characters or the audience.

Trans people should be viewed as fully formed human beings, rather than mere objects of fascination or controversy, and they should be allowed to speak in their own voices about issues that are important to them.

Finally, media makers should recognize that transgender people vary widely with regard to ethnicity, class, identity, background, and so forth. Media coverage should reflect this diversity, rather than relying primarily on white, middle-class trans women who neatly fit the woman-trapped-in-a-man's-body stereotype that the public is most familiar with.[6]

Activist Scholarship in the Media Justice Movement

BY CAROLYN M. BYERLY, PHD,
Department of Journalism, Howard University

Are you an academic or independent communications researcher? If so, you can play a significant role in the media justice movement. First, you can help develop theories, i.e., overarching explanations, for gender and race issues in media, and standards for evaluating media performance. For example, in *Women and Media: A Critical Introduction,*[7] Karen Ross and I created the Model of Women's Media Action to describe patterns of women's media activism in twenty nations. After the 2008 election, I posed a Theory of Feminist Social Responsibility,[8] which states that socially responsible news organizations must

* provide coverage of issues and events affecting women's status and well-being;
* include a range of women's views in such coverage;
* offer a forum for exchange, comment, and criticism on gender-related issues;
* include equal gender representation in all levels of professional practice, governance, and ownership.

Second, applied research is invaluable. Media justice activists need scholarship that provides data and other information for reshaping federal communications law. A 2006 study I conducted with Kehbuma Langmia and Jamila A. Cupid in Washington DC neighborhoods revealed that nonwhite news consumers want news content from the perspective of Black or other nonwhite communities. The two hundred people we interviewed didn't see such journalism on major TV channels or in newspapers. Such a perspective goes to the heart of both media ownership and localism (meeting of the informational needs of local audiences). Applied research helps make the case that media policy activism should advance gender- and race-conscious standards for ownership and operation, particularly in broadcast arenas.[9]

Third, by adopting a media-conscious pedagogy, academics can acquaint their students with the impact of media on issues related to justice, inequality, and activism. Develop curricula that include readings from the perspective of those doing media justice work and opportunities to critically analyze news and entertainment media with respect to gender and race.

Empowering Youth to Make Media

BY MAILE MARTINEZ,
program manager, Reel Grrls

Youth: Are you tired of the sensationalized drama and harmful stereotypes that mark most depictions of young people in reality TV, scripted programs, and movies? If so, the youth media movement may be for you! Young people are responding to mainstream media in increasingly sophisticated ways. At Reel Grrls in Seattle, teens are trained to use professional-quality video cameras, audio equipment, lights, and editing software to create short films, TV shows, vlogs, and web series showcasing their own authentic values and issues. Other after-school programs teach youth radio production, audio recording, graphic design, and more. If your school does not offer media production classes, consider taking a class at a local community college or technology center, or visit ListenUp.org to find a youth media organization in your area. For a DIY approach, Andrea Richards's book *Girl Director*[10] will get you started making your own video for very little money.

Adults: Support young people making their own media. Donate your time, skills, and/or money. Volunteer filmmakers, video editors, camera operators, sound technicians, and screenwriters can make a huge difference in the life of a young person—and in our media landscape—by teaching their skills. But you don't need to have expertise in those areas to empower young people to tell their stories: You can plan, promote, and host public screenings of youth-produced work, help a young person find interview subjects, be a story consultant or editor, fundraise, and more.

Youth Media in Action: In 2007, Sami Muilenburg, a teen filmmaker and Reel Grrls participant, decided to make a documentary about media consolidation. She understood that although media economics directly impact young people, many of her peers had never thought about who actually owns the media. Her film, *A Generation of Consolidation,* has screened at festivals nationwide and won a Student Emmy award! Other Reel Grrls participants created a *Top Model* spoof, *America's Next Top Dork,* to ask the question: What if, instead of competing with other women to be crowned the most beautiful, reality TV contestants demonstrated who was the smartest, the most compassionate, and the most individualistic?*

Many Ways to Bite Back

I hope you will be inspired to learn more about these projects and issues, and that you will get involved in one or more of these crucial media justice and independent media arenas.

If the strategies, projects, and issues outlined here don't speak to you, know this: The dedicated women and men above represent just a small sample of the vast array of work being tackled within the media justice and media reform movements.

Along with a team of independent journalists and women's rights advocates, I founded Women In Media & News in October 2001 to increase women's presence and power in the public debate. We offer media literacy presentations and workshops for students and communities across the country and provide media

---

* You can view *Generation of Consolidation* and learn more at www.generationofconsolidation.org, and watch *America's Next Top Dork* at Youtube.com/reelgrrls.

training for women's, social justice, and youth groups. We help journalists and media producers diversify their Rolodexes with qualified women experts through our POWER Sources Project. We host WIMN's Voices, a dynamic group blog on women and the media, where we welcome your questions and observations. And since media content is the direct result of institutional problems, we advocate systemic changes that can result in a more just, open, democratic media climate. We envision a landscape in which unfettered journalism features a broad range of perspectives and serves the public good, while pop culture amuses us, connects us, and pushes us to think and feel in new ways. Just like all nonprofits, we need your support—financial (for the reasons Tracy Van Slyke mentioned above) as well as your volunteer time, energy, and ideas—to help us pursue that vision. The feminist media justice movement can't succeed without you.

I know some readers may not necessarily get why I'm closing a book about reality television with a selection of short essays about topics as seemingly unrelated as low-power radio, independent magazines, broadband policy, and the like. We need to understand that all of these issues are inextricably linked. The problems afflicting contemporary commercial media—and, as a result, negatively impacting the lives of women, people of color, youth, LGBT people, and the poor, among others—are varied and interconnected. Therefore, one of WIMN's founding principles is a strong belief in the importance of multiple strategies to achieve lasting change. While I believe deeply in the importance of WIMN's mission and programs, we are only one important piece of a larger puzzle. That's why I've opened *Reality Bites Back* to the contributors above. They are just a few of the folks who have inspired me during the nineteen years I've been doing independent journalism and media activism. Each offers a way for you to jump in . . . and that's just the beginning.

It's only for want of space that this chapter didn't also include contributions from advocates for copyright policies that protect artists but don't stifle innovation or information, ethnic press publishers, indie zine makers, hip-hop activists, local pirate radio operators, communities organizing against hate speech, municipal broadband activists, Internet neutrality and digital inclusion activists, lawyers working on media policy regulation, men doing profeminist media literacy education . . . you see where I'm going with this? We could fill an entire book just with how-tos from an ever-growing list of racially, geographically, and age-diverse individuals and organizations whose practical and powerful strategies are helping to create the kind of media we all deserve.

Remember, you don't need to turn off your TV. I'm certainly not going to give up mine! Anyone who tells me to sacrifice my *Buffy the Vampire Slayer* or *Arrested Development* DVDs will have a fight on their hands. You want to watch *Project Runway* or *What Not to Wear?* You'll get no argument here; just watch with your critical filters intact. Television can be a fun, cathartic, and yes, a source of much pleasure (guilty or otherwise).

And when it's not . . . that's your cue to bite back.*

---

* If the advocacy areas described in this chapter don't speak to you, scan through the resource guide—or see RealityBitesBackBook.com for more media justice organizations, media producers, and media associations that can offer you additional avenues toward change.

Resource Guide

Detailed descriptions of the following books, media outlets, and media activist projects are available at www.RealityBitesBackBook.com.

Additional resources, including independent TV and radio programs and social justice advocacy organizations, are available at Women In Media & News (www.wimonline.org).

BOOKS

Adproofing Your Kids: Raising critical thinkers in a media saturated world, Tania Andrusiak and Daniel Donahoo

Backlash: The Undeclared War Against American Women, Susan Faludi

Beyond the Echo Chamber: How a Networked Progressive Media Can Reshape American Politics, Jessica Clark and Tracy Van Slyke

Bitchfest: Ten Years of Cultural Criticism from the Pages of Bitch Magazine, Lisa Jervis and Andi Zeisler

Can't Buy My Love: How Advertising Changes the Way We Think and Feel, Jean Kilbourne

Conscious Women Rock the Page, Marcella Runell Hall, Black Artemis, E-Fierce, and J-Love

Critical Studies in Media Commercialism and *Consumer Culture and TV Programming*, Robin Andersen

Don't Believe the Hype: Fighting Cultural Misinformation About African Americans, Farai Chideya

Enlightened Racism: The Cosby Show, Audiences, and the Myth of the American Dream, Sut Jhally and Justin M. Lewis

Feminism and Pop Culture: Seal Studies, Andi Zeisler

From Black Power to Hip Hop: Racism, Nationalism and Feminism, Patricia Hill Collins

Girl Director: A How-to Guide for the First-Time, Flat-Broke Film and Video Maker, Andrea Richard

Hey Kidz! Buy This Book: A Radical Primer on Corporate and Governmental Propaganda and Artistic Activism for Short People, Anne Elizabeth Moore

Lessons from the Fat-o-Sphere: Quit Dieting and Declare a Truce with Your Body, Kate Harding and Marianne Kirby

Media Literacy: A Reader, Donaldo Macedo and Shirley Steinberg

Real Majority, Media Minority: The Costs of Sidelining Women in Reporting, Laura Flanders

Selling Anxiety: How the News Media Scare Women, Caryl Rivers

Share This!: How You Will Change the World with Social Networking, Deanna Zandt

So Sexy, So Soon, Jean Kilbourne and Diane Levin

Style and Status: Selling Beauty to African American Women, 1920–1975, Susannah Walker

Teaching Youth Media, Steven Goodman

The Media Monopoly, Ben Bagdikian

Toxic Sludge Is Good for You: Lies, Damn Lies, and the Public Relations Industry, John Stauber

Unmarketable: Brandalism, Copyfighting, Mocketing and the Erosion of Integrity, Anne Elizabeth Moore

Whipping Girl: A Transsexual Woman on Sexism and the Scapegoating of Femininity, Julia Serano

White Weddings: Romancing Heterosexuality in Popular Culture, Chrys Ingraham

Women and Media: A Critical Introduction, Carolyn Byerly, PhD, and Karen Ross

PRINT AND ONLINE MAGAZINES

AdBusters—www.adbusters.org

Alternet—www.alternet.org

Bitch: Feminist Response to Pop Culture magazine—www.bitchmagazine.org

Bust—www.bust.com

ColorLines: Race Culture Action—www.colorlines.com

Columbia Journalism Review—www.cjr.org

Extra!—www.fair.org/extra/index.html

In These Times—www.inthesetimes.com/

Make/Shift—www.makeshiftmag.com/

Media and Gender Monitor—www.waccglobal.org/en/resources/media-and-gender-monitor.html

Media Report to Women—www.mediareporttowomen.com

Ms. Magazine—www.msmagazine.com/

New Moon: A Magazine for Girls and Their Dreams—www.newmoon.org/

On the Issues—www.ontheissuesmagazine.com

PR Watch—www.prwatch.org/cmd/prwatch.html

Salon—www.salon.com

$pread magazine—www.spreadmagazine.org/

Teen Voices—www.teenvoices.com/tvhome.html

The Nation—www.thenation.com/

The Progressive—www.progressive.org

Women's Enews—www.WomensEnews.org

World Pulse magazine—www.worldpulsemagazine.com

Yes! Magazine—www.yesmagazine.org/default.asp

WEBSITES & BLOGS WITH A FOCUS ON GENDER, RACE, AND MEDIA

About Face: www.about-face.org

Bitch magazine blogs: http://bitchmagazine.org/blogs

BroadSheet: www.salon.com/life/broadsheet

Feministing: www.feministing.com

Gender Ads: Ads, Education, Activism: www.genderads.com/Gender_Ads.com.html

IndyMedia movement: www.indymedia.org

Jack & Jill Politics: www.jackandjillpolitics.com

Jean Kilbourne's Resources for Change: http://jeankilbourne.com/?page_id=49

Jezebel: http://jezebel.com

Media Matters for America: http://mediamatters.org

Pop and Politics: www.popandpolitics.com

Pop Culture Pirate: http://elisakreisinger.wordpress.com

PopPolitics.com: www.poppolitics.com

Racewire, the *ColorLines* blog: www.racewire.org

Racialicious: www.racialicious.com

Sociological Images: http://contexts.org/socimages

Who Makes the News: www.whomakesthenews.org

WIMN's Voices: www.wimnonline.org/WIMNsVoicesBlog

INDEPENDENT TV, RADIO, AND FILM

American Documentary: www.amdoc.org

California Newsreel: www.newsreel.org

CounterSpin: www.fair.org/index.php?page=5

Democracy Now!: www.democracynow.org/

Feminist International Radio Endeavor (FIRE): www.fire.or.cr/indexeng.htm

Free Speech TV: www.freespeech.org

GRITtv with Laura Flanders: http://lauraflanders.firedoglake.com

Listen Up!: http://listenup.org/index.php

Making Contact/Women's Desk: www.radioproject.org/desks/women.html

Media Education Foundation: www.mediaed.org

On the Media: www.onthemedia.org

Paper Tiger TV: http://papertiger.org

Uprising Radio: www.uprisingradio.org

WINGS: Women's International News Gathering Service: www.wings.org

Women Make Movies: www.wmm.com

FILMS ABOUT MEDIA ISSUES

A Girl Like Me, Directed by Kiri Davis

America the Beautiful, Directed by Darryl Roberts

Class Dismissed, Directed by Pepi Leistyna

Ethnic Notions, Directed by Marlon Riggs

Generation of Consolidation, Directed by Sami Muilenburg

Hip Hop: Beyond Beats and Rhymes, Directed by Byron Hurt

Killing Us Softly, Directed by Jean Kilbourne

Slip of the Tongue, Directed by Karen Lum

The Souls of Black Girls, Directed by Daphne Valerius

Tough Guise, Directed by Jackson Katz

MEDIA LITERACY AND MEDIA ADVOCACY ORGANIZATIONS

Action Coalition for Media Education (ACME): www.acmecoalition.org

Alliance for Community Media (ACM): www.ourchannels.org

Allied Media Conference: www.alliedmediaconference.org

Benton Foundation: www.benton.org/

BeyondMedia: www.beyondmedia.org

Campaign for a Commercial-Free Childhood: www.commercialexploitation.org

Center for Digital Democracy: www.democraticmedia.org

Center for Investigative Reporting: www.muckraker.org

Center for Media and Democracy: www.prwatch.org

Center for Media Justice: http://centerformediajustice.org

Center for Media Literacy: www.medialit.org

Children's Media Coalition: www.kidsfirst.org

Commercial Alert: www.commercialalert.org

Common Sense Media: www.commonsensemedia.org

Electronic Frontier Foundation: www.eff.org

Fair Use Network: http://fairusenetwork.com

Fairness and Accuracy in Reporting (FAIR): www.fair.org

Fairness and Integrity in Telecommunications Media Coalition (FIT Media): http://fitmedia.org/

Free Press: www.freepress.net (also see: www.StopBigMedia.com)

Future of Music Coalition: http://futureofmusic.org

Girls, Women + Media Project: www.mediaandwomen.org

GLAAD—Gay & Lesbian Alliance Against Defamation: www.glaad.org

Global Action Project: Youth Make Media: www.global-action.org

GoLeft.org: www.goleft.org

Guerrilla Girls: www.guerrillagirls.com

List of Journalism Associations, Coalitions, Ethnic Media, and other organizations for media makers: www.wimnonline.org/press/#groups

MAG-NET Media Action Grassroots Network: www.mediagrassroots.org

Marin Institute: www.marininstitute.org/

Media Access Project: www.mediaaccess.org

Media Alliance: www.media-alliance.org

Media Justice League: www.MediaJusticeLeague.org

Media Literacy Project: www.nmmlp.org

National Organization for Men Against Sexism: www.nomas.org

NOW Media Hall of Shame: www.now.org/issues/media/hall-of-shame/index.php

NYC Grassroots Media Coalition: www.nycgrassrootsmedia.org

Parents for Ethical Marketing: http://parentsforethicalmarketing.org

People's Production House: www.peoplesproductionhouse.org

Prometheus Radio Project: http://prometheusradio.org

Reclaim the Media: www.reclaimthemedia.org

Reel Grrls: www.reelgrrls.org

Shaping Youth: www.shapingyouth.org

The Media Consortium: www.themediaconsortium.org

WAM! Women, Action & the Media: www.womenactionmedia.org

Women & Girls Collective Action Network and FUFA (Females United For Action) Youth: http://womenandgirlscan.org

Women's Institute for Freedom of the Press: www.wifp.org

Women's Media Center: www.womensmediacenter.com

Writers Guild of America: www.wga.org

Notes

INTRODUCTION

1. *Enlightened Racism: The Cosby Show, Audiences, and the Myth of the American Dream,* Westview Press. June 10, 1992. Jhally, Sut and Lewis, Justin M.

2. "On Fox, Making Reality a Reality; How Network Exec Mike Darnell Took a Programming Concept All the Way to the Bank," *The Washington Post,* Feb. 10, 2003. Farhi, Paul.

3. "Reality Kings," *Vanity Fair,* July 2003. Seal, Mark.

4. Nielsen News FAQs, http://en-us.nielsen.com/main/news/news_faqs.

5. "Millionaire Groom's Dirty Secret," TheSmokingGun.com (no date). www.thesmokinggun.com/millionaire/millionaire.html.

6. "Fox's Point Man for Perversity; 'World's Scariest Programmer,' Starring Mike Darnell as Himself," *The New York Times,* Feb. 26, 2000. Kuczynski, Alex and Cater, Bill.

7. *Vanity Fair,* July 2003. Seal, Mark.

8. "Fox Idols," *LA Weekly,* Mar. 7, 2003. Finke, Nikki.

9. "On the Air: The latest news from the TV beat," *Entertainment Weekly,* Mar. 28, 2003. Rice, Lynette and Keck, William. "When Reality Attacks; Who are the victims now that unscripted shows rule TV land? Producers of sitcoms and dramas. Six of the best strike back. Look out, Joe Millionaire," *Entertainment Weekly,* Mar. 14, 2003. Rice, Lynette, interviewing Wilmore, Larry; Herskovitz, Marshall; Robbins, Brian; Bowser, Yvette Lee; Helford, Bruce; and Keyser, Christopher.

10. "Reality Chief Mike Darnell Let Fox Stew, But Renewed," *The Washington Post,* Aug. 7, 2007. de Moraes, Lisa.

11. "Top 10 most-watched shows of the decade," Reuters, Dec. 2, 2009. Hibbard, James.

12. "*The Real World*—Just Your Regular Reality Show Racism," Racialicious.com, May 8, 2008. Peterson, Latoya. www.racialicious.com/2008/05/08/the-real-world-just-your-regular-reality-show-racism/.

13. *Vanity Fair,* July 2003. Seal, Mark.

14. *The New York Times,* Feb. 26, 2000. Kuczynski, Alex and Cater, Bill; "Joe Mastermind; Brilliant programmer or evil genius bent on destroying American culture? Either way, Fox's reality guru Mike Darnell (the brains behind 'Joe Millionaire') is changing TV," *Entertainment Weekly,* Mar. 28, 2003. Snierson, Dan.

15. "Blood, Sweat, and Ratings," *Business Week,* May 15, 2006. Lowry, Tom.

16. *Backlash: The Undeclared War Against American Women.* Faludi, Susan. p. xxii.

17. "Jackass Nation: No shame, no fame is the new mantra of reality tv. But when will too much reality be too much?" *Entertainment Weekly,* July 13, 2001. Rice, Lynette; "Is Trash TV Bad for Women? a Producer's Defense of Celebreality," Jezebel.com, Jan 15, 2010. Carmon, Irin.

18. "Anatomy of a Disaster; The strange tale of how *Commander in Chief* went from a smash to the brink of cancellation in just one season," *Entertainment Weekly,* May 19, 2006. Shaw; Jessica. *Entertainment Weekly,* Mar. 14, 2003. Rice, Lynette. Also see *Firefly* entry on Wikipedia http://en.wikipedia.org/wiki/Firefly_%28TV_series%29.

19. *Vanity Fair,* July 2003. Seal, Mark. "Nielsens: Big bucks, big start for '10'," *USA Today,* Aug. 14, 2007. Levin, Gary; "Final Renewals & Cancellations For The 2008-9 Season," TVByTheNumbers.com, May 27, 2009. Gorman, Bill.

20. "Unreal World; The fear factor sets in as reality-TV ratings head south," *Entertainment Weekly,* Nov. 2, 2001. Brown, Scott; "Are You SELLING to Me?: Stealth Advertising in the Entertainment

Industry," Writers Guild of America, Nov. 14, 2005; "NBC's new head honcho says 'more product placement, please,'" WIMN's Voices, June 4, 2007. Pozner, Jennifer L; "You're . . . Rehired?" *Entertainment Weekly*, July 20, 2007. Armstrong, Jennifer.

21. *The New York Times*, Feb. 26, 2000. Kuczynski, Alex and Carter, Bill; *The Washington Post*, Feb. 10, 2003. Farhi, Paul.

22. *Variety*, Jan. 16, 2007. Adalian, Josef. "Women Rule New Fox Show."

23. "Humiliation sells on the road to fame," *CBS Evening News*, Jan. 24, 2007. Reported by Schlesinger, Richard; "The case for reality TV: what the snobs don't understand," *The Atlantic Monthly*, May 1, 2007. Hirschorn, Michael.

24. *Fix Me Up: Essays on Television Dating and Makeover Shows*, McFarland Publishing, 2010. Edited by Lancioni, Judith.

25. "Reception analysis," according to The Museum of Broadcast Communications, uses "qualitative (and often ethnographic) methods of research" and "explor[es] the active choices, uses and interpretations made of media materials, by their consumers." See David Morley, "Audience Research: Reception Analysis," part of the Encyclopedia of TV on www.museum.tv.

26. *Enlightened Racism*, Jhally and Lewis, p. 35.

27. Ibid, pp. 19, 30.

28. Ibid, p. 17.

29. "Reporting on writers' strike reinforces myth of 'unscripted' reality TV genre," WIMN's Voices blog, Nov. 5, 2007. Pozner, Jennifer L.

30. "Are You SELLING to Me?" 2005, WGA.org "Product Integration" site.

31. *Vanity Fair*, July 2003. Seal, Mark.

32. "The Bachelor and Other Delights," NPR's MonitorMix blog, Apr. 28, 2008. Brownstein, Carrie.

33. "It Wasn't the Editing," *Television Without Pity*, July 5, 2007. Sars, "How Reality TV Fakes It," *Time*, Jan. 29, 2006. Poniewozik, James.

34. "How Reality TV Fakes It." Poniewozik.

35. Jezebel.com, Jan. 15, 2010.

36. Variety, Jan. 16, 2007. Adalian, Josef.

37. "Reality Check: The revolution in 'unscripted' fare has Hollywood asking, Just what exactly is a writer?" *Broadcasting & Cable*, July 16, 2005. Higgins, John M. and Benson, Jim. "How Reality TV Fakes It." Poniewozik; "It Wasn't the Editing." Sars.

38. "Reality Check," Jan. 29, 2006. Higgins and Benson. "Fast Track," *Broadcasting & Cable*, Aug. 29, 2005. Staff. "WGA showcasing reality TV workers; Guild is holding news conference on Tuesday," *Variety*, Apr. 7, 2008. McNary, Dave. Also see www.wga.org/content/default.aspx?id=2630.

39. "A Portrait of 'Generation Next': How Young People View Their Lives, Futures and Politics," Pew Research Center For The People & The Press in association with The Generation Next Initiative and Documentary produced by MacNeil/Lehrer Productions. Jan. 9, 2007.

CHAPTER ONE

1. "Reality: 'Joe Millionaire' Was a Faker From the Start," *Daily Press*, Feb. 1, 2004. Jicha, Tom. "Is Mr. Smith Going to Washington? Not Yet," *The Wichita Eagle*, June 17, 2003; "Evan Marriott suggests 'Joe Millionaire' producers 'fixed' Zora Andrich as the winner," RealityTVWorld.com, June 19, 2003. Rogers, Steve. www.realitytvworld.com/news/evan-marriott-suggests-joe-millionaire-producers-fixed-zora-andrich-as-winner-1321.php.

2. *True Hollywood Story: America's Next Top Model,* Mar. 26, 2006.

3. Ibid.

4. "What Were They Thinking?" as told to Dan Snierson, *Entertainment Weekly,* Aug. 8, 2008.

5. Web search retrieved November 15, 2008, http://gallery.bahamas.com/bahamas/island/templrgstandard.aspx?sectionid=63274&level=3.

6. "Again, what's love got to do with it?; 'The Bachelor' is back for Season 10, with a Navy doctor as bait, and so is all the guile a girl could muster," *Los Angeles Times,* Apr. 15, 2007. Caramanica, Jon.

7. "What Were They Thinking?" as told to Jennifer Armstrong, *Entertainment Weekly,* Aug. 8, 2008.

8. "Disney Dream Weddings Special," TheTrueDisneyFan.blogspot.com, Dec. 18, 2009. Lady Aurora Yensid.

9. "Joe Mastermind; Brilliant programmer or evil genius bent on destroying American culture? Either way, Fox's reality guru Mike Darnell (the brains behind 'Joe Millionaire') is changing TV," *Entertainment Weekly,* Mar. 28, 2003. Snierson, Dan.

10. "The Gay Deceivers, Again," PopMatters.com, Mar. 22, 2004. Abernethy, Michael.

11. "Playing It Straight: Reality dating shows and the construction of heterosexuality," *Journal of Popular Film & Television,* June 22, 2009. Tropiano, Stephen.

12. Fox press release reprinted on TheFurtonCritic.com, May 5, 2004. www.thefutoncritic.com/news.aspx?id=6579 and "Fox Puts Foot in Its Mouth, Kicks Self," *The Washington Post,* May 14, 2004. de Moraes, Lisa.

13. "What Were They Thinking?" as told to Dan Snierson, *Entertainment Weekly,* Aug. 8, 2008.

14. In nearly every lecture I've given on reality TV since 2002, I've drawn connections between the fight for lesbian and gay marriage rights and the trivial depiction of marriage in reality TV dating shows. I was pleasantly surprised in December 2009 when New York Senator Diane Savino made a similar argument on the Senate floor, in favor of same-sex marriage. "Turn on the television. We have a wedding channel on cable TV devoted to the behavior of people on the way to the altar. They spend billions of dollars, behave in the most appalling way, all in an effort to be princess for a day. You don't have cable television? Put on network TV. We're giving away husbands on a game show. You can watch *The Bachelor,* where thirty desperate women will compete to marry a 40-year-old man who has never been able to maintain a decent relationship in his life," Savino said. "That's what we've done to marriage in America, where young women are socialized from the time they're five years old to think of being nothing but a bride. . . . So if there's anything wrong with the sanctity of marriage in America, it comes from those of us who have the privilege and the right and have abused it for decades." For video of Savino's speech, see "Heroine Alert: Diane Savino, NY State Senator," *Jezebel,* Dec. 3, 2009. Robertson, Lindsay. http://jezebel.com/5417973/heroine-alert-diane-savino-ny-state-senator.

CHAPTER TWO

1. "Low ratings another Miss America Pageant problem," *The Ledger* (Lakefield, FL), Sept. 13, 1984. Lin, Jennifer.

2. *TLC GIVES MISS AMERICA A MAKEOVER IN ORIGINAL REALITY PROGRAM* MISS AMERICA: REALITY CHECK, Dec. 5, 2007. TLC Press Release.

3. "Miss America reality: Can reality television save a cultural relic?" *Ottawa Citizen,* Jan. 26, 2008. Srikanthan, Thulasi.

4. "Breast Implant Questions and Answers," FDA.gov; "Government Studies Link Breast Implants to

Cancer, Lung Diseases, and Suicide." Zuckerman, PhD, Diana and Flynn, Rachael. MPHBreast-ImplantInfo.org, citing Brinton, L. A., Lubin, J. H., Burich, M. C., Colton, T., Brown, S. L., and Hoover, R. N.; "Cancer Risk at Sites Other Than the Breast Following Augmentation Mammoplasty." *Annals of Epidemiology* 11: 248-256. (2001).

5. "The Ageing Dilemma," *Women & Hollywood* blog, Apr. 4, 2009. Silverstein, Melissa.

6. "Fast Food Chains Say Sexy Ads 'Generate Positive Consumer Sales,'" *Jezebel*, July 8, 2009. Egan Morrissey, Tracie; "Sex, Lies, and Advertising," *Ms. Magazine*, July/Aug. 1990. Steinem, Gloria.

7. Report of the APA Task Force on the Sexualization of Girls, Executive Summary, 2007.

8. *Can't Buy My Love: How Advertising Changes the Way We Think and Feel* (New York: Free Press, 2000). p. 135. Kilbourne, Jean. Also see: "The Effect of Experimental Presentation of Thin Media Images on Body Satisfaction: A Meta-Analytic Review," *International Journal of Eating Disorders* 31 no. 1: 1–16 (Jan. 2002). Groesz, Lisa M., Levine, Michael P. and Murnen, Sarah K.

9. "Sexist/Racist Ad Watch: Skin Whitening Edition," *Feministing*, Mar. 4, 2009. Valenti, Jessica. "Asian-Americans Criticize Eyelid Surgery Craze," *WomensENews*, Aug. 15, 2004. Kobrin, Sandy. *Style and Status: Selling Beauty to African American Women, 1920-1975* (Lexington: University Press of Kentucky, 2007), p.9. Walker, Susannah.

10. "Study: Tanning beds as deadly as arsenic," *The Associated Press,* July 28, 2009. Cheng, Maria.

11. "Q&A: Darnell and Fleiss talk 'More to Love'" *THRFeed, Hollywood Reporter* blog, Mar. 29, 2009. Hibberd, James.

12. Ibid.

13. "On 'The Biggest Loser,' Health Can Take Back Seat," *New York Times,* Nov. 25, 2009. Wyatt, Edward.

14. "National Eating Disorders Association/Next Door Neighbors Puppet Guide Book" and "Statistics: Eating Disorders and their Precursors," a NEDA online fact sheet.

15. "Fashion's invisible woman," *Los Angeles Times,* Mar. 1, 2009. Vesilind, Emili; "Advance Data from Vital and Health Statistics, Number 347, October 27, 2004," Division of Health and Nutrition Examination Surveys, Center for Disease Control. Ogden, Cynthia L., PhD, Fryar, Cheryl D., MSPH, Carroll, Margaret D., MSPH, and Flegal, Katherine M., PhD.

16. "Tyra Banks Wants Plus-Sized Teens for New Modeling Competition," *UsMagazine.com,* Jan. 26, 2010.

17. National Eating Disorders Association, www.nationaleatingdisorders.org/p.asp?WebPage_ID=286&Profile_ID=41143 and the University of Maryland Medical Center, www.umm.edu/patiented/articles/how_serious_anorexia_nervosa_000049_5.htm.

18. "Images continue to entice kids to smoke; Research shows depictions in movies are rising," *Ventura County Star,* May 16, 007. Parker-Pope, Tara.

19. "Weight a Minute: Dickinson scorns efforts to rehabilitate modeling," *New York Post,* Feb. 4, 2007. Starr Seibel, Deborah.

20. See www.ProThinSpo.com and www.FastingAddictBlog.Blogspot.Com.

21. Team WWK (Watch With Kristin), "ANTM's London Levi Discusses Eating Disorders," *E! News Online,* Apr. 16, 2009. "ANTM Interview: London Levi," TopModelGossip.com, Apr. 18, 2009. Balser, Erin.

22. "ANTM's London Levi," *E! News Online.*

23. "Statistics: Eating Disorders and their Precursors," NEDA online. NEDA cites the source of these statistics, respectively, as: *I'm, Like, SO Fat!* (New York: The Guilford Press, 2005). Neumark-Sztainer, D. p. 5; "Weight-related behaviors and concerns of fourth-grade children," *Journal of*

American Dietetic Association (1992). Gustafson-Larson, A. M. and Terry, R. D. pp. 818–822; "A longitudinal study of the dietary practices of black and white girls 9 and 10 years old at enrollment: The NHLBI growth and health study," *Journal of Adolescent Health* (1991). Mellin, L., McNutt, S., Hu, Y., Schreiber, G. B., Crawford, P., and Obarzanek, E. pp. 27–37.

24. "Small Wonders; TV WINNERS & LOSERS—Men with superpowers, women with super power, and networks with super—make that modest—hits. A report on the fall season," *Entertainment Weekly*, Nov. 25, 2005. Armstrong, Jennifer; "Who Is America's Next Top Model, Really?" *The New York Times*, Nov. 6, 2005. Trebay, Guy; CW Press Release, Sept. 10, 2009, via TVByTheNumbers. com. Seidman, Robert.

25. Anonymous comment posted on the "Beat Bulimia" bulletin board of the Healthy Place Support Network, Healthyplace.com.

26. *Can't Buy My Love*. Kilbourne, pp. 132–133.

27. "The elastic body image: The effect of television advertising and programming on body image distortions in young women," *Journal of Communication* (1992). Myers, P. and Biocca, F. A. pp. 109–130; "Women 'suffer poor self-esteem due to airbrushing in advertising,'" *Telegraph*, Nov. 27, 2009.

28. "So you think you can sing," *SFGate.com.*, Jan. 25, 2007. Wiegand, David.

29. "American Idol or big fatty? Ask the diet-obsessed talking head!" WIMN's Voices blog, May 25, 2007. Zeisler, Andi.

30. TheSmokingGun.com, "Fox Doctor's Diploma-Mill Degree," May 14, 2004.

31. "Cosmetic Plastic Surgery Research: Statistics and Trends for 2001-2008," www.cosmeticplastic-surgerystatistics.com/statistics.html. "Model's death highlights plastic surgery risks," CNN, Jan. 7, 2010. Tutton, Mark. "Early Mortality Among Medicare Beneficiaries Undergoing Bariatric Surgical Procedures," *JAMA* 294: 1903–1908 (2005). Flum, David R., MD, MPH; Salem, Leon, MD; Broeckel Elrod, Jo Ann, PhD; Patchen Dellinger, E., MD; Cheadle, Allen, PhD; Chan, Leighton, MD, MPH.

CHAPTER THREE

1. "In Rape Debate, Controversy Trumps Credibility: 'Natural' sexual assault theory 'irresistible' to profit-driven media," *Extra!*, May/June 2000. Pozner, Jennifer L.

2. "The Bachelor and Other Delights," NPR's MonitorMix, Apr. 28, 2008. Brownstein, Carrie.

3. "Mean Girls: Tamra Barney explains why she thinks she was the 'mean girl' this season!" Bravo.com blog, Feb. 17, 2009. Barney, Tamra; "WTF, Atlanta! Did NeNe Really Choke Kim?" E! Online, Jul. 31, 2009. "DeShawn Snow No Longer a "'Real' Housewife: 'I Didn't See It Coming,'" *Essence* online, Jan. 14, 2009. Byrd, Kenya N.

4. "On Reality TV, Tired, Tipsy and Pushed to Brink," *New York Times*, Aug. 2, 2009. Wyatt, Edward.

5. "The Real Housewives of Atlanta; Cast Members Put the Real in Reality," *Jet*, Sept. 7–14, 2009. Hoffman, Melody K.

6. "Interview: Kortnie Coles talks about 'America's Next Top Model,'" *Reality TV World*, Mar. 31, 2009. Bracchitta, John.

7. See "I'm Not Here to Make Friends," a remix video by Rich Juzwiak, consisting of nothing but reality TV participants uttering that ubiquitous phrase. http://fourfour.typepad.com/fourfour/2008/07/im-not-here-to.html. Juzwiak discussed his video on NPR's *This American Life* on Sept. 11, 2009.

8. "The Big Lie: False Feminist Death Syndrome, Profit, and the Media," in *Catching a Wave: Reclaim-*

ing Feminism for the 21ˢᵗ Century (Boston: Northeastern University Press, 2003). Pozner, Jennifer L. Eds. Dicker, Rory and Piepmeier, Alison.

9. *Today in New York*, NBC. May 7, 2006; "My Bosses From Hell—And They Were All Women," *London Daily Mail*, Aug. 23, 2004. Platell, Amanda; "Do All Women Make Bad Bosses?" posted on the news blog of the British edition of *Marie Claire* magazine, Dec. 8, 2009.

10. "Mommy vs. Mommy," *Newsweek*, June 4, 1990. Darnton, Nina; "Scary rise of the 'sancti-mommy,'" *Washington Times*, June 8, 2008. Miller, Cheryl; "The Mommy War," *Texas Monthly*, July 1989. Russell, Jan Jarboe. "LOVE & MONEY; Is My Mom Better Than Yours?" *The New York Times*, July 1, 2001. Spragins, Ellyn; "The Opt-Out Revolution," *The New York Times*, Oct. 26, 2003. Belkin, Lisa.

11. "The Mommy War Machine," *The Washington Post*, Apr. 29, 2007. Graff, E. J.

12. *Getting Even: Why Women Don't Get Paid Like Men and What to Do About It*, Touchstone, Sept. 27, 2005. Murphy, Evelyn and Graff, E. J. Also see the National Organization for Women's "Wal-Mart: Merchant of Shame" campaign: www.now.org/issues/wfw/wal-mart.html.

13. *A Place on the Team: the Triumph and Tragedy of Title IX*, Princeton University Press, Jan. 31, 2005. Suggs, Welch. p. 2–3. "Education and Title IX," fact sheet of the National Organization for Women, www.now.org/issues/title_ix/index.html; "Rally 'Round the Boys: PBS's National Desk enlists in the 'Gender Wars,'" *Extra!* Sept./Oct. 1999. Pozner, Jennifer L.

14. "WELL; What Are Friends For? A Longer Life," *The New York Times*, Apr. 21, 2009. Parker-Pope, Tara.

15. "Anna Nicole Smith: A very slow news day," BobHarris.com, Feb. 8, 2007. www.bobharris.com/component/content/article/68/1294-anna-nicole-smith-a-very-slow-news-day. His critique was later produced as an animated video for Salon.com. "Bob Harris vs. the damn news: Puppies! Baby pandas! Britney! And something about North Korea," Oct. 10, 2007.

16. "The Simpsons; Making of superstar sisters Jessica and Ashlee Simpson," *Dateline*, NBC News. May 8, 2005. Kotb, Hoda; "She's having a blonde moment," *USA Today*, Oct. 28, 2003. Thomas, Karen; "'Dumb blonde' as an art form," *Arizona Daily Star*, Nov. 7, 2003. Bailey, Rob.

17. "Is Tyra Banks Racist: The peculiar politics of *America's Next Top Model*," Slate.com, May 18, 2006. Dahl, J. E.

18. *Understanding Inequality: the Intersection of Race/Ethnicity, Class, and Gender*, (New York: Rowman & Littlefield, 2007). Arrighi, Barbara A. p. 230.

19. "Larry Summers Is Not the Change I Was Expecting," Women's Media Center, Nov. 7, 2008. Arreola, Veronica.

20. "Ready for its closeups? Tyler, TX going national in Fox's Anchorwoman," on the TV Press Tour, July '07 website of former *Dallas Morning News* veteran TV critic Ed Bark. July 7, 2007.

21. Feminist Law Professors blog, Jan. 14, 2010 and Jan. 17, 2010.

22. "New Blouse, New House, I Need a New Spouse: The Politics of Transformation and Identity in Television Makeover and Swap Shows," in *Fix Me Up: Essays on Television Dating and Makeover Shows* (Jefferson, NC: McFarland Publishing, 2009). Tarrant, Shira, PhD. Ed. Lancioni, Judith. p. 181.

23. "The Tax on Being Female: .23 Cents per Hour and Counting," and "Media Discrimination Begets Biased Content," *Women's Review of Books*, May/June 2006. Pozner, Jennifer L.

24. "Mad Men's Secret Product Placements," *Brandweek*, Aug. 17, 2009. Wasserman, Todd.

25. "TV Guide Proves Summer Is Here," Media Bistro's Fishbowl LA blog, June 16, 2008.

26. "How to marry your own millionaire," *USAToday.com*, Feb. 10, 2003. Maxwell, Alison. (Found on Zap2it.com, Dec. 2, 2002.)

27. "Top 10 most-watched shows of the decade," Reuters, Dec. 2, 2009. Hibbard, James.

28. "According to U.S. Government estimates, 600,000 to 800,000 victims are trafficked globally each year and 14,500 to 17,500 are trafficked into the United States. Women and children comprise the largest group of victims [and] are often physically and emotionally abused." From "Distinctions Between Human Smuggling and Human Trafficking," U.S. Department of State, Apr. 1, 2006. See GEMS: Girls Education & Mentoring Services, publications and film, *Very Young Girls*. Also see: "Sex Slaves: Estimating the Numbers" on PBS's website for the 2006 *Frontline* film, *Sex Slaves*.

29. "Who're You Calling a Whore?: A Conversation with Three Sex Workers on Sexuality, Empowerment, and the Industry," by Susan Lopez, Mariko Passion, and Saundra in *Yes Means Yes!* (Berkeley, CA: Seal Press, 2008).

30. "Waiting for Mr. REALLY Right," *Sirens*, Aug. 10, 2008. Goode, Erich.

31. *Fix Me Up: Essays on Television Dating and Makeover Shows*. Tarrant. p. 173.

32. *A2/M2 Three Screen Report*, Volume 6, 3rd Quarter 2009. Updated Dec. 18, 2009. The Nielsen Company. *How Teens Use Media: A Nielsen report on the myths and realities of teen media trends*, June 2009. The Nielsen Company.

CHAPTER FOUR

1. "America to Watch Family Pick Mate for Glendale Dad," *The Cincinnati Enquirer*, July 1, 2003. Kiesewetter, John.

2. "Dear Suitor: A House Isn't Always a Home," *Television Week*, August 4, 2003. Gates, Anita; "Looking for a Date, and Some Public Humiliation," *The New York Times*, July 22, 2002. Gates, Anita.

3. "Dear Suitor." Gates.

4. "True Love on TV: A Gendered Analysis of Reality-Romance Television," Poroi: An Interdisciplinary Journal of *Rhetorical Analysis* and Invention 4.2 (2005): 17-51. Brophy-Baermann, Michelle.

5. "Employment Situation Summary," Jan 8, 2010. Bureau of Labor Statistics. "Wealth, Income, and Power," Sept. 2005, updated Oct. 2009. Domhoff, G. William. "Let America be American Again: Racial Wealth Equity," *Huffington Post*, Dec. 18, 2007. www.huffingtonpost.com/amaad-rivera/let-america-be-american-a_b_77417.html. Rivera, Amaad. For extensive data, see *Foreclosed: State of the Dream 2008*, a report by the Racial Wealth Divide Program at United for a Fair Economy.

6. Lui also notes that "Single women of each race have less than half the wealth as men of their own race, but due to the racial wealth gap, women of color are at the bottom." Meizhu Lui, "Feminomics: A Woman's Place—Still in the (Poor) House," NewDeal20.org, The Franklin and Eleanor Roosevelt Institute, citing *Shortchanged: Why Women Have Less Wealth and What Can Be Done about It*, (London: Oxford University Press, Aug. 2010). Chang, Mariko. "Improving Pay Equity Would Mean Great Gains for Women," Institute for Women's Policy Research news release, July 10, 2008. For detailed breakdowns of poverty, earnings, education, and healthcare differences between women of color and other population groups, see "Data Tables on the Economic Status of Women of Color in the United States: Key Data Points," the Institute for Women's Policy Research, May 20, 2008, www.iwpr.org/femstats/wocdata.htm.

7. *Flavor of Love Girls: Charm School*. VH1.com.

8. Ibid.

9. "New Blouse, New House, I Need a New Spouse. Tarrant.

10. "Triumph of the Shill, Part 2: Reality TV Lets Marketers Write the Script," *Bitch: Feminist Response to Pop Culture* 24 (2004). Pozner, Jennifer.

11. "This New House," *Mother Jones*, Mar./Apr. Illustration by Fox, Nathan. 2005.

12. See Walker, Rob. "The Product Is You," Murketing blog, 6/15/07 (www.murketing.com/journal/?p=605), "The Product Is You, No. 2," 6/27/07 (www.murketing.com/journal/?p=629), and "Selling audiences," Gus Andrews' Flickr photostream (http://flickr.com/photos/37071176@N00/2577219794/).

13. "Americans spend every cent—and more," CNN Money, Dec. 21, 2006. Isidore, Chris; "U.S. savings rate hits lowest level since 1933," Associated Press wire story published at MSNBC.com, Jan. 30, 2006.

14. "Fighting Off Depression," *The New York Times*, Jan. 4, 2009. Krugman, Paul.

15. An "All News" search of the Nexis news database turns up 2,394 references to the word *staycation* in 2008, the year *First Class All the Way* premiered.

16. "Study Ties Bankruptcy to Medical Bills," *The New York Times*, Feb. 2, 2005. Abelson, Reed. "Record Number Receive Food Stamps," National Public Radio, Aug. 10, 2009. "Now Casting Women Living Extravagant Lifestyles!" RealityWanted.com, Dec. 16, 2009.

17. "Given a Shovel, Americans Dig Deeper Into Debt," *The New York Times*, July 20, 2008. Morgenson, Gretchen.

18. *First Class All the Way* press release, reprinted at www.thefutoncritic.com.

19. Bravo.com websites for *Million Dollar Listing* Season 2 and *First Class All the Way*; "Over One Million People Lost Their Home in 2008," *Business Week* Hot Property blog, Jan. 14, 2009. Palmeri, Chris; United for a Fair Economy report: *Foreclosed: State of the Dream 2008*. Additionally, for a wealth of information on the vanishing middle class, rising poverty rates, and the growing gap between the nation's rich and poor, see: Economic Policy Institute, Lawrence Mishel, Jared Bernstein, and Heidi Shierholz. *The State of Working America 2008/2009* (Ithaca, NY: Cornell University Press, Jan. 2009). Economic Policy Institute, Mishel, Lawrence, Bernstein, Jared and Shierholz, Heidi, excerpts available on EPI's website at www.stateofworkingamerica.org/. Also see "By the Numbers" at Demos.org.

20. "Is Greed Ever Good?: No, Say Ethicists; and It's Not Even Good for Capitalism, Some Argue," *ABC News*, Aug. 22, 2002. James, Michael S.

21. "ABC Drops Controversial 'Neighborhood' Reality Show," CivilRights.org, July 6, 2005.

22. "The (Female) Cost of Living," *Daily Worth* blog, Dec. 16, 2009. Dunleavy, M. P., www.dailyworth.com/blog/312-the-female-cost-of-living#.

23. *Taking On the Big Boys: Or Why Feminism Is Good for Families, Business, and the Nation*, The Feminist Press at CUNY. Apr. 1, 2007. Bravo, Ellen.

24. www.emailbrain.com/Archive/Default.aspx?Mode=2&s=37478&n=246151&c=1 and http://drloisfrankel.com/fee_schedule.html.

25. "The dark underside of Oprah's Big Give; Generous? No doubt. But the mogul's approach only underscores a shameful story on social infrastructure," Toronto Star, Apr. 19, 2008. Diebel, Linda.

26. "The dark underside of Oprah's Big Give." Diebel; *Fix Me Up*. Tarrant.

27. "Undercover Boss: Advertainment's Fourth Wave," Gawker.com's Defamer blog, Feb. 8, 2010. Nolan, Hamilton.

28. "With "Extreme Makeover" Homes, Some Get Foreclosure Instead of Happy Ending," FindingDulcinea.com, June 5, 2009. Lovett, Haley A.

29. *All You Can Eat: How Hungry Is America*, (New York: Seven Stories Press. 2008) Berg, Joel. p. 191.

30. Organizations such as the National Housing Law Project, Housing Works, the Insight Center for Community Economic Development, and the Women's Institute for Policy Research propose a variety of public policy approaches to the institutional problems of poverty, homelessness, and gender and racial disparities in these areas.

31. TMZ.com, "Adrianne Curry on 'Top Model': They 'F***ed' Me," Feb. 6, 2007. TMZ Staff.

32. "The 'Idol' Advantage," *The Philadelphia Inquirer*, Sept. 1, 2002. Hiltbrand, David.

33. "Reinventing Reality; He made millions with American Idol and other watch-'em-squirm shows. But TV viewers are fickle—so SIMON FULLER will parody what he has built," *Time*, Jan. 1, 2003. James, Jennie.

34. *VH1 News Presents: Reality TV Secrets 2;* "Star struck; Elementary students are rapt audience for 'Idol' contestant," *Grand Rapid Press*, Apr. 30, 2004.

CHAPTER FIVE

1. "An Island Divided," *St. Petersburg Times*, Sept. 21, 2006. Deggans, Eric.

2. Indeed, Kabir was attractive enough to be cast on an Indian wedding episode of the short-lived Alicia Silverstone vehicle *Miss Match*. (Like so many other reality show participants, Kabir was revealed post-*Joe* to be an actor.) The letter of complaint, addressed to NBC's president and *Average Joe*'s producers, appeared on October 30, 2003 on the websites Reality TV World and Fans of Reality TV.

3. "Have Fook Yu and Fook Mi hit the big time?" *SF Gate*, Sept. 29, 2005. Yang, Jeff.

4. "Performing Race in *Flavor of Love* and *The Bachelor*," *Critical Studies in Media Communication* 25, No. 4, Oct. 2008. Dubrofsky, Rachel E. and Hardy, Antoine. pp. 373–392.

5. *Navigating Interracial Borders: Black-White Couples and Their Social Worlds*, (Piscataway, New Jersey: Rutgers University Press, 2005). Childs, E. C.

6. "Deranged Marriage," *ColorLines* RaceWire. May, 2003. Sen, Rinku. "The Millennials: A Portrait of Generation Next," Pew Research Center, Dec. 11, 2009. Keeter, Scott and Taylor, Paul.

7. "Bachelor Winner Arrested for Assaulting Fiancé," *People* online, Nov. 24, 2007. Helling, Steve.

8. The Jim Crow Museum of Racist Memorabilia at Ferris State University, www.ferris.edu/jimcrow/sapphire/.

9. "TV Guide Top Ten Reality TV Villains," PopCrunch.com, June 16, 2008. Castina; TVGuide.com photo gallery: www.tvguide.com/PhotoGallery/Evil-Reality-TV-1001885/12.aspx; "Natural Born Villain," *Mahogany*, Winter 2006–2007. "'The Donald' Plays Trump Card on NBC," *Pittsburgh Post-Gazette*, Apr. 11, 2004. Owen, Rob. "Commentary," *Newhouse News Service*, May 26, 2006. Cornog, Evan. "You can't keep it real on TV without race," *Fort Worth Star Telegram*, Apr. 23, 2004. Parish Perkins, Ken.

10. "Star Democrats steal the show: In Boston, celebrities go to work at their real job: politics," *National Post*, July 29, 2004.

11. Alberts, Sheldon. "If We Ran Reality TV; Black is beautiful . . . so is Asian," *Entertainment Weekly*, May 21, 2004.

12. "False accusation of racism stings as much as real slur," Chicago Sun-Times, Mar. 25, 2004. Roeper, Richard.

13. "Omarosa played too many cards and got Trumped," *Chicago Sun-Times*, Mar. 21, 2004. Mitchell, Mary.

14. *The Bitch Switch: Knowing How to Turn It On and Off*, (Beverly Hills, CA: Phoenix Books, 2008). Manigault-Stallworth, Omarosa; "Donald J. Trump Partners with TV One on a Groundbreaking New Reality Series Entitled, 'Omarosa's Ultimate Merger,'" *PR Newswire*, Nov. 10, 2009.

15. "How Reality TV Fakes It," *Time,* Jan. 29, 2006. Poniewozik, James; Jim Crow Museum.

16. "Misperceptions, the Media, and the Iraq War," WorldPublicOpinion.org, Oct. 2, 2003.

17. *The Terror Dream: Fear and Fantasy in Post-9/11 America,* (New York: Metropolitan Books, 2007). Faludi, Susan. pp. 3–4.

18. "Demographic Profile of Service Members Ever Deployed: Operation Iraqi Freedom and Operation Enduring Freedom," Jan. 31, 2009. Fact sheet from Iraq and Afghanistan Veterans of America, citing Contingency Tracking System. The racial backgrounds of an additional 20.5 percent of service members were listed as "unknown."

19. *The Terror Dream.* Faludi, Susan. pp. 165–195. "A Double Standard for Heroes," AlterNet, Nov. 14, 2003. Chideya, Farai. "The Private War of Women Soldiers," Salon, Mar. 7, 2007. Benedict, Helen.

20. *Slave in a Box: The Strange Career of Aunt Jemima,* (Charlottesville, VA: University of Virginia Press, 1998). Manring, M. M.

21. Museum of Broadcast Communications online Encyclopedia of TV. Entry written by Bodroghkozy, Aniko.

22. "Nell Carter Is Dead at 54; Star of 'Ain't Misbehavin'," *The New York Times,* Jan. 24, 2003. Holden, Stephen.

23. "More Than Skin Deep: FX's 'Black. White.,'" *The Washington Post,* Mar. 8, 2006. Crews, Chip; "Six-part FX documentary tries to bring racism out into the open," *Oakland Tribune,* Mar. 7, 2006. Young, Susan; "Reality show challenges racial perceptions Black and white television," *Contra Costa Times,* Mar. 7, 2006. Barney, Chuck; "FX puts a new face on its upcoming six-part documentary 'Black. White.,'" *Call and Post (Cleveland),* Dec. 21, 2005.

24. "Fox Plays the Race Card," TruthDig.com, Mar. 9, 2006. Avni, Sheerly.

25. "Commodifying Africa on U.S. Network Reality Television," *Communication, Culture & Critique* 1 no. 4, Dec. 2008. Steeves, H. Leslie pp. 416–446. *Culture and the Ad: Exploring Otherness in the World of Advertising* (Boulder, CO: Westview Press, 1994). O'Barr, William.

26. "Why I'm Starting to Love *The Amazing Race,*" BobHarris.com, Dec. 4, 2009.

27. "Cosmetic Surgery and the Televisual Makeover: A Foucauldian feminist reading," *Feminist Media Studies* 7 no. 1, Mar. 2007. Heyes, Cressida J. p. 23.

28. *Style and Status: Selling Beauty to African American Women, 1920–1975* (Lexington, KY: University Press of Kentucky, 2007). Walker, Susannah. p. 2.

29. "Butch Voices Conference Closing Keynote," Aug. 23, 2009. Transcript on OaklandLocal.com.

30. "Addicted to 'Love,' Fans savor Flavor with a side of guilt," *Contra Costa Times,* Oct. 14, 2006. Barney, Chuck.

31. "A Ladies' Man Everyone Fights Over," *The New York Times,* Oct. 1, 2006. Ogunnaike, Lola; "Flavor Flav: Totally Cuckoo? The real story behind what makes the rapper-turned-reality star tick," *Entertainment Weekly,* Aug. 11, 2006. Watson, Margeaux.

32. "The Immortals—The Greatest Artists of All Time," *Rolling Stone,* Apr. 15, 2004. Yauch, Adam.

33. PR Newswire, October 17, 2006; "A Ladies Man." Ogunnaike, "Reality TV Loving It Hating It Living It," *Entertainment Weekly,* June 12, 2009.

34. *Love and Theft: Blackface Minstrelsy and the American Working Class* (New York: Oxford University Press, 1993). Lotte, Eric.

35. Internet Movie Database biography for Stepin Fetchit, accessed Feb. 9, 2010; *Stepin Fetchit: The Life and Times of Lincoln Perry* (New York: Pantheon, 2005). Watkins, Mal.

36. "Slaves to the Clock," *Essence,* Nov. 2006. Dickerson, Debra.

37. "Film To Expose MTV, BET & VH1," HipHopDx.com, Feb. 27, 2007. Springer Jr., Anthony. Watch *Turn Off Channel Zero* here: www.myspace.com/turnoffchannelzero.

38. "Love Him, Or Leave Him?; Flavor Flav's Popular Show Sets Off Passionate Debate on Comedy and Race," *The Washington Post*, Nov. 2, 2006. Wiltz, Teresa; *Tavis Smiley*, PBS, Aug. 15, 2007; Lynn Elber, "Producing duo spices up VH1 with 'Flavor of Love,' more; only sin for channel 'to be boring,'" The Associated Press, Oct. 3, 2007.

39. "The Real World—Just Your Regular, Reality Show Racism," Racialicious.com, May 8, 2008. Peterson, Latoya.

40. "The Fake Maui," AngryAsianMan.com blog, Jan. 26, 2007; "Locals Object to New MTV Reality Show 'Maui Fever, '" *The Insider*, Jan. 23, 2007.

41. *"I Love New York*: Does New York Love Me?" *Journal of International Women's Studies* 10 no. 2. Nov. 2008. Campbell, Shannon B., Giannino, Steven S., China, Chrystal R. and Harris, Christopher S. Also see the Jim Crow Museum's extensive "Jezebel Stereotype" photo gallery and essay, at www.ferris.edu/jimcrow/jezebel/.

42. *"I Love New York*: Does New York Love Me?" Campbell et al.

43. "'I Love New York' premiere draws VH1's best series debut ratings ever," RealityTVWorld.com, Dec. 1, 2007.

44. Spectrum PR, *Biography for Tariq Nasheed*, Internet Movie Database, IMDB.com.

45. "Producing duo spices up VH1." Elber.

46. "Love Him, or Leave Him." Wiltz.

47. "Anything but Racism: Media make excuses for 'whitewashed' TV lineup," *Extra!* Jan./Feb. 2000. Jackson, Janine; *Out of Focus, Out of Sync Take 4: A Report on the Television Industry*, Dec. 2008. NAACP Hollywood Bureau; "TV's Great Black Hope," *Entertainment Weekly*, June 20, 2008. Armstrong, Jennifer and Watson, Margeaux.

48. Fairness & Accuracy In Reporting, *Extra!* magazine's publisher, has monitored representation of women and people of color in journalism since 1986: www.fair.org/index.php?page=12 for extensive studies and reports. Statistics about women in journalism, TV fiction, film—and in media production, management, and ownership—can be found on WIMN's Field Guide to Media Research (www.wimnonline.org/education/media_research.html) and Media Report to Women (www.mediareporttowomen.com/statistics.htm).

49. "Producing duo spices up VH1." Elber.

50. *From Mammy to Miss America and Beyond: Cultural Images and the Shaping of U.S. Social Policy* (London: Routledge, 1993). Jewell, K. Sue.

51. Oregon Coalition Against Domestic and Sexual Violence online fact sheet, http://www.ocadsv. com/OCADSV_WhatYouShouldKnow_CommunitiesOfColor.asp; "A New Generation of Native Sons: Men of Color and the Prison-Industrial Complex," Belk Jr., Adolphus G.; Also see notes from chapters 3 and 4 for research on women of color and economics; a Dellums Commission report excerpted at NAACP.org.

CHAPTER SIX

1. "Tyra Banks Apologizes Over Bi-Racial Episode of 'ANTM,'" StyleList.com, Nov. 18, 2009. Oliver, Dana.

2. *The Asian Mystique: Dragon Ladies, Geisha Girls, & Our Fantasies of the Exotic Orient*, (New York: PublicAffairs, 2006). Prasso, Sheridan. p. 87.

3. "Ethnic Magazine Editors Discuss Health, Hollywood Buzz," Sept. 12, 2007. National Public Radio. "Can she stay on *Top?*" *Time Out Chicago*, no. 163 : Apr. 10–16, 2008. Aeh, Kevin; "Hidden potential; Reaching consumers," *International Cosmetic News*, Mar. 1, 2008. Guilbault, Laure.

4. *Black Beauty: Aesthetics, Stylization, Politics* (Surrey, UK: Ashgate, 2009). Tate, Shirley Anne.

5. "Bitch poured beer on my weave," *Vanity Fair* contributing editor James Wolcott's blog, Sept. 23, 2004.

6. *Extra!*, the magazine published by media watch organization Fairness & Accuracy In Reporting, produced some of the most well-documented debunking of 1980s and 1990s news coverage scapegoating "welfare queens" and criminalizing youth of color. See: "Five Media Myths About Welfare," *Extra!* May/June, 1995; "Public Enemy Number One? Media's Welfare Debate Is a War on Poor Women," *Extra!* May/June, 1995. Jackson, Janine and Flanders, Laura; "Wild in Deceit: Why 'Teen Violence' Is Poverty Violence in Disguise," *Extra!* Mar./Apr., 1996. Males, Mike; "Superscapegoating: Teen 'superpredators' hype set stage for draconian legislation," *Extra!* Jan./Feb, 1998. Templeton, Robin; "The Smell of Success: After 10 years of 'welfare reform,' ignoring the human impact," *Extra!* Nov./Dec. 2006. deMause, Neil.

7. "Eartha Quake," the avatar of a member of the TelevisionWithoutPity.com fan community, left this comment in the discussion forum devoted to Tiffany during *ANTM*'s fourth season. Apr. 14, 2005.

8. "'Ugly Betty' recast: 'Top Model' is Willi's daughter!" EW.com, Aug. 11, 2009. Ausiello, Michael.

9. "The Resisting Monkey: 'Curious George,' Slave Captivity Narratives, and the Postcolonial Condition," *Ariel: A Review of International English Literature* 28, no. 1 (Jan. 1997): 69–83. Cummins, June.

10. See: *Ethnic Notions,* 1987, directed by Marlon Riggs; and the Jim Crow Museum of Racist Memorabilia at Ferris State University.

11. The Gender Ads Project. Lukas, Scott A., PhD. www.genderads.com/Gender_Ads.com.html.

12. "Obama as witch doctor: Racist or satirical?" CNN.com, Sept. 18, 2009. Fantz, Ashley.

13. "Naomi Campbell in Yet Another 'Out of Africa' Spread," *Black Voices*' BV On Style blog, Aug. 13, 2009.

14. "Caged Black Women: Grace Jones & Amber Rose," FashionBombDaily.com, Aug. 13, 2009. "Iman @ Thierry Mugler in 1985," MakeFetchHappen.blogspot.com, Aug. 22, 2008. Brigitte. "Why Photograph a Black Woman in a Cage?" Jezebel.com, Aug. 14, 2009. Jenna.

15. "Africa Is Wild, and You Can Be Too," SociologicalImages.blogspot.com, July 5, 2009. Wade, Lisa. Also see http://wildafricacream.blogspot.com/search/label/ADVERTISING.

16. "Is Tyra Banks Racist? The peculiar politics of America's Next Top Model," Slate.com, May 18, 2006. Dahl, J. E.

17. "Prime-Time's Top-Earning Women," Forbes.com, Oct. 12, 2009. Rose, Lacey; "Who's the Next Oprah?" E! Online, Nov. 27, 2009. Gornstein, Leslie; "Tyra Banks On It," Forbes.com, July 3, 2006. Blakeley, Kiri.

18. "Tyra Banks to leave talk show," Variety.com, Dec. 28, 2009; "Tyra Banks Says Goodbye to Talk Show," People.com, Dec. 28, 2009.

CHAPTER SEVEN

1. "2003 Ventura Rape Victim Awarded $20 Million in Suit," *Los Angeles Times* (California Local section; no author byline) Aug. 31, 2006. Early details reported by MSNBC's *Countdown with Keith Olbermann,* Nov. 4, 2004.

2. "Woman Says She Was Drugged, Raped at San Diego House for MTV's 'Real World'," *Los Angeles Times*. Nov. 26, 2003. Perry, Tony. Anyone curious about this case can sift through reports in reputable news outlets via the Nexis Lexis news database, and in reality TV fan sites such as Reality TV World (www.real-

itytvworld.com/news/police-raid-real-world-san-diego-house-after-date-rape-allegation-2035.php and www.realitytvworld.com/news/authorities-decline-file-charges-in-alleged-real-world-san-diego-rape-case-2770.php) and Wikipedia (http://en.wikipedia.org/wiki/The_Real_World:_San_Diego).

3. "And the Hot Tub Goes to . . . Austin," *The New York Times.* June 19, 2005. Nielsen research referenced in Patosky, Joe Nick.

4. "Reality TV Hunk's Military Indiscretion: Drunken grope led to 'For Love or Money' star's Marine demise," TheSmokingGun.com. June 9, 2003. www.thesmokinggun.com/archive/campos1.html.

5. "The Bachelor Stewardess Says 'Buh Bye,'" TV Guide Online. Oct. 28, 2002. Coleridge, Daniel.

6. "Millionaire Groom's Dirty Secret," TheSmokingGun.com (no date). www.thesmokinggun.com/millionaire/millionaire.html "Murder suspect raises reality TV questions," The Associated Press, Aug. 21, 2009. Lang, Derrik J.

7. "Did Megan Want a Killer Millionaire?" *Huffington Post,* Aug. 27, 2009. Sax, Robin; "Reality TV: When Casting Goes Wrong," *Entertainment Weekly,* Sept. 4, 2009. Schwartz, Missy.

8. "Global Big Bother; Violence, orgies, riots—it's not just our Big Brother that causes outrage," *The Express,* Jan 20, 2007. Ridley, Mike; "What Your Reality Show Isn't Telling You," AOL SmartMoney.com. Willis, Kedon. (not dated.)

9. "Flavor Flav: Totally Cuckoo? The real story behind what makes the rapper-turned-reality star tick," *Entertainment Weekly,* Aug. 11, 2006. Watson, Margeaux; And, "Hip-Hop, you don't stop: Public Enemy were the Sex Pistols of rap—but they're still seeking the respect they deserve. Johnny Davis talks fighting the power and milking cows on TV with Flavor Flav and Chuck D," *Guardian* online, June 18, 2006. David, Johnny. www.guardian.co.uk/music/2006/jun/18/urban. Accessed Nov. 24, 2009.

10. "Mark Consuelos Talks of Love (and His Kelly Girl)," TVGuide.com, June 18, 2007. Mitovich, Matt Webb.

11. NBC's official *Age of Love* show promo site, www.nbc.com/Age_of_Love/bios/bio_bachelor.shtml.

12. See "Statutory Rape Laws by State," OLR Research Report. April 14, 2003. Norman-Eady, Sandra, with Reinhart, Christopher and Martino, Peter. www.cga.ct.gov/2003/olrdata/jud/rpt/2003-R-0376.htm.

13. "Reality TV." Schwartz.

14. From the "HollaFAQ" at http://hollabacknyc.blogspot.com/, a group blog that allows women who experience street harassment to post cell phone pictures of the people who verbally or physically assault them as they go about their day, along with narrative descriptions of exactly what transpired. The site, dedicated to creating communities in which public spaces are safe for all people, offers women a place to share their experiences, vent, get catharsis, and find support, while also sending a message to perpetrators that they may not be guaranteed the anonymity they assume when catcalling, yelling at, rubbing up against, pinching, grabbing, groping, following, or otherwise assaulting women—in fact, they may be photographed and caught online doing just that. The Street Harassment Project, an organization in New York that holds public actions against what they consider gender-based violence, offers the following as the first of its founding principles: "That street harassment, rape and assault are connected issues; that all stem from attitudes of dehumanization of women that are part of a bigger social picture: the system of male supremacy and sexism under which we still live." More information is available at www.streetharassmentproject.org/.

15. "If We Ran Reality TV; Paris, you're in. Trista, you're out. We've got an extreme makeover for television's most popular—and polarizing—genre." *Entertainment Weekly,* May 21, 2004. Sidewater, Nancy.

16. BarStoolSports.com, posted by elpresidente. Dec. 7, 2009. http://boston.barstoolsports.com/random-thoughts/the-countdown-to-snookie-getting-punched-in-the-face-is-on/.

17. "MTV Pulls Punch Clip from Next Episode of *Jersey Shore*," TVGuide.com, Dec. 11, 2009. Stanhope, Kate.

18. According to a year 2000 UN Study on the Status of Women, www.feminist.com/antiviolence/facts.html Bureau of Justice Statistics Crime Data Brief, Intimate Partner Violence, 1993–2001, Feb. 2003, via Family Violence Prevention Fund: http://endabuse.org/resources/facts/. Fact sheet from RAINN, the Rape, Abuse & Incest National Network. www.rainn.org/statistics.

19. You can find such images on offer in virtually any issue of most glossy fashion mags, and even in the style sections of major news outlets such as *The New York Times Sunday Magazine*. For a small sample of these sorts of visuals, and for critiques of advertising content, see "Killing Us Softly 3," an excerpt of Jean Kilbourne's video-clip-filled lecture, www.youtube.com/watch?v=ufHrVyVgwRg&feature=related (Kilbourne's discussion of violent ads begins at minute 3:23). Several young women have taken Kilbourne's lead and are using new media tools to create their own slideshows shining a spotlight on this problem, such as "Sexism and Violence in Advertising" by Canadian feminist writer Jenna Owsianik, www.youtube.com/watch?v=ft67TI9Wstc, and "Exploitation of women in ads" by a communications student whose YouTube handle is hertrippyness, www.youtube.com/watch?v=WgGiB-o84sk&feature=related. *Ms. Magazine*'s "No Comment" section offers a rich archive of such images over several decades in the magazine itself, while a few print and video ads per issue from Spring 2006 to the present are available on their website at www.msmagazine.com/nocommentarchive.asp; several of the ads mentioned in this paragraph can be found in the archive, including a Foot Petals ad featuring a woman's stilleto-clad, disembodied legs hanging from a noose, a Marc Jacobs ad centered on the lower half of an apparently abandoned woman's dead body lying on the ground, and a somewhat infamous Jimmy Choo ad in which singer Quincy Jones is shown digging a grave to get rid of model Molly Simms, dead in the trunk of his car.

20. "America's Next Top Model Obsessed" on Oxygen Struts to Double and Triple Digit Increases among Key Demos," Oxygen press release, Jan. 22, 2009, on TheFutonCritic.com.

21. "Next Top Model Champ CariDee Shares Her Blonde Ambitions," TVGuide.com, Dec. 12, 2006. Katner, Ben.

22. One notable exception is *Fix Me Up: Essays on Television Dating and Makeover Shows*, an anthology of scholarly essays edited by Judith Lancioni, published by McFarland & Company, Nov. 13, 2009.

23. "Top Model's beautiful corpses: the nexus of reality TV misogyny and ad industry ideology," WIMN's Voices: The Group Blog on Women, Media, and . . . , Mar. 22, 2007. Pozner, Jennifer L. www.wimnonline.org/WIMNsVoicesBlog/?p=462.

24. Can't Buy My Love. Kilbourne. p. 64.

25. Ibid., p. 64.

26. Ibid., p. 59.

CHAPTER EIGHT

1. *Enlightened Racism*. Jhally and Lewis. p. 133.

2. *Backlash*. Faludi. pp. xx–xxii.

3. "History of Women in Sports Timeline, 2003," St. Lawrence Country branch of the American Association of University Women. www.northnet.org/stlawrenceaauw/time14.htm.

4. "Wedding Porn Doesn't Turn Us On: Age at 1st Marriage Has Never Been Higher," *Psychology Today* blog, *Living Single*. Jan. 17, 2010. DePaulo, Bella, PhD.

5. "Employment Situation Summary," Bureau of Labor Statistics, Mar. 5, 2010.

6. Clip excerpted on *Anderson Cooper 360 Degrees*, CNN, July 30, 2009.

7. *White Weddings: Romancing Heterosexuality in Popular Culture*, 2nd edition, 2008. Ingraham, Chrys. pp. 38–43.

8. *Backlash*. Faludi. pp.100–101; "Newsweek: Sorry for the spinster scaremongering 20 years ago," *Shakesville*, May 26, 2006. McEwan, Melissa.

9. *Backlash*. Faludi.

10. "New Blouse, New House, I Need a New Spouse." Tarrant.

11. "The Mommy War Machine," *The Washington Post*, Apr. 29, 2007. Graff, E. J.; *The Mommy Myth: The Idealization of Motherhood and How It Has Undermined All Women* (New York: Free Press, 2004). Douglas, Susan and Michaels, Meredith.

12. "Is Our Sexed-up Society Creating Prosti-Tots?" *AlterNet.org*, Mar. 11, 2010. Harris, Lynn; *The Lolita Effect: The Media Sexualization of Young Girls and What We Can Do About It* (New York: Overlook, 2008). Durham, Meenakshi Gigi.

13. The National Resource Center on Child Sexual Abuse, "Fact Sheet on Child Sexual Abuse," Huntsville: NRCCSA, 1994.

14. "New Blouse, New House, I Need a New Spouse." Tarrant.

15. "Queer Women on Reality TV Are Making a Difference," AfterEllen.com, Oct. 16, 2006. Lo, Malinda.

16. "Tweeting Tips for Tila Tequila," AfterEllen.com, Nov. 12, 2009. Hogan, Heather; "Interview: Tila Tequila," CherryGrrl.com, Nov. 30, 2009.

17. *Transgender: What Does It Mean?* and *Bad Questions to Ask a Transsexual* appeared on VideoJug and YouTube, respectively, and are available at Calpernia.com.

18. "Women rule new Fox show: Rocket Science producing reality project," *Variety*, Jan. 16, 2007. Adalian, Josef.

19. Ibid.

20. "Boxed In: Employment of Behind-the-Scenes Women in the 2008–09 Prime-Time Television Season," Center for Study of Women in TV and Film, San Diego State University, 2009. Lauzen, Martha M., PhD.

21. "The Glass Ceiling Persists," Annenberg Public Policy Center, Dec. 22, 2003.

22. "Progress or No Room at the Top?: The Role of Women in Telecommunications, Broadcast, Cable and E-Companies," Annenberg Public Policy Center, Mar. 2001.

23. Ibid.

24. "Women in Film celebrates female achievements," *The Hollywood Reporter* online, June 16, 2008. Bowen, Shannon L.

25. *Enlightened Sexism: The Seductive Message That Feminism's Work is Done* (New York: Times Books, 2010). Douglas, Susan. p.14.

26. *Enlightened Sexism*. Douglas.

CHAPTER NINE

1. "America's Next Top Model Struts Into Walmart: First Branded Line Based on Hit Reality Series in Select Stores Now," CBS Press Release posted at The Futon Critic.com, Dec. 3, 2008.

2. *Why the Comcast/NBC Merger Poses a Major Threat to Video Competition That AntiTrust Authorities Cannot Ignore*, a report from Consumer Federation of America and Free Press. Cooper, Mark and

Wright, Corie. Referenced in "New Report: Comcast/NBC Merger Is Bad News for the Public," StopBigMedia.com, Dec. 2, 2009. Stearns, Josh.

3. *Can't Buy Me Love: How Advertising Changes the Way We Think and Feel* (New York: The Free Press, 2000). Kilbourne, Jean. p. 33.

4. For extensive documentation of this phenomena, see the "Advertiser Influence" section of Fairness & Accuracy In Reporting at FAIR.org. For a discussion specific to media content related to women and women's issues, see "Sex, Lies & Advertising," *Ms. Magazine*, July/Aug. 1990. Steinem, Gloria.

5. "Anything but Racism; Media make excuses for 'whitewashed' TV lineup," *Extra!* Jan./Feb. 2000. Jackson, Janine.

6. "Ad buyers back off reality programs," *USA Today*, May 12, 2003. McCarthy, Michael; "A-list Advertisers Reconsider Reality; Less concern over content as ratings deliver key demos," *ADWEEK*, Feb. 3, 2003. Consoli, John.

7. "Brian Stelter, Product Placements, Deftly Woven into the Story Line," *The New York Times*, Mar. 2, 2009.

8. "Are You SELLING to Me?: Stealth Advertising in the Entertainment Industry." Nov. 14, 2005. Writers Guild of America.

9. Research assistant Anita Sarkeesian found forty lines of dialog, twenty-two visual integrations and on-air presence for a CoverGirl corporate spokesperson on *America's Next Top Model* cycle 11, episode 9. Every *ANTM* episode includes product placement, but their CoverGirl commercial shoots are the most intensive examples.

10. "The Donald Drives a Deal; Chrysler the sole auto sponsor of NBC's Trump reality vehicle *The Apprentice*; Network TV," *Mediaweek*, Jan. 5, 2004. Greenberg, Karl; "Marketers dive into 'Apprentice 3'; Sony, Visa, Verizon sign up for $2.5M deals, despite ratings slide and worries about clutter," *Advertising Age*, Nov. 29, 2004. Atkinson, Claire; "Idol Signs Three Major Sponsors; Ford, Coke, AT&T Wireless pay record $20M each," *Broadcasting & Cable*, Jan. 13, 2003. McClellan, Steve. *Buyology: Truth and Lies About Why We Buy* (New York: Doubleday, 2008). Lindstrom, Martin. pp. 40, 41, 49.

11. "Seventeen Magazine and MTV Join for a Reality Show," *The New York Times*, Oct. 10, 2005. Bosman, Julie.

12. *Madison and Vine: Why the Entertainment and Advertising Industries Must Converge to Survive* (New York: McGraw Hill, 2004). Donaton, Scott. p. 64.

13. "The Nielsen Company Issues Top Ten U.S. Lists for 2008," Press release, Dec. 12, 2008. Nielsen.

14. Steven J. Heyer, quoted in *Madison and Vine*. Donaton.

15. 2008 and 2009 programming percentages provided to author via email from Fox Corporate Communications, Jan. 20, 2010; CBS, Jan. 25, 2010; The CW, Jan. 22, 2010; and phone communication from NBC, Jan. 26, 2010. Information about NBC's full 2009 broadcast year was unavailable at press time due to the upheaval caused by the *Jay Leno Show* being added to, then removed, from the prime-time lineup. ABC would not supply data, but a significant portion of their 2009 and 2010 roster were unscripted shows including *The Bachelor, Dancing with the Stars, Extreme Makeover: Home Edition, Find My Family, Supernanny,* and *Wife Swap,* and stunts like *Conveyor Belt of Love*.

16. "Series Let Advertisers 'Boldly Go' Where Few Have Gone Before," *Advertising Age*, May 7, 2009. Steinberg, Brian. "'Survivor': Mark Burnett," *Advertising Age*, Oct. 8, 2001. Pendleton, Jennifer.

17. "Superstar Joe Abruzzese: 'Survivor's' win-win mentality scores big; Abruzzese throws the bag of

tricks wide open for tie-in partners, and all benefit from incredible buzz," *Advertising Age,* Mar. 26, 2001. Fitzgerald, Kate.

18. "Sponsors on 'Restaurant' menu; Product placement gets NBC reality series on the air," *The Hollywood Reporter,* July 18, 2003. Hiestand, Jesse.

19. "A Serving Of Reality 'Drama' You Can Eat Up," *The Boston Globe,* July 20, 2003. Graves, Amy; "Making it real: 'The Restaurant'; TV cameras are there through it all for Rocco's on 22nd in New York," *The Baltimore Sun,* July 16, 2003. Lu-Lien Tan, Cheryl.

20. "NBC Recasts Its Office; New entertainment bosses plan to climb out of fourth place," May 31, 2007. Battaglio, Stephen; "Jay Leno Is #1," *Tuned In* blog, *Time,* Dec. 11, 2009.

21. "The Commercial Tidal Wave," *Monthly Review* 54, no. 10 (2003). McChesney, Robert W. and Bellamy Foster, John.

22. "Mitsubishis on the Menu; Product Placement Takes a Leap Forward with NBC's "'The Restaurant,'" *St. Louis Post-Dispatch,* Aug. 3, 2003. Pennington, Gail.

23. "10 Things Your Reality Show Won't Tell You," AOL Money & Finance, Money, Aol.com (undated). Willis, Kedon.

24. "MAGNA Global Entertainment Announces Sponsors of NBC's "'The Restaurant,'" July 2, 2003. Business Wire; "NBC Cooks Up a Meal Ticket," *Daily Variety,* Jan. 17, 2003. Adalian, Josef.

25. "When Reality Attacks; Who are the victims now that unscripted shows rule TV land? Producers of sitcoms and dramas. Six of the best strike back. Look out, Joe Millionaire," *Entertainment Weekly,* Mar. 14, 2003. Rice, Lynette.

26. Quoted in *Philadelphia Daily News* and "Triumph of the Shill, Part 2: Reality TV Lets Marketers Write the Script," *Bitch: Feminist Response to Pop Culture* 24, Spring 2004. Pozner, Jennifer L.

27. "Marketers dive into 'Apprentice 3.'" Atkinson. "Product Placement Pacts Cut for 'Stewart,'" *MediaWeek.com,* Aug. 26, 2005. McClellan, Steve; "'Apprentice' viewers tell Pontiac: You're hired," *Automotive News,* May 2, 2005. LaReau, Jamie.

28. "'The Shaken Self': Product Choices as a Means of Restoring Self-View Confidence," *Journal of Consumer Research* 36, no. 1 (2009). Gao, Leilei, Wheeler, S. Christian and Shiv, Baba. p. 29.

29. "America's Next Top Model Struts into Wal-Mart: First Branded Line Based on Hit Reality Series in Select Stores Now," press release at TheFutonCritic.com, Dec. 3, 2008. The film *Wal-Mart: The High Cost of Low Price* provides information on Wal-Mart's hiring and environmental practices.

30. "Wounded Disney Co. Vows to Bounce Back," *Orlando Sentinel* (Florida), Sept. 22, 2001. Johnson, Robert and Verrier, Richard. "The 'Big Lie': False Feminist Death Syndrome, Profit, and the Media," in *Catching a Wave: Reclaiming Feminism for the 21st Century,* ed. Dicker, Rory and Piepmeier, Alison. (Boston: Northeastern University Press, 2003). Pozner, Jennifer L.

31. Leierwood family website, "Wife Swap" page. http://leierwood.com/swap.html.

32. "Superstar Joe Abruzzese." Fitzgerald.

33. "An Eye-Land Paradise: CBS sets summer record with socko 'Survivor'," *Daily Variety,* Aug. 25, 2000. Kissell, Rick.

34. "Is this any way to make music?" *St. Petersburg Times,* Apr. 13, 2001. Deggans, Eric; "Television; New Faces of Synergy 2001; AOL Time Warner's TV, Music and Web Units Are Taking Cross-Promotion to a New Level with 'Popstars,'" *Los Angeles Times,* Mar. 11, 2001. Lowry, Brian.

35. "Pussycat Dolls: Pussy Galore!" Blender.com, June 19, 2006. Raftery, Brian.

36. Writers Guild of America, Nov. 14, 2005.

37. "Product Placement Is on the Menu of This 'Restaurant' a New Twist in Marketing," *The Boston Globe,* July 20, 2003. Wallenstein, Andrew.

38. "Soap Opera: How Ponds infiltrated The Starter Wife writers' room," *Slate*, May 30, 2007. Stevenson, Seth. "Excruciatingly bad dialogue, insufferably elitist characters, and glaring product placement: 'Starter Wife' makes me gag." WIMN's Voices, June 7, 2007. Pozner, Jennifer L.

39. "Writers Guild Strikes Back; Guerilla Protests Only Start of Action on Reality, Product Placements," *Television Week*, Nov. 28, 2005. Hibberd, James.

40. *Bitch*. Pozner.

41. Email correspondence from Nancy Marsden, Jan. 25, 2009. Marsden organizes FIT Media, a bipartisan consortium of health, media, and child advocacy organizations and professionals seeking regulation of embedded advertising.

42. *Unmarketable* (New York: New Press, 2007). Moore, Anne Elizabeth.

43. Korby Siamis letter to FCC, http://fjallfoss.fcc.gov/ecfs/document/view?id=6520170200.

44. For information on advertising and children, see the Campaign for a Commercial-Free Childhood, www.commercialexploitation.org/, the Media Education Foundation documentary *Captive Audience*, and Fairness & Accuracy in Reporting's archives on Channel One, www.fair.org/index.php?page=19&media_outlet_id=22.

45. "Joe Mastermind; Brilliant programmer or evil genius bent on destroying American culture? Either way, Fox's reality guru Mike Darnell (the brains behind 'Joe Millionaire') is changing TV," *Entertainment Weekly*, Mar. 28, 2003. Snierson, Dan.

46. "What Do Prisoners Make for Victoria's Secret? From Starbucks to Microsoft: a sampling of what US inmates make, and for whom," *Mother Jones*, July/Aug. 2008. Winter, Caroline.

CHAPTER TEN

1. See www.racialicious.com/2007/05/31/antm-the-drinking-game/.

2. (New York: Perigee Trade, 2009). Harding, Kate and Kirby, Marianne.

3. Anita Sarkeesian was a research assistant for several chapters of this book. Her website, Feminist Frequency: Conversations with Pop Culture, can be found at www.feministfrequency.com/.

4. I first became interested in writing *Reality Bites Back* after publishing "The Unreal World: Why women on 'reality TV' have to be hot, desperate and dumb" in the Fall 2004 issue of *Ms. Magazine*. So I was pleasantly surprised when I read in the description of *The Bachelor: Tool Edition* parody that "Character-types are based on concepts from 'The Unreal World' by Jennifer Pozner." You can watch the video on YouTube: www.youtube.com/watch?v=ZG-sDcInThY. My hope is that if you are reading this book, and especially this chapter, you will find some way to put your interest in this subject into creative action, whether by producing your own media literacy projects or by engaging in any of the media activism strategies detailed in chapter 11.

5. "Girl Talk: A new book posits zines as the founding documents of third-wave feminist political culture," *The American Prospect* web feature. Nov. 12, 2009. Clark, Jessica. Review of *Girl Zines: Making Media, Doing Feminism, NYU Press*, Nov. 18, 2009. Piepmeier, Alison.

6. *Hey Kidz! Buy This Book: A Radical Primer on Corporate and Governmental Propaganda and Artistic Activism for Short People* (Berkeley, CA: Soft Skull Press, 2004). Moore, Anne Elizabeth. p. 152.

CHAPTER ELEVEN

1. *Applicability of Sponsorship Identification Rules*, Public Notice, 40 F.C.C. 141 (1963).

2. Sponsorship Identification rules are set forth in Sections 317 and 507 of the Communications Act of 1934 and subsequent FCC rules. See FCC. *Notice of Inquiry and Notice of Proposed Rulemaking on*

Sponsorship Identification and Embedded Advertising (2008) at 3. http://fjallfoss.fcc.gov/edocs_public/attachmatch/FCC-08-155A1.pdf.

3. Citizens and consumer groups calling for disclosure of embedded ads have suffered defeats at the FTC in 1992 and 2005. In 1992, the FTC ruled that embedded ads are not deceptive and do not inflict substantial harm any more than conventional advertising. In 2005, the FTC reiterated that opinion, adding that because product placements generally do not make claims about a product's efficacy or attributes, they cannot be misleading.

4. FAIR's archive of action alerts and *Extra!* magazine articles about Don Imus dating back to March 1, 2000 is available at www.fair.org/index.php?page=19&media_outlet_id=58. WIMN's Voices blogger Jill Nelson's two influential posts on Imus's "nappy headed hos" comments and fallout, "Imus Protest! Unruly-Haired Hater," Apr. 8, 2007, www.wimnonline.org/WIMNsVoicesBlog/?p=490 and "Black Women: First Dissed, Then Disappeared," Apr. 10, 2007, www.wimnonline.org/WIMNsVoicesBlog/2007/04/10/black-women-first-dissed-now-disappeared/.

5. *Beyond the Echo Chamber: How a Networked Progressive Media Can Reshape American Politics,* New Press, Feb. 9, 2010. Clark, Jessica and Van Slyke, Tracy.

6. For more resources, see GLAAD Media Reference Guide: Transgender Glossary of Terms, www.glaad.org/Page.aspx?pid=376 and "Skirt Chasers: Why the Media Depicts the Trans Revolution in Lipstick and Heels." Serano, Julia. www.juliaserano.com/outside.html#skirtchasers. Originally published in *Bitch* magazine, Issue 26, Fall 2005.

7. *Women and Media: A Critical Introduction* (Malden, MA: Blackwell, 2006). Byerly, C. M. & Ross, K. (2006).

8. Women, the Economy and News: Analysis of the 2008 U.S. Primary Coverage," *St. John's Journal of Legal Commentary* 24 no. 2 (Fall 2009). Byerly, C. M. pp. 387–402.

9. "Media Ownership Matters. Localism, the ethnic minority news audience, and community participation," in *Does bigger media equal better media?* (Report) Social Science Research Council and Benton Foundation, 2006. Byerly, C. M., Langmia, K. and Cupid, J. A. www.ssrc.org/programs/media.

10. *Girl Director: A How-to Guide for the First-Time, Flat-Broke Film and Video Maker* (Berkeley, CA: Ten Speed Press, 2005). Richard, Andrea.

Index

A

ABC: *The Bachelor* on, 10; as Disney owned, 45; ideological agenda of, 289; *Miss America Pageant* on, 61; *Profiles from the Front Line*, 169
Abdul, Paula, 91
Abrego, Cris, 185, 217
abuse. *See* sexual abuse
Access Hollywood, 261
activism, media: campaign ideas, 333–335; curbing embedded ads, 327–329; DIY media, 314–318, 335–336; intergenerational, 105; multi-faceted, 345; against racist entertainment, 184; talking back to the media, 318–324; tools for, 32, 325–342; by young people, 31
Addams, Calpernia, 50, 265
A Different World, 65
advertising: activism, 327–329; as-seen-on shopping, 147; Aunt Jemima, 172; as banking on apathy, 295–296; as basis of reality TV, 26, 141–142, 274, 280, 281; beauty as worth, 67–68; bodily "fixes", 66, 78; bogus promises of, 159–160; "Bravo Affluencer Effect", 143–144; cattiness, 100; as editorial, 292–293; effectiveness of embedded, 285–286, 298; fueling jealousy, 107; industry statistics, 275; to insecurity, 56; magazines, 279; methods, 276–280; models of women in, 19; Nielsen ratings for, 9; prescription drugs, 277; psychological manipulation via, 286–287; questioning, 314; racial essentialism, 207, 208–209; as scripted, 28; and self-esteem drops, 89; sexualized, 120, 131; as skewing economic reality, 19; unconscious reception of, 235–237; via *ANTM*, 89, 228, 273–274; via hyperconsumption displays, 139; violence against women in, 227–229, 233; wedding industry, 250–251; *See also* corporate sponsors; product placement
Advertising Age, 236, 281
aesthetic procedures, 94
African American women: angry Black woman trope, 102–103, 166–169, 199, 200–203; asses of, 70; as "black bitches", 166–169; hair of, 67–68, 177–179, 203; humbling proud, 203–204; "mammy" stereotype, 169–172; as savages, 206–209; as "welfare queens", 202
age: ageism, 247; and couple pairings, 63

agency, women's: as given to men, 244; princesses as without, 48; as punishable, 47–48
A Generation of Consolidation, 344
Age of Love: cattiness as advertized on, 100; contestant age on, 40, 72; male contestant background, 218
Alexander, J., 230
Ali, 243
All-American Girl, 60, 95
Alliance for Community Media (ACM), 337
Alston, Joshua, 23
Alter, Jonathan, 202
Amanda, 153
The Amazing Race, 174–175, 262
American Documentary/POV, 339–340
American Express, 283
American Idol: advertising on, 279, 281; bogus payouts, 159; buzz for, 292; contestant poverty, 136; crazy-making on, 28; critical responses to, 31; "homogenator", 177–178; humiliation of women on, 55; Nielsen ratings of, 132; viewing statistics, 18; women's weight as focus of, 90–92
American Psychological Association's Task Force on the Sexualization of Girls, 67
Americans: bad behavior abroad, 175; ethnicity vs. nationality for, 197, 198–199
American Society for Aesthetic Plastic Surgery, 94
America's Most Smartest Model, 216
America's Next Top Dork, 318, 344
America's Next Top Immigrant, 317
America's Next Top Model: abuse as handled on, 212–213, 219; addresses beauty bias, 196–197; airtime statistics, 228; audience, 88, 234–235; bigotry on, 204; bogus payouts, 158; commercials as plot, 273, 278, 280; crazy-making on, 28; critical responses to, 31; eating disorders on, 84–86; ethnicity vs. nationality on, 198–199; ethnic props, 173, 174; ethnic stereotypes on, 166, 199–203, 200–203; as a "fairytale", 34; handling of sexual abuse, 228–229; humiliation of women on, 55; judge Jane Dickinson, 83–84; Keenyah Hill, 86–87; lesbians on, 262; marketers behind, 233; media literacy drinking game, 306; models as mannequins, 137; necrophiliac shoot, 232–233, 235, 237; objectification on, 8; punishes intelligence, 111–112, 115; season 11, 63; skinniness on, 76–79; Toccara Jones, 79–83; token "plus sized" slot, 78; transgender Isis on, 264; values imparted, 287, 313; violence against women on, 137, 227–229; "wild" women

photo shoot, 208–209; Yaya DaCosta, 203–204; *See also* Banks, Tyra
America's Regal Gems, 256
Ames, Richard, 293
Amos & Andy, 166, 183
Anchorwoman, 120–122, 123
Anderson, Robin, 286
Andrich, Zora, 33–34
anger: channeled as activism, 325; righteous, self-protecting, 82–83
Aniston, Jennifer, 107
The Anna Nicole Show, 109
anorexia. *See* eating disorders
antifeminism: as backlash to gains, 240–242; humiliation as spreading, 53; by women, 110
antiharassment laws, 125
antitrust violations, 274
The Apprentice: advertising on, 15, 126, 278, 286; Black women stereotypes on, 166–169; extreme wealth portrayals, 134; sexual-harassment environment of, 125–126; women's bodies as success on, 119
Arab Americans, 176
Are You Hot? The Search for America's Sexiest People, 75
Arianna, 148–149
Arreola, Veronica, 117
Arrested Development, 284
arrogance, 204
The Art of Gold Digging (Nasheed), 190
The Art of Mackin' (Nasheed), 190
A Shot at Love with Tila Tequila, 14, 49, 164, 262
The Asian Mystique, 199
Atalanta, 45
athletes, female, 241
The Atlantic Monthly, 18
attractiveness: to prevent sexual abuse, 220–222; qualifications for, 62; as thin, 74; via pricey clothing, 153; of women's pain, 231; as women's worth/power, 235
audience, female: *America's Next Top Model*, 88; finance as measure of love for, 42; internalize backlash against women, 252; life as a beauty contest for, 61–62; as "wanting" reality TV, 14
audience, TV: belief in "reality" TV, 22, 204; critical viewing by, 268, 300, 310–311; desensitized to violence against women, 233; generational development of, 17–18; given what "they want", 14, 270, 280, 290; identifying, 312; LGBTQ, 316; long-term impact on, 21, 29; as mislead by "unscripted" shows, 26; for the *Miss America Pageant*,

60–61; playing catfights to, 102; take-home messages, 251; talking back by, 318–324; target demographics, 10, 275; as "unaffected" by TV, 235–236; view-time statistics, 132; *See also* young audiences
Aunt Jemima, 172
"authenticity", of reality TV: as defining perception, 97–98; as detrimental veneer, 68–69; as scripted, 24
Average Joe, 164, 224
Avni, Sheerly, 174
Axe, 284

B

Bachelet, Michelle, 241
The Bachelor: advertising during, 275, 276; "as seen on" packages, 39; bachelor screenings, 214–216; vs. the "Black-chelor", 180–181; cattiness of women on, 99; crazy-making on, 28; faux sincerity of, 41; female subservience on, 239–240; Latinas on, 164–165; male validation as pursued on, 53; media literacy drinking game, 307–308; primary qualification for, 71; punishes female desire, 259; pushes princess culture, 45; reunion specials, 56; as "revolutionary" TV, 10; season 10, 42–44; season 2, 36–37; as white, 49, 163
The Bachelorette: Ali, 243; gender stereotypes, 244–246; men with money on, 38; whitewashing on, 164, 275
The Bachelor: Tool Edition, 318
The Bachelor: Where Are They Now?, 252
background checks, 218–219
Backlash Bingo, 301–305
Backlash: The Undeclared War Against American Women (Faludi), 13, 240
backstabbing, 100
Baldwin, Andy, 42–43
Ball, Lucille, 110
"Balloon Boy" hoax, 255
Bankable Productions, 211
Banks, Tyra: address of ED, 84–85; advertiser's co-option of, 210–211; apologizing for blackface, 196; bio of, 210; on body weight, 78, 81; humbling of Yaya DaCosta, 204; on Isis King, 264; mocks models pain, 230; on post-show opportunities, 158; racist complicity of, 112, 204, 205–206, 209–210; victim blame game, 230–231; yells at contestants, 201–203; *See also America's Next Top Model*
bariatric surgery, 94
Barker, Chrissy, 273
Barker, Nigel, 197, 230, 273
Barney, Tamra, 102

Bartsch, Jeff, 28
The Beulah Show, 172
beauty: *ANTM* as shaping ideals of, 88, 211; "correcting" non-white, 176–179, 205–206; finding flaws in, 75; ideals, 62, 67–68, 150; industry, as home of Tyra Banks, 210–211; of lesbians, 262; myths on reality TV, 68–69; racial bias in, 70, 90, 196–197; on *The Swan*, 11; thin as, 48, 67; of women in danger, 231–232, 233; as women's worth, 67, 72, 94–95; as worth the pain, 92
Beauty and the Geek, 114
beauty pageants: *American Idol* as, 91; bucking the system of, 95–96; for children, 75–76, 102, 257–258; life as, 61–62; *Miss America Pageant*, 60; popularity of, 95; in prison, 299
Bee, Samantha, 121
Behar, Robert, 339
belief: in being "unaffected" by ads, 235–236; in "reality"-embedded ads, 287; in TV's fictions, 8, 22–23, 68–69, 239
Benton Foundation, 327
Berg Joel, 157
Bernie Mac, 285
BET, 82, 277
Bethenny's Getting Married?, 315
Big Brother, 27, 217
The Biggest Loser, 78
Birleanu, Andre, 216
bisexuality: misrendering of, 49–50; misrepresentation on TV, 261–262; *A Shot at Love with Tila Tequila*, 14, 49, 164, 262
Bitch: Feminist Response to Pop Culture, 322, 329
The Bitch Switch: Knowing How to Turn It On and Off, 168
blackface, 173, 183, 196
Black Like Me, 173
Black. White., 173
blaxploitation, 19, 49, 181, 186
blogging, 327–328
blond, "dumb", 109
Bloomberg, Mike, 291
body image: ads as eroding, 286; insecurities, 205; as learned from *ANTM*, 287; media effects on, 89–90; of young women, 88
body mass index, 77, 83
body weight: average American, 78; body dismorphic syndrome, 77; buying to "fix", 66; cautionary tales about, 74; and desirability, 70–71; historical embrace of curves, 65; loss on *The Biggest Loser*, 78; *More to Love* reinforces stereotypes about, 73–74; pro-anorexia, 83–90; skinniness and health,

76–78; thin as beautiful, 48, 64–65; *See also America's Next Top Model*
Boesky, Ivan, 146
Bouwer, Marc, 85, 86
Boy Meets Boy, 51
Bravo, 139, 140, 141, 143–144
"Bravo Affluencer Effect", 143–144
breast cancer, 108
breast implants, 62
Bridezillas, 11, 118, 254–255
Brown, Cleveland, 193
Brownstein, Carrie, 101
Bruckheimer, Jerry, 124, 169
Buffy the Vampire Slayer, 14, 317
Buffy vs. Edward, 317
bulimia. *See* eating disorders
Bunim/ Murray Productions, 214
Bunny Ranch, 260
Bureau of Labor Statistics, 106
Burnett, Mark, 124, 281
Burruss, Kandi, 103
business, women in: *Anchorwoman*, 121–122; contestant, 243; facing gender discrimination, 116–117; vs. love, 252–253; as mothers, 106; portraying ineptness of, 126; sexuality as only asset to, 119; statistics of, 267; workplace abuse, 125–126
Byerly , PhD, Carolyn, M., 342–343
Byram, Amanda, 221
Byrd, Ayana, 178

C

cable, 19, 49, 61, 70, 162, 275
Camay Soap, 67
Camille, 200
Campaign for a Commercial-Free Childhood, 327, 328
Campbell, Naomi, 207, 208
Campos, Rob, 129, 214–215, 219
Can't Buy My Love: How Advertising Changes the Way We Think and Feel (Kilbourne), 67, 236
CariDee, 230
Carracedo, Almudena, 339
Carrie, 152
Carter, Nell, 172
casting: importance of, 27; irresponsible, 219; liabilities in, 71–72; people of color, 193; questioning, 313; the rich, 145; sexual predators, 213–214; stunt casting, 122; unintelligent women, 114
catfights, 99–100
Cathouse, 260
CBS: Lauren Jones on, 120; as media owner,

274; president, on Darnell, 13; prime time programming statistics, 282; reality TV airtime, 281; suing of, 217
CDC, 77
Celebrity Fit Club, 82
Center for Media Justice, 179
Center for Study of Women in TV and Film, 267
The Celebrity Apprentice, 15, 168
change, charity vs., 155–157
Channel One, 298
characters: as "real", 68–69; scripting stereotyped, 22–23, 72
charity shows, 154–155
Charles, London, 70
Charm School: bigotry on, 137; business segment, 120; premise, 161, 188; reunion special, 192; Saaphyri on, 112, 137–138; weekly lessons, 190–191
Chicago Sun Times, 168
child rearing, 106, 125
children: beauty pageants for, 75–76, 102; effects of beauty ideals on, 67; hypersexualized girls, 75–76, 257–258; as media creators, 343–344; media literacy for, 23, 309–310, 332–333; princess culture as ingrained in, 45; protection against embedded ads, 327, 328; women as made into, 24
"China Doll", 199
Chisholm, Shirley, 123
Cho, Margaret, 95
The Cho Show, 95, 96
Choe, Gina, 198
cisgender, 263
Clarkson, Kelly, 295
class issues: digital divide, 314; documenting, 339; reinforcing bias, 19; *See also* poverty; wealth
Clinton, Bill, 202
Clinton, Senator Hillary Rodham, 242
Closing the Racial Wealth Gap Initiative, 135
clothing, 167
Coca-Cola, 279, 281
Coffey, Tabatha, 262
Coles, Kortnie, 104
Columbia Journalism Review, 21
Comcast, 168
comedy: violence against women as, 222–223; women's pain as, 229
Commander in Chief, 14, 284
Commercial Alert, 327, 328
Community Media Centers (CMCs), 336–337
competition shows: goal of, 52; *Popstars*, 293–294; postelimination interviews, 104;

prey on financial insecurity, 136; prizes, 294; tourist, 174–175; women as untrustable on, 99; women's looks on business-based, 119
competitiveness, female, 105
Complex, 208
confession cam, money shot for, 54, 56
confidence: as anti-consumer, 56; as eroded on *ANTM*, 87; of Toccara Jones, 79–80, 81; *See also* self-esteem
Conger, Darva, 9–10
Consuelos, Mark, 218
consumption: activist-led, 328; conspicuous, 139–143; encouraging excessive, 153–154; limiting media, 309; media, sophisticated, 300; TV-generated, 285–286, 288
contestants: audience identification with, 234; celebrating non-normative, 310; gender-different treatment of, 91; lying to, 41, 127–128; molded into stereotypes, 28; as product placements, 295; psychological experimentation on, 103; safety, 218; why people chose to be, 136–137
contestants, female: antagonism as nurtured among, 100–101, 103; desperate loneliness of, 249, 252–253; as domestic failures, 254–255; endangering, 229–231; financial insecurity of, 136; friendship among, 104, 108; nicknames for, 224; sexuality of, 258–259
contestants, male: on *The Bachelorette*, 245; domination by, 255–256; predatory history of, 213–219; prey on women's intelligence, 113–114
controversy: advocacy group baiting, 12; casting to create, 27; mommy wars, 105–106; ratings as generating by, 185; *Real World* rape, 214
Cooper, Anderson, 246
Coors, 283
Cops, 281
corporate sponsors: control of content, 275, 283–284; FCC bypass by, 293; media created by/for, 283–284, 296–298; placement methods, 276–277; profit controlled by, 293, 294; *See also* advertising
Corwin, Lola, 164
The Cosby Show, 22
cosmetic surgery. *See* plastic surgery
Council of Fashion Designers of America, 83
counterads, 315
Couric, Katie, 241
CoverGirl, 233, 273, 287
Cowell, Simon, 90–91, 177
Cox, Laverne, 265

Cranford, Heather, 216
Crest, 286
critical thinking, 310, 311–312, 330
Crittenden, Danielle, 110
Cronin, Mark, 184, 185, 192–193, 217
cross promotion, 276
Csincsak, Jesse, 38
cultural appropriation, 174–175
cultural conditioning: about people of color, 194–195; about women and money, 130; entertainment as, 192–193; hegemony, 97, 126; to massive consumption, 142–143; promoting violence, 225–227; reality TV as reinforcing, 47, 270–271; via advertising, 236–237, 286
Cupid, Jamila A., 342–343
Curious George, 206
Curl Girls, 50
Curry, Adrianne, 35, 158, 212–213
Cusanelli, Katelynn, 265
CW, 282, 294
Cyril, Malkia, 179

D

D, Chuck, 182, 184
DaCosta, Yaya, 116, 203–204
Dahl, J. E., 112, 210
The Daily Show, 121
Darnell, Mike: as a cash cow, 13; cultural conditioning by, 270–271; on in-prison beauty pageant, 299; reality TV origins with, 9–12; on social responsibility, 15–16; women's rights as viewed by, 266
The Dating Experiment, 27
dating shows: cable, 70, 185; faux sincerity of, 41; *Flavor of Love*, 180; fostering female competition on, 100; gay male, 51; as heterosexual only, 50; humiliation of women on, 52–56; racial template for, 69–70, 163; relationship advice for women, 246–247; selling women's stupidity on, 114–115, 116; stigmatizing singleness, 118; take-home messages, 251; violent relationship dynamics in, 225; women as without agency on, 244; for women of color, 48–49; *See also* fairytale shows
Davis, Albert, 283
debate, stimulating, 20–21
debt, credit card, 145
defeatist attitude, 203
Deggans, Eric, 183
dehumanization: of Black models, 205; of Blacks as "wild", 206–207; consequences of, 209; as cultural conditioning, 194–195; of women, via violent ads, 233

de la Renta, Oscar, 139
Delgado, Mary, 164–165
DePaulo, Bella, 242
desire, female, 258–259
dialogue, advertising via, 278
Dickerson, Debra, 184
Dickinson, Jane, 83–84
Diebel, Linda, 155
digital divide, 314, 334
Dillon, Kate, 85
DiSanto, Tony, 26
Disney: ideological agenda of, 288–289; as media owner, 274; princess culture as created by, 45
Disney Dream Weddings, 45
DiSpirito, Rocco, 283
divas, Black, 166–169
documentaries, 339–340
domestic violence: on *Charm School*, 190; early signs of, 125; by Flavor Flav, 217–218; isolation in, 108; for laughs, 222–223; in the media, 225–227; statistics, 225; trauma exploitation, 219–222; *See also* sexual abuse
domination: politics of, 131; scripting relational, 225; in slavery, 184
Donaton, Scott, 281
Douglas, Susan, 268, 272
Doyle, Brandy, 338
Dr. 90210, 8
"Dragon Lady", 199
Draper, Don, 297
drug dealing, 192
Dukes v. Wal-Mart Stores, 107
dumb blond trope, 109–110
dysmorphic syndrome, body, 77

E

eating disorders: body image and, 67; health risks, 77; promoting, 83–90; and self-confidence, 87; in young women, 88
eBay, 152
economics: financial inequity, 155–156; financial statistics, 135; gendered, of sex and money, 130–131; modern-day statistics, 135; personal savings, 144; recession, U.S., 19, 144–145; status quo of, 157; teaching high-end shopping, 150–154; unrealistic "reality" TV, 145
Eden's Crush, 292–293
editing: disguising, 28; to re-arrange the truth, 26
Eisner, Michael, 289
Elliott, Shelley, 172
Elyse, 115
emotions: as entertaining, 23; exacerbating negative, 28; exploitation of trauma, 219–220;

male, 37; manipulation of, 16, 93; selling fear, 231–232; setup of women's humiliated, 54–55
E! News Online, 87
Enlightened Racism (Jhally and Lewis), 8, 239
Enlightened Sexism (Douglas), 268
entertainment: commercialization of, 295, 297–298; commercials masked as, 26, 235–236; cultural context of, 26, 192–193; ideological dissemination via, 97; vs. journalism, 122; mindless, banishing, 311; as misogynist infotainment, 237; myths, 14; as power without responsibility, 22; racist, 187; socially responsible, 226; social responsibility as exempted from, 15–16
Entertainment Tonight, 261
Entertainment Weekly: "5 Best Reality TV Moments", 222; on casting people of color, 193; Darnell interview, 16; Evan Marriott interview, 37; on *Flavor of Love*, 181, 183, 217; on Omarosa, 167
Essence, 184
essentialism, gender, 99
ethnic cleansing, 177
Eva, 200
Evans, Danielle, 112, 229
exercise, vs. plastic surgery, 92
Extra!, 193, 331
Extreme Makeover, 35, 93–94
Extreme Makeover: Home Edition, 140, 142, 156–157, 280–281

F

FAIR, 301, 331
Fairness and Integrity in Telecommunications Media Coalition (FIT Media),, 327
Fair Use, 340
fairytale shows: commerce as key to, 39; emotional response to, 46; false endings on, 33–34; feminist rethinking of, 45; *Flavor of Love* as different from, 179–180; formula fed to contestants, 42; homosexuality as excluded from, 47; humiliation as flip side of, 52–56; infantalization of women in, 39–40; *Joe Millionaire* as, 40; mainstream violence against women, 137–138, 225; short-lived conclusions of, 38, 58–59, 158; undermining women's rights, 256; as white only, 48–49; *See also* dating shows; *The Bachelor*
Faludi, Susan, 13, 170, 240
fantasy: escapist, 16–17; hip-hop, 182; straight male, 49; of wealth, 135, 146
Farmer Wants a Wife, 101, 224
fashionistas, making, 150–154
Faust, Drew Gilpin, 242

FCC, 298, 327, 328, 333–335, 338
fear, 231–232
Fear Factor, 52, 276
Fechit, Stephin, 184
feminism: backlash to gains of, 240–242; media declares death of, 105; media effects of, 226; scare tactics against, 253; social responsibility of, 342–343
fiction: believing TV's, 22–23, 239; of "real ity" caricature, 204; of reality TV endings, 157–158
Field, Sally, 284
51 Minds, 216
Fiore, Jasmine, 216
Firefly, 14, 284
Firestone, Andrew, 54
First Class All the Way, 145
The First Wives Club, 63
Fitchner, Christy, 254
Flanagan, Caitlin, 110
Flav, Flavor, 179–180, 217, 224
Flavor of Love: bigotry on, 137; Black sexuality caricatures, 139, 186–187; breaks whitewashing mold, 69–70; catfights on, 99; critical responses to, 30, 307; as a minstrel show, 183, 184; nicknames on, 182, 189, 224; post-, 179–195; pre-, 162–179; racial stereotypes on, 179–182; sex as required and demonized on, 259; spinoffs, 138, 185–186, 192; success of, 182–183; verbal abuse on, 224; *See also Charm School*
flaw finders, 75, 205
Fleiss, Mike: avoids facts, 26; *The Bachelor*, 10; *The Bachelorette*, 245; on crying women, 23; on humiliation of women, 55; *More to Love*, 73; *Who Wants to Marry a Multi-Millionaire?*, 9; *Who Wants to Marry a Multi-Millionaire?* producer, 12; on women's qualifications, 71
Flipping Out, 146
For Love or Money, 99, 129, 214–215, 219
Foster, David, 292
Foster, John Bellamy, 283
Fox: cancels *Firefly*, 14; Darnell's work for, 9, 11; prime time programming statistics, 282; *Who Wants to Marry a Multi-Millionaire?*, 9–10
Frakes, Cy, 113
Frankel, Bethenny, 315
Frankel, Dr. Lois, 154
Frankenbiting, 27
Free Press, 327
frenemies, 98
Friends, 65, 66
From G's to Gents, 138, 191

From Mammy to Miss America and Beyond: Cultural Images and the Shaping of U.S. Social Policy (Jewell), 194
FTC, 328
FX, 173

G

Galán, Nely, 93, 220
The Gamekillers, 284
games, media literacy, 301–308
Gandinsky, Brian, 123
Gaspin, Jeff, 15
Gekko, Gordon, 146
gender binary, 263
gender discrimination, 116–117
gender equality, 107–108, 247
gender essentialism, 99, 125, 126
gender inequality: economics of, 130–131; in executive roles, 267; mainstreaming, 137–138; as societal, not personal, 126–127; as worldview of TV executives, 266–267
General Electric, 274
Gere, Richard, 44
Gimme a Break!, 172
Gimme Sugar, 50
Girl Director (Richards), 343
The Girls Next Door, 62, 258
The Girls of Hedsor Hall, 138
Givens, Kamal and Ahmad, 113, 224
GLAAD (Gay & Lesbian Alliance Against Defamation), 52, 265
Global Action Project (GAP): Youth Make Media, 317
"gold diggers", 127–131
GoLeft.org, 330
Gonzalez, Jaslene, 84, 199
The Good Life, 145
Gottlieb, Lori, 253
Goude, Jean-Paul, 208
Graff, E. J., 106
The Graduate, 63
gratification, immediate, 147
"Greed is Good", 146
Griff, Professor, 184
Grisham, Cassie, 84–86
Grodner, Allison, 145
group dates, 54
Guiney, Bob, 42, 164–165

H

Hair Story: Untangling the Roots of Black Hair in America (Byrd and Tharps), 178
Hantz, Russell, 113
Harding, Kate, 77, 311

Harlem Heights, 277
Harper's Bazaar, 207
Harris, Bob, 109, 175
Harrison, Chris, 37, 41, 100, 246
Hatchett, Matt, 247–248
health: and body weight, 76–78; eating disorders and, 83–84
health insurance, 135
Heene, Falcon, 255
Heene, Richard, 255
Hefner, Hugh, 258
hegemony, cultural, 97, 126
Helford, Bruce, 285
heterosexuality, as normative, 24
Hill, Keenyah, 86–87
The Hills, 98, 104, 308
Hilton, Paris, 35, 110, 135
hip-hop: Cronin on, 217; socially conscious, 182
Hip Hop: Beyond Beats and Rhymes, 182
Hirschorn, Michael, 14, 18, 183, 192
Holla Back NYC, 220
Hollar, Julie, 331
The Hollywood Reporter, 282
homosexuality: as exempt from fairytale shows, 49; gay men, 51; in reality TV spoofs, 315–316; same-sex relationships, 59, 249
hooks, bell, 131
Horst, Tessa, 42–44
Houle, Billie Jeanne, 42, 54
House, Yoanna, 200
housework: on *Flavor of Love*, 161; as "natural" role of women, 117–118; women as ineffective at, 119, 255; as women-only, 125
Howard University, 342
Hudson, Jennifer, 90
humiliation, female, 52–56, 157, 224
hunger, 157
Hurley, Phil, 122
Hurt, Byron, 182

I

Ianni, Dr. Lynn, 93, 220
Ice Cube, 173
I Love Lucy, 110
I Love Money, 216
I Love New York: bigotry on, 137; humiliation of women on, 18; Jezebel stereotype on, 187; success of, 187–188
"*I Love New York*: Does New York Love Me?", 187
Imadeen, 68
Imam, 207–208
"I'm not here to make friends", 104

Imus, Don, 331
inauthenticity, teaching, 76
independence, women's: cautionary tales about, 53, 253; media attacks on, 252; men's respect for, 247–248
independent media, 335–336
Ingraham, Chrys, 250
The Insider, 223
"inspirational" shows, 192
intelligence: discrimination against women's, 116–117; humbling African American, 203–204; on pause, 31, 32; women as without, 108–117
Internet access, 314
Interpublic, 283
Interscope A&M Records, 294
interviews: gathering misinformation for, 101; portraying women's stupidity in, 113; poste-limination, 104, 243, 291; record your own, 315; Tiffany Richardson on, 202
Iraq War, 169, 288, 289–290
Ish Entertainment, 18, 192
isolation, fostering female, 107–108
"Is Tyra Banks Racist?" (Dahl), 112
I Want to Work for Diddy, 265

J

Jackson, Janine, 275
James, Andrea, 50
The Jay Leno Show, 283
jealousy, 107
Jenkins, Ryan, 216
Jericho Communications, 285–286
Jerido, Patricia, 330
Jersey Shore , 19, 223
Jessica, 151
Jewell, K. Sue, 194
jewelry, 43
Jezebel, 186, 187, 194
Jhally, Sut, 8, 21, 239, 286
Jillian, 246
Jim Crow Museum of Racist Memorabilia, 169
Joe Millionaire: advertising during, 276; conclusion, 33–34, 58; humiliation of women on, 53, 224; portrayal of women, 11, 99, 128–129; premise as a deception, 37, 127–128; stages a sex scene, 261; success of, 12, 129
Johnson, Army Specialist Shoshana, 171
Jolie, Angelina, 107
Jones, Grace, 208
Jones, Lauren, 120, 123
Jones, Sergeant First Class Danette, 124, 170–172
Jones, Toccara, 79–83, 158

Joseph, Anchal, 196–197
journalists: becoming a, 335–336; Constitutional protection of, 333; inhibition of, 301; reality TV, 121–122
Journal of Consumer Research, 286
Journal of the American Medical Association, 94
Jungle Fever (Goude), 208

K

Kabir, Tareq, 164
Kanisha, 244
Katarina, 234–235
Keeping up with the Kardashians, 308
Kelle, 205–206
Kellner, Jamie, 13
Kelly, Clinton, 142, 150
Kentucky Fried Chicken, 181
Keoghan, Phil, 174
Kilbourne, Jean, 66, 89, 233, 286
King, Isis, 264
King of the Crown, 113
Kirby, Marianne, 311
Kleinfeld, 147
Kmart, 287
Knight, Gladys, 91
Kozer, Sarah, 127, 261
Kreisinger, Elisa, 315–316, 340–341
Kressley, Carson, 286
Kristen, 151
Krugman, Paul, 144
Kucher, Aston, 114
KYTX, 120, 122

L

Lachey, Nick, 110
Ladies Home Journal, 67
Lamas, Lorenzo, 75
Langmia, Kehbuma, 342–343
La Perla, 287
Latina, 200
Lauze, Dr. Martha M., 267
Lawson, Jonathan, 333–335
Leach, Robin, 146
Leakes, NeNe, 103, 104, 110
Leierwood, Mina, 289–290
Lepore, Nanette, 85
lesbians: as excluded from fairytales, 47; misrepresentation on TV, 261
Lessons from the Fat-o-Sphere: Quit Dieting and Declare a Truce with Your Body (Harding and Kirby), 311
Leuschner, Lisa, 90, 91
Levi, Lauren "London", 87

Lewis, Justin M., 8, 21, 239
Lewis, Keith, 138
liberation, co-option of: to attack plus-sized women, 74; to "correct" non-white features, 177; as lonely heartache, 253; on makeover shows, 25, 94–95; for plastic surgery industry, 94
lifestyle shows, 104, 140–141
Lifestyles of the Rich and Famous, 146
Liguori, Peter, 266
The Little Mermaid, 48
Little Miss Perfect, 75, 257
Live with Regis and Kelly, 34
Living Single, 65
local TV, 336–337
Locke, Kimberley, 90, 177
Logo, 50
London, Stacey, 142, 150
Lopez, Cynthia, 339–340
Los Angeles Times, 41
love: as absent from blaxploitation shows, 181; vs. career, for women, 243, 252–253; fairytale, as white only, 49; reality TV manipulates need for, 57–58; reality TV version, 59, 130; verbal abuse in the name of, 202, 203; as violent power imbalance, 226–227
Lui, Meizhu, 135
Lynch, Private Jessica, 171

M

Made in L.A., 339
Mad Men, 126
Madrid Fashion Week, 83
Magna Global Entertainment, 283
Maher, Charlie, 245
makeover shows: copying *ANTM*, 228; false therapists on, 93; *The Real Housewives of Atlanta*, 92; self-help as consumption on, 139–140; spending as encouraged on, 149–150; stereotyping femininity on, 76; takeaway lesson from, 154; unnecessary plastic surgery, 39; vs. usable skill, 95; *What Not To Wear*, 150–154; women of color on, 176; *See also The Swan*
makeup: age-defying, 107; for children's pageants, 75–76; to erase ethnicity, 173–174, 177
Maldonado, Leiomy, 265
"mammy" stereotype, 169–172
Manhattan Neighborhood Network, 336
Manigault-Stallworth, Omarosa, 160, 166–169
Manring, M.M., 172
Manuel, Jay, 80, 230, 231–232
Marie Claire, 105

Marin, Nolé, 80
Marine Corps Judge Advocate General (JAG), 215
Marin Institute, 328
Mark Burnett Productions, 167
marriage: as completing a woman, 249, 253–254; as dating show conclusion, 38; as fixation of women, 249–250; over forty, 251; redefinitions of, 249; rise in median age of, 242; same-sex, 59, 241; stereotypes of, 8; unlikelihood of, 58–59; *See also* weddings
Married by America: Fleiss on, 12; Houle on, 42; humiliation of women on, 54; insecurity about weight on, 70; Latinas on, 165; premise of, 11
Marriott, Evan, 33–34, 37, 58, 128
Marry Him: The Case for Settling for Mr. Good Enough (Gottlieb), 253
Marsden, Nancy, 298
Marshall, Garry, 124
Martindale, Wink, 115
Martinez, Maile, 318, 343–344
masturbation, 259
Maui Fever, 185
McCauley, Christie, 332
McChesney, Robert W., 283
McHale, Joel, 209
McIntosh, Jonathan, 316
"Me, Inc.", 168
media, the: Big Six owners, 274, 288, 325, 326; corporate control of, 274, 275–276, 283; deconstructing, 312; dehumanizes people of color, 206–207; diet, 311; distribution, 334; diversity erosion, 297; DIY media, 314–318, 335–336; effects on body image, 89–90; executives, as male, 194, 267; feminist backlash in, 240–242; hype for reality shows, 290–295; internalizing messages from, 21; make your own media, 314–318; mergers, 272; "mirroring" social bias, 272; moguls, 21; playing the dimwit to, 110; requiring accountability for, 331; socialization by, 21, 97; spoofs, 315–316; superficiality of, 18; talking back to, 318–324, 329; Telecommunications Act of 1996, 66; transgender bias, 50; Tyra Banks as influenced by, 210; violence against women in, 225–227; vs. women's independence, 251–252; vs. women's solidarity, 104–105
Media Consortium, 335
"Media Justice: A Women's Issue", 301
media literacy: education, 29–31, 301, 344–345; games to serve, 300–308; group film screenings for, 330; importance of, 23, 234–235;

justice movement, 300; key to, 313; positive effect of, 268; for young people, 309–310, 332–333
Media Literacy Project, 301, 312, 332
Meet My Folks, 114–115; fake residences on, 133–134
Megan Wants a Millionaire, 216
Melaney, Molly, 38
men: advertising to, 139; appearance-based judgments of, 71; child rearing by, 125; as executives, 194, 267; as *Idol* contestants, 136; as leaders, 124, 247; reality TV education for, 46, 225; respect for women, 247–248, 256; stereotypes of, 37, 247; undermining intelligence of, 256; wealth as requirement for, 24, 42
men of color: Asian, 164; as drug dealers, 192; *From G's to Gents*, 191–192; stereotyped roles for, 49, 190–192; *See also* people of color
Mesnick, Jason, 38, 246
Messing, Debra, 35, 296
Millennial Generation, 31
Miller, Portia Simpson, 241
Million Dollar Listing, 146
The Millionaire Matchmaker, 247–249, 259
Mindless Entertainment, 16, 184
minstrel shows, 179, 183, 185, 186
misfortune, pleasure in, 16
misogyny: documenting, 331; in hip-hop, 182; as introduced to children, 257; on *More to Love*, 73; reality TV as built on, 19–20; scripting in, 214–215
Miss America Pageant, 60–61
Miss Seventeen, 279, 280
Miss South Carolina Teen USA, 113
Miss USA, 254
Mitsubishi, 283
modeling: by plus-sized women of color, 79–83; pro-anorexia in, 83–90; on reality TV, effects of, 88–89; smoke and mirrors of, 206; "wild" Black women, 207–208; *See also America's Next Top Model*
Mok, Ken, 34, 78
mommy wars, 105
money: encouraging spending, 149, 151; makes Mr. Right, 256; as a man's "love", 43–44; as primary target of studios, 13; as promise in fairytale romance, 38; societal bias of women and, 130; withholding advertising, 275
Mo'Nique: addresses domestic violence, 190; as *Charm School* host, 137; on *Charm School* premise, 161, 188–189; criticizes female sexuality, 259; "sisterhood" of, 192

Moonves, Les, 13
Moore, Anne Elizabeth, 286, 318
Mora, Naima, 200
More to Love: breaks the thin mold, 48; media literacy drinking game, 307–308; premise of, 73–74; punishes intelligence, 116
Morghan, 256–257
motherhood: mommy wars, 105–106; women as ineffective at, 118
movies, 124
Mr. Personality, 12
Mr. Right: as rich, 256; as white, 163
MTV, 49, 191, 223, 265
Mueller, Don, 133, 160
Muilenburg, Sami, 344
Murphy Brown, 65
music: industry, Cronin on, 217; reality TV marketing of, 293; socially conscious, 182
Myeong-Sook, Han, 241
My Fair Wedding with David Tutera, 45, 254
Mystery Science Theater 3000, 301

N

NAACP, 172, 184, 193
Nanny 9-11, 118
Nasheed, Tariq, 190–191
National Crime Victimization Survey, 225
National Eating Disorders Association, 78, 88
National Economic Council, 117
National Writers Guild, 328
Native Americans, 176
Naval Criminal Investigative Service (NCIS), 215
NBC, 282, 283
Neal, Mark Anthony, 193
networks, TV: buzz generation by, 290–295; commercial revenue, 276; content decline, 295; dating shows, 185; decrease in scripted TV shows, 284–285; ideological agendas governing, 288; as pimps, 260; prime time programming chart, 281, 282; resist embedded advertising, 284; self-regulation by, 298
Newlyweds, 109–110
news, TV: *Anchorwoman*, 120–122; "Balloon Boy" hoax, 255; for/by people of color, 342–343; Iraq War obfuscation, 169; mommy wars as selling, 106; people of color in the, 193; pop culture coverage, 18; scapegoats "welfare queens", 202; women's looks on, 64
NewsCorp, 274
Newsweek, 251
New York Goes to Work, 187
The New York Times, 13, 103, 181

Next Entertainment, 29
Nielsen ratings, 9, 15, 132
nonunion workers, 23, 126
NYC Prep, 145

O

Obama, President Barak, 117
obesity, 77
objectification: of children, 258; on *Flavor of Love*, 181–182; going along with, 25
O'Connell, Charlie, 100
O'Donnell, Larry, 156
Omarosa's Ultimate Merger, 168
"Once in a Lifetime" (Talking Heads), 133
On the Lot, 124
Oprah's Big Give, 154
"Our City, My Story", 317

P

pain, 229–232
Palmer, Jesse, 100
Paradise Hotel, 28
Paris Hilton's My New BFF, 35
passivity, female, 48
payouts, 158
Pelosi, Representative Nancy, 241
Pennington, Ty, 142, 280
people of color: acting roles for, 193; all-alike-Asians, 197, 198; Darnell's shows as marginalizing, 12; dehumanization of, 206–207; ethnicity as skin deep, 173–174; financial statistics, 135; Flavor Flav as stand-in for, 193; in the media, 193–194; mockery of, 180–181; mocking poverty of, 136–138; news for/by, 342–343; pre-*Flavor of Love* roles, 162–179; in *Profiles from the Front Line*, 169–170; in reality TV casts, 30–31; reality TV implications for, 194–195
Perry, Lincoln Theodore Monroe Andrew, 184
Peterson, Latoya, 12
Pew Research Center, 32
Philippousis, Mark, 58, 218
The Pickup Artist, 14, 37, 319
plastic surgery: to achieve "femininity", 263; as beauty standard, 62; to combat domestic violence, 220–222; to "correct"' non-white features, 176–177; industry, 94; on *The Real Housewives of Atlanta*, 92; *See also The Swan*
Platinum Weddings, 45, 250
Playboy, 62, 258
Playing it Straight, 51
plus-sized models, 79–83

politics: of backlash against women, 253–254; of domination, 131; racist cartoons in, 206–207; of religion, 289; of TV, 18, 288–290; women in, 241–242
Pollard, Tiffany "New York", 130, 187
Ponds, 296
Poniewozik, James, 27
Pontiac Solstice, 286
pop culture: activism improving, 329; feminist backlash in, 240–242; hip-hop commentary on, 182; perceptions of people of color, 194; socialization by, 97
Pop Culture Pirate, 340
Popstars, 292–293
Porter, Felicia "Fo", 199
poverty: co-opting, 174; mocking, 136–138; and sex work, 260; as unserved by charity shows, 155–156; "welfare queens", 202
power: as all men's, 57; of corporate sponsors, 275, 283–284; fantasy of, 135; mainstreaming discriminatory, 138; in violent relationship dynamics, 225–226
Pretty Woman, 44
princess fantasy: Disney as pushing, 45; "fairytale" shows for, 34–35; infantalization of women in, 39–40; as limited to thin white women, 48
pro-ana, 84
product placement: activism against, 327–329; "as seen on" packages, 39; contestants as, 295; embedded, 275; as goal of reality TV, 142–143; methods of, 276–280; network regulation of, 298; reality TV as hour-long, 235–236; reality TV as revolutionary for, 281; in *The Restaurant*, 283; in scripted shows, 296; statistics, 281
Profiles from the Front Line: gender stereotyping on, 124; ideological agenda of, 288–289; "mammy" stereotype, 169–172
Project Runway, 139
Prometheus Radio Project, 338
pro-mia, 84
"prostitots", 257
prostitution, 260
protest letters, 319–322
Public, Educational and Governmental (PEG) Access TV, 336–337
Public Enemy, 182
publicity, controversy as, 12
public service, charity vs., 155–157
Pussycat Dolls, 293–294

Q

Quakers, 289
"Queen Melisssa", 254–255

Queer Eye for the Straight Guy, 139, 279, 285–286
The Queer Housewives of NYC, 315–316
Quijada, Andrea, 332

R

RaceWire, 317
The Rachel Zoe Project, 35, 139, 145, 308
racism: advertising, 67–68; beauty bias, 196; Black complicity in, 183–184; of Blacks as "wild", 206–207; *Black. White.* addresses, 173–174; discrimination, 194; as entertainment, 184–185; foregrounding, 162; *From G's to Gents* reinforces, 191; hip-hop commentary on, 182; internalized, 205; of minstrel shows, 183–184; naming, 167; racial essentialism, 208–209; reinforcing, 19; remorse for, 175; in TV's fictions, 22; of the white Prince Charming, 10; *See also* men of color; people of color; women of color
radio, 338
Ramos, Luisel, 82, 84
rape: attempted, 215; on *The Real World*, 213–214; statutory, 218
ratings, 223
Real Chance of Love, 224, 307
real estate, 146
Real Housewives franchise: catfights as viewership draws, 102; media literacy drinking game, 308; misrepresentation on, 118; no "friends" on, 104; women as portrayed on, 98–99; *See also The Real Housewives of Atlanta*
The Real Housewives of Atlanta: Black stereotypes on, 166, 186; casting of African Americans, 30; catfights on, 102–103; dumbing down of women on, 110–111; Zolciak on, 92
The Real World: Black stereotyping on, 185; casting devolution, 12; early seasons, 265; as marginal, 281; rape on, 213–214; as reality TV precursor, 9; *The Real World: Brooklyn*, 63; violence against women on, 222
Reality Bites Back, 20
RealityBitesBackBook.com, 32
reality TV: advertising as basis of, 281; airtime statistics, 11; as altering identity perception, 97–98; central conceit of, 24; cheap cost of, 14, 285, 292, 321; critical thinking response to, 29–31, 310–313; escape of sociological scrutiny, 233–234; as heteronormative, 52; ideological basis, 326; implications of, 17; means for "drama" creation, 103; media hype for, 290–295; non-exploitative, 175; romancing violence against women, 225–227; social

belief as secret to, 47; stereotype enforcement, 98–108
Reality TV's Sexiest Vixens, 260
Reclaim the Media, 333
Redstone, Sumner M., 274
Reel Grrrls, 318, 343–344
Reisenberg, Robert, 284, 285
relationships, redefined, 249
religion, politics of, 289
remix videos, 315–316, 340–341
respect for women, 57
The Restaurant, 15, 140, 283, 284
Reston, Ana Carolina, 83, 84
Reveille, 283
Revlon, 158
Rice, Condoleeza, 241
Richards, Andrea, 343
Richardson, Tiffany, 200–203
Richie, Nicole, 110, 135
Rivers, Caryl, 252
Roberts, Julia, 44
Robinson, D'eva, 166
Rocket Science Laboratories, 29
Rock of Love Bus, 16
Rock of Love: Charm School, 138
Rockwell, Rick, 9–10, 216
romance: as a deception, 37; homosexuality as excluded from, 24; humiliation as part of, 57; as linked to finance, 36, 38; rejected, as punchline, 55
Rose, Amber, 208
Roseanne, 65
Ross, Karen, 217
Rubenstein, Atoosa, 279–280
Rubinelli, Jayla, 232
Run, Rev, 249
Run's House, 249
Ruzicka, Greg, 155
Rycroft, Melissa, 38

S

Saaphyri, 112, 137–138
Sakai, Sheena, 199
Salley, John, 60, 92
Sapphire trope, 166, 169
Sarkeesian, Anita, 316–317
Satin, Scott, 134
Saunders, Sakura, 338
savings, personal, 144–145
Sawyer, Diane, 202
Say Yes to the Dress, 147, 250, 279
Scantlin, Melana, 164
Schadenfreude, 16–17, 128
Scherzinger, Nicole, 293–294

Schneider, Trish, 127
The Scholar, 154
scholarly activism, 342–343
Schuster Institute for Investigative Journalism, 106
scripting: as being puppeteers, 28; cancellation
    of scripted shows, 284–285; as done for real-
    ity TV, 26–27; "lack" of, 23; as misleading
    viewers, 26; product placement, 296–297;
    questioning, 313; to reinforce stereotype, 18
Seacrest, Ryan, 65, 90, 136
The Search for the Next Pussycat Doll, 294
Sears, 280, 281
Sebik, Justin, 217
The Secret Millionaire, 155
security checks, 218–219
seduction, 190, 239
SeenOn.com, 147
self-acceptance: on camera, 197; as laziness, 93
self-esteem: ads as eroding, 89, 286; body-
    based, 71–72; as eroded in plus-sized mod-
    els, 81; externally-induced, 35; friendship
    as fostering, 108; media effects on, 66–67;
    net worth as conflated with, 158; systematic
    crushing of, 56; via high-end shopping, 153;
    via male validation, 220
self-help shows, pseudo: "counseling" on, 93,
    220, 221; exploitation on, 138, 192
self-loathing, 81
*Selling Anxiety: How the News Media Scare
    Women* (Rivers), 252
Serano, Julia, 341–342
Seriously, Dude, I'm Gay, 51
Seventeen, 233, 279, 280, 287
sex: bisexual female, for men, 262; *Cat-
    house*, 260; consenting, in teenagers, 218;
    vs. female desire, 258–259; on *Flavor of
    Love*, 180–181; gender and, 263; industry,
    130–131, 260, 294; on *Joe Millionaire*, 261;
    money and, 130–131
sexism. *See* misogyny
sexual abuse: *ANTM*'s handling of, 212–213;
    of children, 258; glamorizing, 234; as good
    publicity, 12; isolation in, 108; mainstreaming,
    137–138; in the media, 225–227; plastic sur-
    gery to combat, 220–222; rape, 213–214, 215,
    216; by reality show contestants, 213–219; by
    slave masters, 186; statistics, 225; trivialized,
    219; verbal, 223–224; in the workplace,
    125–126; *See also* domestic violence
sexuality: as advertising, 120; Black women's,
    186, 208–209; gendered double standards,
    246; hyper-, as beauty standard, 62; margin-
    alizing nonnormative, 263; for news ratings,
    120–121; of playmates, 258; as required

and demonized in women, 259; as taught
    to children, 257–258; as women's business
    asset, 119; women's stereotyped, 24
Shapiro, Adam, 27, 217
Sheehan, Cindy, 241
She's Got the Look, 63
shopping: high-end, 149, 150–154; as seen on
    TV, 147; TV-responsive, 297
Siamis, Korby, 298
Silverman, Ben, 15, 283–285
The Simple Life, 110, 135
Simpson, Jessica, 109
Simpson, Joe, 110
Sinclair, Emily, 28
single women: financial statistics, 135; humili-
    ation of, 55; as losers, 118, 242; over forty,
    as doomed, 251; self-loathing loneliness of,
    249, 252
Sirleaf-Johnson, Ellen, 241
sisterhood, 105
skinniness: on *ANTM*, 76–79; as aspirational,
    64–65; as beauty standard, 62; as lovable, 74;
    pro-anorexia, 83–84
slackers, 203
slavery, 184, 186, 206
Sleeping Beauty, 48
Smiley, Tavis, 184
Smith, Anna Nicole, 109
TheSmokingGun.com, 215
Snookie, 223
Snow, DeShawn, 103, 111, 186, 189
soap operas, 297
social issues, on TV: 1970-1990, 297; devolution
    of, 12; disappearance of diversity, 297
social bias: on beauty, 176; becoming norma-
    tive, 30–31; gender essentialism, 125; hip-
    hop commentary on, 182; media as reinforc-
    ing, 272; reality TV as resurrecting, 25
social experiments, 23, 24
socialization, by the media, 97
social norms: as context of reality TV, 16–17; as
    learned behavior, 98
social responsibility: conservative rollback of,
    202; feminist, 342–343; marketer power as
    trumping, 205–206; power without, 22; real-
    ity TV as exempt from, 15–16
social rights: charity does not further, 155;
    erosion of sisterhood as harming, 108; reality
    TV as scripted to erase, 18
*Soul Babies: Black Popular Culture and the
    Post-Soul Aesthetic* (Neal), 193
The Soup, 209
South, plantation-era, 172
So You Think You Can Be President?, 317

Sparks, Jordin, 92
spending, U.S., 144
Stacy, 152
Stanger, Patti, 247–248
The Starter Wife, 296
statutory rape, 218
Steeves, H. Leslie, 174
Stegall, Krista, 217
Stepford wives, 248
stereotypes, female: by age, 63–64; Asian, 199; on beauty shows, 76; of the "black bitch", 200–203; of bridal fixation, 249–250; capitalizing on, 168–169; effects of exposure to, 131; of the "gold digger", 127–131; Jezebel, 187; Latina, 199–200; "mammy", 169–172; protesting, 204; as servants, 238–239; as untrustable backstabbers, 98–108; verbal abuse perpetuating, 223; of women as incompetent, 117–127; women as stupid, 108–117
stereotypes, gender: advertising, 39–40, 287–288; of Africans, 174, 208–209; anti-Black, 183–184, 186; of Asian men, 164; on *The Bachelorette*, 245; becoming social truths, 97; as binary, 50, 261; Black male, 190–192, 217–218; Cold War era, 170; Darnell establishes reality-TV, 11; emotional response to, 46; in fairytales, 57; gay, 51; of husbands/fathers, 256; molding, 28; naturalizing, 98, 117; in *Profiles from the Front Line*, 170; reality TV exaggerates, 24–25, 26; reinforcing, 17, 246–247, 255–256; shopping for, 152; signaling abuse, 125; socially-conditioned, 47; spoofs on, 316–317; of transgender people, 265
Stockholm syndrome, 210
Stolz, Kim, 262
story editing, 28
St. Petersburg Times, 183, 292
street harassment, 220
Studdard, Ruben, 91
success: backlash to women's, 241; masking below-average show, 319; of Tyra Banks, 210; via consumption, 147–148; via non-Black hair, 178–179; of women, 241–242
Sullivan, Brittany "McKey", 232
Sulmers, Claire, 207, 208
Summers, Lawrence, 117
superficiality, 18
Supernanny, 118, 125, 241
The Surreal Life, 16
Survivor: buzz for, 290–292; cultural appropriation on, 174–175; embedded advertising, 281–282; ethnic casting on, 185; *Survivor: Africa*, 174

The Swan: enforcing femininity ideals on, 263; exploitation of trauma, 219–222; as a "fairytale", 34; premise, 11, 93; sadism of, 257
sweatshop practices, 339
synergy, 289
Szish, Katrina, 148–149

T

Tabatha's Salon Takeover, 262
tabloids, 23
Tacori, 38
talent, 140–141
Talking Heads, 133
Tarrant, Shira: on heteronormativity of TV, 261; on Katrina survivor charity shows, 156; on price of change, 140; on transmission of ideals, 126, 131; on TV depictions of homemakers, 255
Taylor, Mikki, 120
Telecommunications Act of 1996, 66
Television Without Pity, 27, 203
Temptation Island, 11, 164, 260
10x10 Entertainment, 294
Tequila, Tila, 262
The Terror Dream (Faludi), 170
Texas Monthly, 105
Tharps, Lori, 178
Thompson, Whitney, 80
Tieri, Nicole, 159
Time, 27
TimeWarner, 274, 292
Tim Gunn's Guide to Style, 36, 139, 148
Tina, 244
T.I.'s Road to Redemption, 192
Title IX, Education Amendment, 107
TLC, 61, 147
Toddlers & Tiaras: fostering female competition on, 101–102; sexual exploitation on, 63, 75, 256–258
Tool Academy, 138
Top Chef, 140
Top Design, 139
torture, 103
Tough Love: 1950s gender binaries on, 246; career vs. marriage on, 253; female submissiveness on, 244; marital fixation on, 249; media literacy drinking game, 307–308
tourism, 174–175
Trading Spouses, 255
train wreck TV, 18
Transamerican Love Story, 50, 265
transgender people: expand beauty definitions, 63; improving representation for, 341–342;

on Logo, 50; media invisibility of, 25; reality TV portrayal of, 264–265
Tribeca Film Festival, 317
Tropic Thunder, 199
True Hollywood Story: The Bad Girls of Reality TV, 260
Trump, Donald: bankruptcies of, 159–160; misogyny of, 119; on Omarosa, 168; on wealth, 134
Trump Organization, 119
Truth in Advertising Guidelines, 328
Turn off Channel Zero, 184
Tutera, David, 45
TV One, 168
Twilight, 317
The Tyra Show, 210, 211

U

Ugly Betty, 204
Undercover Boss, 156
unions: actions against workers, 156; reality TV as reducing jobs in, 11, 285; for reality workers, 296
United for a Fair Economy, 135
University of Massachusetts–Amherst, 22
UPN, 13
Upright Citizens Brigade, 296
Upton, Caitlin, 113

V

values: for children, 102; and media representation, 195; media shaping of, 21; on TV, identifying, 312, 313; white beauty, 176
Vanity Fair, 201
van Slyke, Tracy, 335–336
Vaughn, Jessica, 154
Velvick, Byron, 163, 165
VH1: Black sexuality caricatures, 186–187; casting diversity on, 180; celebrates violence against women, 222; media literacy drinking game, 307; *Tough Love*, 244; transgender people on, 265
Viacom, 274, 290
Victoria's Secret, 211
voiceovers, 27
von Furstenberg, Diane, 139

W

Wade, Lisa, 208–209
Walker, Susannah, 178–179
Wal-Mart, 233, 273, 287
Ward, Steve, 242, 244
Warner, Jackie, 262
Waste Management, Inc., 156

WB, 13, 293
WE, 45, 254
The Weakest Link, 14
wealth: change via, 140; conspicuous consumption of, 139–143; makes Mr. Right, 256; as marketers advantage, 134; misrepresentation on TV, 135, 146; promise of instant, 157–158; as "realistic", 146
weddings: as-seen-on-TV wedding dresses, 147; to bridezillas, 254; Disney, 45; industry, 250–251
Welcome to the Neighborhood, 146
"welfare queens", 202
The West Wing, 14
WGA, 29, 296, 327
What Not To Wear: advertising on, 140, 279; consumerism on, 142; education in high-end shopping, 145, 150–154; women as portrayed on, 76, 263
"What Would Buffy Do?", 317
Whedon, Joss, 14
When Animals Attack!, 10
When Women Rule the World, 266, 268–270
Whipping Girl: A Transsexual Woman on Sexism and the Scapegoating of Femininity (Serano), 341
White, Mel, 175
White, Ulrick Kevin, 213
whitewashing, 176, 275
White Weddings: Romancing Heterosexuality in Popular Culture (Ingraham), 250
Whitfield, Sheree, 102
Whitson, Dr. Peggy, 242
whores, sexual women as, 259
Who Wants to Be a Millionaire?, 283
Who Wants to Marry a Multi-Millionaire?, 9, 12, 19, 69, 216
Who Wants to Marry My Dad?, 8, 40, 133, 254
"Why Hair is Political" (Walker), 178–179
Wife Swap: Black women stereotypes on, 166; father's roles on, 117, 125; homemaking as "God given" on, 119; "mammy" on, 172; negative depiction of women, 255; politics of, 289–290; women as portrayed on, 73, 241
Wild Africa Cream, 209
Wilkner, April, 198
Williams, Serena, 64
Williams, Vanessa, 60, 64
Wilmore, Larry, 285
Wilson, Dr. Natalie, 310
WIMN (Women In Media & News), 29, 88, 305, 344
WIMN's Voices, 123, 234, 317, 345
Wolf, Johann, 232
Womack, Brad, 41

women: abuse of. *See* domestic violence; sexual abuse; agency as removed from, 35–36; age of, 63; appearance-based judgments of, 71; attacking solidarity of, 104–105, 107–108; creating schisms between, 105; degradation of, 52; Disney as infantilizing, 45; disrespecting, 223–224; executive, 267; "fairytale" shows for, 34–35; as followers, not leaders, 124; glamorizing violence against, 137–138, 227–235; implications for "real" life, 57; as leaders, 270; media scare tactics for, 251–252; as mercenary, 130; need for male validation, 251; preying on insecurities of, 253; reality TV definition of, 20, 25–26; reality TV education on, 47, 97, 98; reality TV portrayal of, 17, 122, 241–242; standing up for themselves, 47–48; submission to men, 244; transgender, 264; *See also* young women
Women and Media: A Critical Introduction (Byerly and Ross), 342
Women in Science and Engineering (WISE), 117
women of color: Asian, 164, 199; on *The Bachelor*, 163–164; as beautiful, 196; beauty bias against, 67–68, 205–206; on cable dating shows, 70; curvaceous, 65; as exempt from fairytale shows, 48; financial statistics, 135; as Flavorettes, 180, 186–187; as "gold diggers", 130; hypersexualization of, 259; Imus's racism toward, 331; Latinas, 164–165, 199–200; makeovers whitewashing, 90, 176–179; "othering", 79; punishing intelligence in, 116; reality TV reinforces stereotypes of, 173; "rehabilitation" of, 188–189; Toccara Jones, 80; as unintelligent, 110–112; in the war effort, 171; *See also* African American women; people of color
women's bodies: advertising via, 131, 294; flaw finders for, 75; impossible beauty ideals for, 25; power via, 235; racist ideology on, 207; reward for thin, 48; valuing beauty over athleticism, 241
women's movement: as collaborative, 107; relational advances, 249–250; and waning beauty contest interest, 60; *See also* activism
women's rights: backlash against, 13, 240–242, 271; disguising attack on, 256; diverting attention from, 104–105; eroded by dividing women, 107–108; internalizing backlash against, 252; lack of, as women's fault, 126; mocking attempts at, 266; reality TV undermines, 17, 20, 25, 125, 132; as uncovered by the news, 18

Work Out, 262
World's Scariest Police Chases, 10
writers, script, 28, 29

Y

Young, Jaeda, 204
young audiences: diminished critical response in, 30–31; high school broadcasts, 298; identification with contestants, 234; as media creators, 343–344; media literacy for, 309–310; of *The Real World*, 214; statistics, 132
young women: as beauty standard, 62; consenting sex by, 218; life goals of, 32; sexual abuse of, 225; weight loss efforts by, 87–88
Your World with Neil Cavuto, 92
Yu, Betty, 336–337
Yvette, Mercedes, 200

Z

Zeisler, Andi, 329
zine-making, 318
Zoe, Rachel, 35, 145
Zolciak, Kim, 92, 102, 111

Acknowledgments

I first want to thank the thousands of students, faculty, and staff I've met doing media education programs at colleges and high schools over the last ten years. It has been a privilege to engage with you about what it means to think critically about media, politics, and pop culture. Your thoughts about reality TV have informed this book.

Heartfelt thanks to Ali Wicks-Lim for her wisdom, humor, and love. She's everything I could want in a sister, which is handy since I don't have any siblings. Thanks also to the endlessly supportive and hilarious Jerry Darcy, for showing me that love can change forms but family remains. I could not have survived writer's block (or much else) without them, or without Heather Carleton, Kristen Harbeson, Beth Murray, Deanne Cuellar, and Veronica Arreola (a wonderful friend and activist, *and* a founding board member of Women In Media & News).

Joe Agostino fed me when I was too exhausted to cook. Jenifer Avery, Keely Savoie, Michelle Garcia, Pat Jerido, Bill Mazza (who designed the Backlash Bingo card), and too many others to mention allowed me to drop off the face of the earth while I was writing and welcomed me back when I was done. My parents and cousins understood when I had to ditch holiday gatherings to keep writing.

Key elements of *Reality Bites Back* wouldn't exist without some amazing people, to whom I am indebted. If you find the resource guide useful, thank Cara Lisa Berg-Powers of By Any Media Necessary. The artwork from the greeting card on page 323 was created by David Dickerson, videoblogger and author of *House of Cards*. Sara Beinert, a founding board member of WIMN, produced an appendix for this book's website, and is a constant source of enthusiasm, encouragement, and friendship. The fabulous Lisa Jervis (another WIMN founder) helped me hone my ideas about embedded advertising for a 2004 *Bitch* magazine series on product placement in pop culture; much of chapter 9 is based on those articles. FIT Media Coalition's N. E. Marsden provided information on public policies governing stealth advertising, which also improved chapters 9 and 11. Feedback from Courtney Young, Bob Harris, Neil DeMause, Cinnamon Cooper, Andi Zeisler, Jennifer Smith, Melanie Klein, Sarah Jaffe, Jamii Claibourne, and several others was invaluable. (And Paula Ivins Kingston of Lucid Salon offered good cheer and a good hair day for that author photo.)

The media justice activists, writers, and media makers who contributed to chapter 11 inspire me every day. I'm honored to learn from and work alongside them, and other progressives too numerous to name. Same goes for all the diverse and dynamic women who blog at WIMN's Voices.

I suffered a catastrophic computer failure halfway through writing this book. Eight years of research—poof. Luckily, Anita Sarkeesian, Brett W. Copeland, Kat Overland, Patricia Johnson, and Jessamyn Lidasan offered speedy research assistance and gathered data crucial to several chapters. Anyone willing to transcribe *Flavor of Love, From G's to Gents, Wife Swap,* and *America's Next Top Model* is really taking one for the team. Speaking of suffering for the cause, Sanford Hohauser came to my apartment several times a month for years, offering snark and sanity checks while I took notes on reality TV. (My apologies, Sanford, for getting you addicted to *The Bachelor.*)

Even as authors Paula Kamen and John K. Wilson kept pushing me to write a book, I didn't consider it for years. I love *having written,* but I'm one of those for whom the process itself has always been rather torturous. My literary agent, Tracy Brown, finally convinced me. He had faith in my ability to take this on, even when I didn't. Tracy is savvy, insightful, and loyal—no wonder so many young feminist writers trust him with our work. Thanks also to journalist Janet Kaye, who helped me believe in my abilities at an early age.

I cannot adequately express how grateful I am to Seal Press. They believed in this book when major publishers told me it would be a great idea to write about the political implications of reality TV—*if only I wouldn't focus on women.* Since then, my incredibly patient editor, Brooke Warner, and generous publisher, Krista Lyons, extended the deadline several times while I wrestled to synthesize ten years of television. They not only understood why a feminist, antiracist analysis of reality TV is important, they were willing to wait for it. That's nearly unheard of. I can't thank them enough for the risk they took with *Reality Bites Back.* (Plus, my writing improved with Brooke's voice in my head, reminding me that sometimes one word is better than, say, seven.)

Finally, reading Susan Faludi, Jean Kilbourne, and Laura Flanders when I was eighteen had a formative impact on my journalism and media criticism. It has been one of the biggest honors of my life to get to know them as colleagues and to learn that they are each as generous as they are brilliant. I can only hope *Reality Bites Back* has a tenth of the meaning for you that *Backlash, Killing Us Softly,* or Laura's body of work has had for me.

About the Author

© THOMAS LASCHER

Jennifer L. Pozner is a media critic, journalist, activist and founder/ executive director of Women In Media & News (WIMN), a media analysis, education and advocacy organization. A noted public speaker, Pozner has conducted interactive multimedia presentations and participated in panels and debates at dozens of high schools, colleges, and conferences across the United States. She has been published in *Newsday, Chicago Tribune, Ms. Magazine, Bitch: Feminist Response to Pop Culture, In These Times,* Alternet, and *Salon,* and has appeared on CNN, FOX, MSNBC, ABC News Now, GRITv, PBS, NPR, and *The Daily Show.* She enjoys *Buffy: The Vampire Slayer,* improv comedy, facilitating media literacy workshops, and winning arguments against blowhards like Bill O'Reilly, Sean Hannity, and Joe Scarborough.

Selected Titles from Seal Press

For more than thirty years, Seal Press has published groundbreaking books. By women. For women. Visit our website at www.sealpress.com. Check out the Seal Press blog at www.sealpress.com/blog.

Feminism and Pop Culture: Seal Studies, by Andi Zeisler. $12.95, 978-1-58005-237-5. Andi Zeisler, cofounder of *Bitch* magazine, traces the impact of feminism on pop culture (and vice versa) from the 1940s to today.

Get Opinionated: A Progressive's Guide to Finding Your Voice (and Taking A Little Action), by Amanda Marcotte. $15.95, 978-1-58005-302-0. Hilarious, bold, and very opinionated, this book helps young women get a handle on the issues they care about—and provides suggestions for the small steps they can take towards change.

Girls' Studies: Seal Studies, by Elline Lipkin. $14.95, 978-1-58005-248-1. A look at the socialization of girls in today's society and the media's influence on gender norms, expectations, and body image.

Yes Means Yes: Visions of Female Sexual Power and a World Without Rape, by Jaclyn Friedman and Jessica Valenti. $15.95, 978-1-58005-257-3. This powerful and revolutionary anthology offers a paradigm shift from the "No Means No" model, challenging men and women to truly value female sexuality and ultimately end rape.

Colonize This!: Young Women of Color on Today's Feminism, edited by Daisy Hernandez and Bushra Rehman. $16.95, 978-1-58005-067-8. An insight into a new generation of brilliant, outspoken women of color—how they are speaking to the concerns of feminism and their place in it.

The Purity Myth: How America's Obsession with Virginity Is Hurting Young Women, by Jessica Valenti. $16.95, 978-1-58005-314-3. With her usual balance of intelligence and wit, Valenti presents a powerful argument that girls and women, even in this day and age, are overly valued for their sexuality—and that this needs to stop.

Find Seal Press Online
www.SealPress.com
www.Facebook.com/SealPress
Twitter: @SealPress